I turned 30. People say that o

stamina, and you can't push yo ... thing.

But I still feel like I can do anything! I'm still going strong!

Naoshi Komi

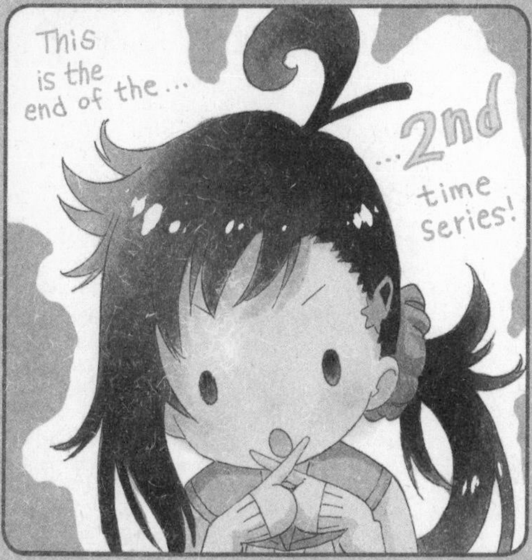
This is the end of the...
...2nd time series!

NAOSHI KOMI was born in Kochi Prefecture, Japan, on March 28, 1986. His first serialized work in *Weekly Shonen Jump* was the series *Double Arts*. His best-selling shonen manga series *Nisekoi* is available in North America from VIZ Media.

NISEKOI:
False Love
VOLUME 22
SHONEN JUMP Manga Edition

Story and Art by
NAOSHI KOMI

Translation ✐ Camellia Nieh
Touch-Up Art & Lettering ✐ Stephen Dutro
Design ✐ Izumi Evers
Shonen Jump Series Editor ✐ John Bae
Graphic Novel Editor ✐ Amy Yu

Printed in the U.S.A.

Published by VIZ Media, LLC
P.O. Box 77010
San Francisco, CA 94107

10 9 8 7 6 5 4 3 2 1
First printing, July 2017

www.shonenjump.com   www.viz.com

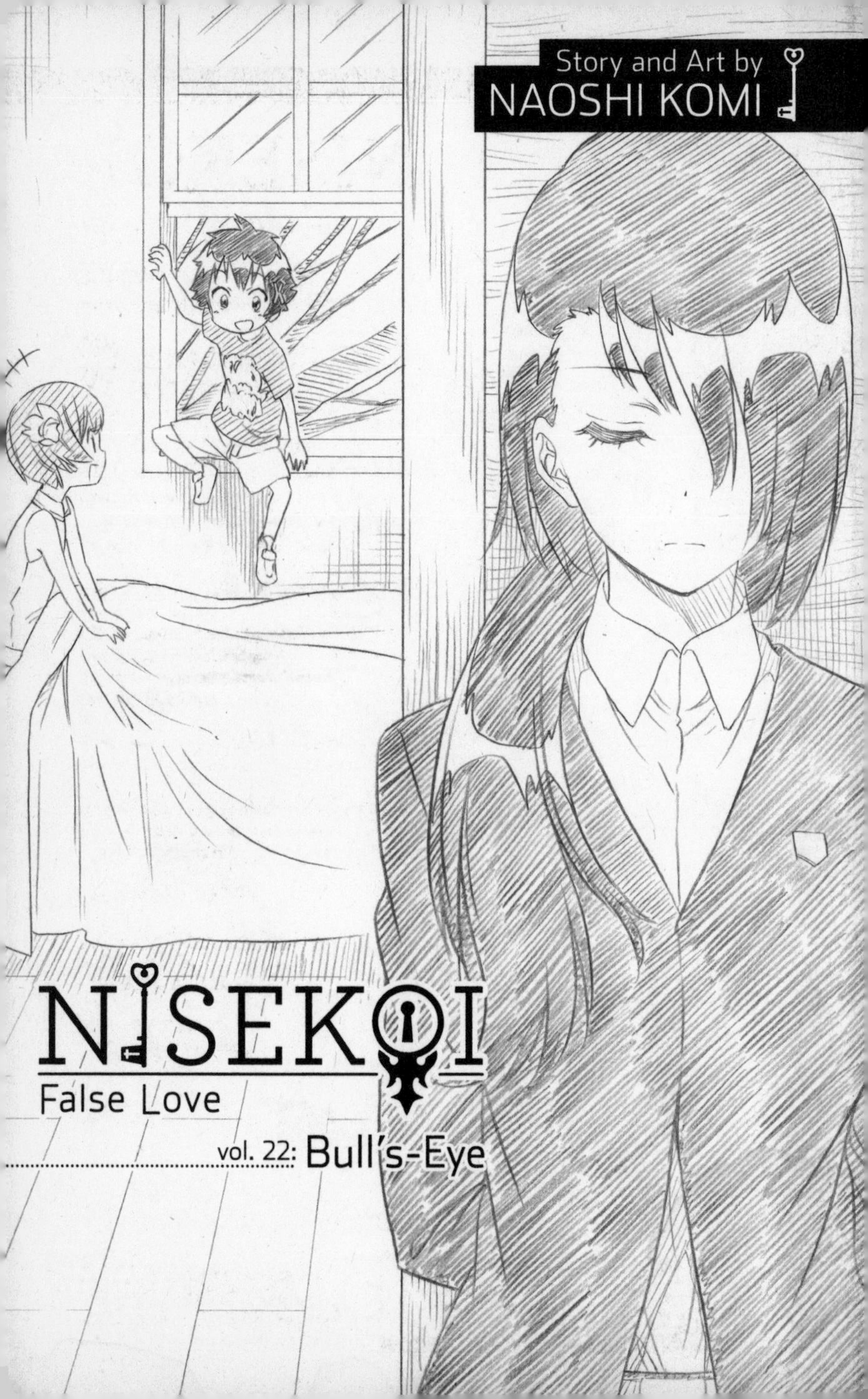
Story and Art by
NAOSHI KOMI
NISEKOI
False Love
vol. 22: Bull's-Eye

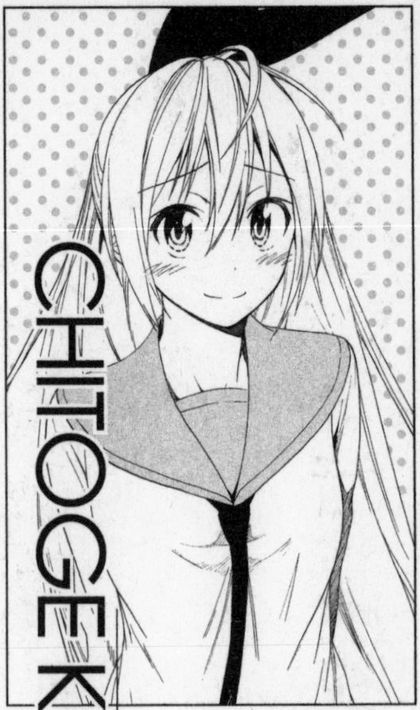

CHITOGE KIRISAKI

A half-Japanese bombshell with stellar athletic abilities. Short-tempered and violent. Comes from a family of gangsters.

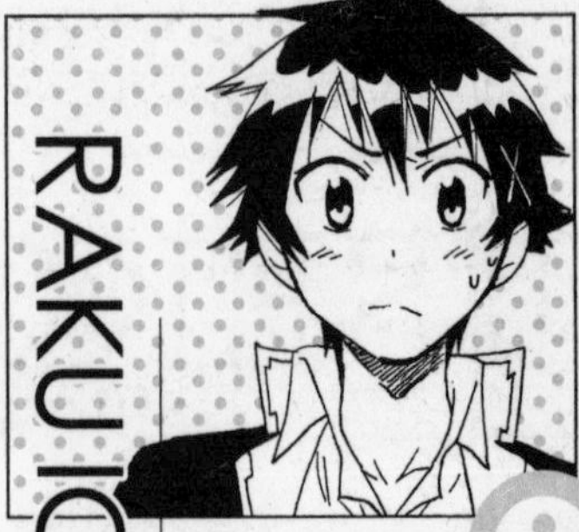

RAKU ICHIJO

A normal teen whose family happens to be yakuza. Cherishes a pendant given to him by a girl he met ten years ago.

KOSAKI ONODERA

A girl Raku has a crush on. Beautiful and sweet, Kosaki has no shortage of admirers. She's a terrible cook but makes food that *looks* amazing.

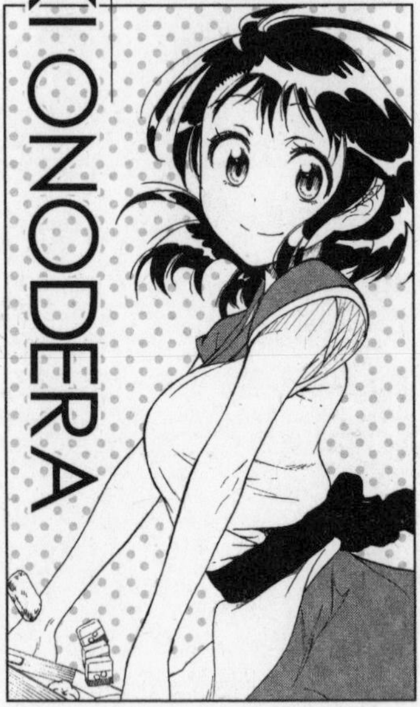

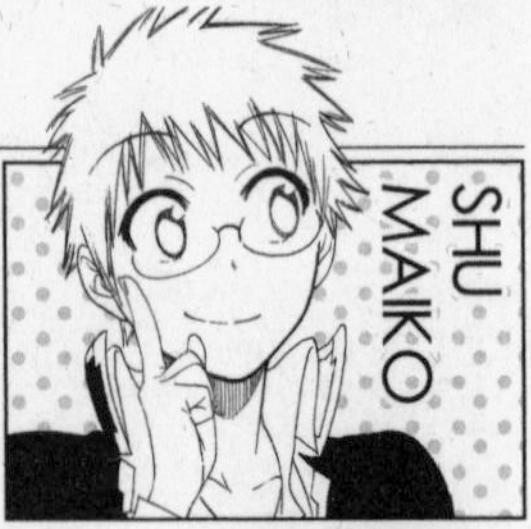

SHU MAIKO

Raku's best friend is outgoing and girl-crazy.

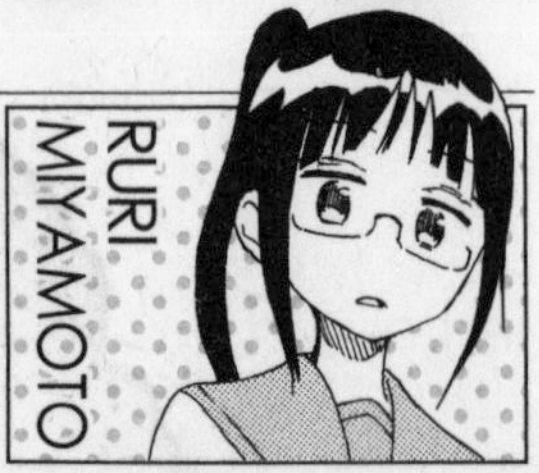

RURI MIYAMOTO

Kosaki's best gal pal. Comes off as aloof, but is actually a devoted and highly intuitive friend.

MARIKA TACHIBANA

Daughter of the chief of police, Marika is Raku's fiancée, according to an agreement made by their fathers—an agreement Marika takes very seriously! Also has a key and remembers making a promise with Raku ten years ago.

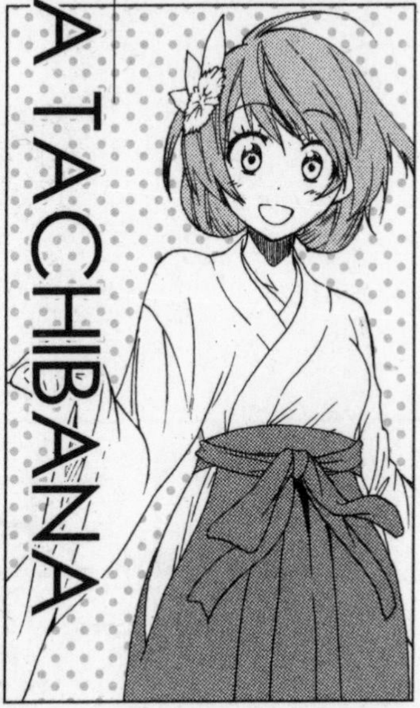

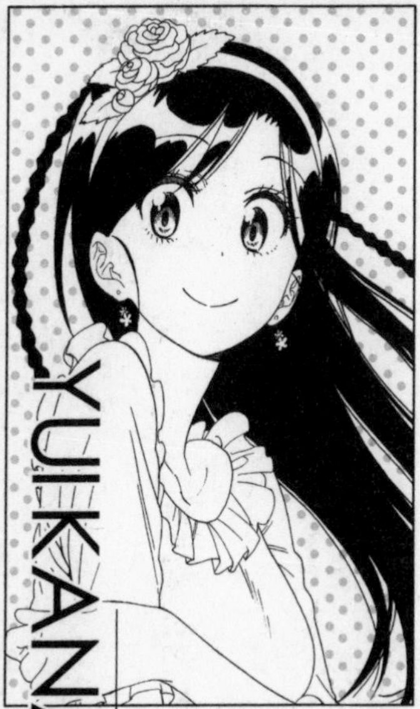

YUI KANAKURA

A childhood friend of Raku's, Yui is the head of a Chinese mafia gang and the homeroom teacher of Raku's class at his school. She was staying at Raku's house and confessed her love to him. Also has a key linked to some kind of promise...

CHARACTERS & STORY

Ten years ago, Raku Ichijo made a promise with a girl he loved that they would get married when they met again...and he still treasures the pendant she gave him to seal their pledge.

Thanks to his family's circumstances, Raku has to pretend he's dating Chitoge Kirisaki, the daughter of a rival gangster. Despite their constant spats, Raku and Chitoge manage to fool everyone. Chitoge also has a token from her first love ten years ago—an old key. Meanwhile, Raku's crush, Kosaki, also has a key, as do Marika, the girl Raku's father has arranged for him to marry, and Yui, a childhood friend who's their homeroom teacher. After Yui's confession of love, Marika also approaches Raku with her sincere feelings. But before Raku gives her an answer, Marika's family forces her to come back to her hometown to get married. With the help of his friends, Raku heads to Kyushu to find out what Marika really wants...

SEISHIRO TSUGUMI

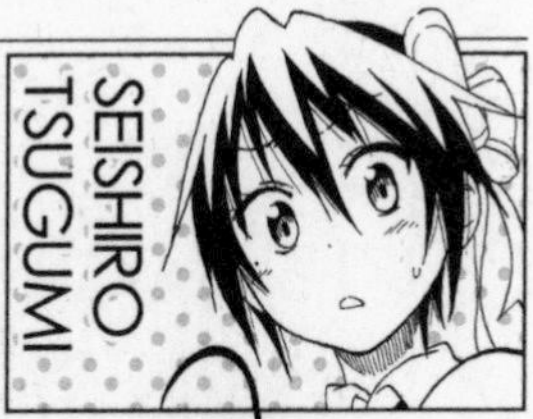

Trained as an assassin in order to protect Chitoge, Tsugumi is often mistaken for a boy.

HARU ONODERA

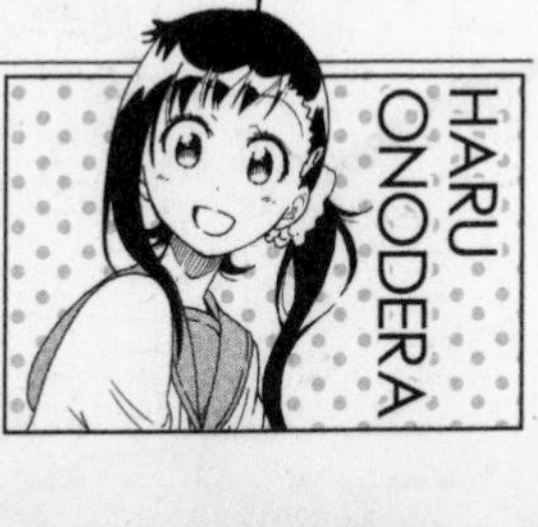

Kosaki's adoring younger sister. Has a low opinion of Raku.

NISEKOI
False Love
vol. 22: Bull's-Eye

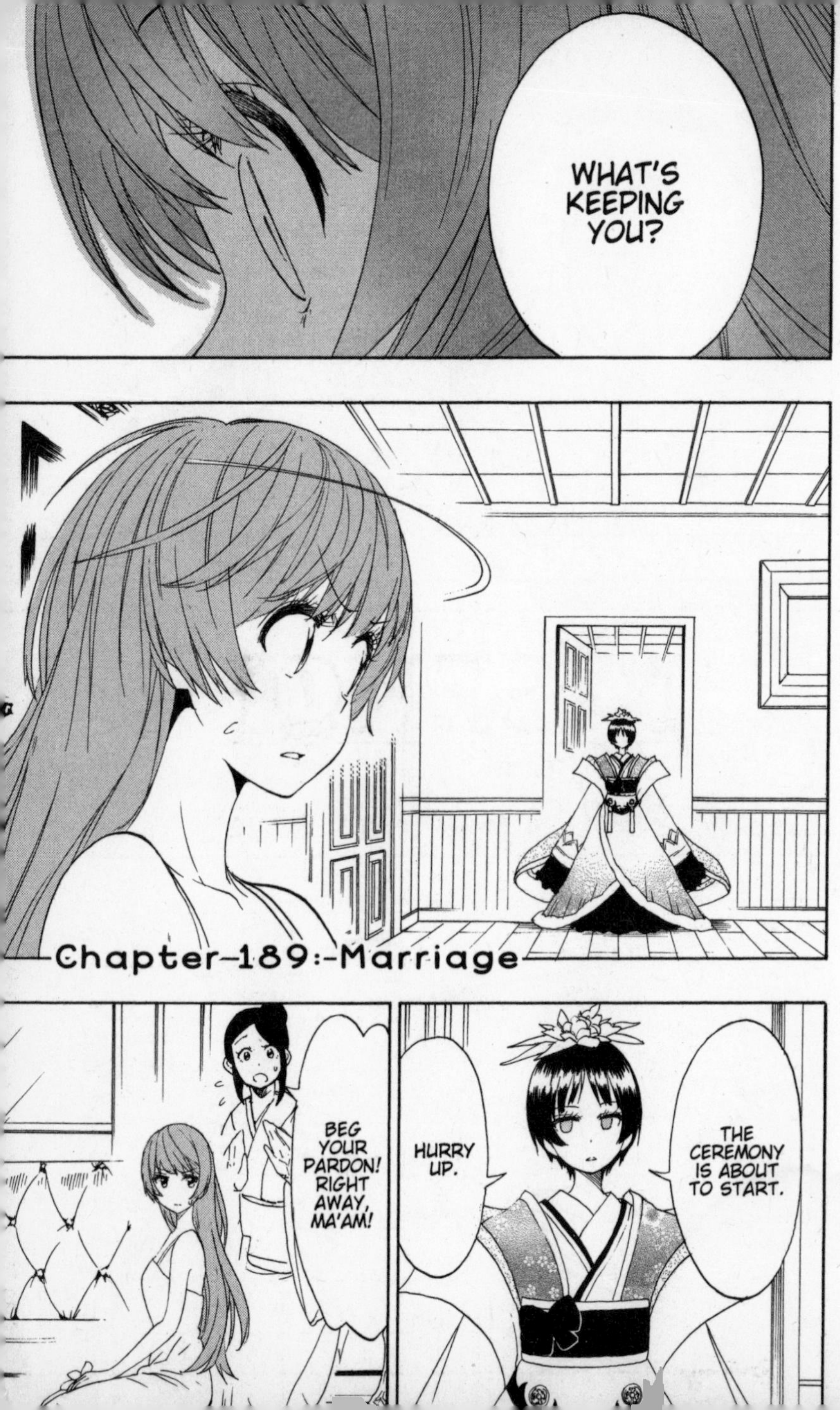
WHAT'S KEEPING YOU?
Chapter 189: Marriage
THE CEREMONY IS ABOUT TO START.
HURRY UP.
BEG YOUR PARDON! RIGHT AWAY, MA'AM!

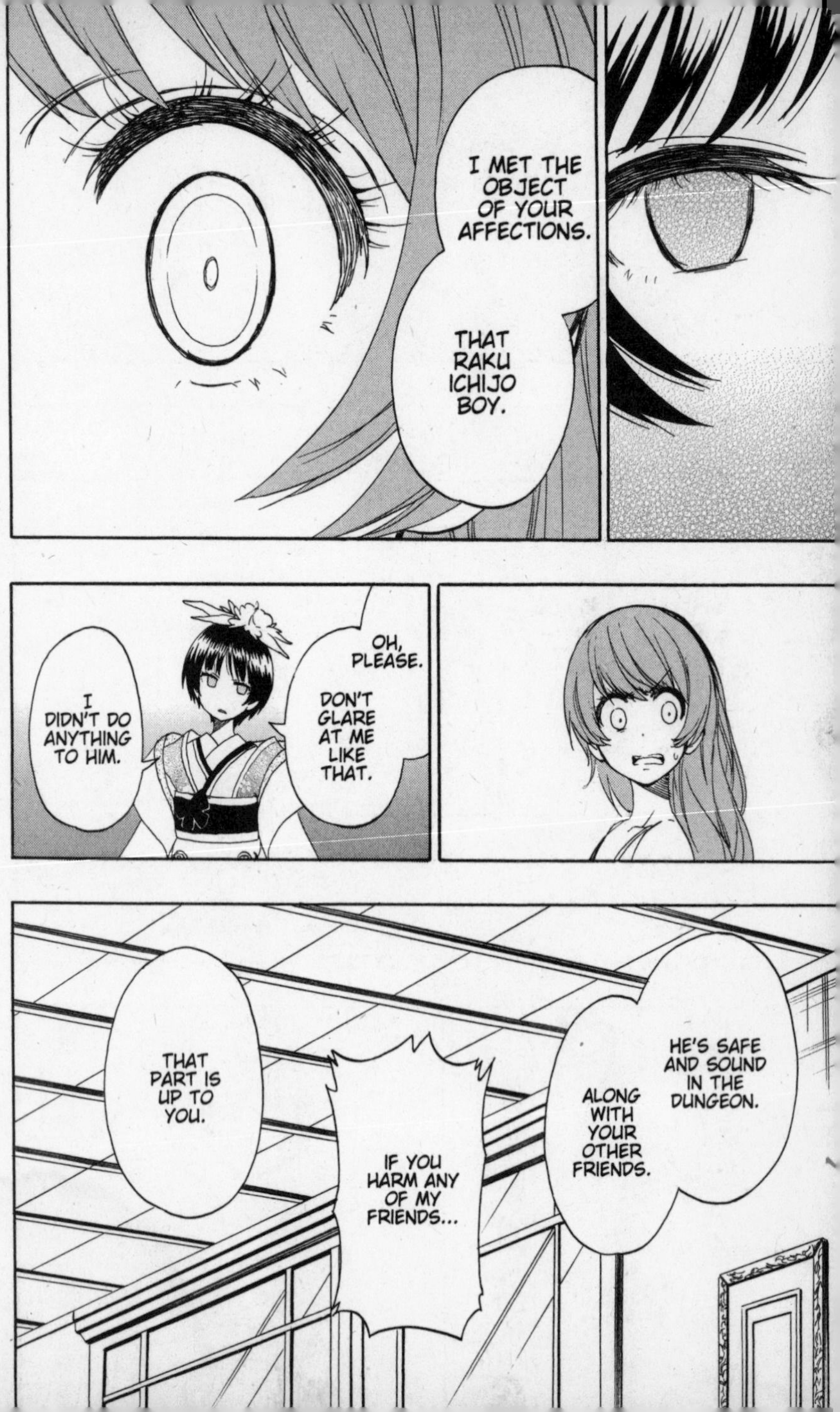
I MET THE OBJECT OF YOUR AFFECTIONS.
THAT RAKU ICHIJO BOY.
OH, PLEASE.
DON'T GLARE AT ME LIKE THAT.
I DIDN'T DO ANYTHING TO HIM.
HE'S SAFE AND SOUND IN THE DUNGEON.
ALONG WITH YOUR OTHER FRIENDS.
IF YOU HARM ANY OF MY FRIENDS...
THAT PART IS UP TO YOU.

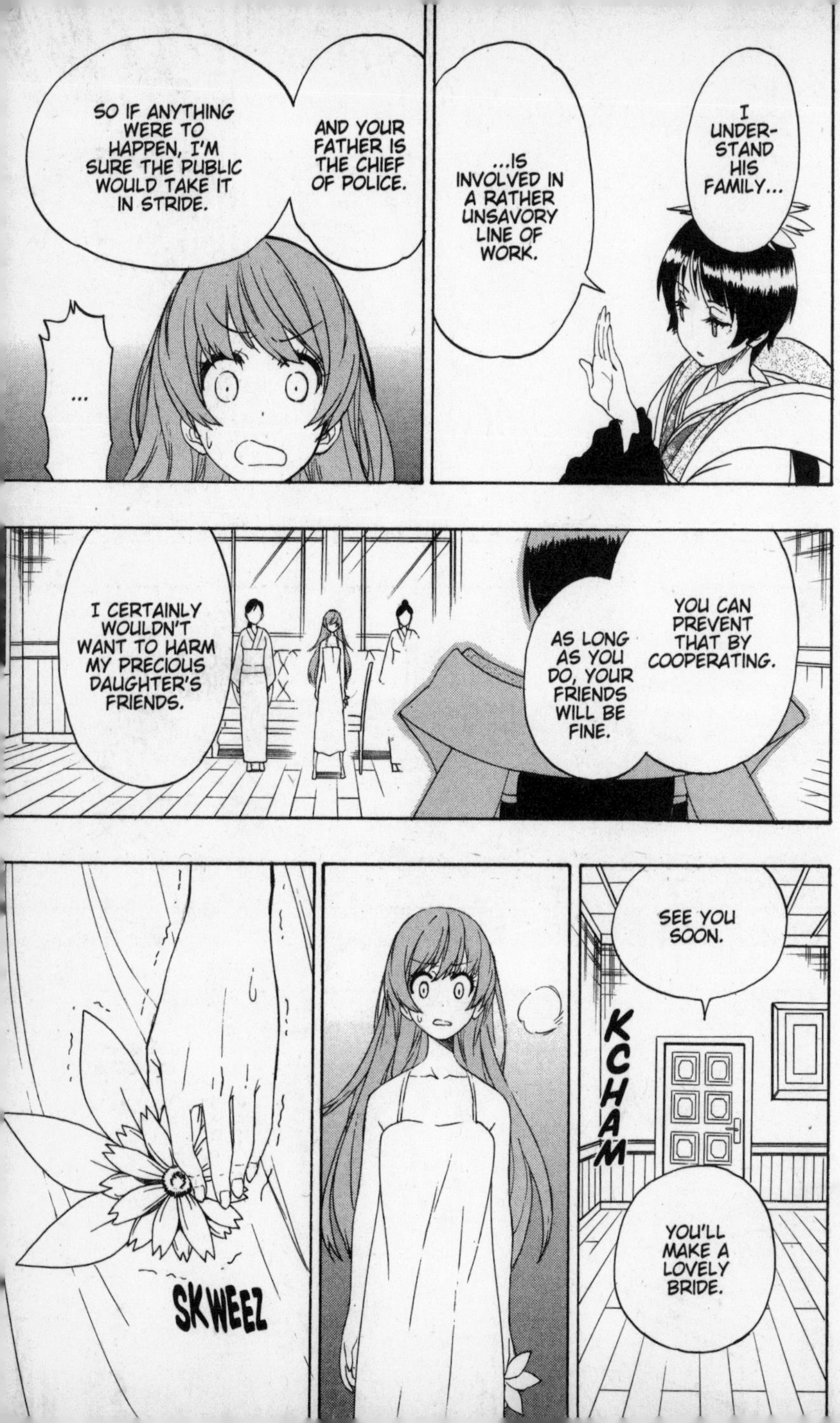
I UNDER-STAND HIS FAMILY...
...IS INVOLVED IN A RATHER UNSAVORY LINE OF WORK.
AND YOUR FATHER IS THE CHIEF OF POLICE.
SO IF ANYTHING WERE TO HAPPEN, I'M SURE THE PUBLIC WOULD TAKE IT IN STRIDE.
...
YOU CAN PREVENT THAT BY COOPERATING.
AS LONG AS YOU DO, YOUR FRIENDS WILL BE FINE.
I CERTAINLY WOULDN'T WANT TO HARM MY PRECIOUS DAUGHTER'S FRIENDS.
SEE YOU SOON.
YOU'LL MAKE A LOVELY BRIDE.
KCHAM
SKWEEZ

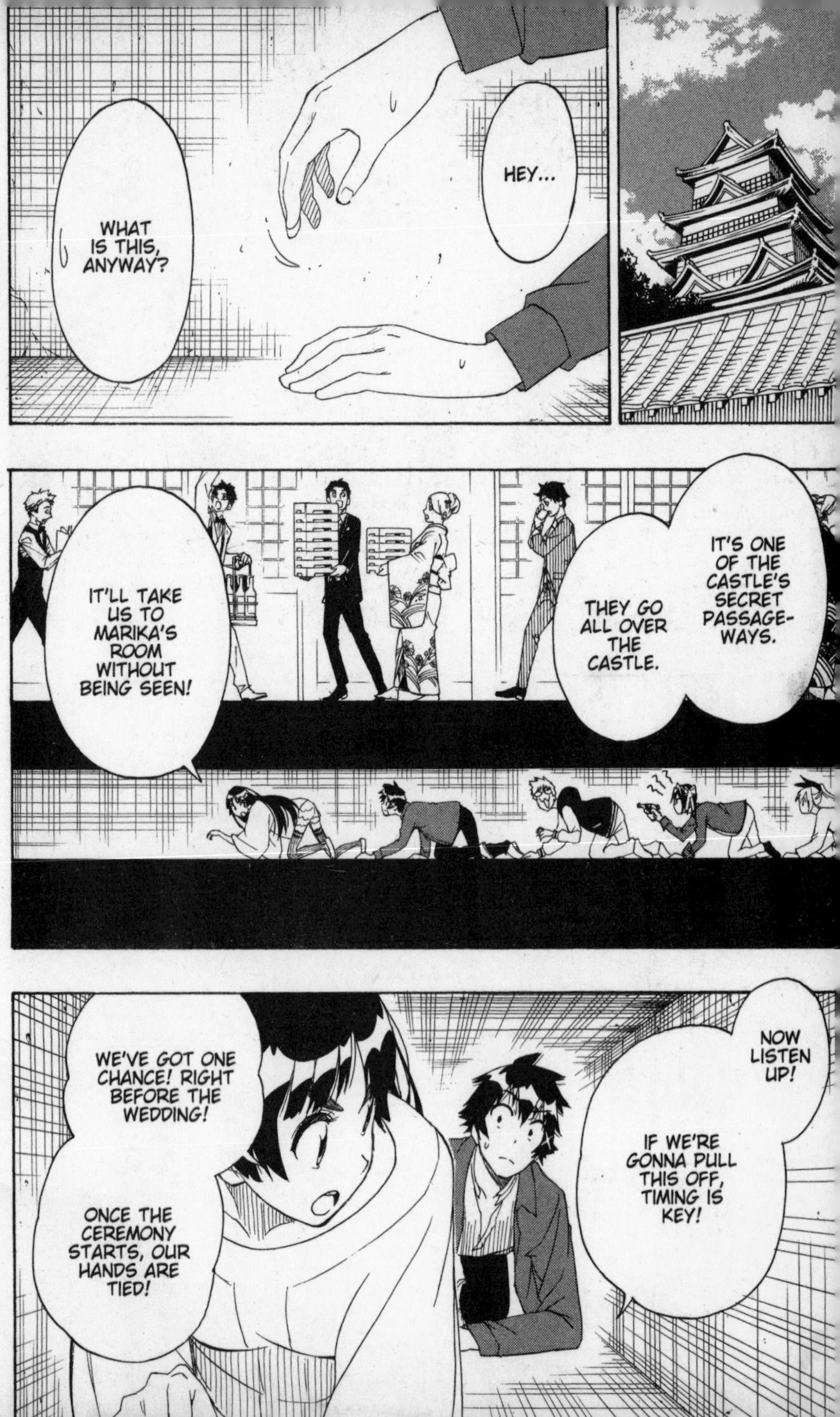
HEY...
WHAT IS THIS, ANYWAY?
IT'S ONE OF THE CASTLE'S SECRET PASSAGE-WAYS.
THEY GO ALL OVER THE CASTLE.
IT'LL TAKE US TO MARIKA'S ROOM WITHOUT BEING SEEN!
NOW LISTEN UP!
IF WE'RE GONNA PULL THIS OFF, TIMING IS KEY!
WE'VE GOT ONE CHANCE! RIGHT BEFORE THE WEDDING!
ONCE THE CEREMONY STARTS, OUR HANDS ARE TIED!

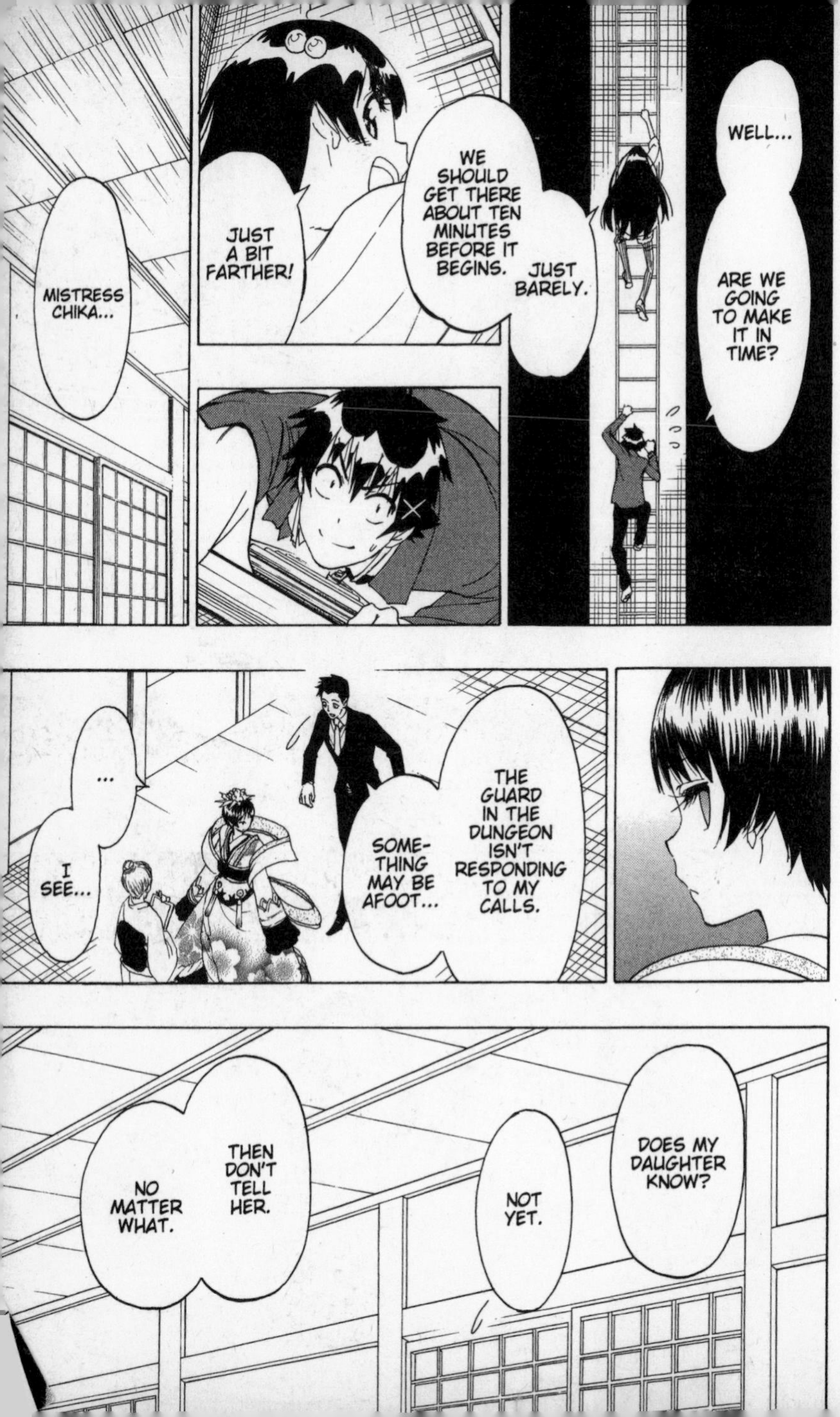
WELL...
ARE WE GOING TO MAKE IT IN TIME?
WE SHOULD GET THERE ABOUT TEN MINUTES BEFORE IT BEGINS.
JUST BARELY.
JUST A BIT FARTHER!
MISTRESS CHIKA...
THE GUARD IN THE DUNGEON ISN'T RESPONDING TO MY CALLS.
SOME-THING MAY BE AFOOT...
...
I SEE...
DOES MY DAUGHTER KNOW?
NOT YET.
THEN DON'T TELL HER.
NO MATTER WHAT.

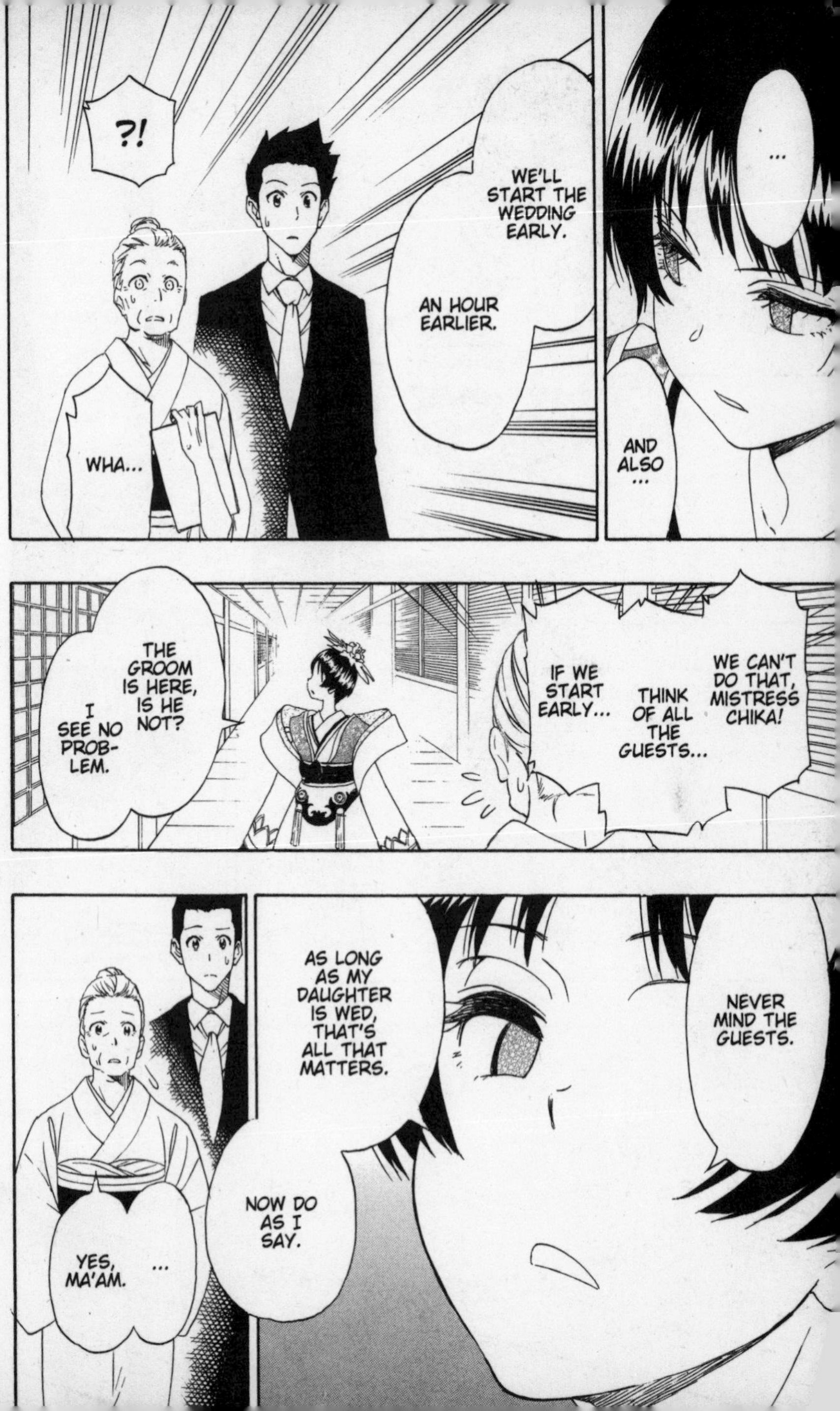
...
AND ALSO ...
WE'LL START THE WEDDING EARLY.
AN HOUR EARLIER.
?!
WHA...
WE CAN'T DO THAT, MISTRESS CHIKA!
THINK OF ALL THE GUESTS...
IF WE START EARLY...
THE GROOM IS HERE, IS HE NOT?
I SEE NO PROB-LEM.
NEVER MIND THE GUESTS.
AS LONG AS MY DAUGHTER IS WED, THAT'S ALL THAT MATTERS.
NOW DO AS I SAY.
...
YES, MA'AM.

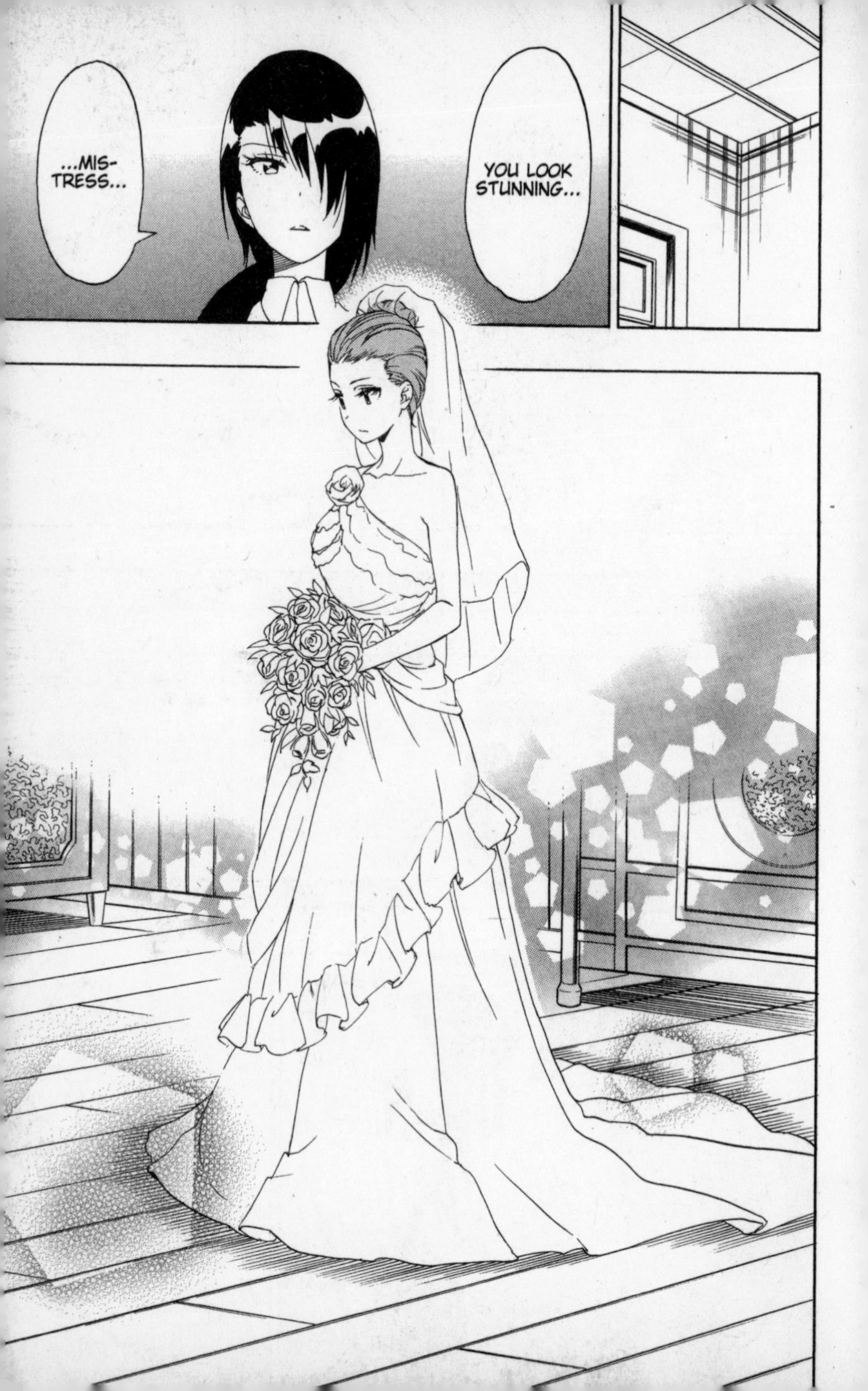
YOU LOOK STUNNING...
...MIS-TRESS...

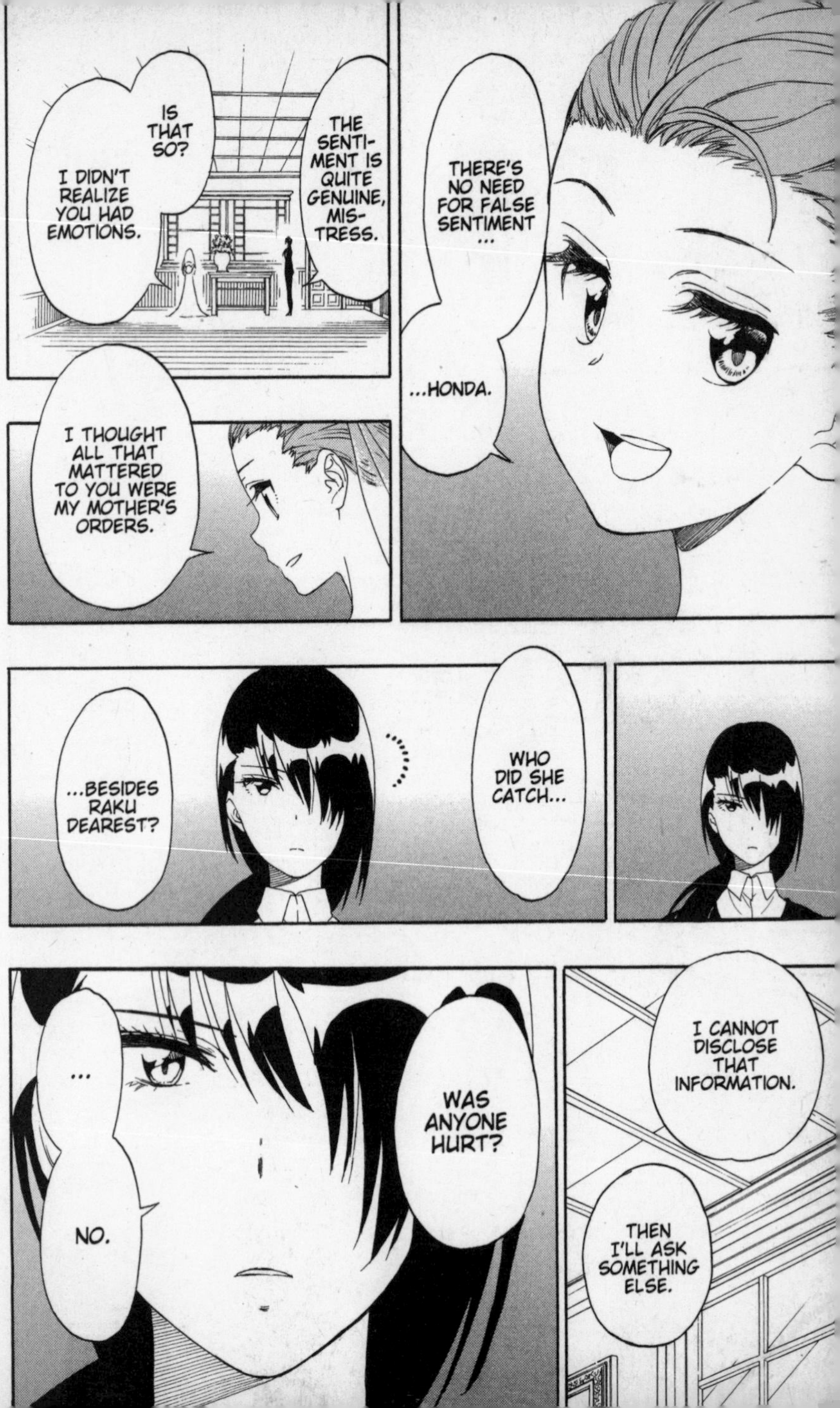
THERE'S NO NEED FOR FALSE SENTIMENT ...
...HONDA.
THE SENTI- MENT IS QUITE GENUINE, MIS- TRESS.
IS THAT SO?
I DIDN'T REALIZE YOU HAD EMOTIONS.
I THOUGHT ALL THAT MATTERED TO YOU WERE MY MOTHER'S ORDERS.
WHO DID SHE CATCH...
...BESIDES RAKU DEAREST?
I CANNOT DISCLOSE THAT INFORMATION.
THEN I'LL ASK SOMETHING ELSE.
WAS ANYONE HURT?
...
NO.

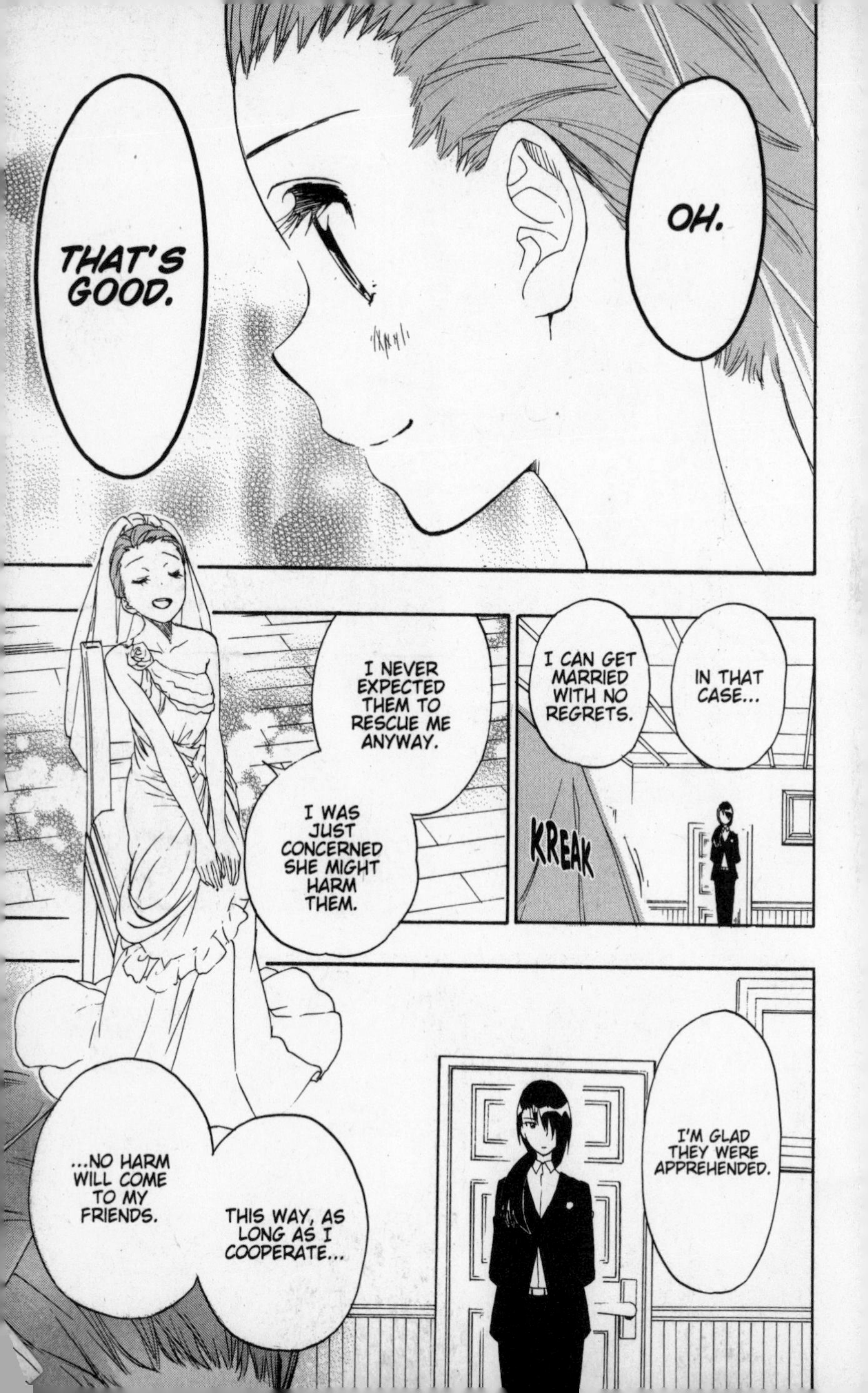
OH.
THAT'S GOOD.
IN THAT CASE...
I CAN GET MARRIED WITH NO REGRETS.
KREAK
I NEVER EXPECTED THEM TO RESCUE ME ANYWAY.
I WAS JUST CONCERNED SHE MIGHT HARM THEM.
I'M GLAD THEY WERE APPREHENDED.
THIS WAY, AS LONG AS I COOPERATE...
...NO HARM WILL COME TO MY FRIENDS.

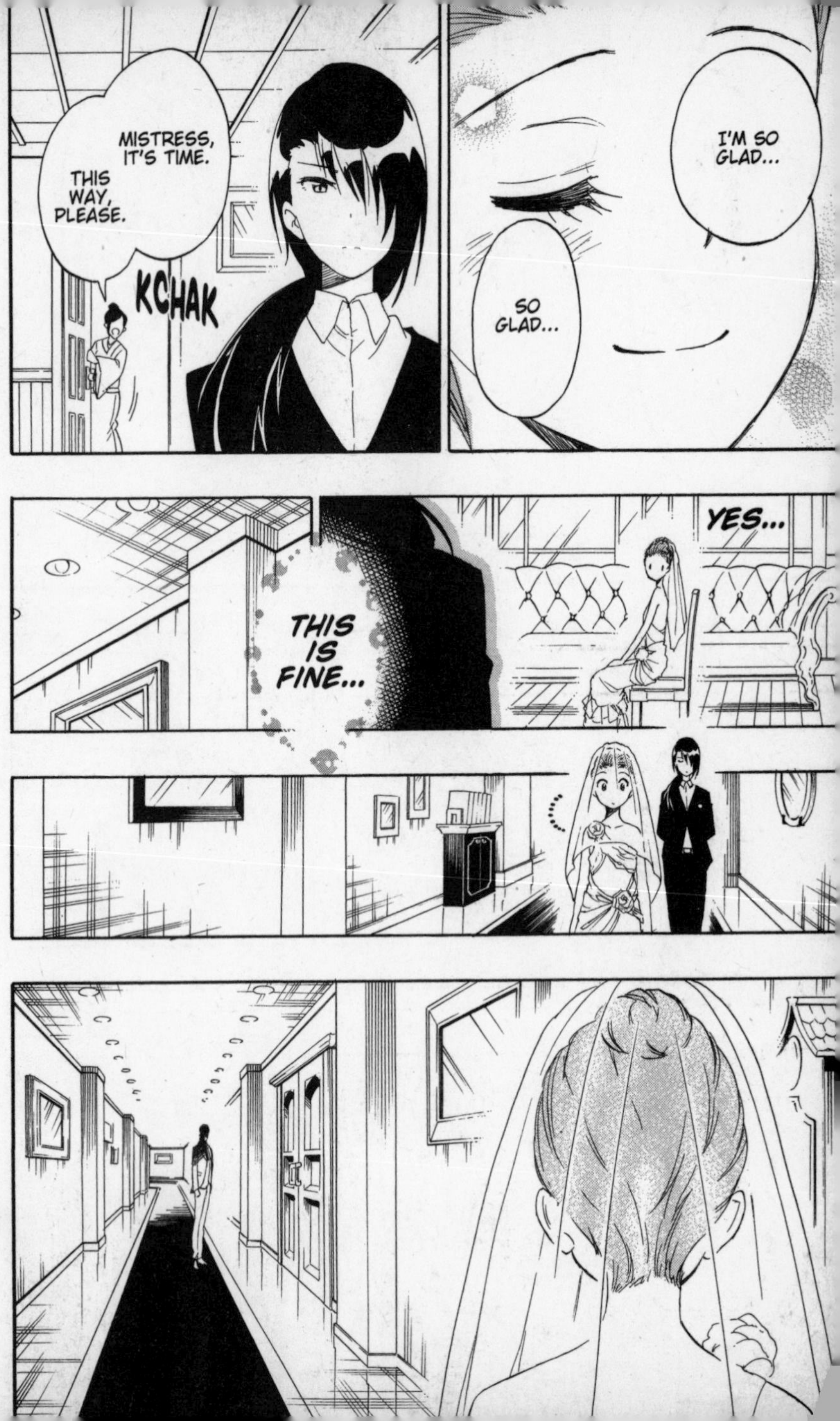
I'M SO GLAD...
SO GLAD...
MISTRESS, IT'S TIME.
THIS WAY, PLEASE.
KCHAK
YES...
THIS IS FINE...

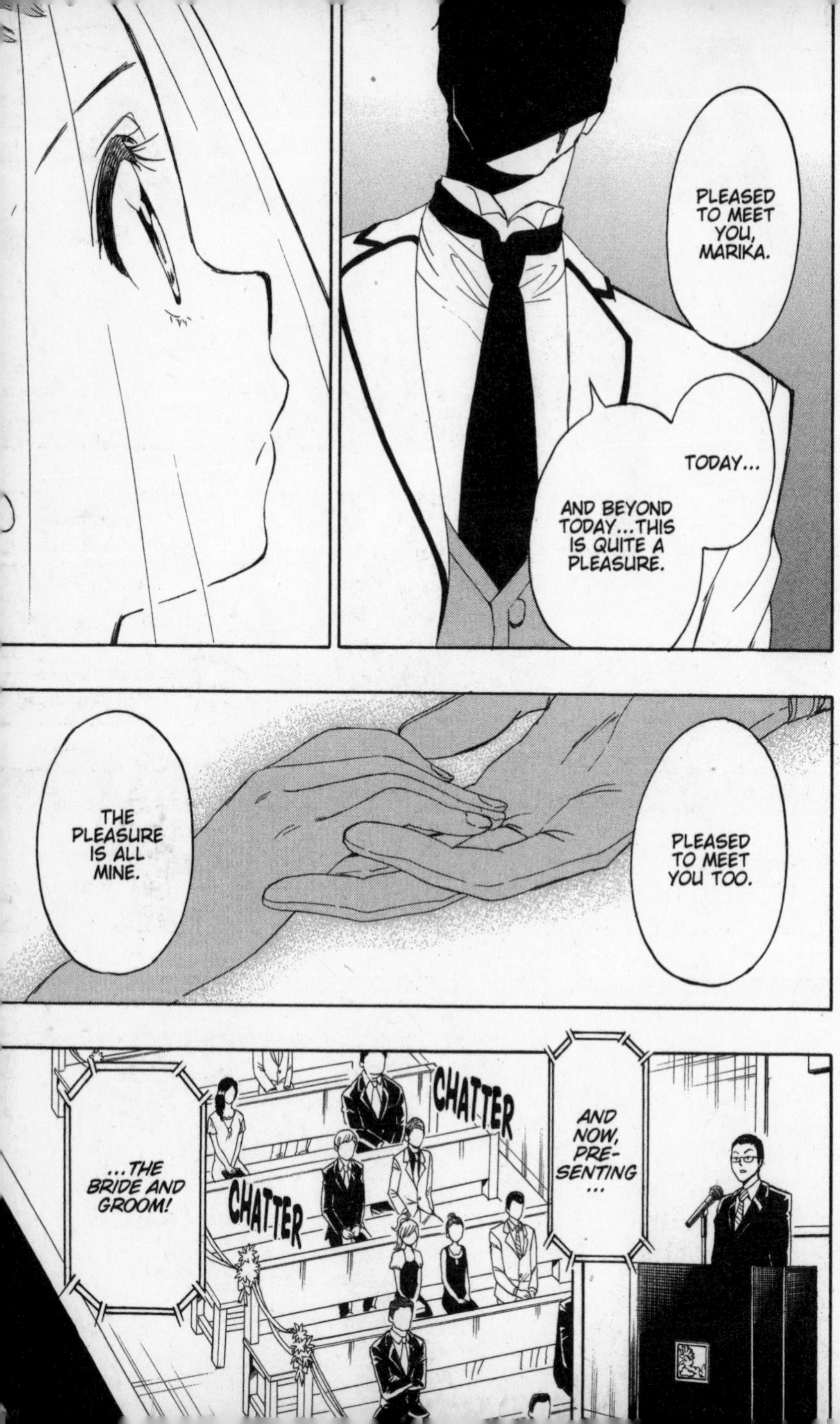
PLEASED TO MEET YOU, MARIKA.
TODAY...
AND BEYOND TODAY...THIS IS QUITE A PLEASURE.
PLEASED TO MEET YOU TOO.
THE PLEASURE IS ALL MINE.
AND NOW, PRE-SENTING ...
CHATTER
CHATTER
...THE BRIDE AND GROOM!

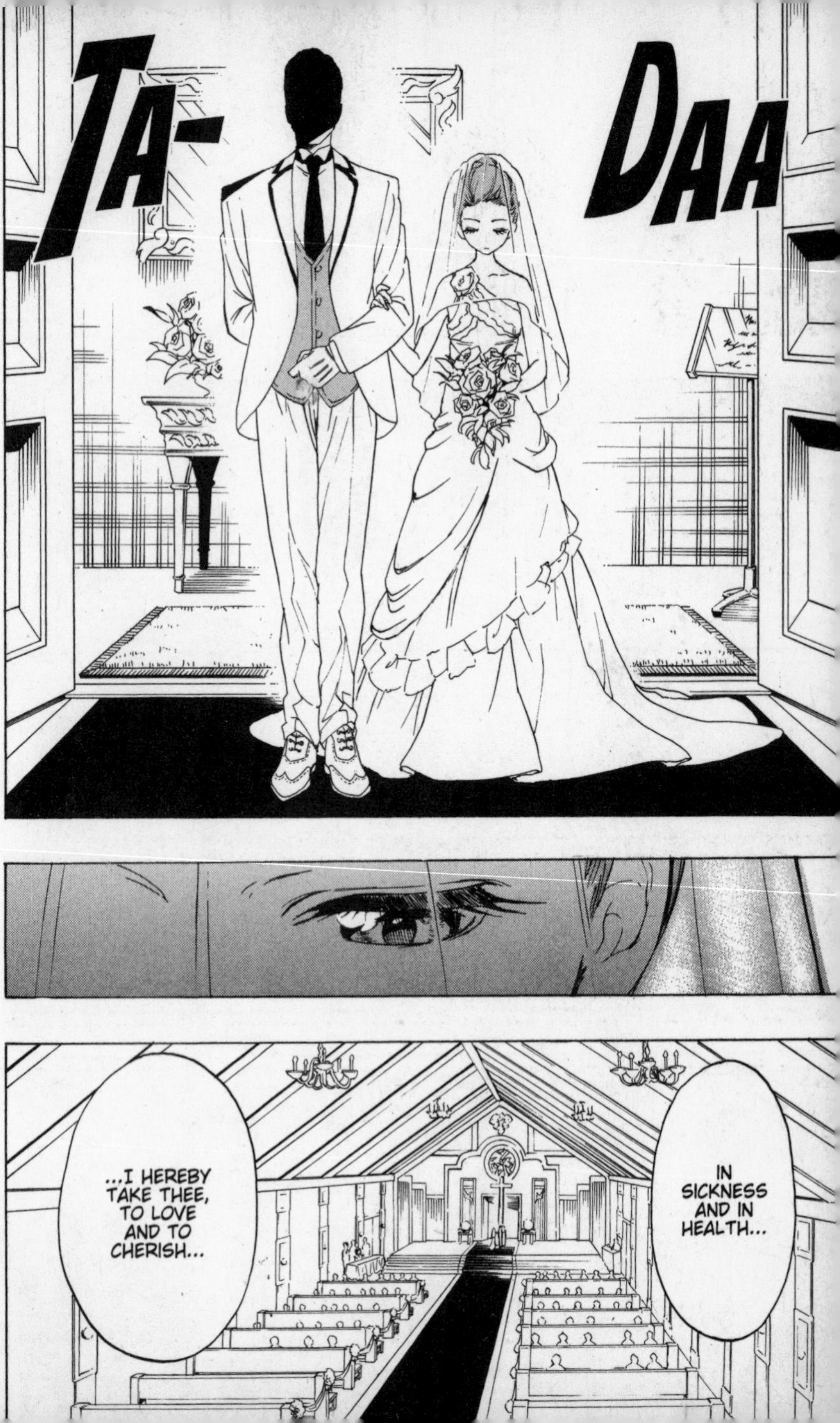
TA-DAA
IN SICKNESS AND IN HEALTH...
...I HEREBY TAKE THEE, TO LOVE AND TO CHERISH...

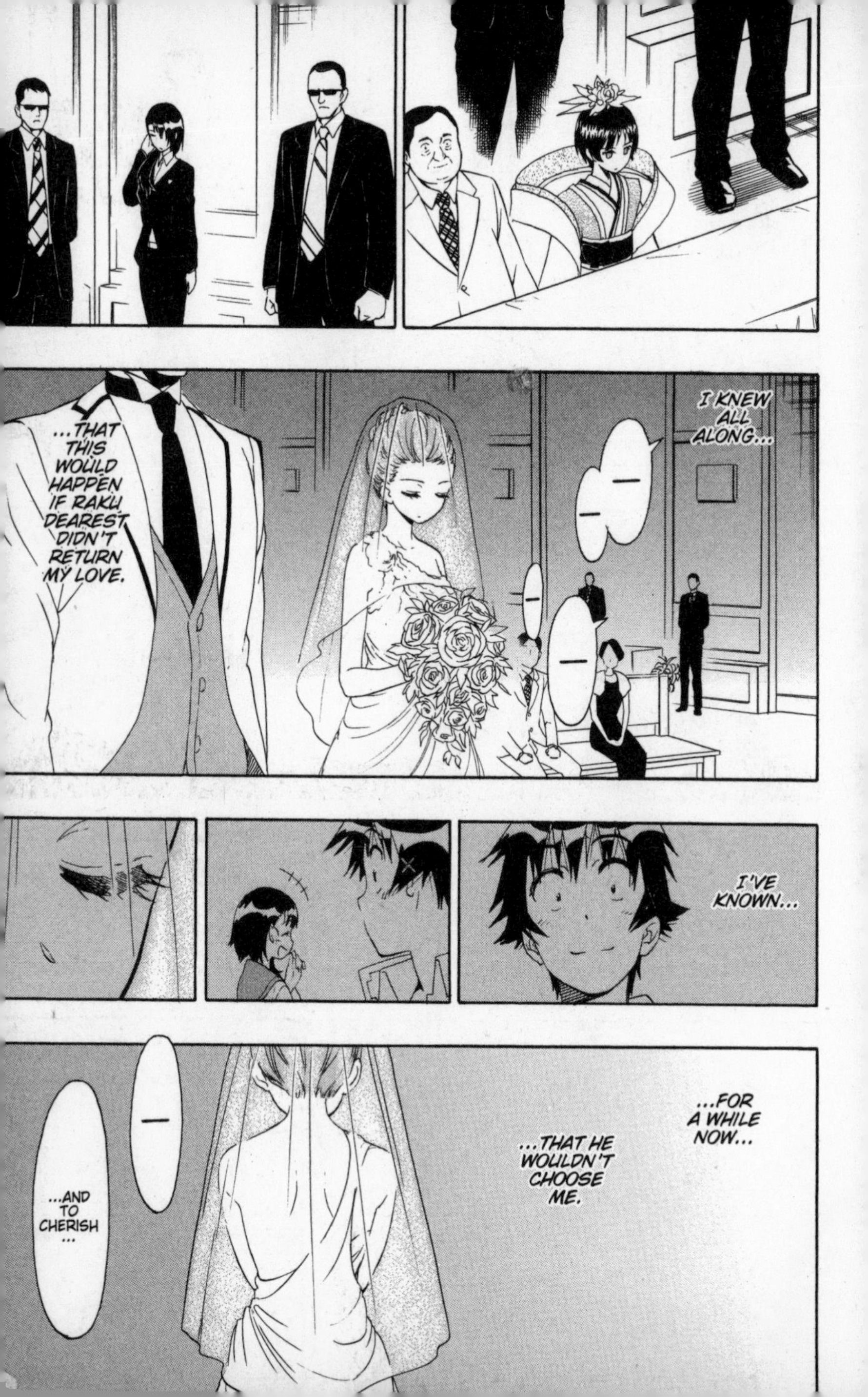
I KNEW ALL ALONG...
——
—
—
...THAT THIS WOULD HAPPEN IF RAKU DEAREST DIDN'T RETURN MY LOVE.
I'VE KNOWN...
...FOR A WHILE NOW...
...THAT HE WOULDN'T CHOOSE ME.
—
...AND TO CHERISH ...

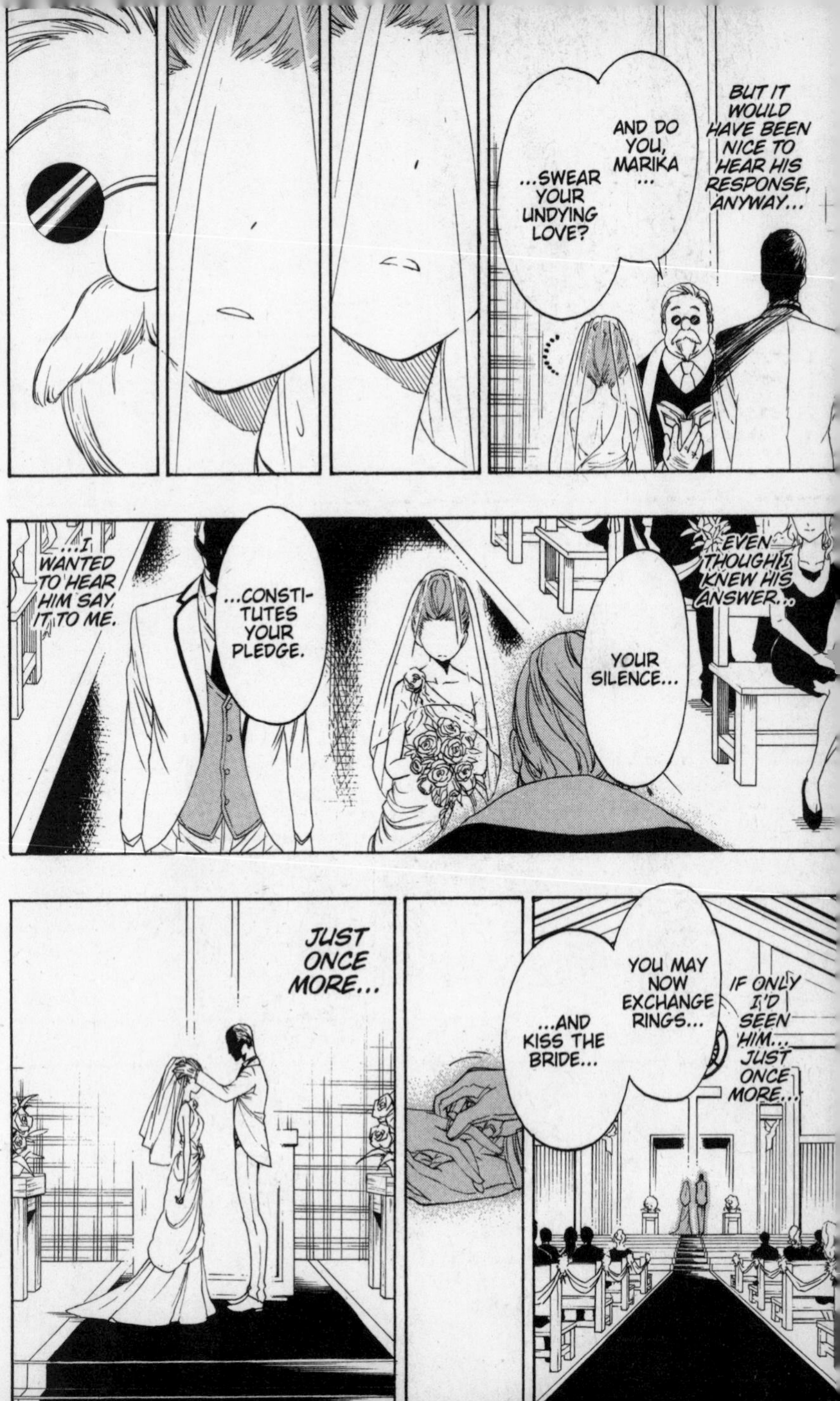
BUT IT WOULD HAVE BEEN NICE TO HEAR HIS RESPONSE, ANYWAY...
AND DO YOU, MARIKA ...
...SWEAR YOUR UNDYING LOVE?
EVEN THOUGH I KNEW HIS ANSWER...
YOUR SILENCE...
...CONSTI-TUTES YOUR PLEDGE.
...I WANTED TO HEAR HIM SAY IT TO ME.
IF ONLY I'D SEEN HIM... JUST ONCE MORE...
YOU MAY NOW EXCHANGE RINGS...
...AND KISS THE BRIDE...
JUST ONCE MORE...

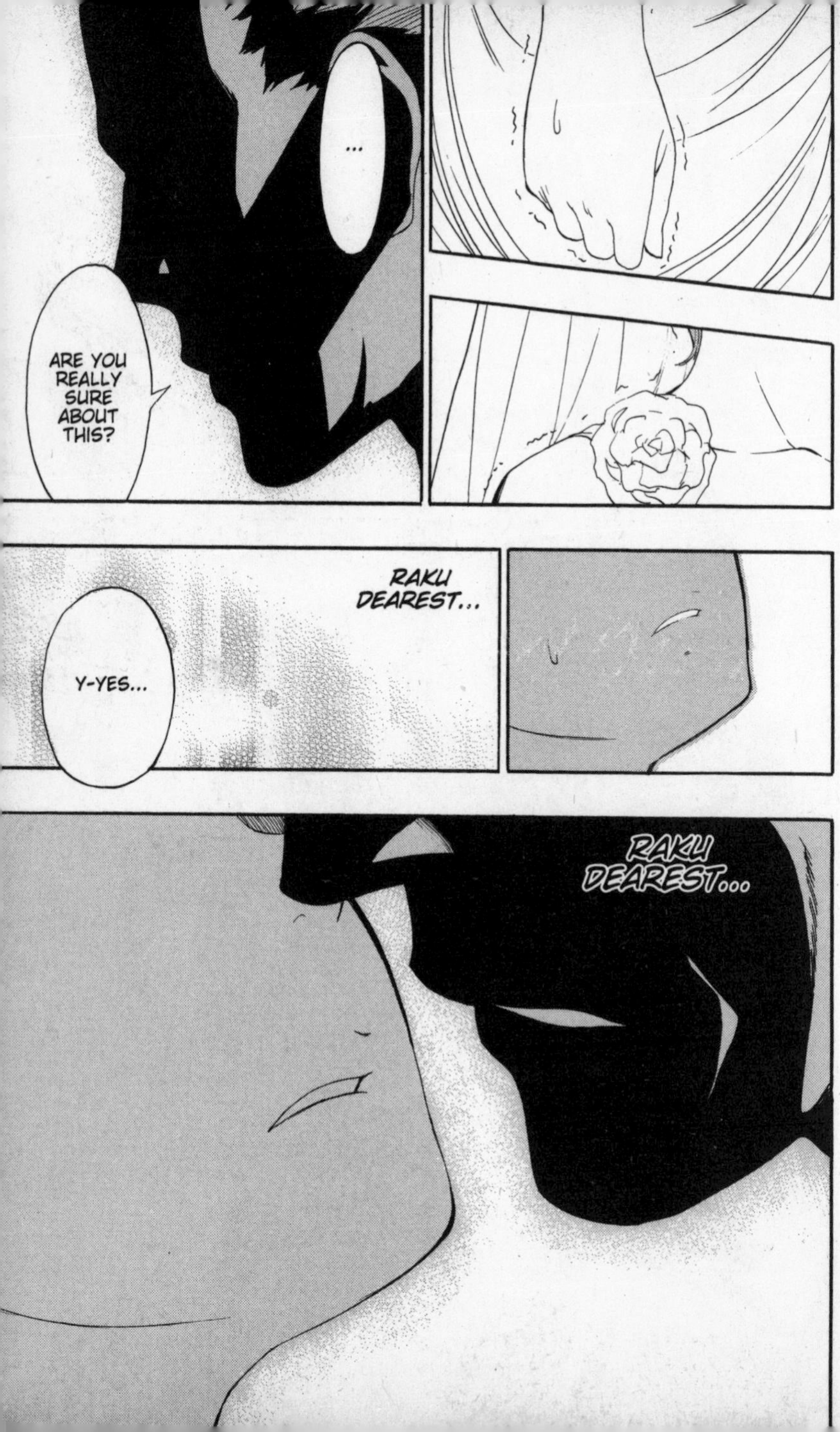
...
ARE YOU REALLY SURE ABOUT THIS?
RAKU DEAREST...
Y-YES...
RAKU DEAREST...

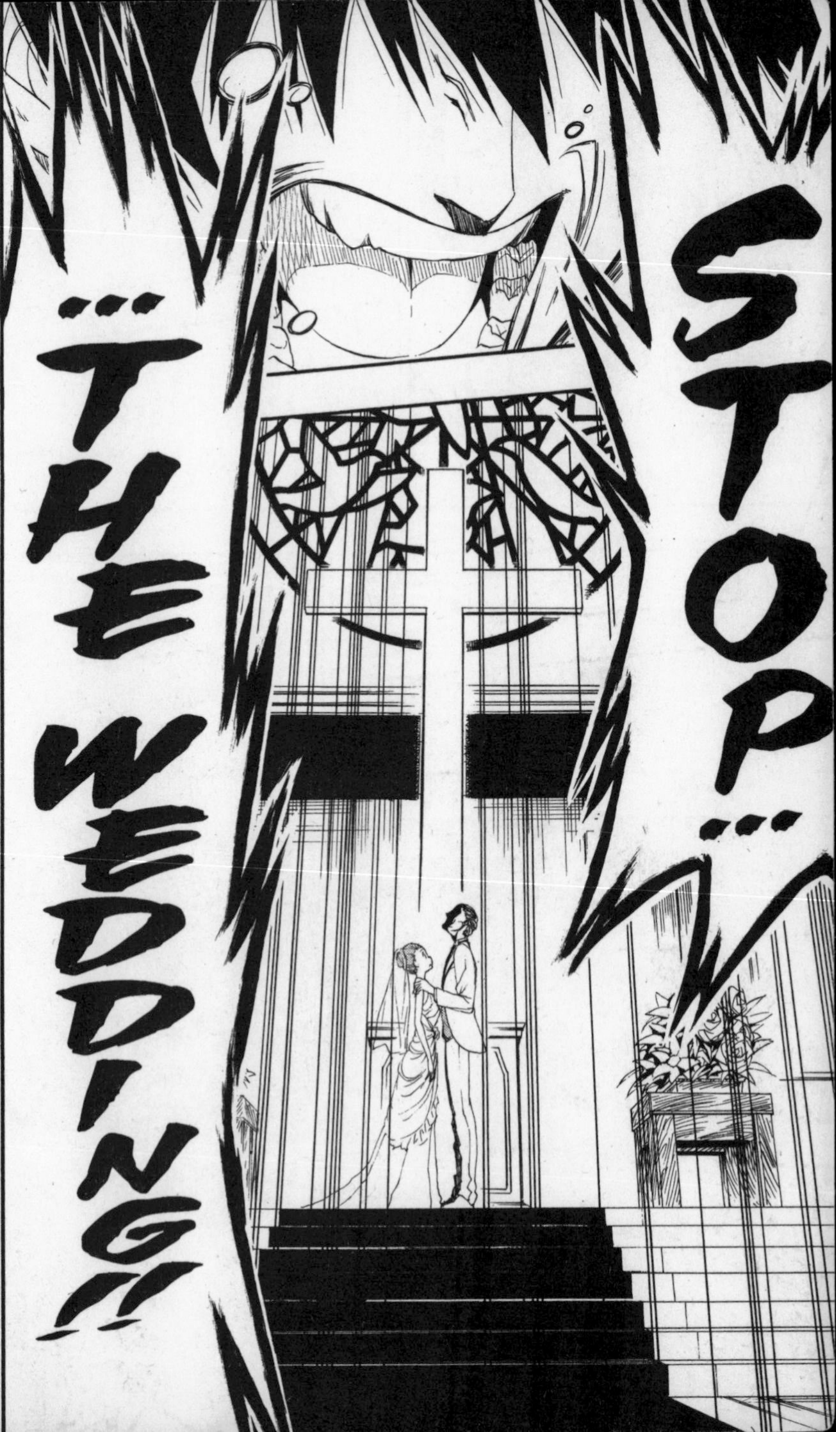
STOP...
...THE WEDDING!!

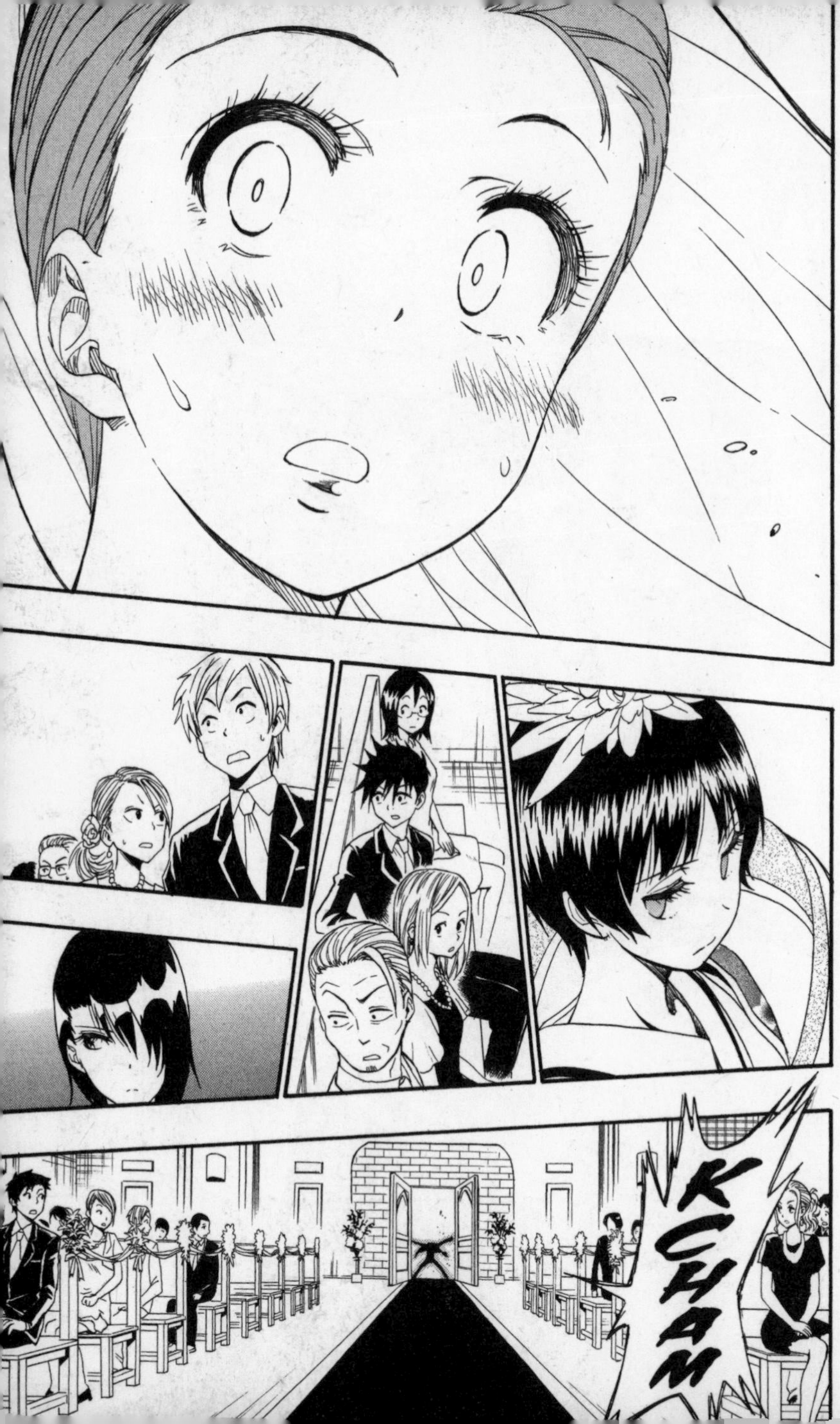
KCHAM

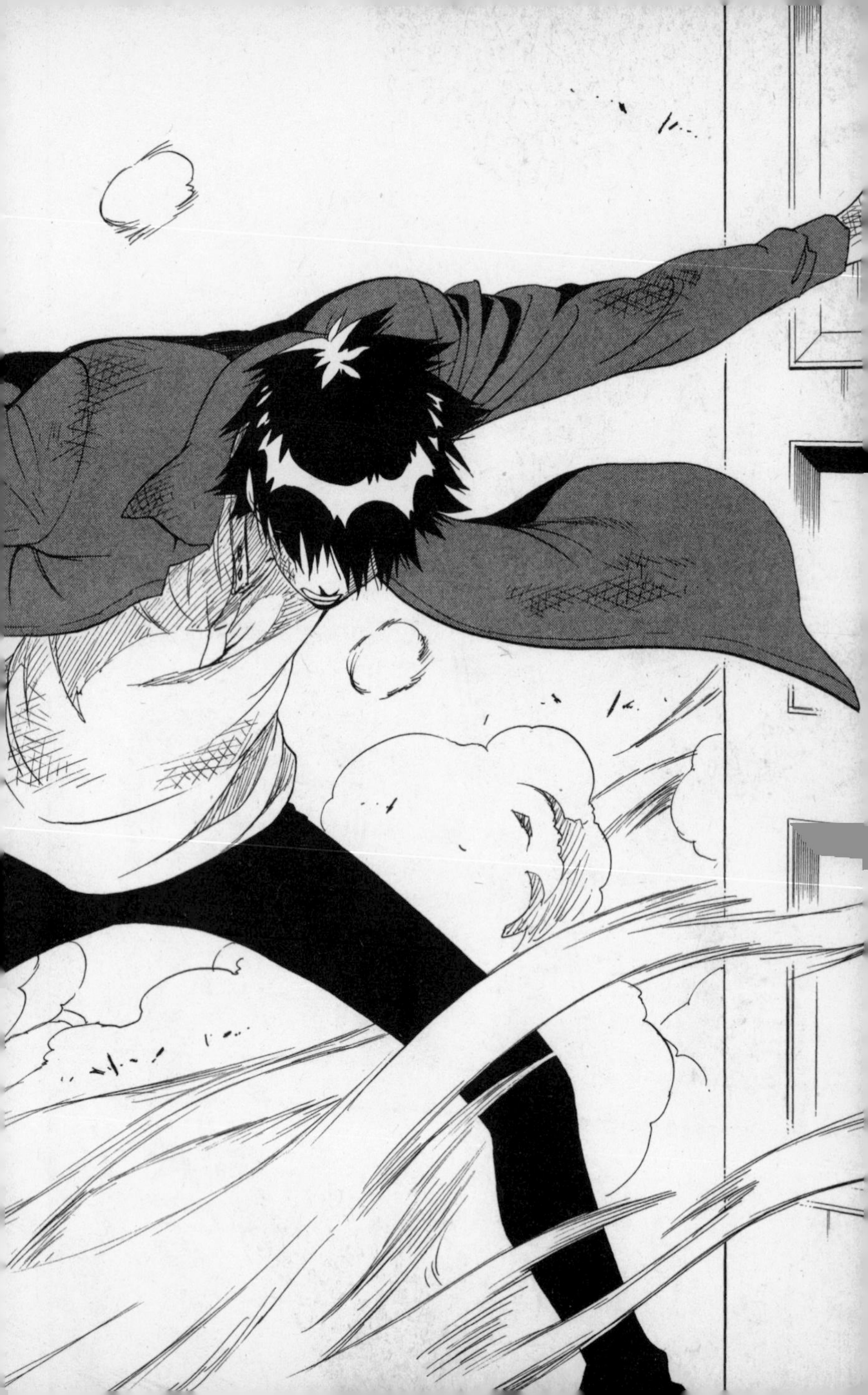

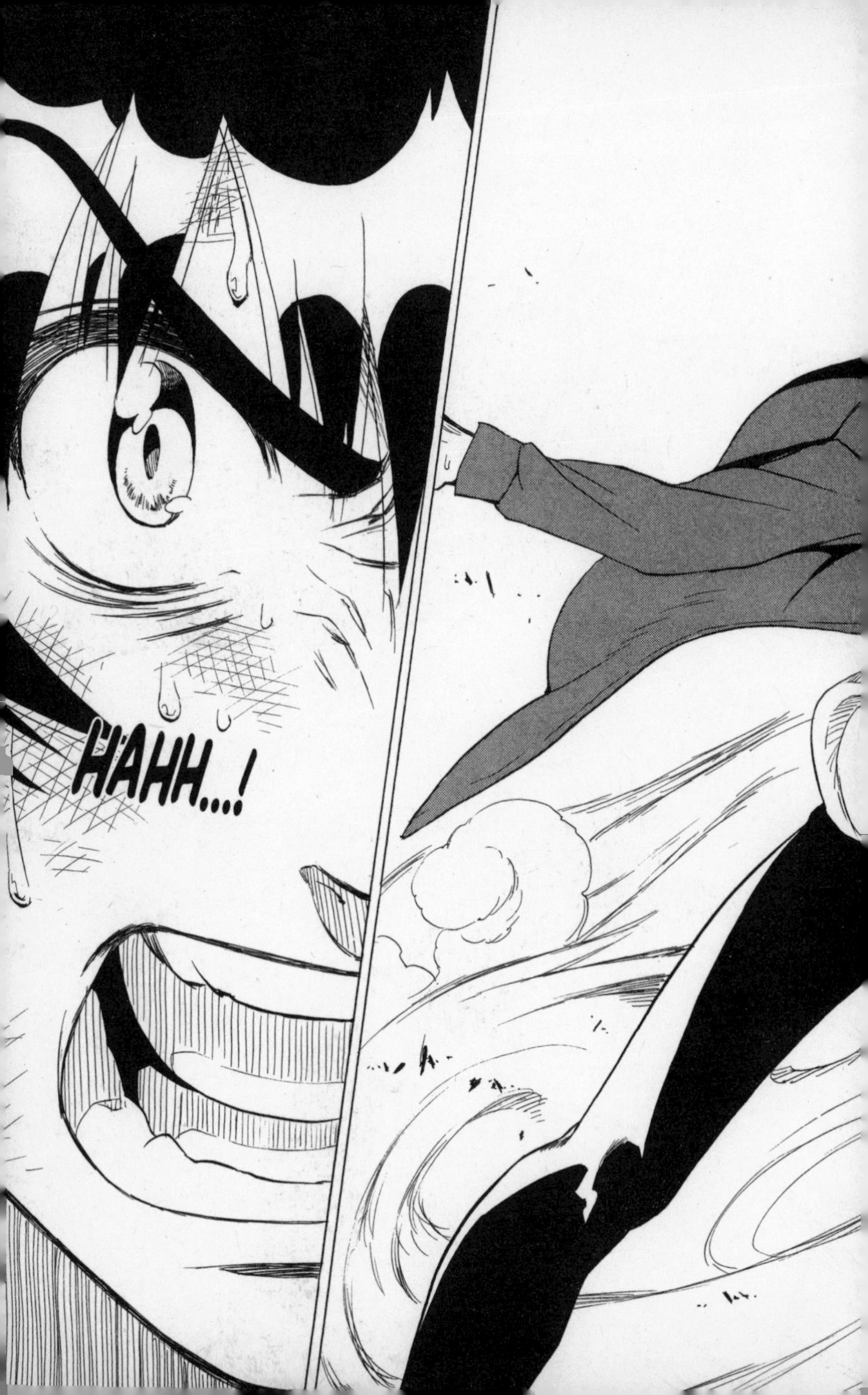
HAHH...!

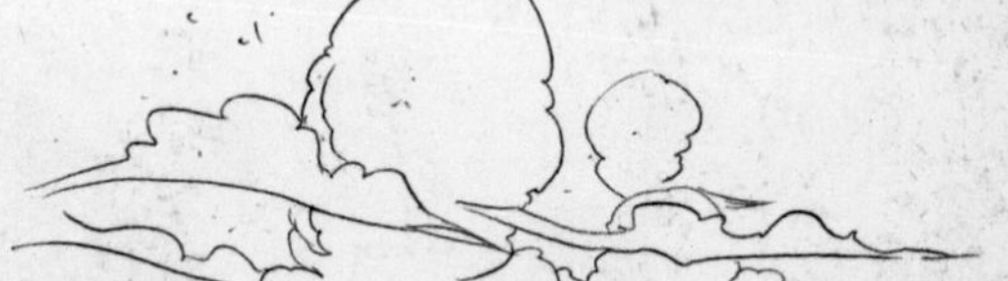

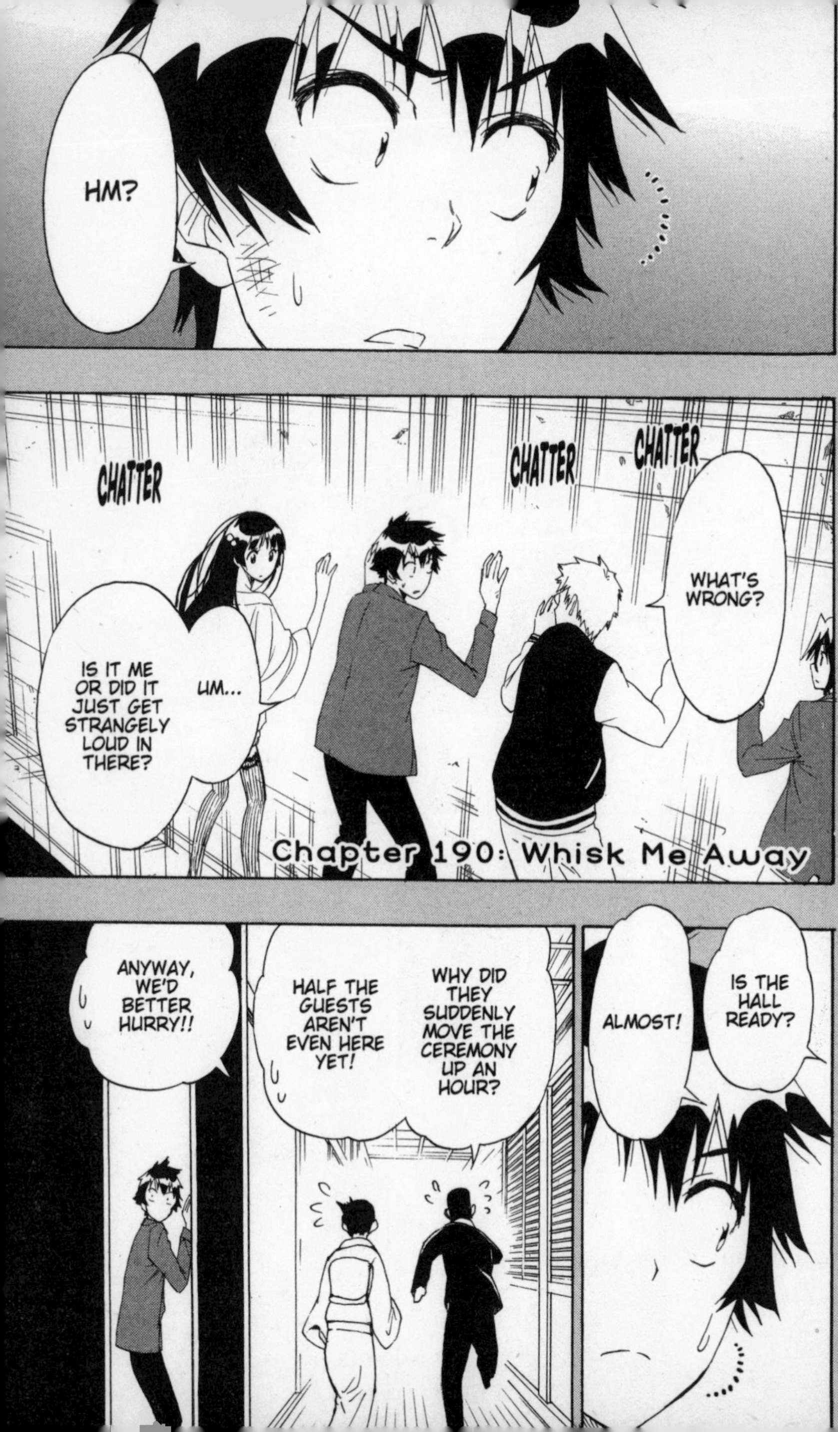
HM?
WHAT'S WRONG?
CHATTER
CHATTER
CHATTER
UM...
IS IT ME OR DID IT JUST GET STRANGELY LOUD IN THERE?
Chapter 190: Whisk Me Away
IS THE HALL READY?
ALMOST!
WHY DID THEY SUDDENLY MOVE THE CEREMONY UP AN HOUR?
HALF THE GUESTS AREN'T EVEN HERE YET!
ANYWAY, WE'D BETTER HURRY!!

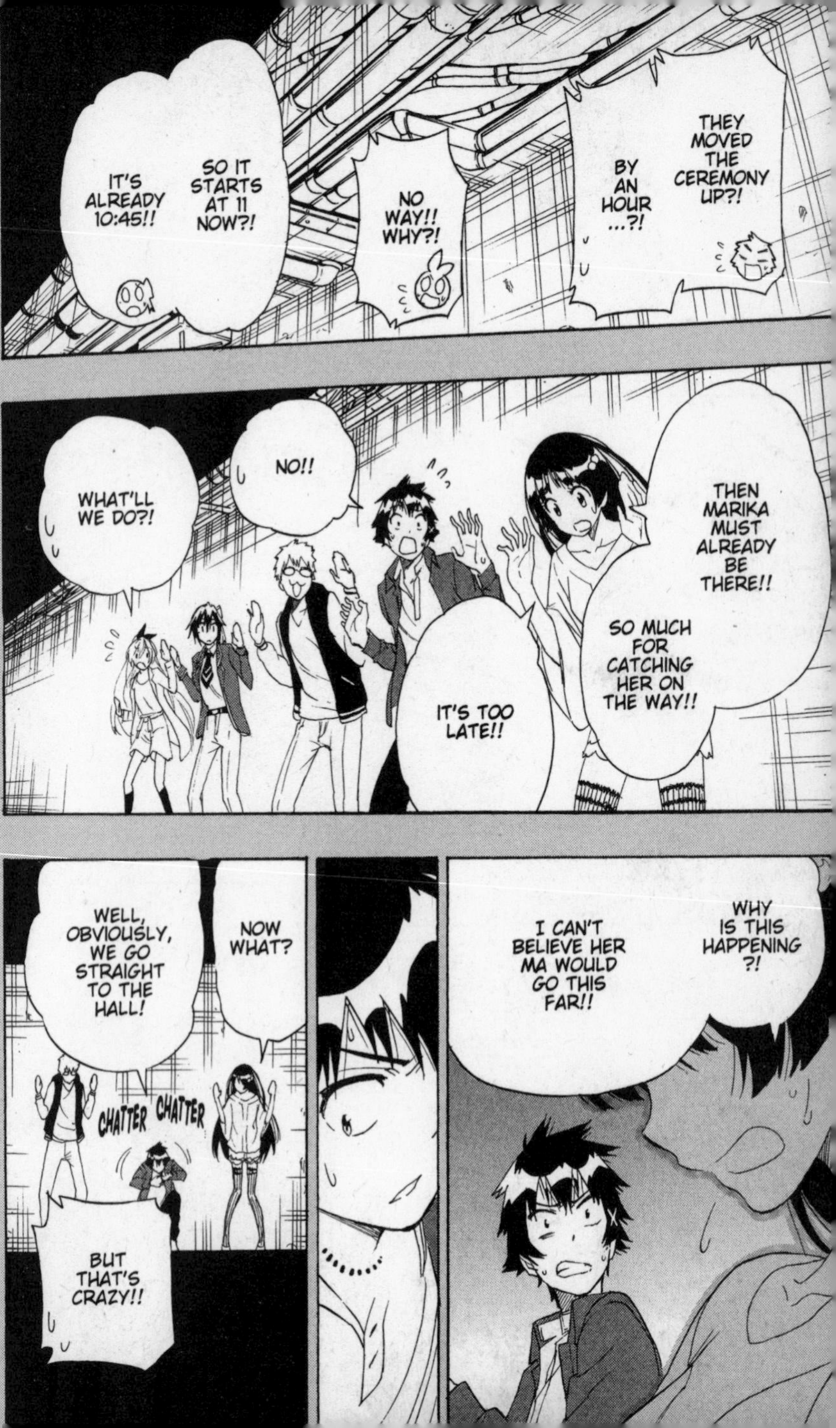
THEY MOVED THE CEREMONY UP?!
BY AN HOUR ...?!
NO WAY!! WHY?!
SO IT STARTS AT 11 NOW?!
IT'S ALREADY 10:45!!
THEN MARIKA MUST ALREADY BE THERE!!
SO MUCH FOR CATCHING HER ON THE WAY!!
IT'S TOO LATE!!
NO!!
WHAT'LL WE DO?!
WHY IS THIS HAPPENING?!
I CAN'T BELIEVE HER MA WOULD GO THIS FAR!!
NOW WHAT?
WELL, OBVIOUSLY, WE GO STRAIGHT TO THE HALL!
CHATTER CHATTER
BUT THAT'S CRAZY!!

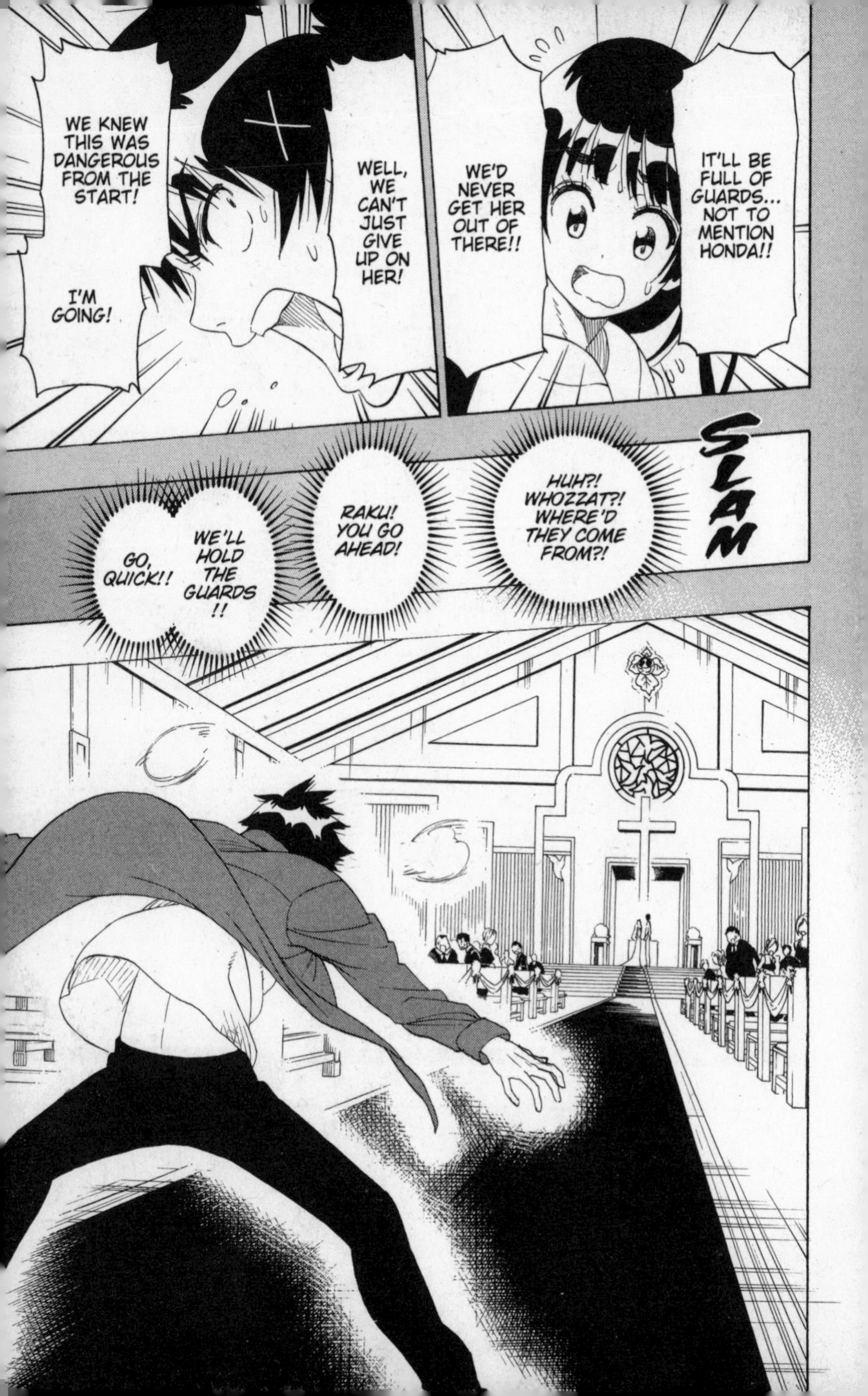
IT'LL BE FULL OF GUARDS... NOT TO MENTION HONDA!!
WE'D NEVER GET HER OUT OF THERE!!
WELL, WE CAN'T JUST GIVE UP ON HER!
WE KNEW THIS WAS DANGEROUS FROM THE START!
I'M GOING!
SLAM
HUH?! WHOZZAT?! WHERE'D THEY COME FROM?!
RAKU! YOU GO AHEAD!
WE'LL HOLD THE GUARDS!!
GO, QUICK!!

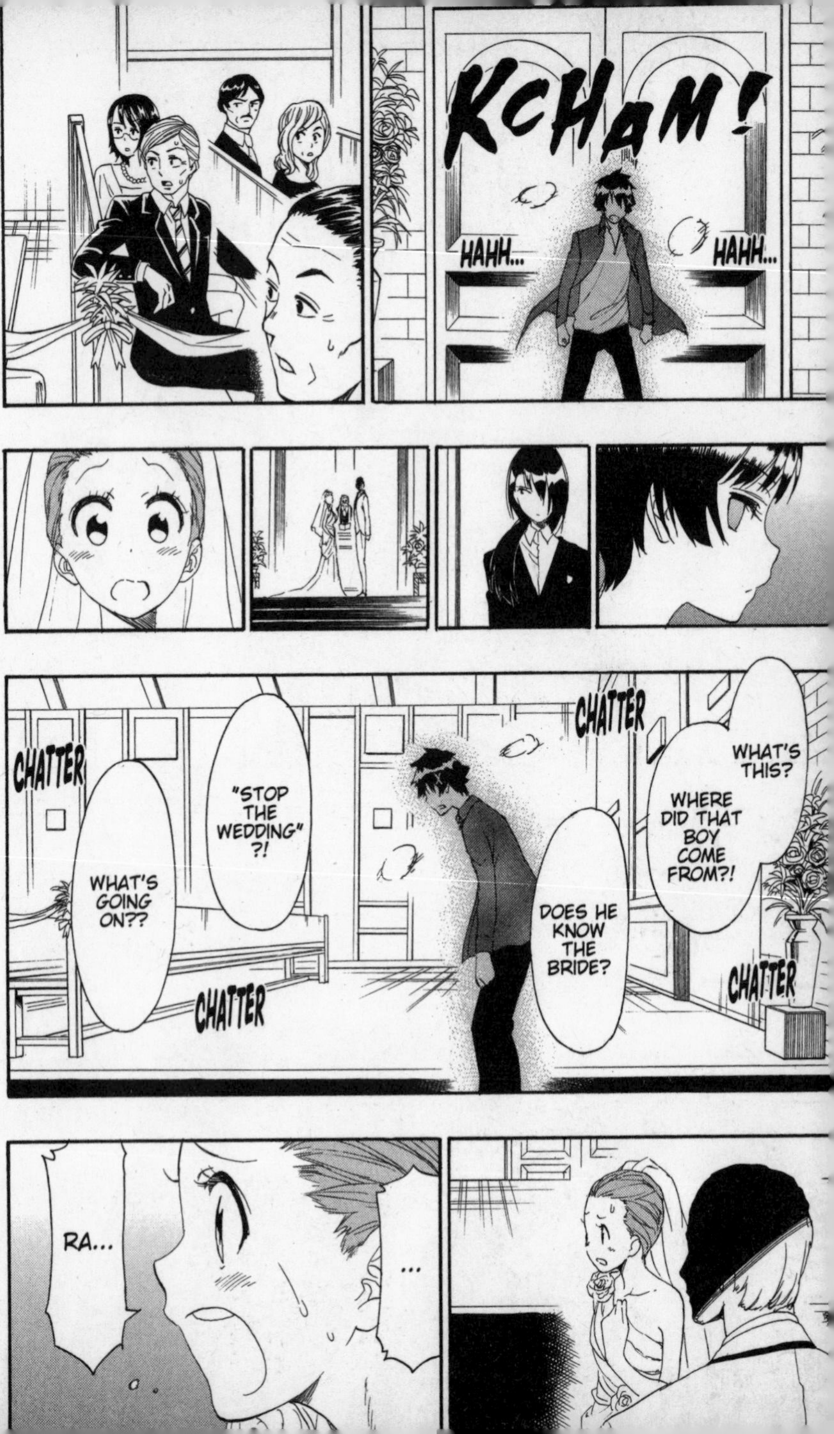
KCHAM!
HAHH...
HAHH...
CHATTER
WHAT'S THIS?
WHERE DID THAT BOY COME FROM?!
CHATTER
DOES HE KNOW THE BRIDE?
"STOP THE WEDDING"?!
CHATTER
WHAT'S GOING ON??
CHATTER
RA...
...

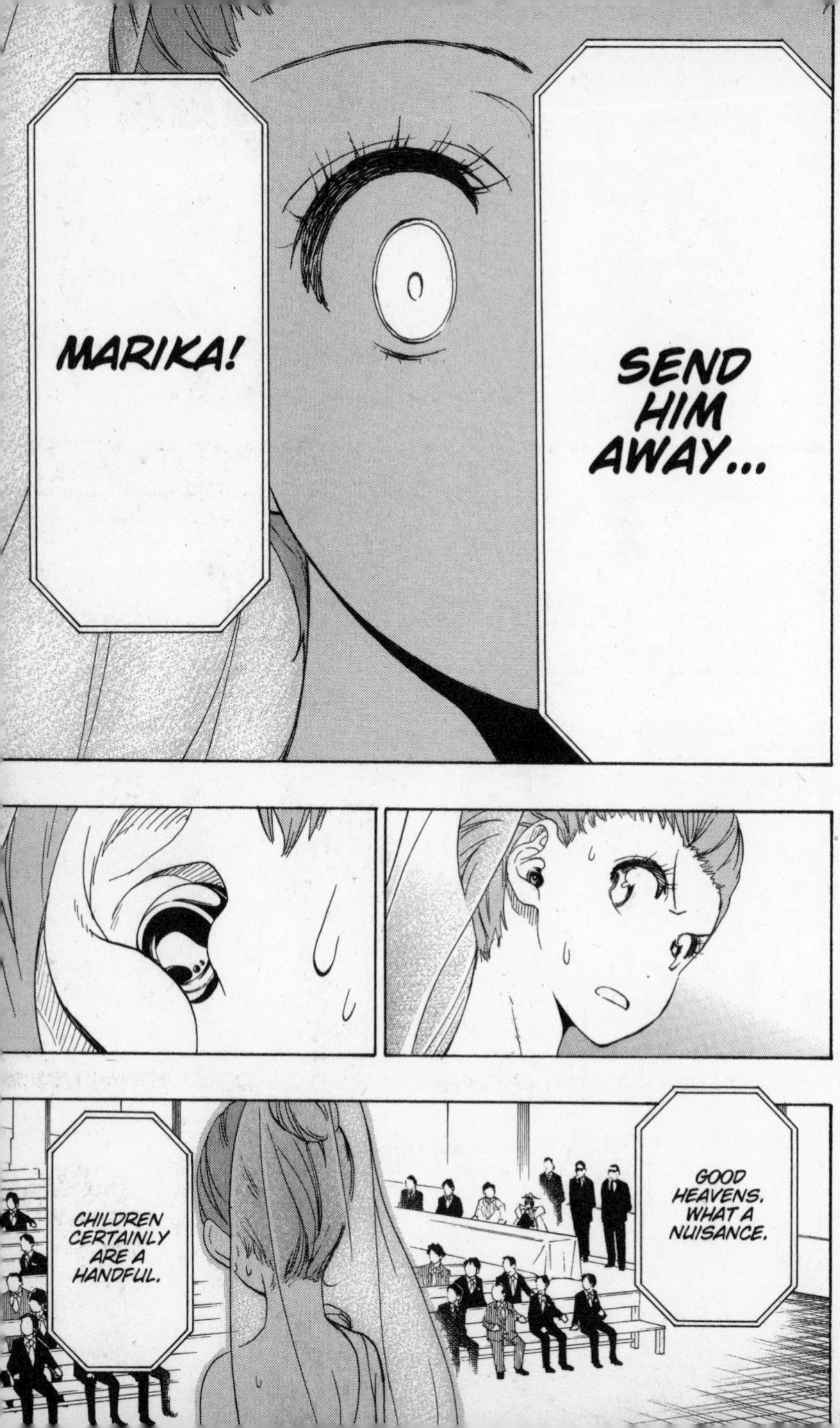
SEND HIM AWAY...
MARIKA!
GOOD HEAVENS. WHAT A NUISANCE.
CHILDREN CERTAINLY ARE A HANDFUL.

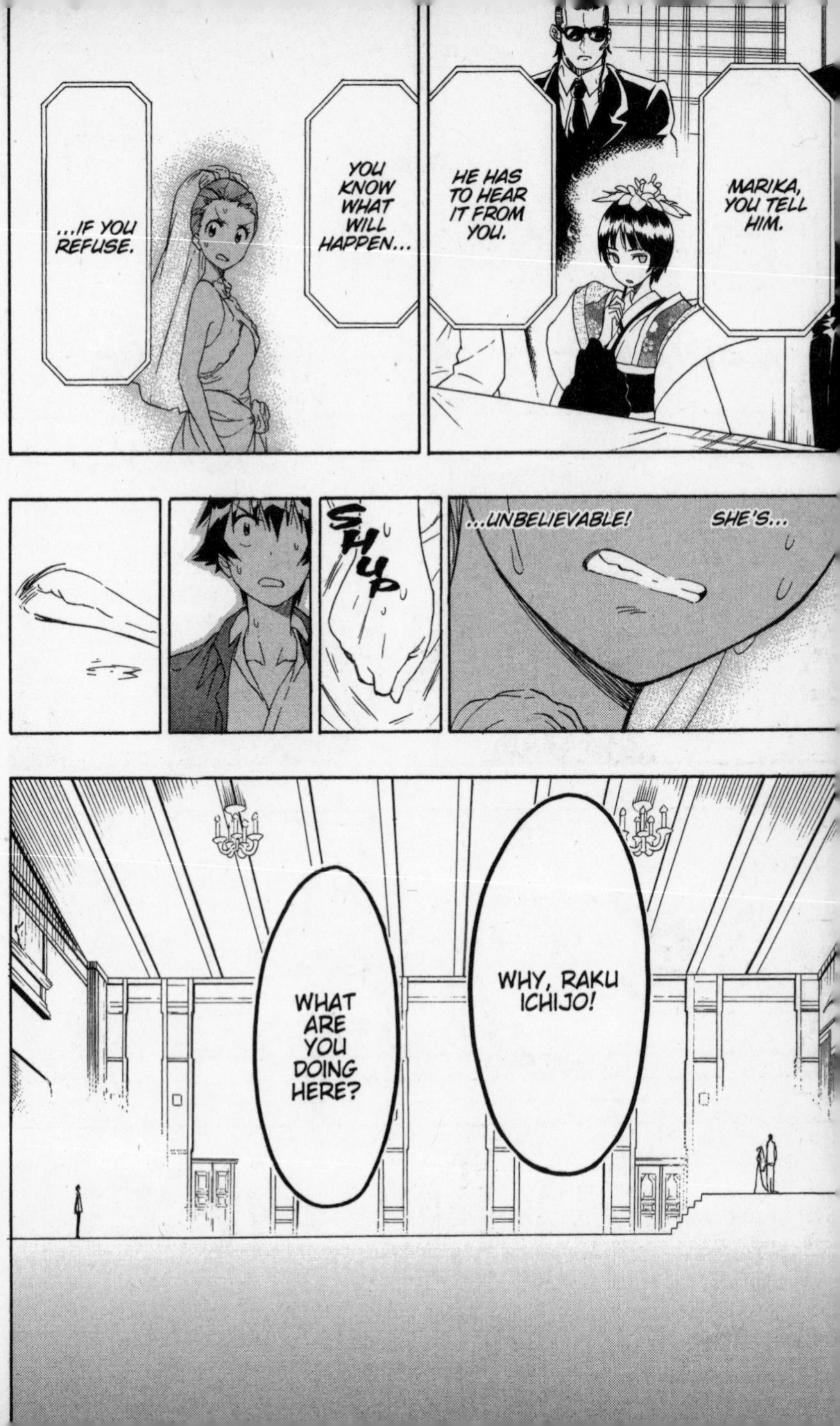
MARIKA, YOU TELL HIM.
HE HAS TO HEAR IT FROM YOU.
YOU KNOW WHAT WILL HAPPEN...
...IF YOU REFUSE.
SHE'S...
...UNBELIEVABLE!
SHUP
WHY, RAKU ICHIJO!
WHAT ARE YOU DOING HERE?

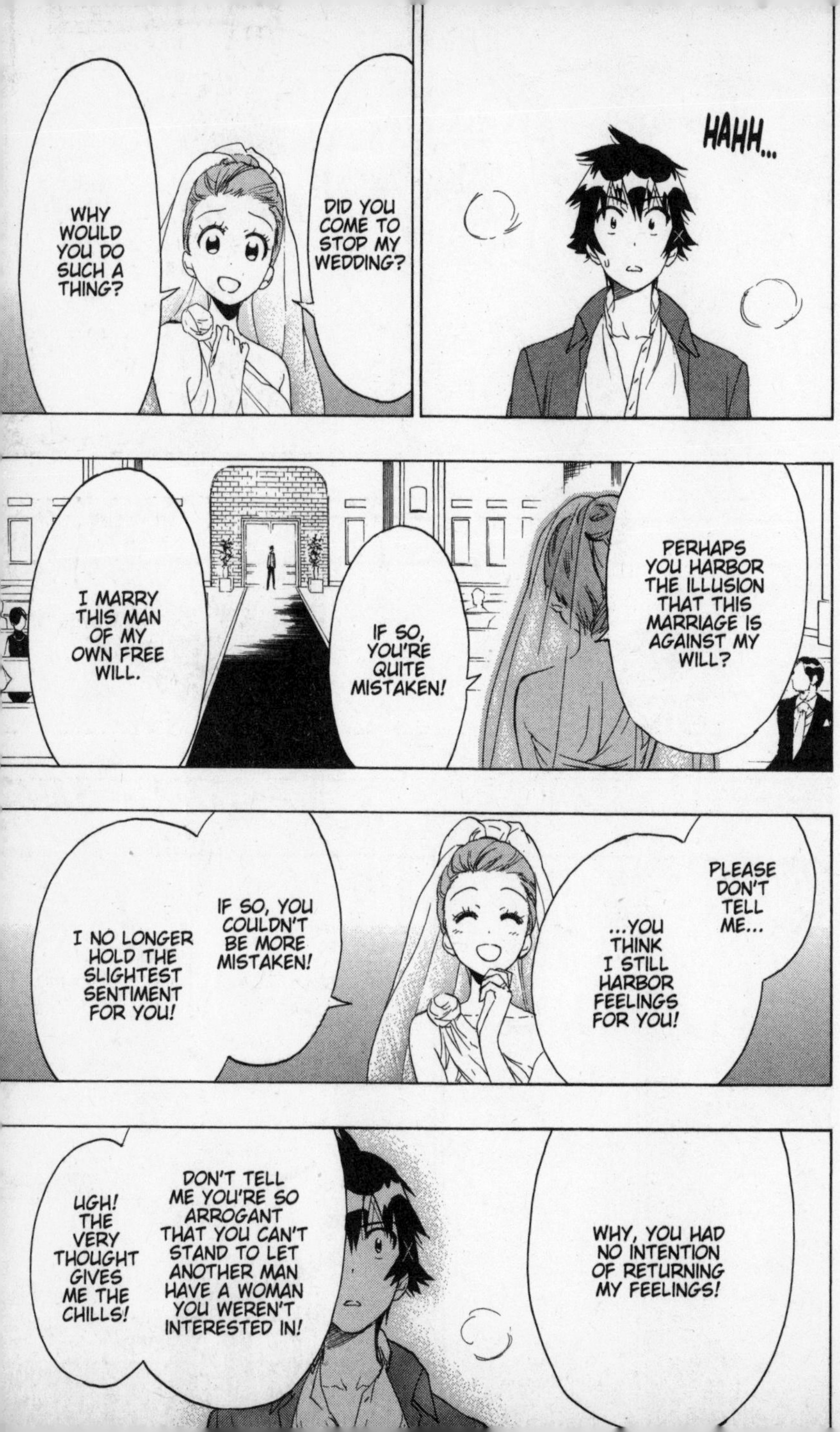
HAHH...
DID YOU COME TO STOP MY WEDDING?
WHY WOULD YOU DO SUCH A THING?
PERHAPS YOU HARBOR THE ILLUSION THAT THIS MARRIAGE IS AGAINST MY WILL?
IF SO, YOU'RE QUITE MISTAKEN!
I MARRY THIS MAN OF MY OWN FREE WILL.
PLEASE DON'T TELL ME...
...YOU THINK I STILL HARBOR FEELINGS FOR YOU!
IF SO, YOU COULDN'T BE MORE MISTAKEN!
I NO LONGER HOLD THE SLIGHTEST SENTIMENT FOR YOU!
WHY, YOU HAD NO INTENTION OF RETURNING MY FEELINGS!
DON'T TELL ME YOU'RE SO ARROGANT THAT YOU CAN'T STAND TO LET ANOTHER MAN HAVE A WOMAN YOU WEREN'T INTERESTED IN!
UGH! THE VERY THOUGHT GIVES ME THE CHILLS!

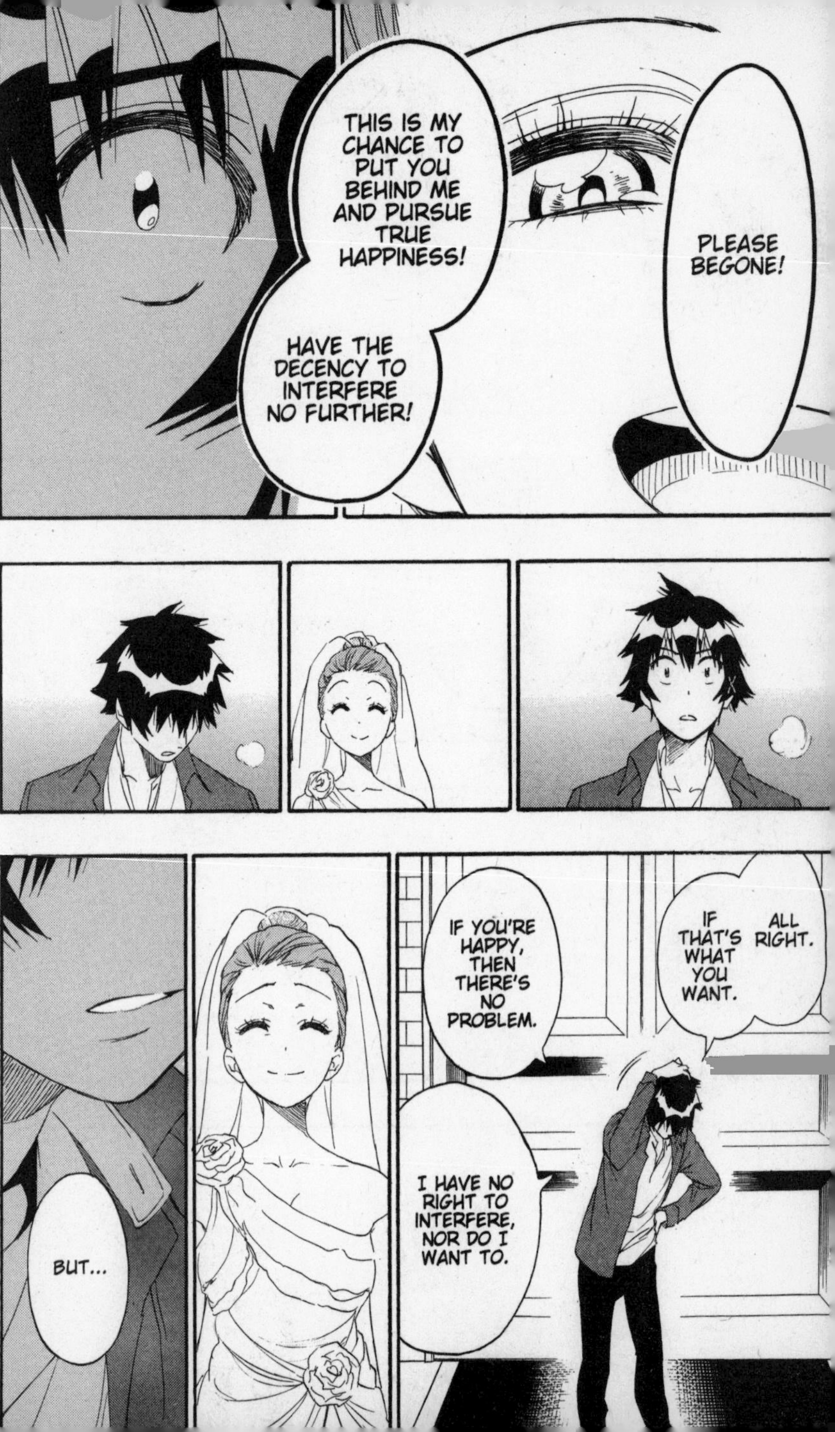
THIS IS MY CHANCE TO PUT YOU BEHIND ME AND PURSUE TRUE HAPPINESS!
HAVE THE DECENCY TO INTERFERE NO FURTHER!
PLEASE BEGONE!
ALL RIGHT.
IF THAT'S WHAT YOU WANT.
IF YOU'RE HAPPY, THEN THERE'S NO PROBLEM.
I HAVE NO RIGHT TO INTERFERE, NOR DO I WANT TO.
BUT...

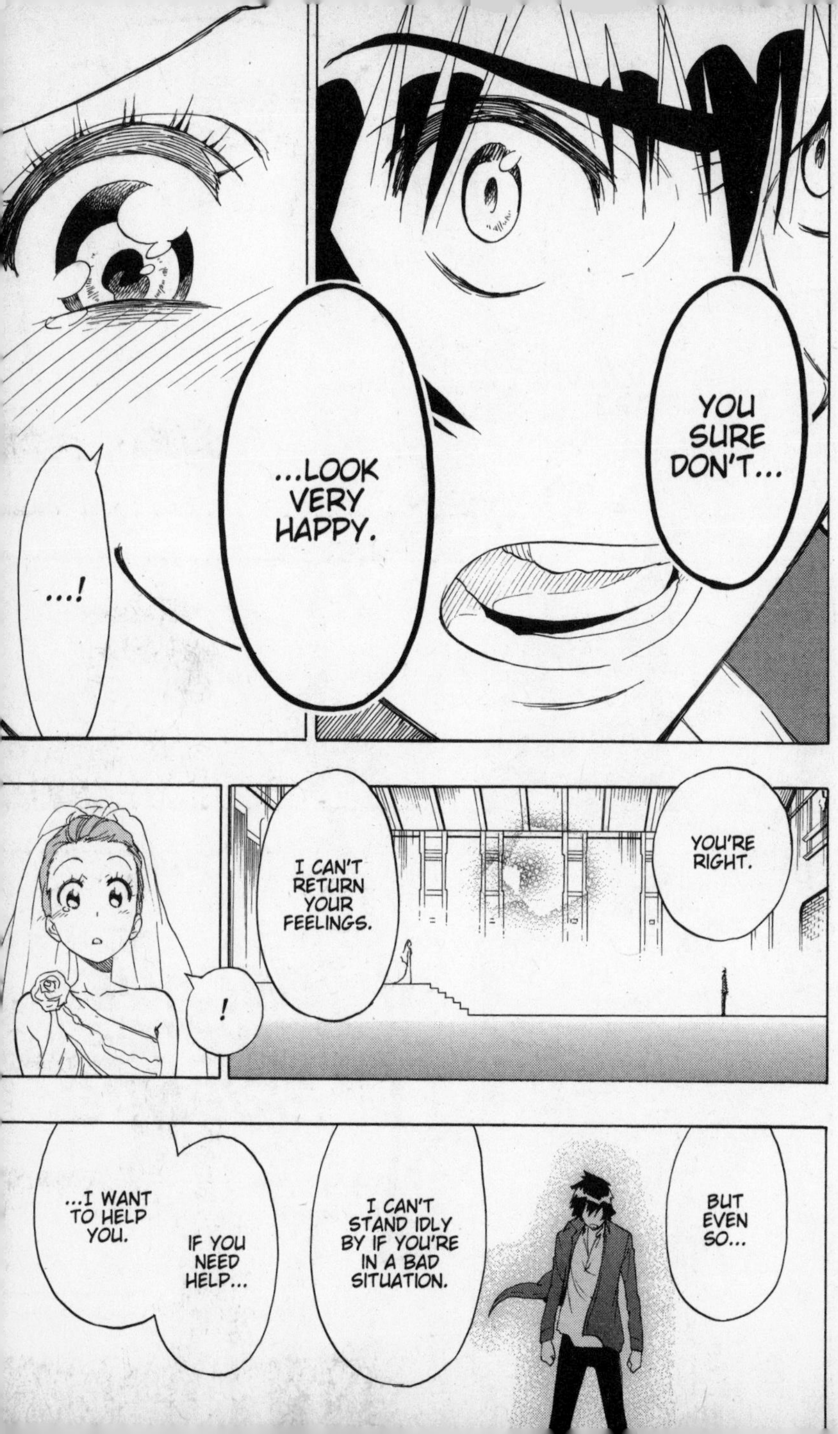
YOU SURE DON'T...
...LOOK VERY HAPPY.
...!
YOU'RE RIGHT.
I CAN'T RETURN YOUR FEELINGS.
!
BUT EVEN SO...
I CAN'T STAND IDLY BY IF YOU'RE IN A BAD SITUATION.
IF YOU NEED HELP...
...I WANT TO HELP YOU.

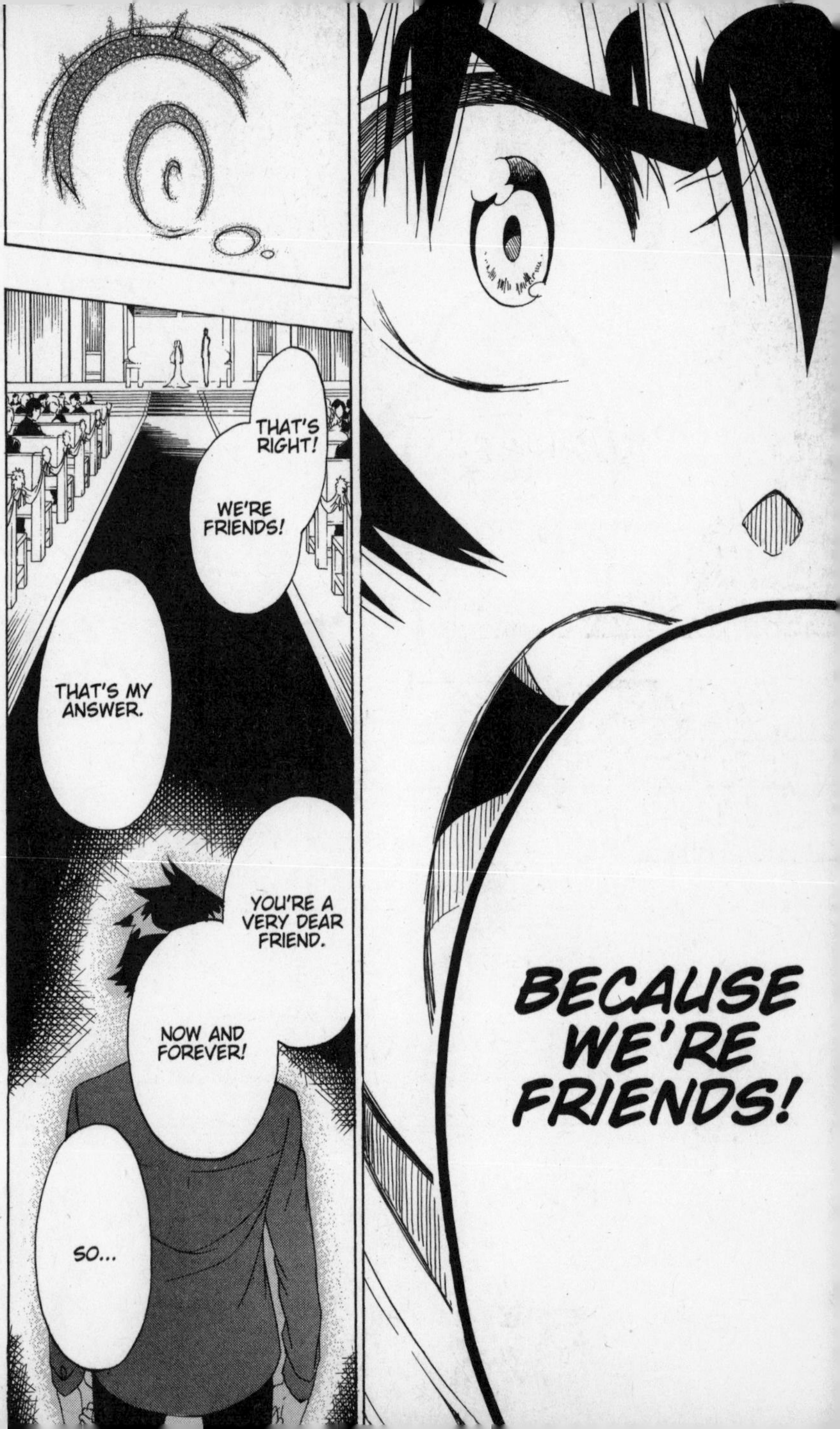

BECAUSE WE'RE FRIENDS!
THAT'S RIGHT!
WE'RE FRIENDS!
THAT'S MY ANSWER.
YOU'RE A VERY DEAR FRIEND.
NOW AND FOREVER!
SO...

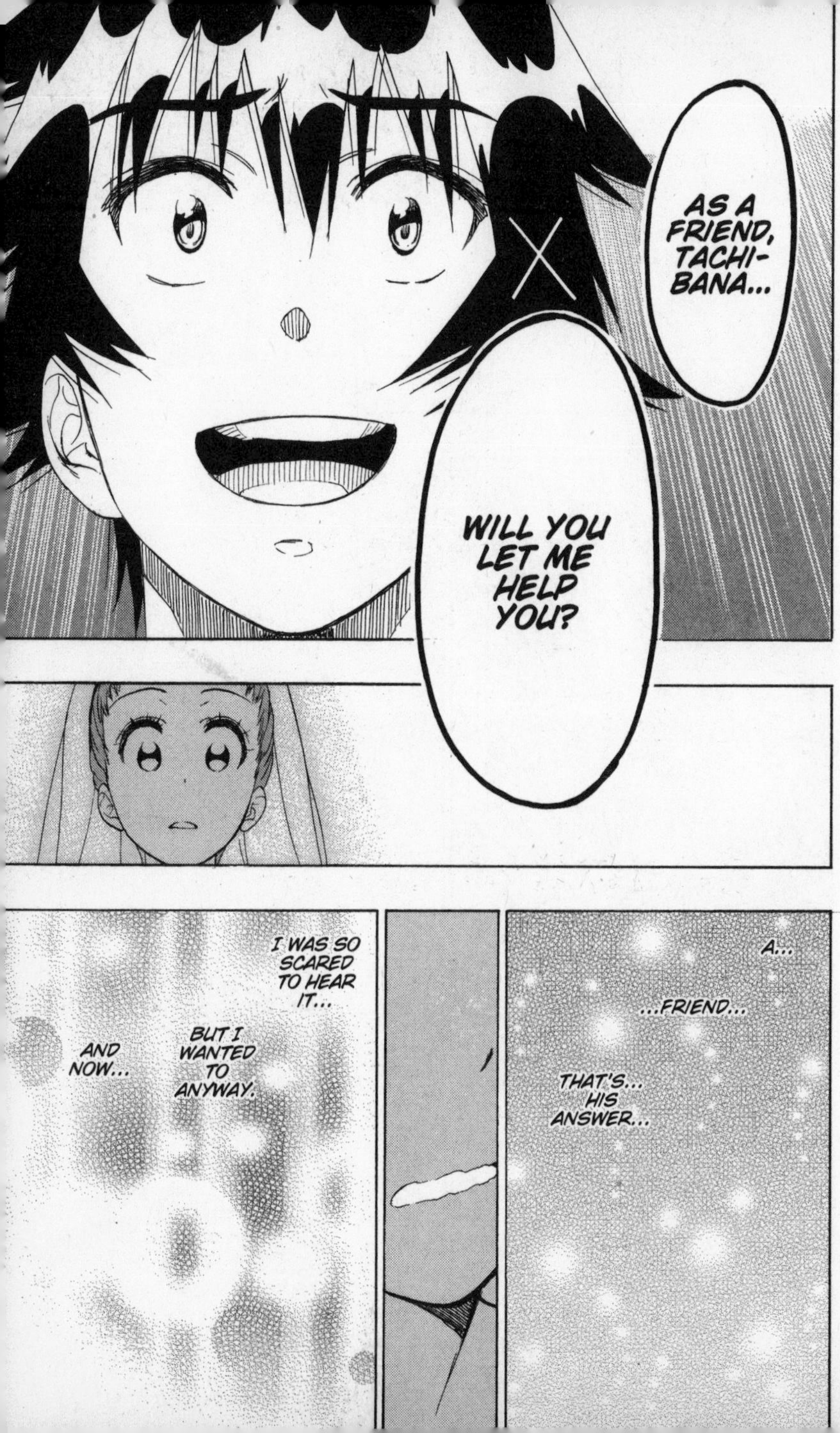
AS A FRIEND, TACHIBANA...
WILL YOU LET ME HELP YOU?
A...
...FRIEND...
THAT'S... HIS ANSWER...
I WAS SO SCARED TO HEAR IT...
BUT I WANTED TO ANYWAY.
AND NOW...

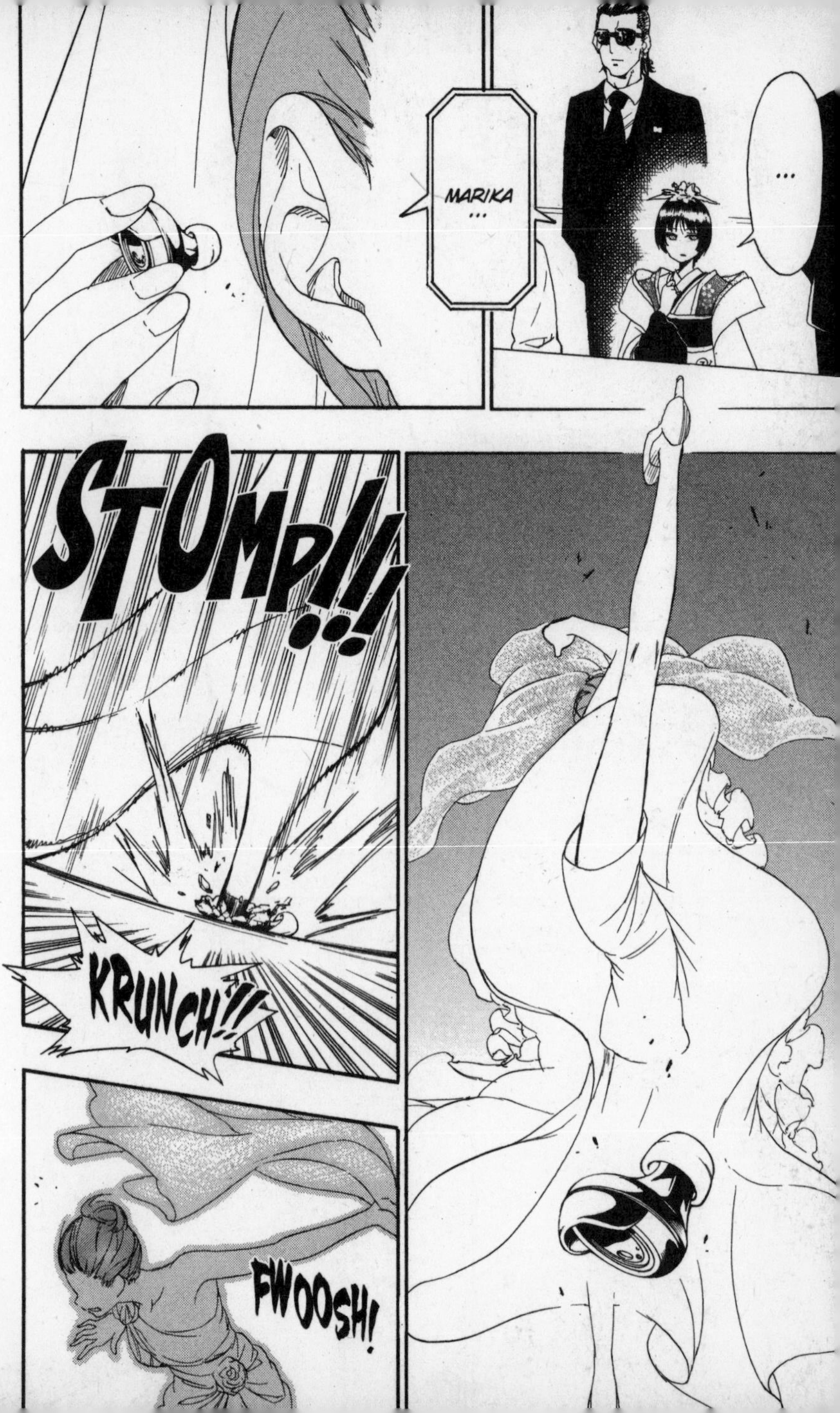
...
MARIKA ...
STOMP!!
KRUNCH!!!
FWOOSH!

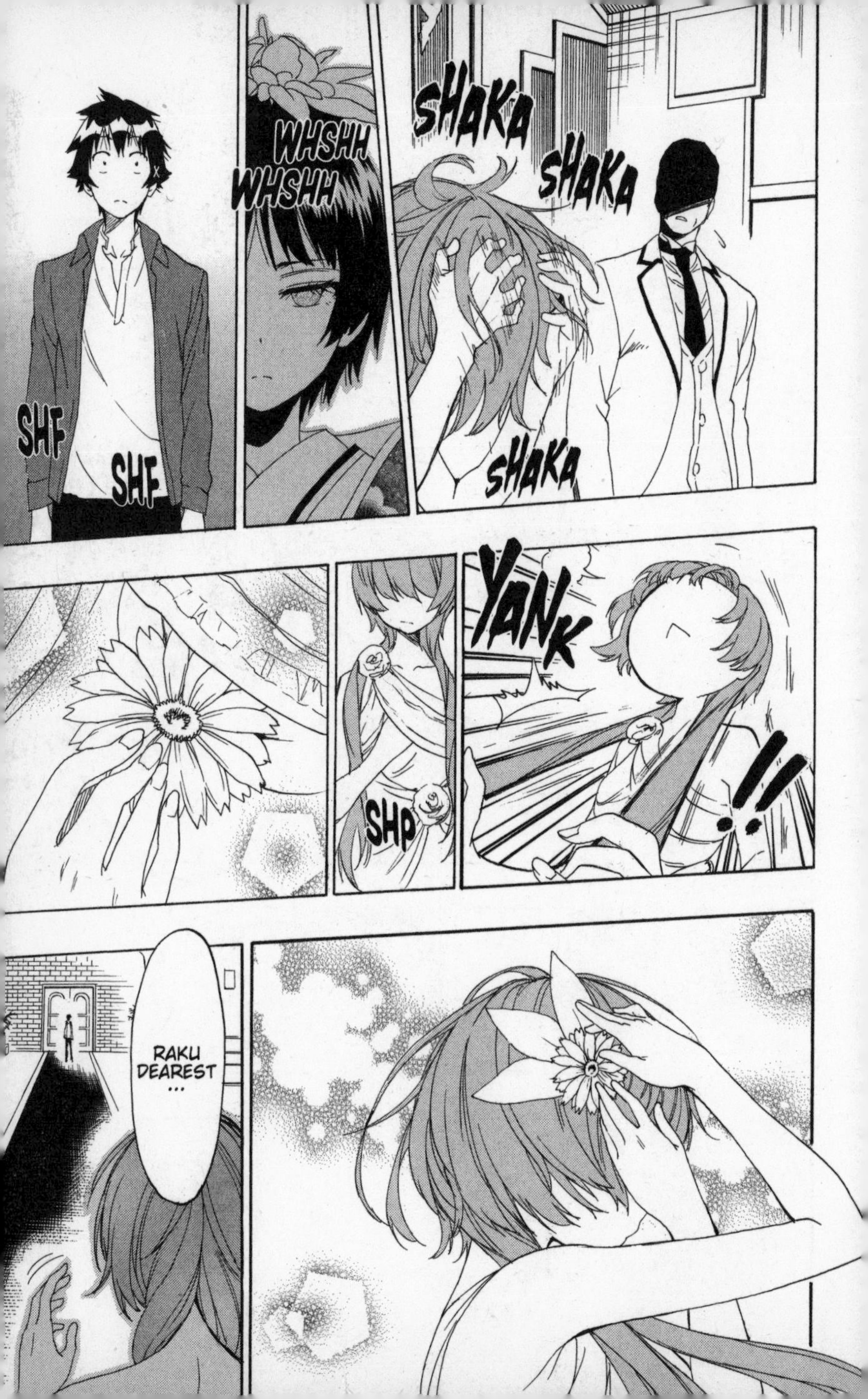
SHAKA
SHAKA
SHAKA
WHSHH
WHSHH
SHF
SHF
YANK
!!
SHP
RAKU DEAREST...

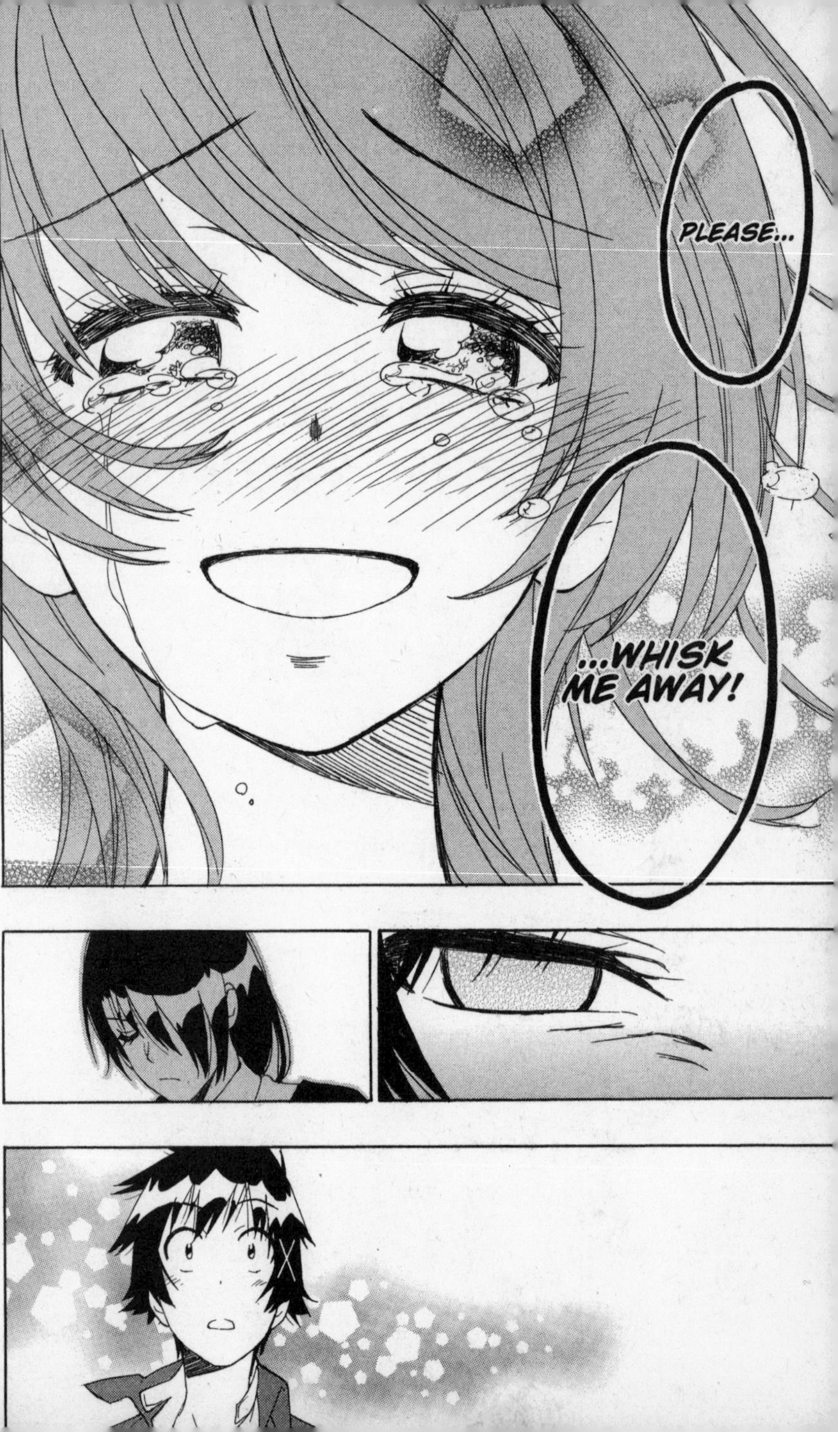
PLEASE...
...WHISK ME AWAY!

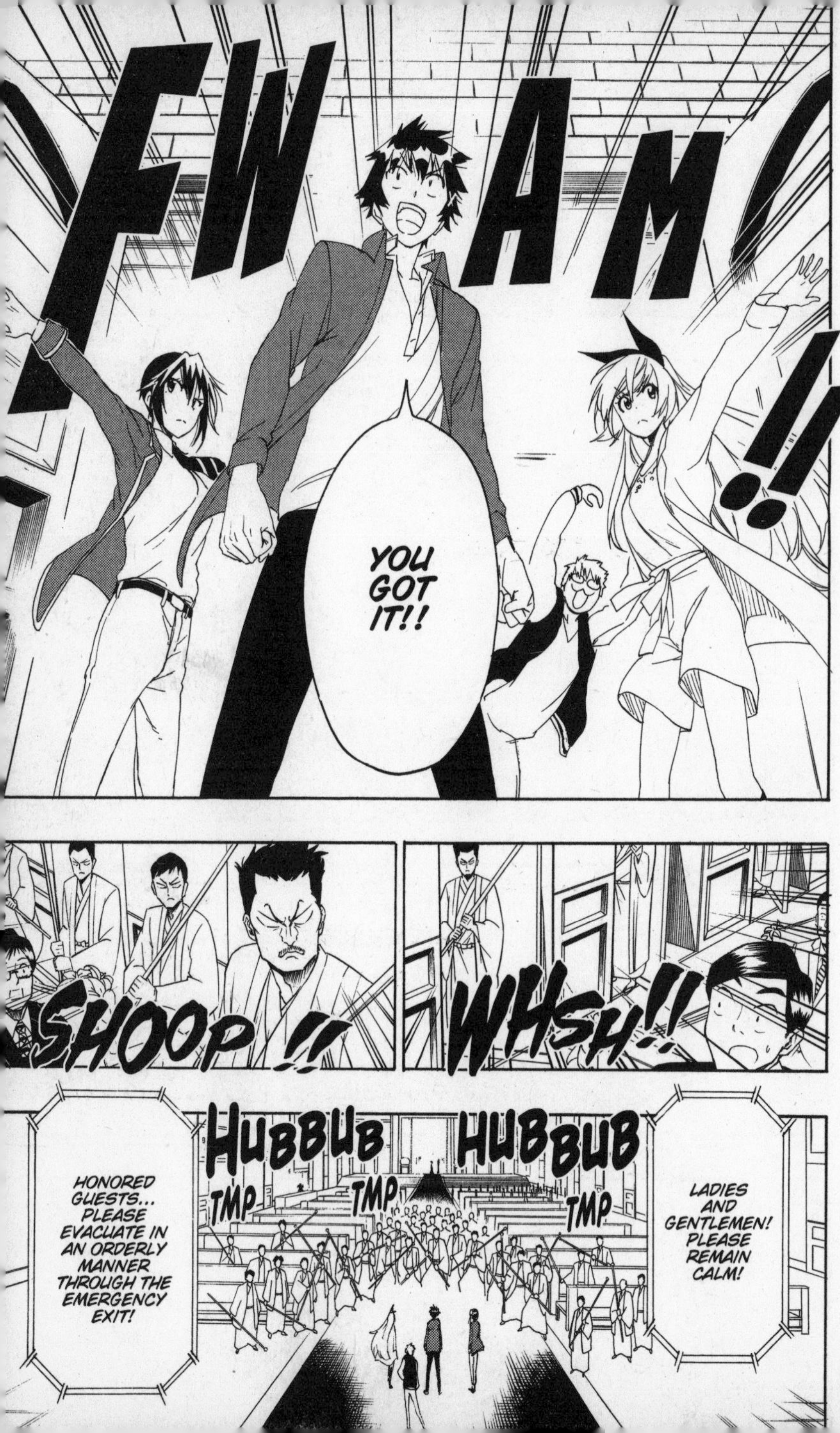
FWAM!!
YOU GOT IT!!
WHSH!!
SHOOP!!
LADIES AND GENTLEMEN! PLEASE REMAIN CALM!
HUBBUB HUBBUB
TMP TMP TMP
HONORED GUESTS... PLEASE EVACUATE IN AN ORDERLY MANNER THROUGH THE EMERGENCY EXIT!

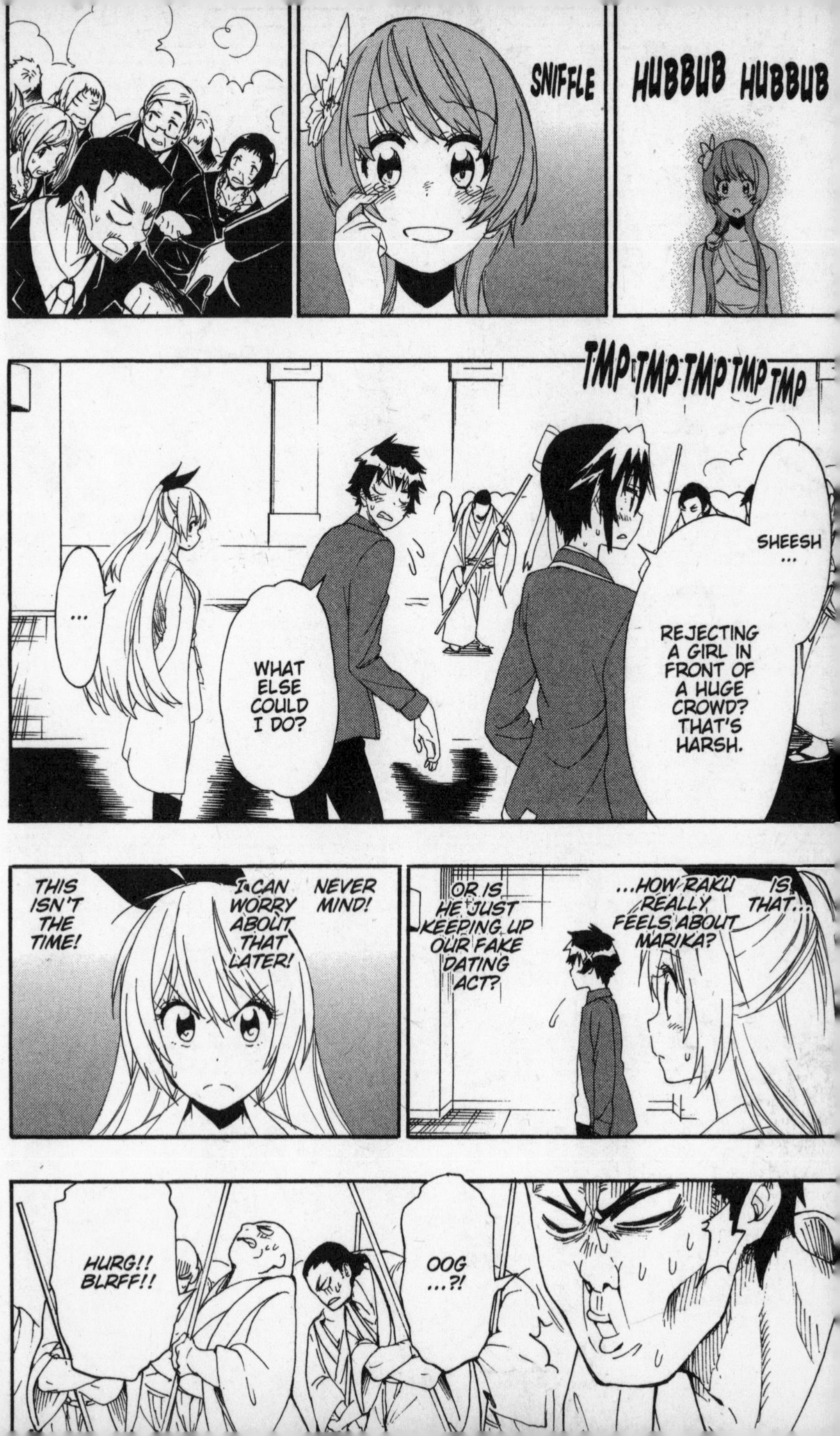
HUBBUB HUBBUB
SNIFFLE
TMP TMP TMP TMP TMP
SHEESH...
REJECTING A GIRL IN FRONT OF A HUGE CROWD? THAT'S HARSH.
WHAT ELSE COULD I DO?
...
IS THAT...
...HOW RAKU REALLY FEELS ABOUT MARIKA?
OR IS HE JUST KEEPING UP OUR FAKE DATING ACT?
NEVER MIND!
I CAN WORRY ABOUT THAT LATER!
THIS ISN'T THE TIME!
OOG...?!
HURG!! BLRFF!!

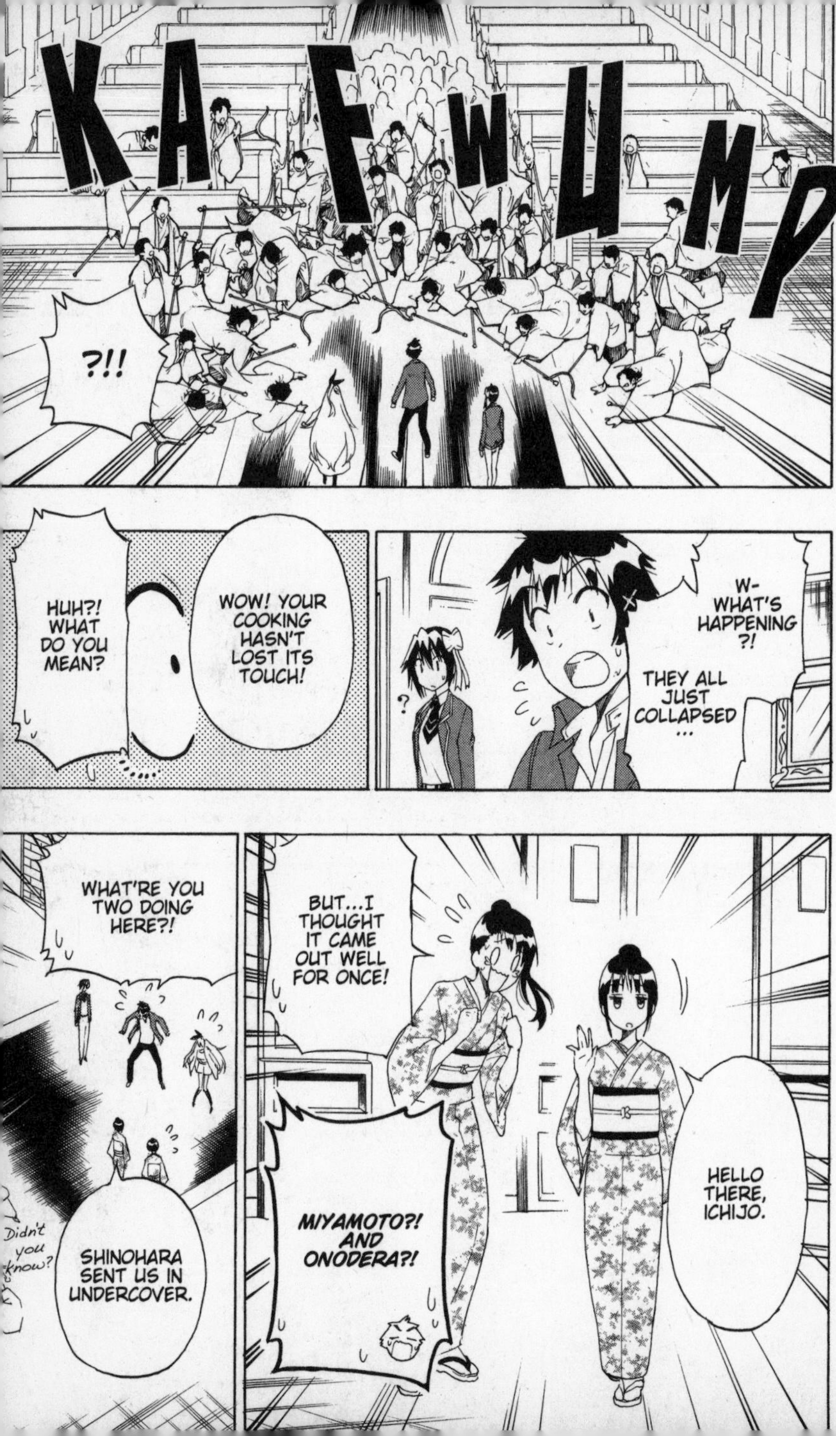
KAFWUMP
?!!
W- WHAT'S HAPPENING?!
THEY ALL JUST COLLAPSED...
WOW! YOUR COOKING HASN'T LOST ITS TOUCH!
HUH?! WHAT DO YOU MEAN?
HELLO THERE, ICHIJO.
MIYAMOTO?! AND ONODERA?!
BUT...I THOUGHT IT CAME OUT WELL FOR ONCE!
WHAT'RE YOU TWO DOING HERE?!
SHINOHARA SENT US IN UNDERCOVER.
Didn't you know?

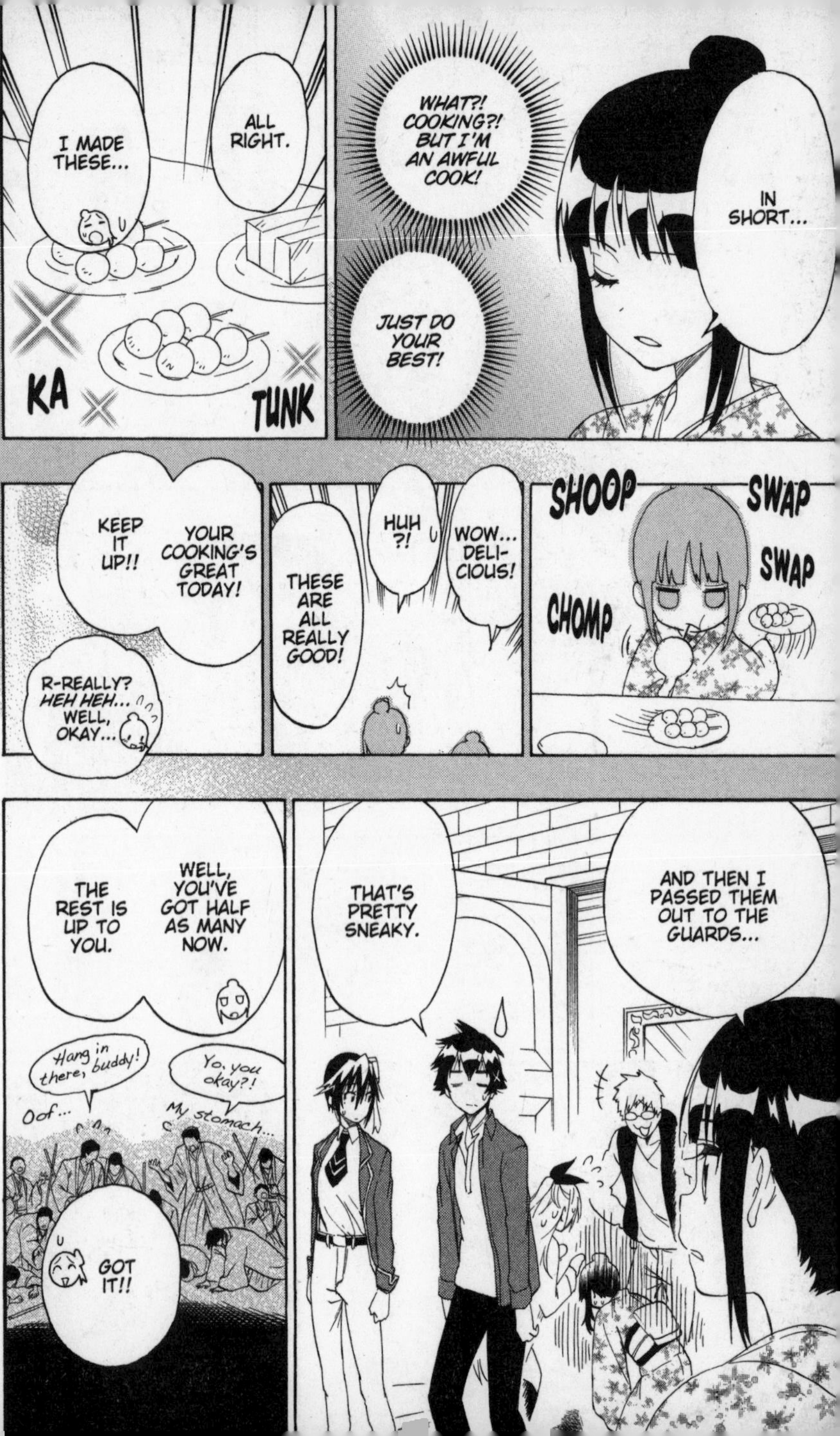
IN SHORT...
WHAT?! COOKING?! BUT I'M AN AWFUL COOK!
JUST DO YOUR BEST!
ALL RIGHT.
I MADE THESE...
KA
TUNK
SWAP
SWAP
SHOOP
CHOMP
WOW... DELI-CIOUS!
HUH?!
THESE ARE ALL REALLY GOOD!
YOUR COOKING'S GREAT TODAY!
KEEP IT UP!!
R-REALLY? HEH HEH... WELL, OKAY...
AND THEN I PASSED THEM OUT TO THE GUARDS...
THAT'S PRETTY SNEAKY.
WELL, YOU'VE GOT HALF AS MANY NOW.
THE REST IS UP TO YOU.
Yo, you okay?!
Hang in there, buddy!
My stomach...
Oof...
GOT IT!!

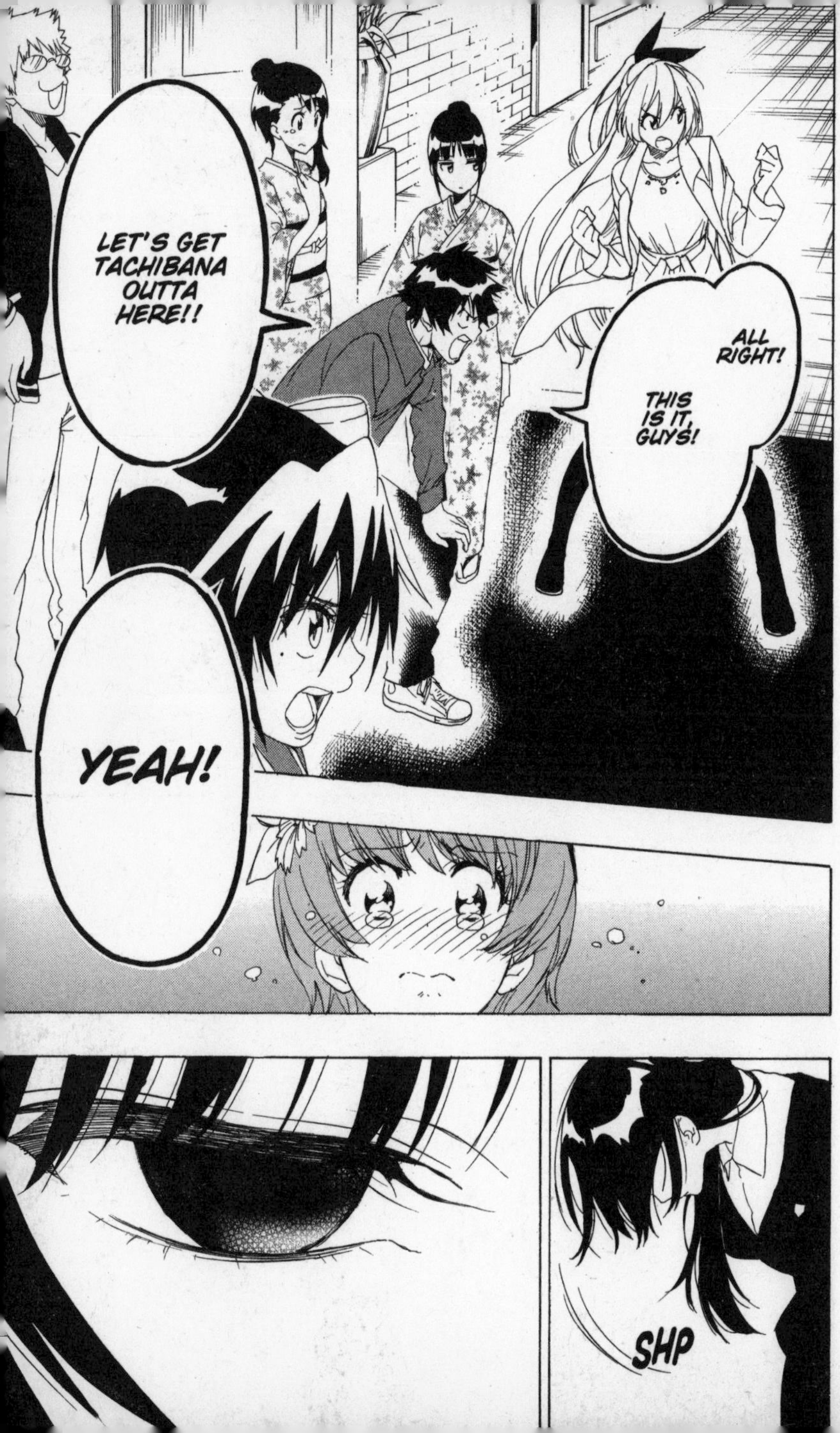
ALL RIGHT!
THIS IS IT, GUYS!
LET'S GET TACHIBANA OUTTA HERE!!
YEAH!
SHP

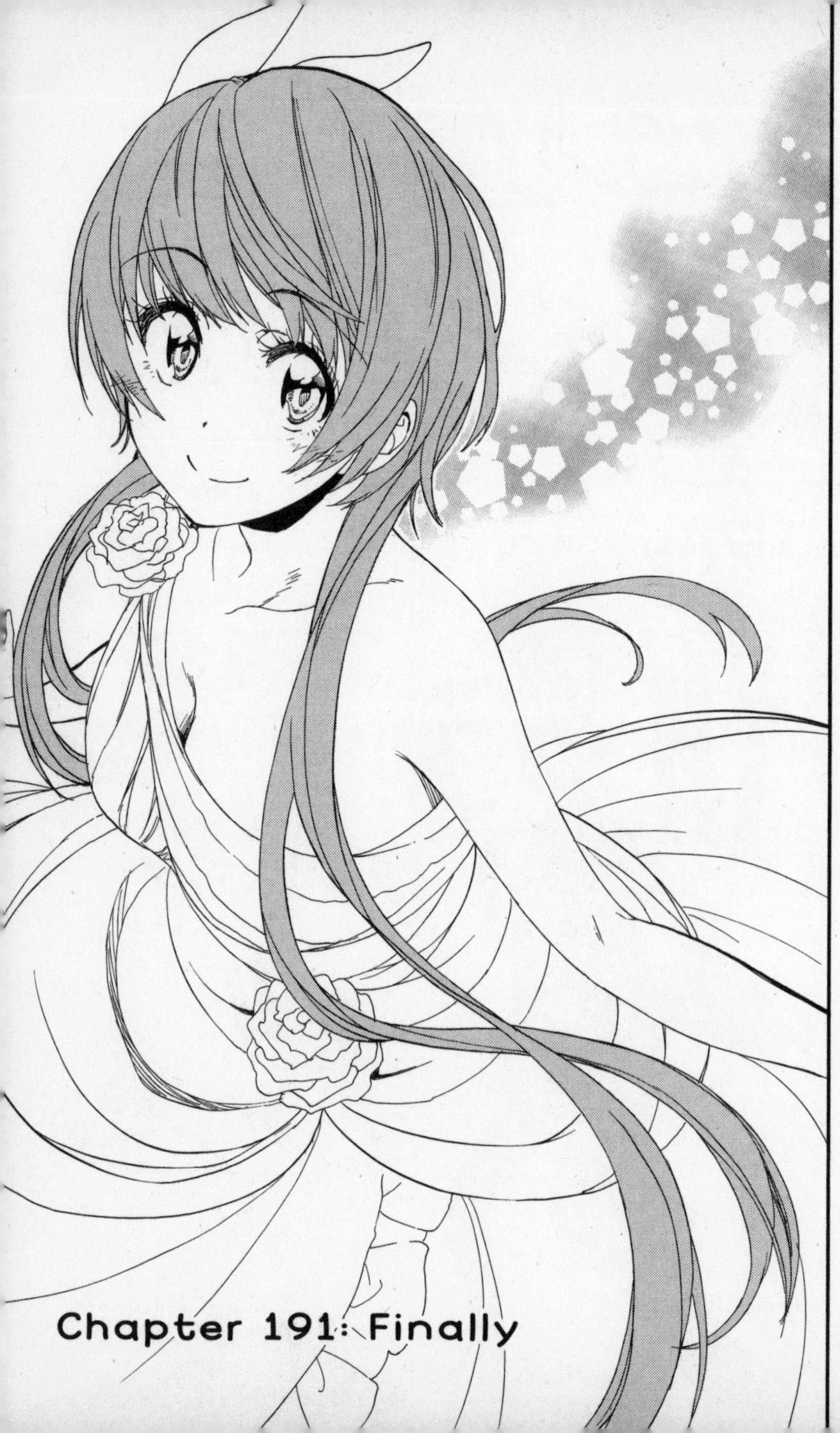

Chapter 191: Finally

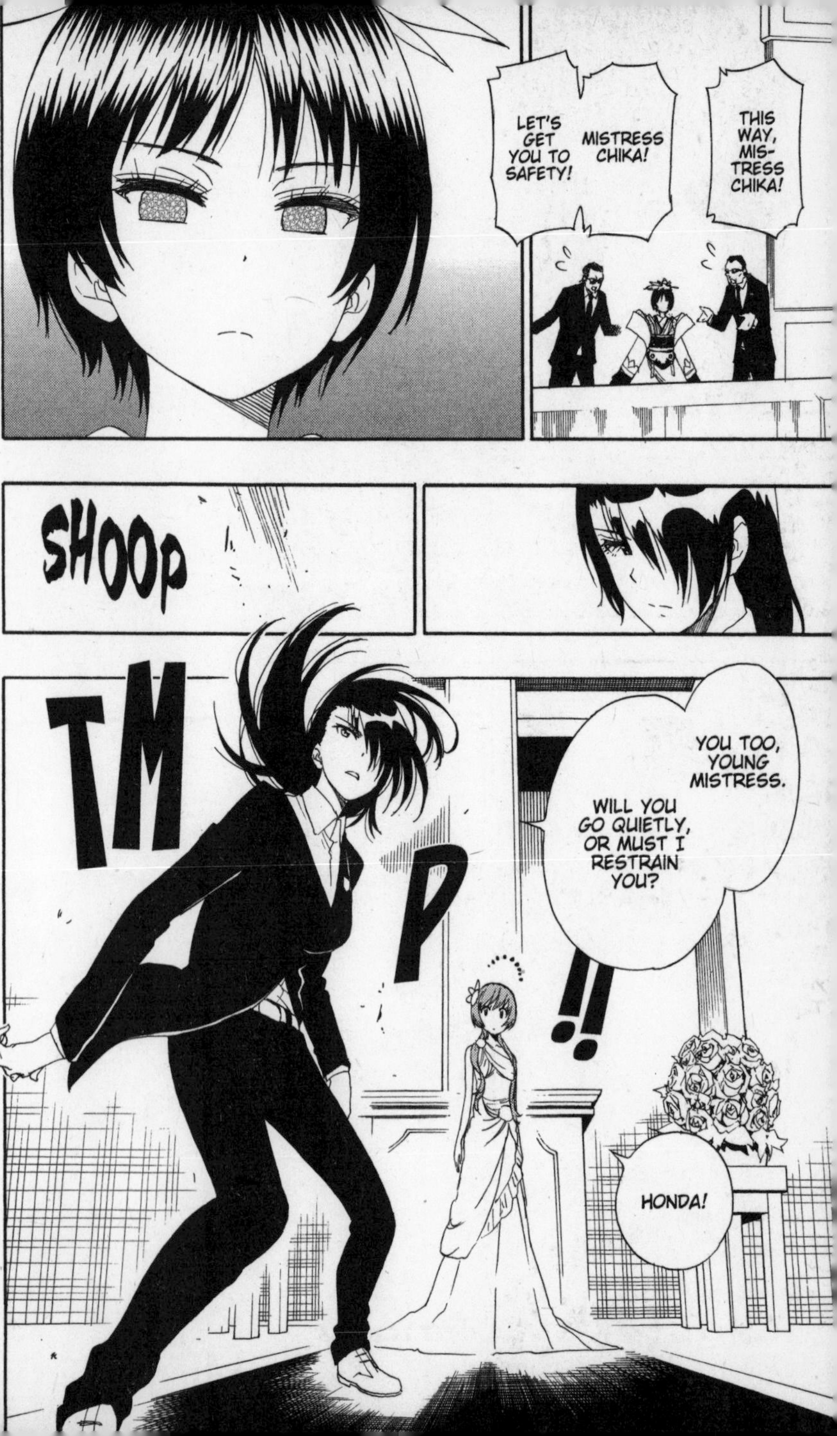
THIS WAY, MIS-TRESS CHIKA!
MISTRESS CHIKA!
LET'S GET YOU TO SAFETY!
SHOOP
YOU TOO, YOUNG MISTRESS.
WILL YOU GO QUIETLY, OR MUST I RESTRAIN YOU?
!!
TMP
HONDA!

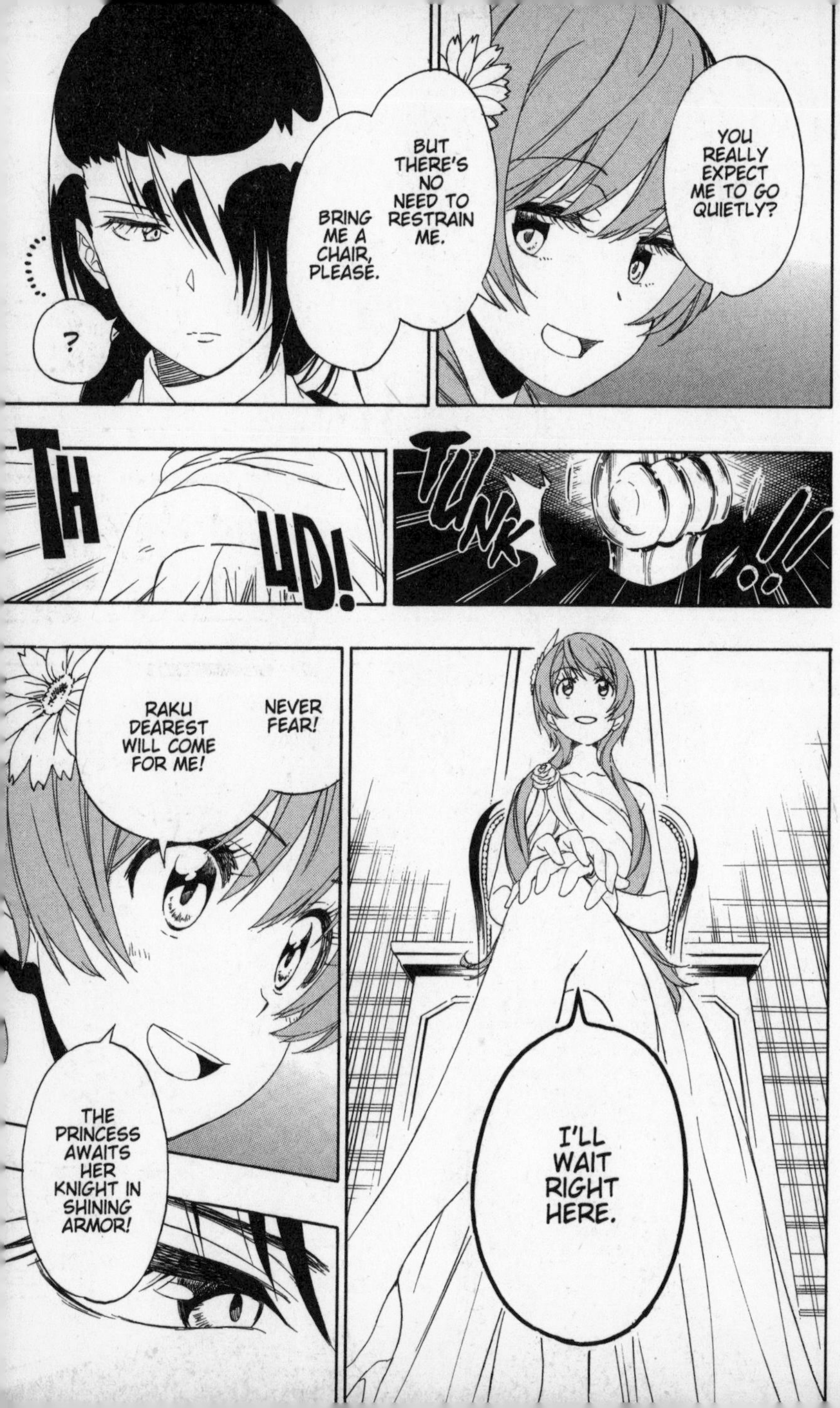
YOU REALLY EXPECT ME TO GO QUIETLY?
BUT THERE'S NO NEED TO RESTRAIN ME.
BRING ME A CHAIR, PLEASE.
......
?
TUNK
!!
THUD!
I'LL WAIT RIGHT HERE.
NEVER FEAR!
RAKU DEAREST WILL COME FOR ME!
THE PRINCESS AWAITS HER KNIGHT IN SHINING ARMOR!

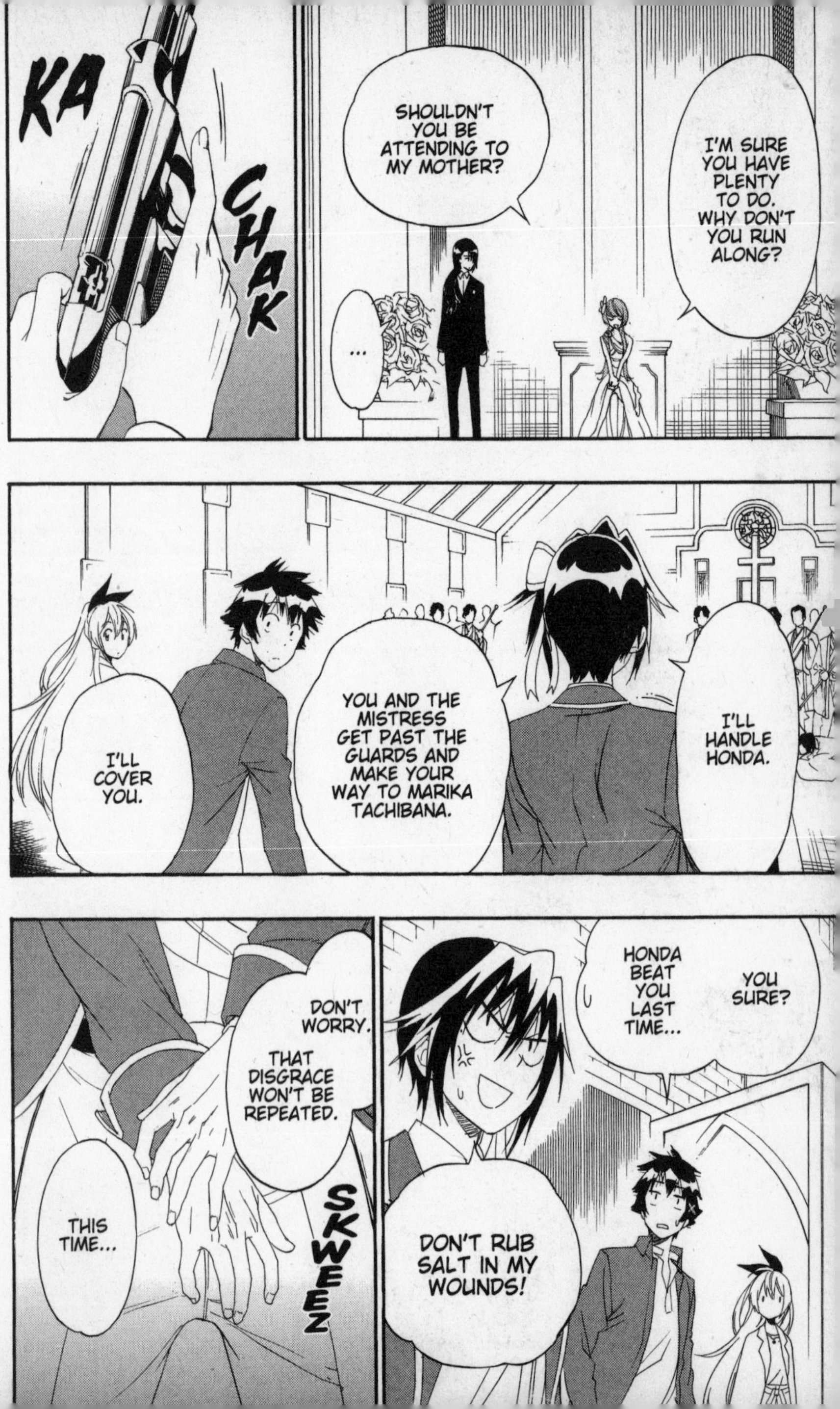
I'M SURE YOU HAVE PLENTY TO DO. WHY DON'T YOU RUN ALONG?
SHOULDN'T YOU BE ATTENDING TO MY MOTHER?
...
KA
CHAK
I'LL HANDLE HONDA.
...
YOU AND THE MISTRESS GET PAST THE GUARDS AND MAKE YOUR WAY TO MARIKA TACHIBANA.
I'LL COVER YOU.
YOU SURE?
HONDA BEAT YOU LAST TIME...
DON'T RUB SALT IN MY WOUNDS!
DON'T WORRY.
THAT DISGRACE WON'T BE REPEATED.
SKWEEZ
THIS TIME...

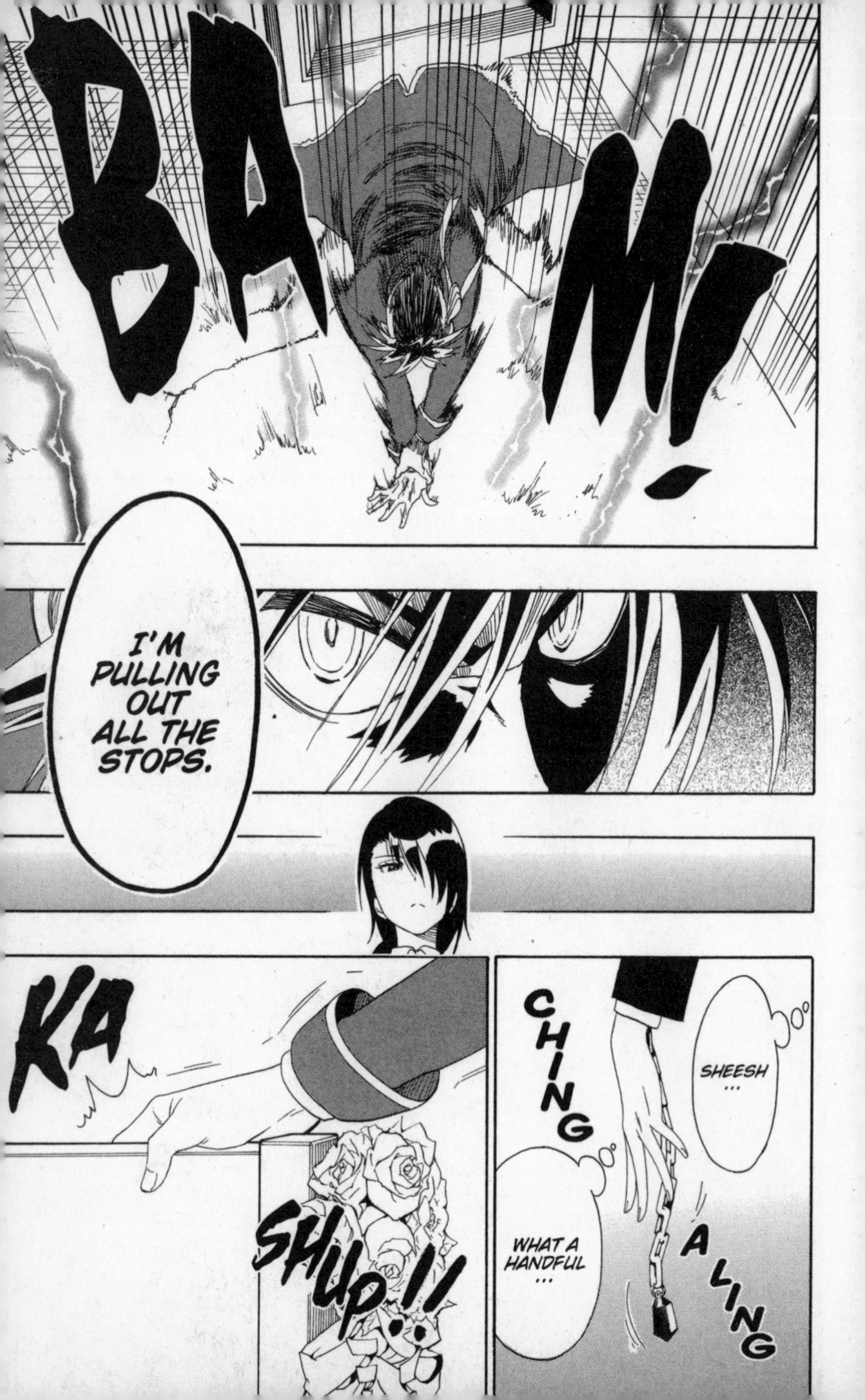
BAM!
I'M PULLING OUT ALL THE STOPS.
SHEESH...
WHAT A HANDFUL...
CHING
A LING
KA
SHUP!!

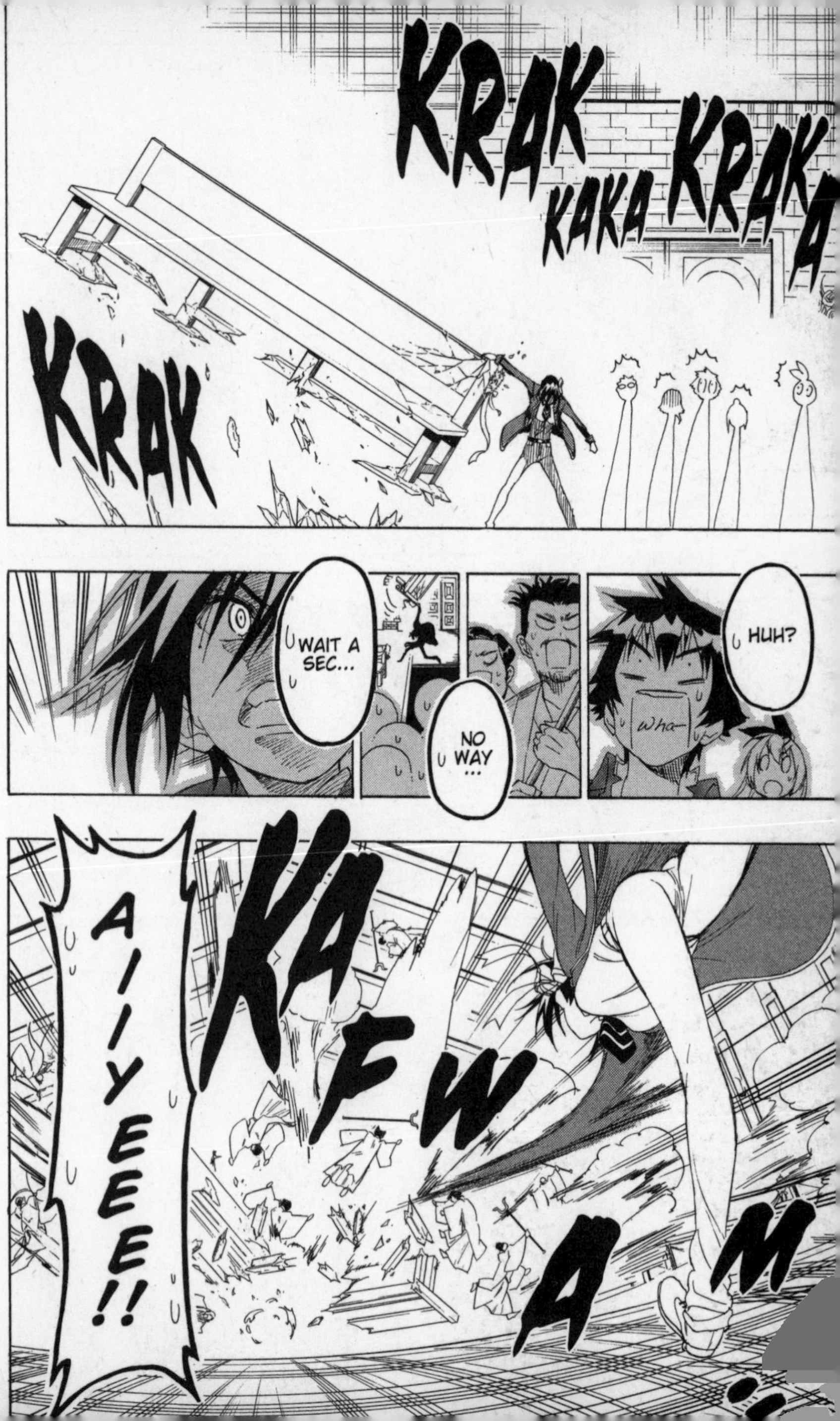
KRAK
KAKA KRAKA
KRAK
HUH?
Wha–
NO WAY...
WAIT A SEC...
KAFWAM
AIIYEEEE!!

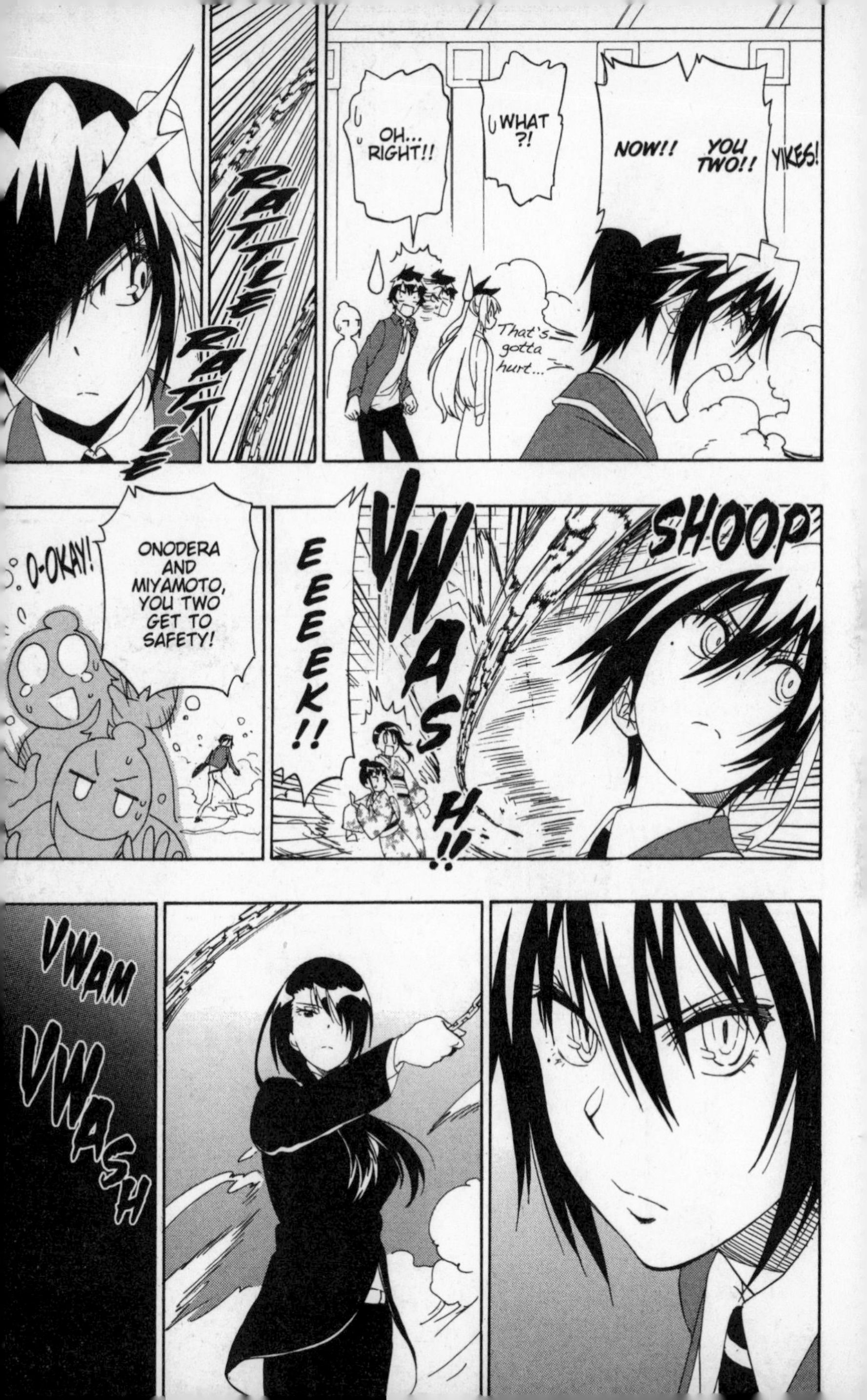
YIKES!
YOU TWO!!
NOW!!
WHAT ?!
OH... RIGHT!!
That's gotta hurt...
RATTLE RATTLE
SHOOP
VWASH!!
EEEEEK!!
ONODERA AND MIYAMOTO, YOU TWO GET TO SAFETY!
O-OKAY!
VWAM
VWASH

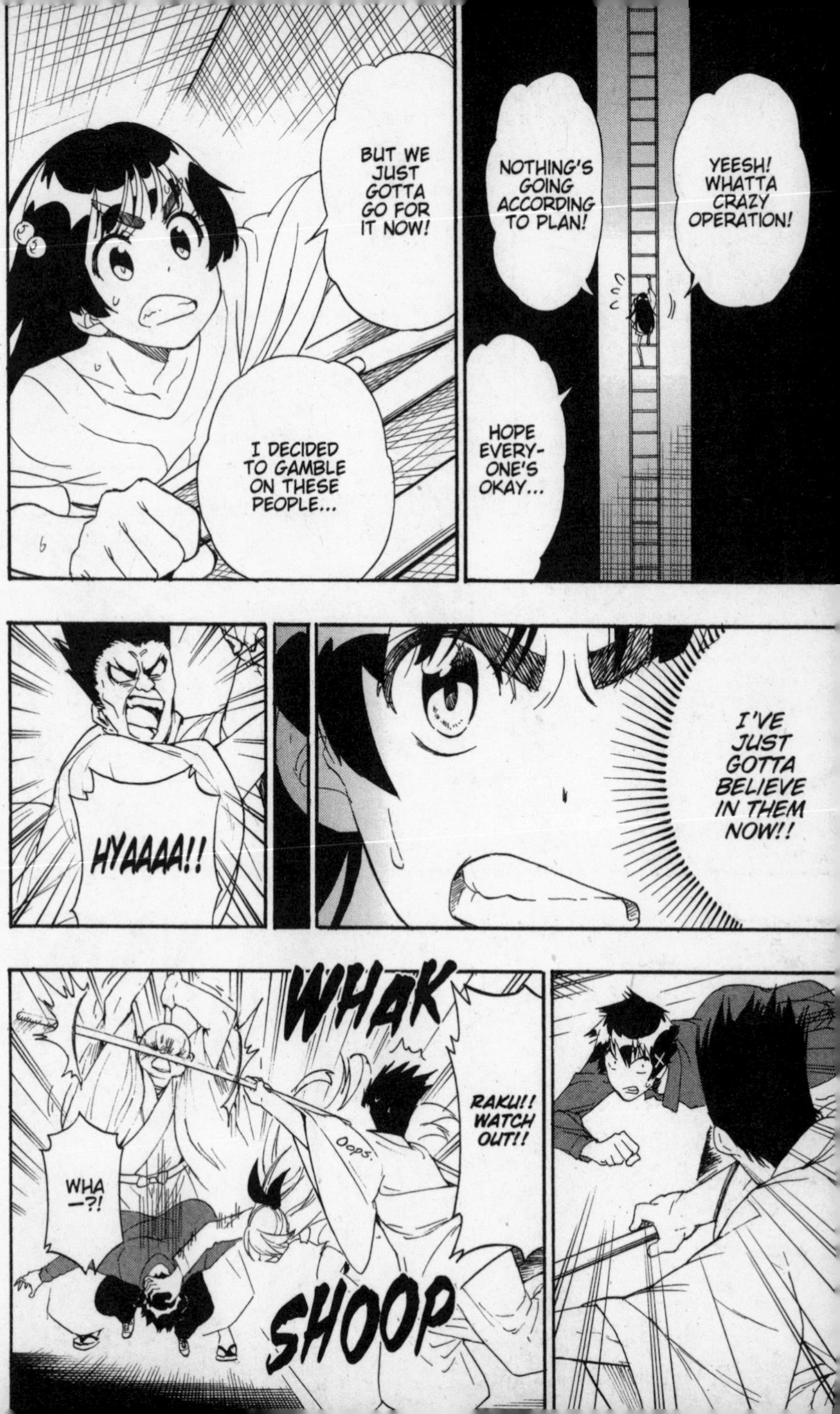
YEESH! WHATTA CRAZY OPERATION!
NOTHING'S GOING ACCORDING TO PLAN!
HOPE EVERY-ONE'S OKAY...
BUT WE JUST GOTTA GO FOR IT NOW!
I DECIDED TO GAMBLE ON THESE PEOPLE...
I'VE JUST GOTTA BELIEVE IN THEM NOW!!
HYAAAA!!
WHAK
RAKU!! WATCH OUT!!
Oops.
WHA—?!
SHOOP

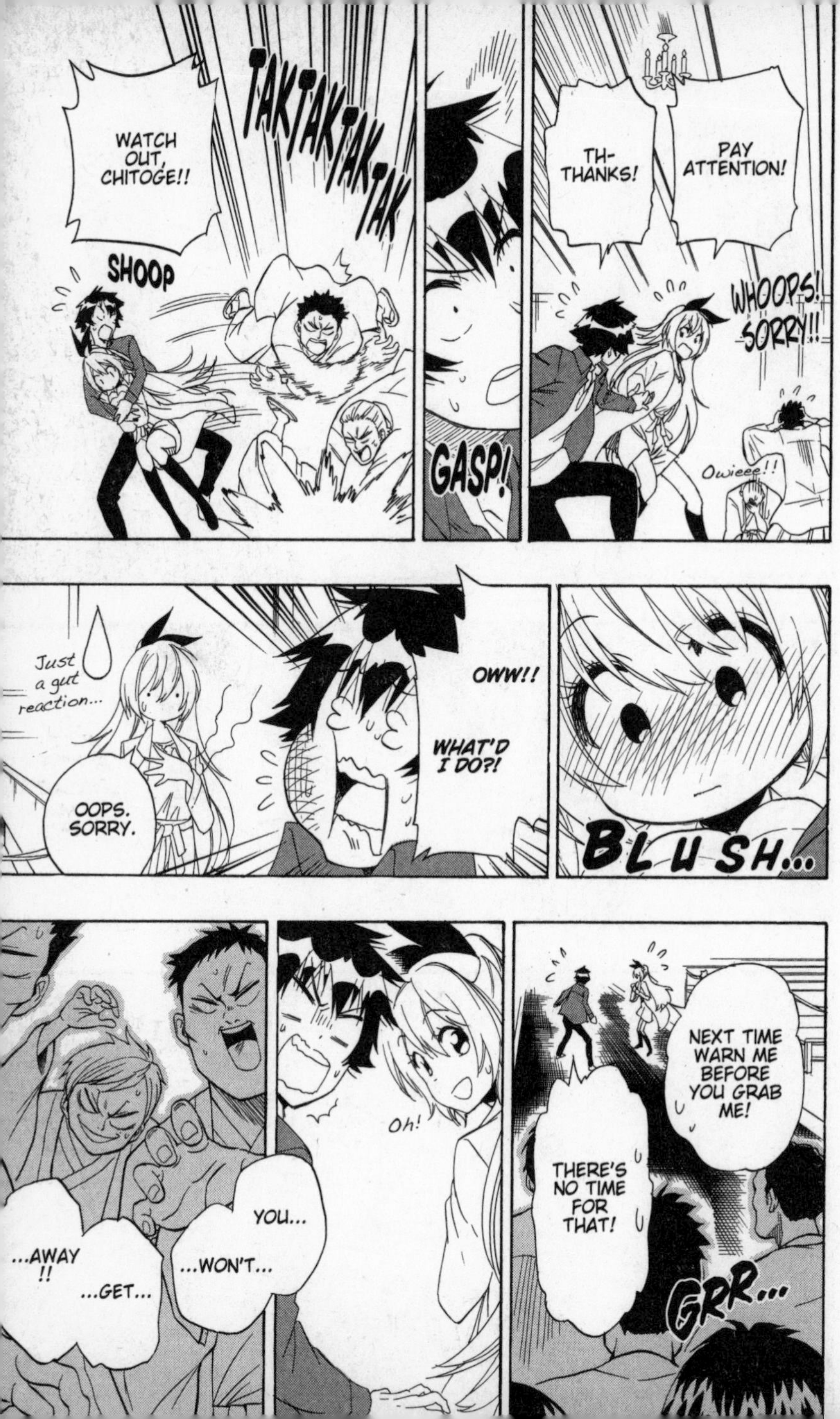
PAY ATTENTION!
TH- THANKS!
WHOOPS! SORRY!!
Owieee!!
GASP!
WATCH OUT, CHITOGE!!
TAKTAKTAKTAK
SHOOP
BLUSH...
OWW!!
WHAT'D I DO?!
Just a gut reaction...
OOPS. SORRY.
NEXT TIME WARN ME BEFORE YOU GRAB ME!
THERE'S NO TIME FOR THAT!
GRR...
Oh!
YOU...
...WON'T...
...GET...
...AWAY!!

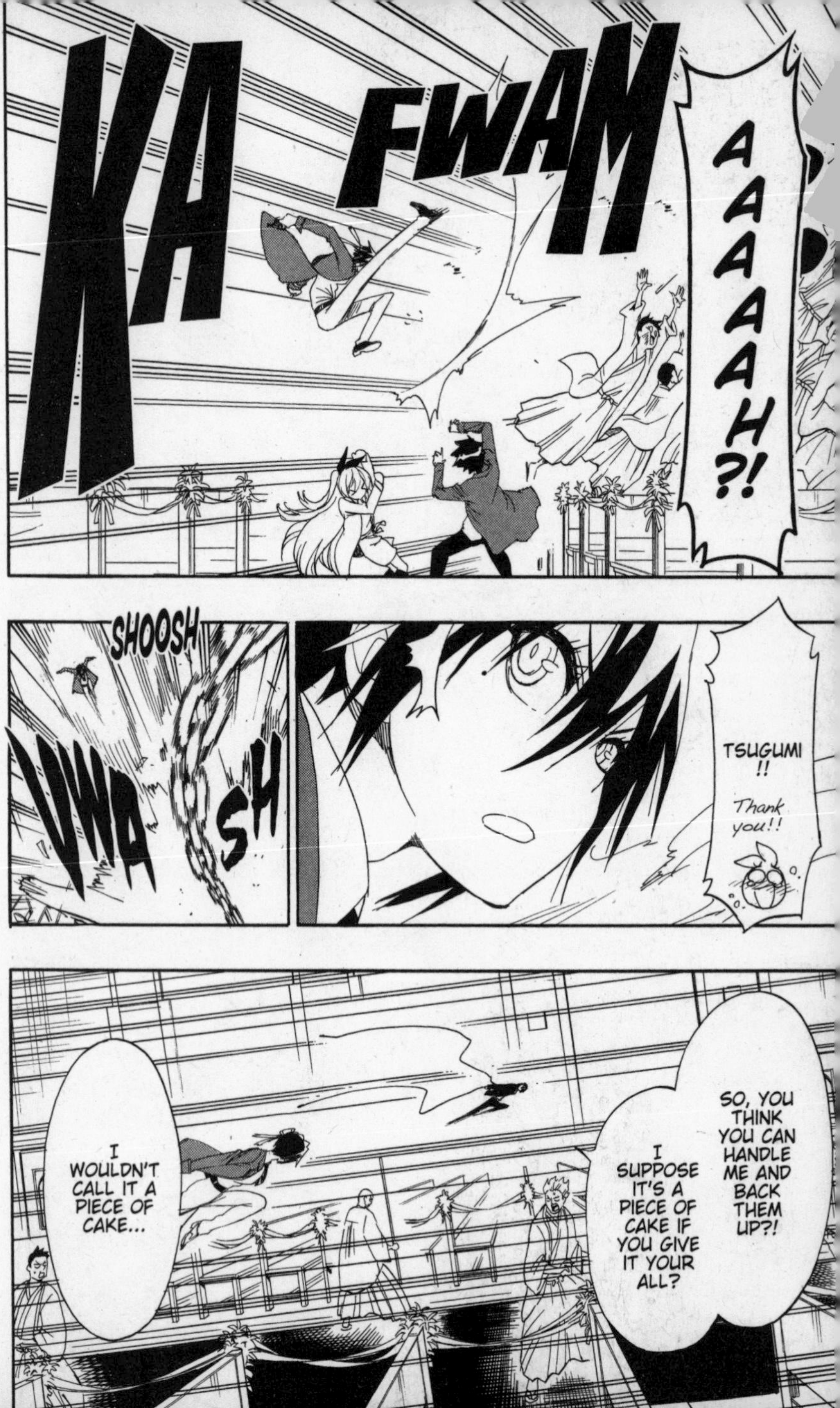
AAAAAH?!
KA
FWAM
TSUGUMI!!
Thank you!!
SHOOSH
WHA
SH
SO, YOU THINK YOU CAN HANDLE ME AND BACK THEM UP?!
I SUPPOSE IT'S A PIECE OF CAKE IF YOU GIVE IT YOUR ALL?
I WOULDN'T CALL IT A PIECE OF CAKE...

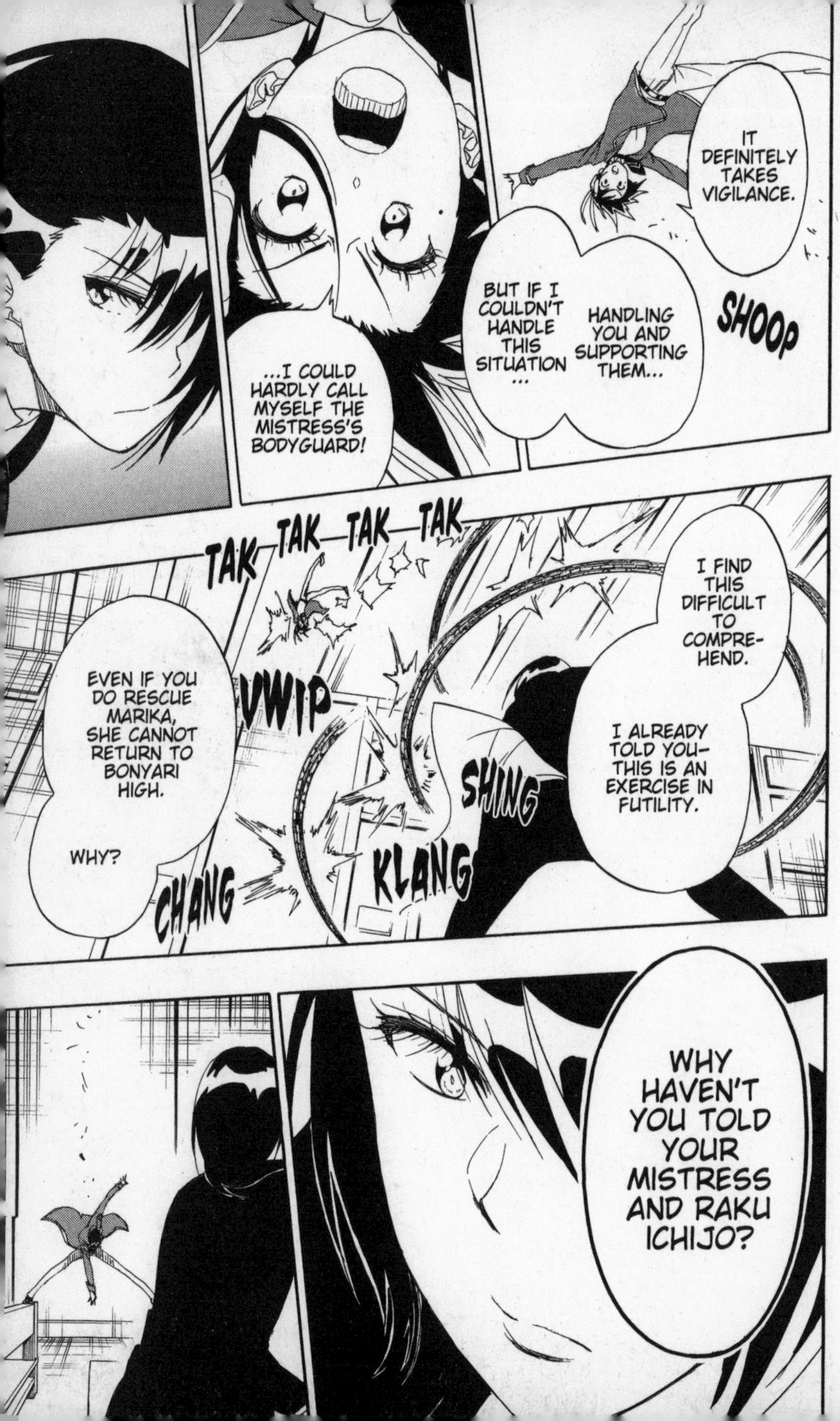
IT DEFINITELY TAKES VIGILANCE.
SHOOP
HANDLING YOU AND SUPPORTING THEM...
BUT IF I COULDN'T HANDLE THIS SITUATION...
...I COULD HARDLY CALL MYSELF THE MISTRESS'S BODYGUARD!
I FIND THIS DIFFICULT TO COMPREHEND.
I ALREADY TOLD YOU- THIS IS AN EXERCISE IN FUTILITY.
TAK TAK TAK TAK
SHING
KLANG
UWIP
CHANG
EVEN IF YOU DO RESCUE MARIKA, SHE CANNOT RETURN TO BONYARI HIGH.
WHY?
WHY HAVEN'T YOU TOLD YOUR MISTRESS AND RAKU ICHIJO?

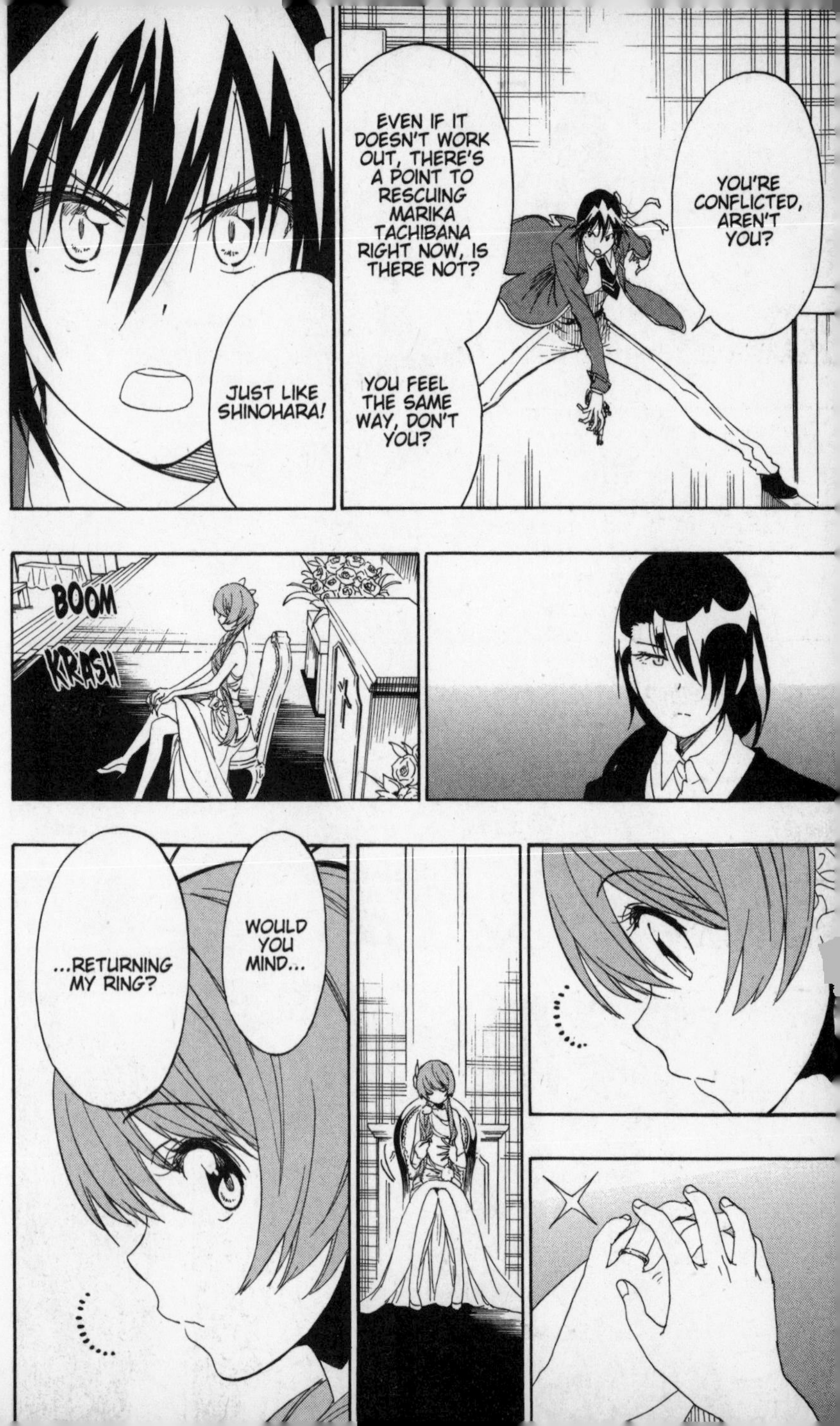
YOU'RE CONFLICTED, AREN'T YOU?
EVEN IF IT DOESN'T WORK OUT, THERE'S A POINT TO RESCUING MARIKA TACHIBANA RIGHT NOW, IS THERE NOT?
YOU FEEL THE SAME WAY, DON'T YOU?
JUST LIKE SHINOHARA!
BOOM
KRASH
WOULD YOU MIND...
...RETURNING MY RING?

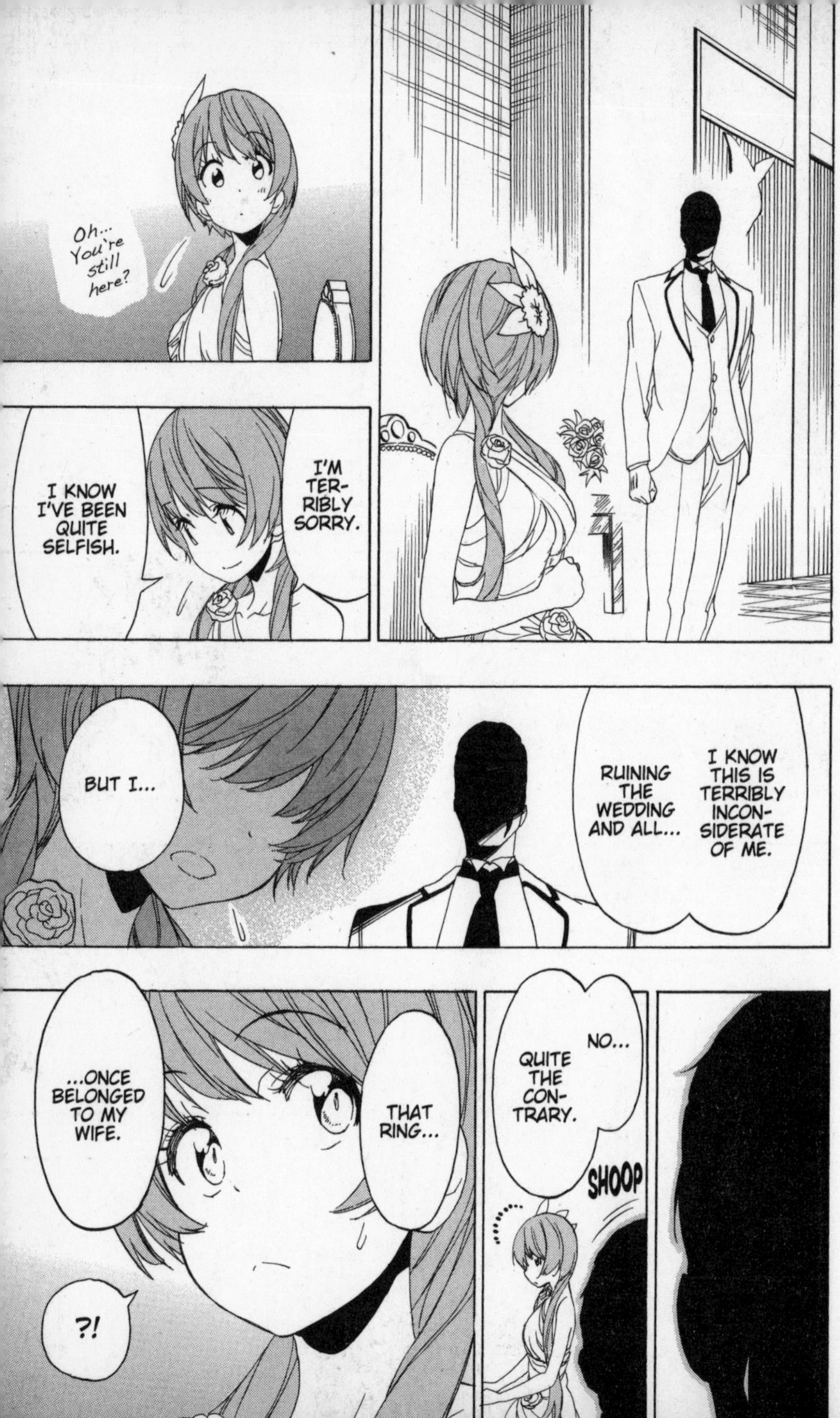

Oh... You're still here?
I'M TERRIBLY SORRY.
I KNOW I'VE BEEN QUITE SELFISH.
I KNOW THIS IS TERRIBLY INCONSIDERATE OF ME.
RUINING THE WEDDING AND ALL...
BUT I...
NO...
QUITE THE CONTRARY.
SHOOP
......
THAT RING...
...ONCE BELONGED TO MY WIFE.
?!

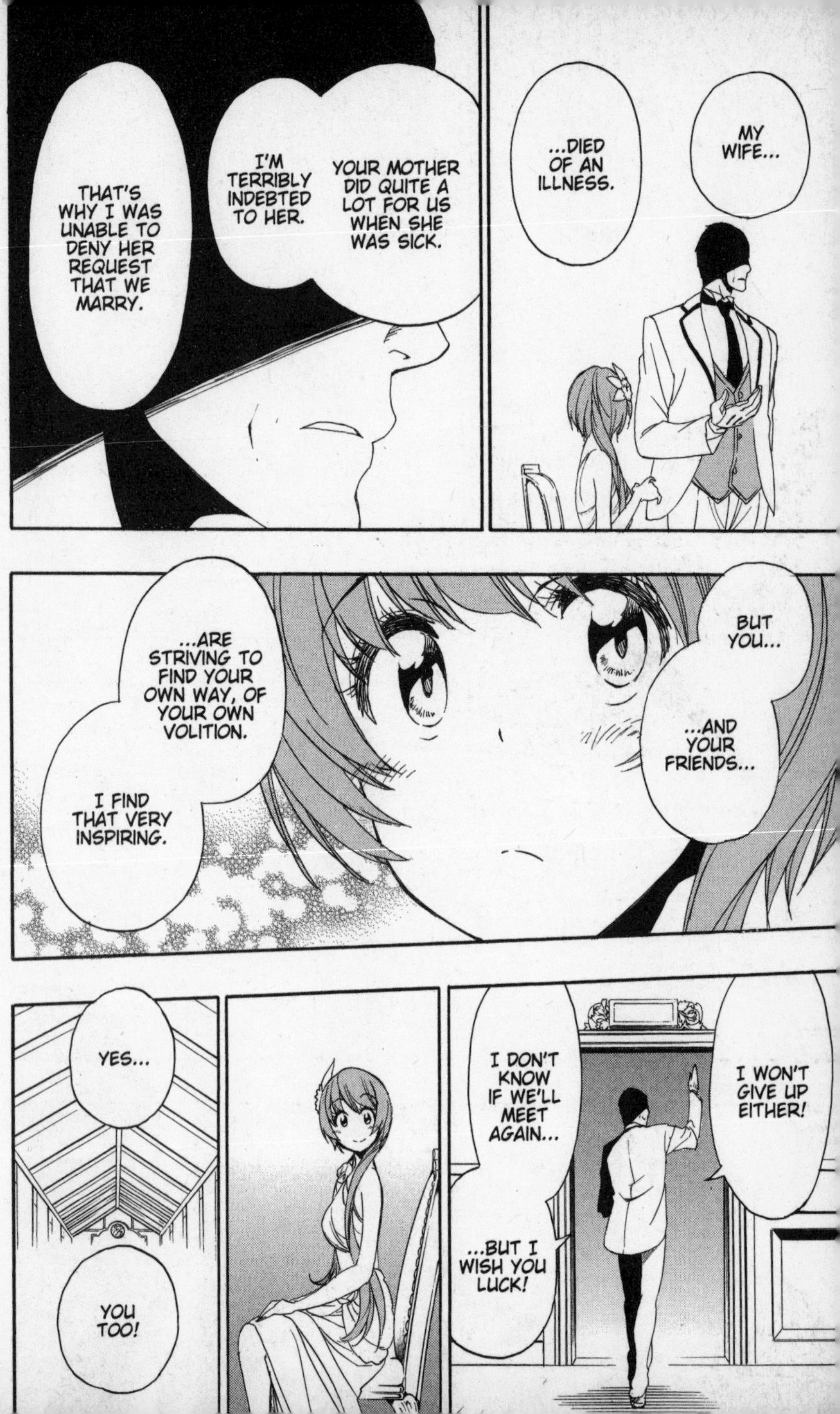
MY WIFE...
...DIED OF AN ILLNESS.
YOUR MOTHER DID QUITE A LOT FOR US WHEN SHE WAS SICK.
I'M TERRIBLY INDEBTED TO HER.
THAT'S WHY I WAS UNABLE TO DENY HER REQUEST THAT WE MARRY.
BUT YOU...
...AND YOUR FRIENDS...
...ARE STRIVING TO FIND YOUR OWN WAY, OF YOUR OWN VOLITION.
I FIND THAT VERY INSPIRING.
I WON'T GIVE UP EITHER!
I DON'T KNOW IF WE'LL MEET AGAIN...
...BUT I WISH YOU LUCK!
YES...
YOU TOO!

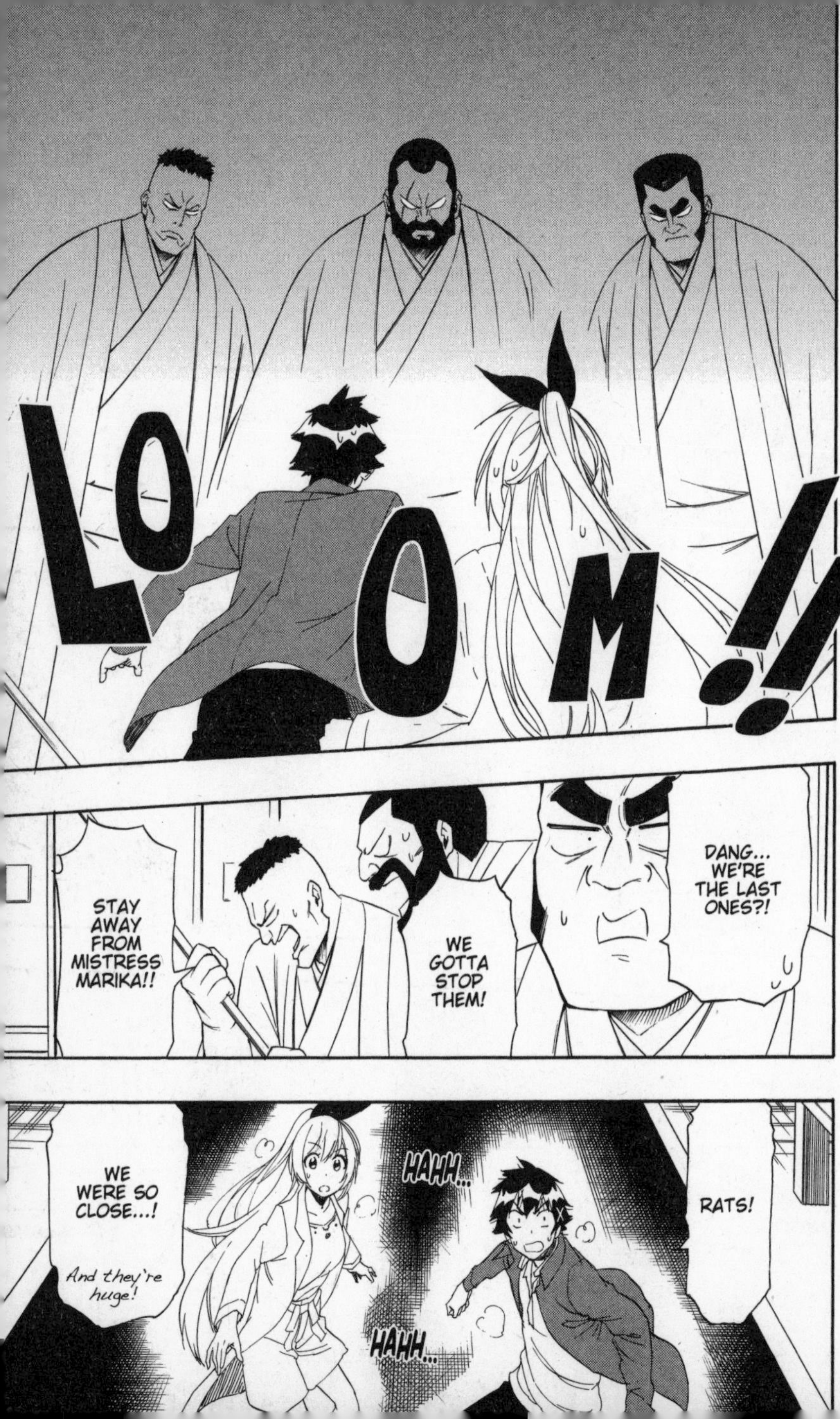
LOOM!!
DANG... WE'RE THE LAST ONES?!
WE GOTTA STOP THEM!
STAY AWAY FROM MISTRESS MARIKA!!
RATS!
HAHH...
HAHH...
WE WERE SO CLOSE...!
And they're huge!

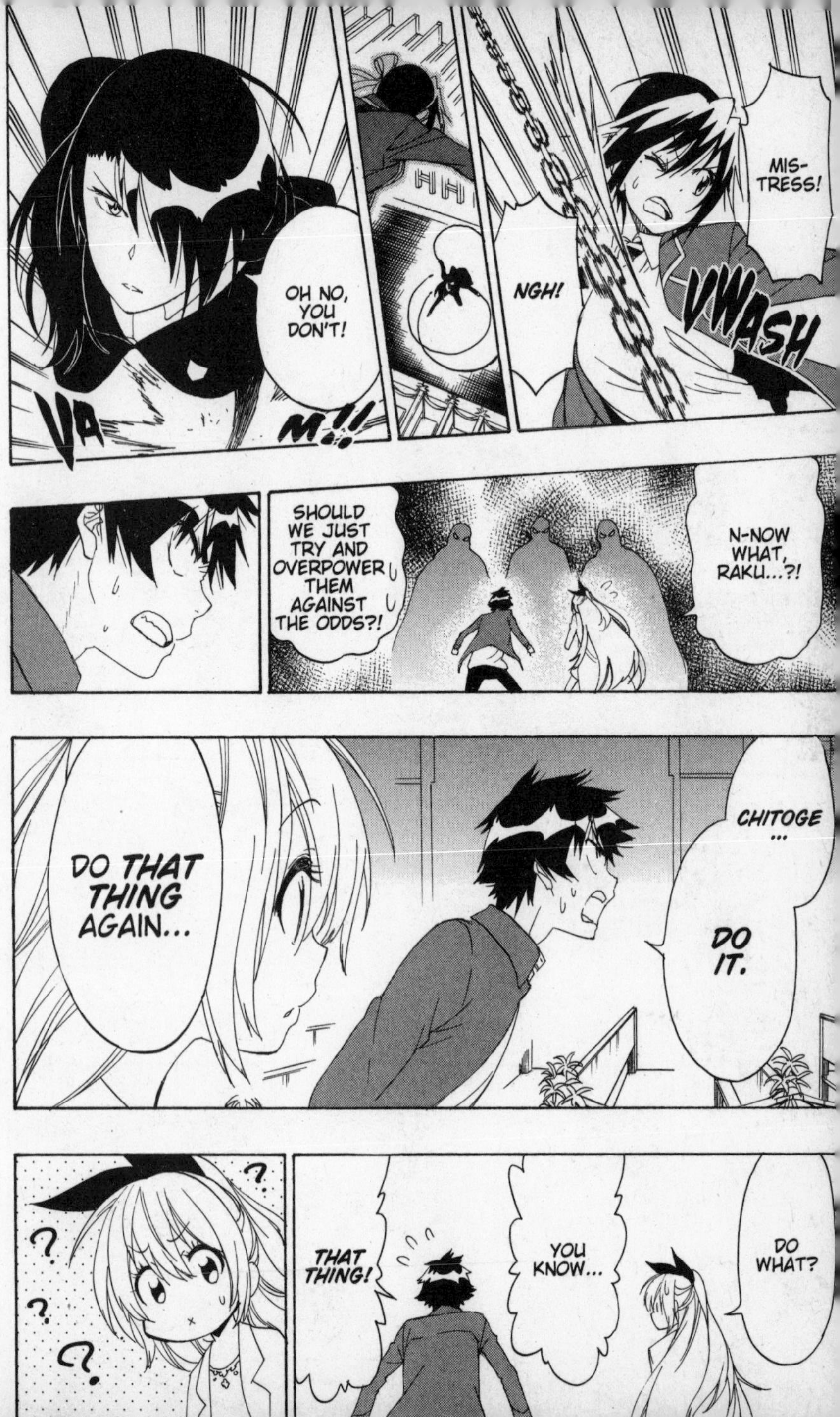
MIS-TRESS!
VWASH
NGH!
OH NO, YOU DON'T!
VAM!!
N-NOW WHAT, RAKU...?!
SHOULD WE JUST TRY AND OVERPOWER THEM AGAINST THE ODDS?!
CHITOGE...
DO IT.
DO THAT THING AGAIN...
DO WHAT?
YOU KNOW...
THAT THING!
? ? ? ?

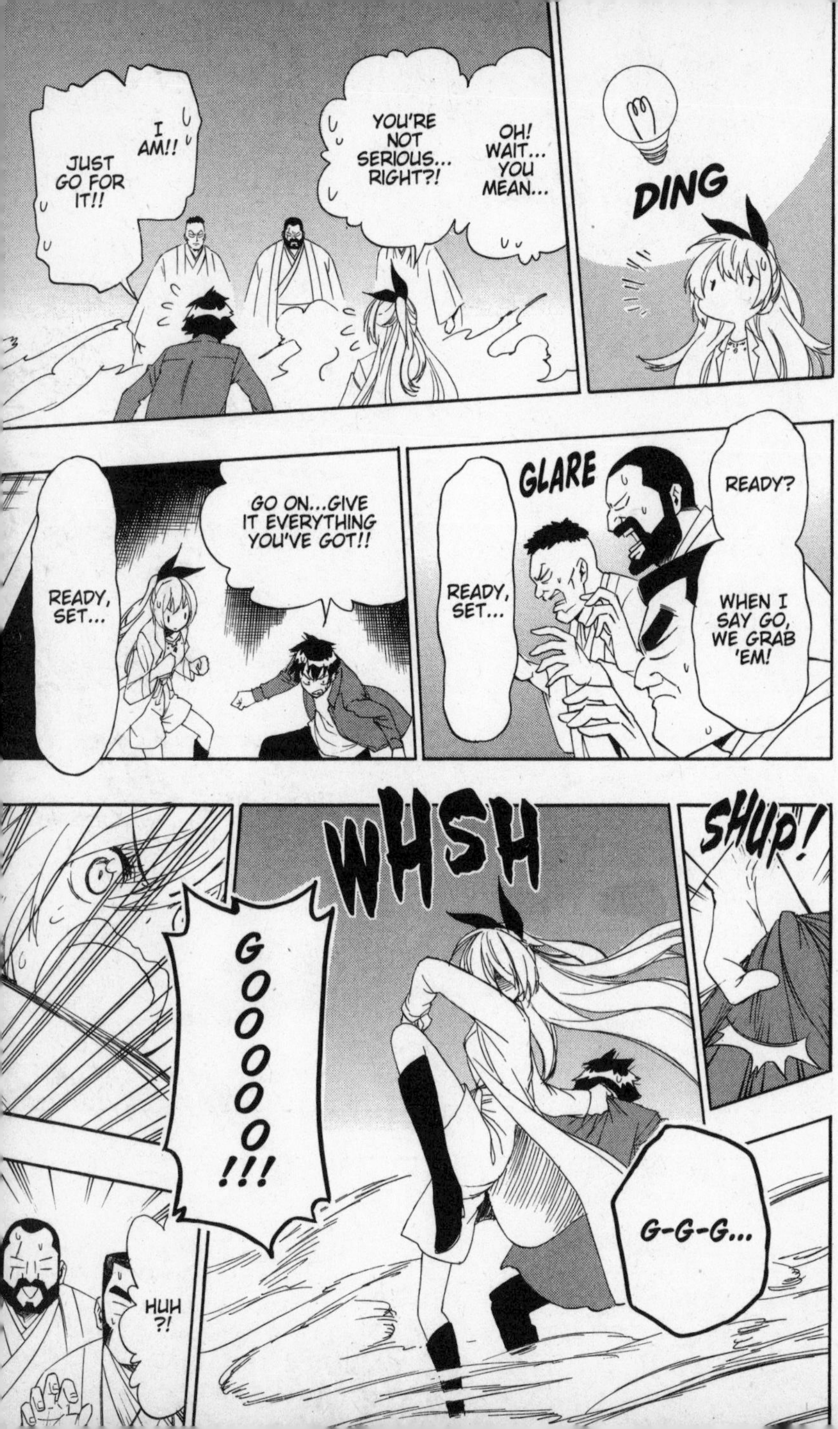
DING
OH! WAIT... YOU MEAN...
YOU'RE NOT SERIOUS... RIGHT?!
I AM!! JUST GO FOR IT!!
READY?
WHEN I SAY GO, WE GRAB 'EM!
GLARE
READY, SET...
GO ON...GIVE IT EVERYTHING YOU'VE GOT!!
READY, SET...
SHUP!
WHSH
GOOOOOO!!!
G-G-G...
HUH?!

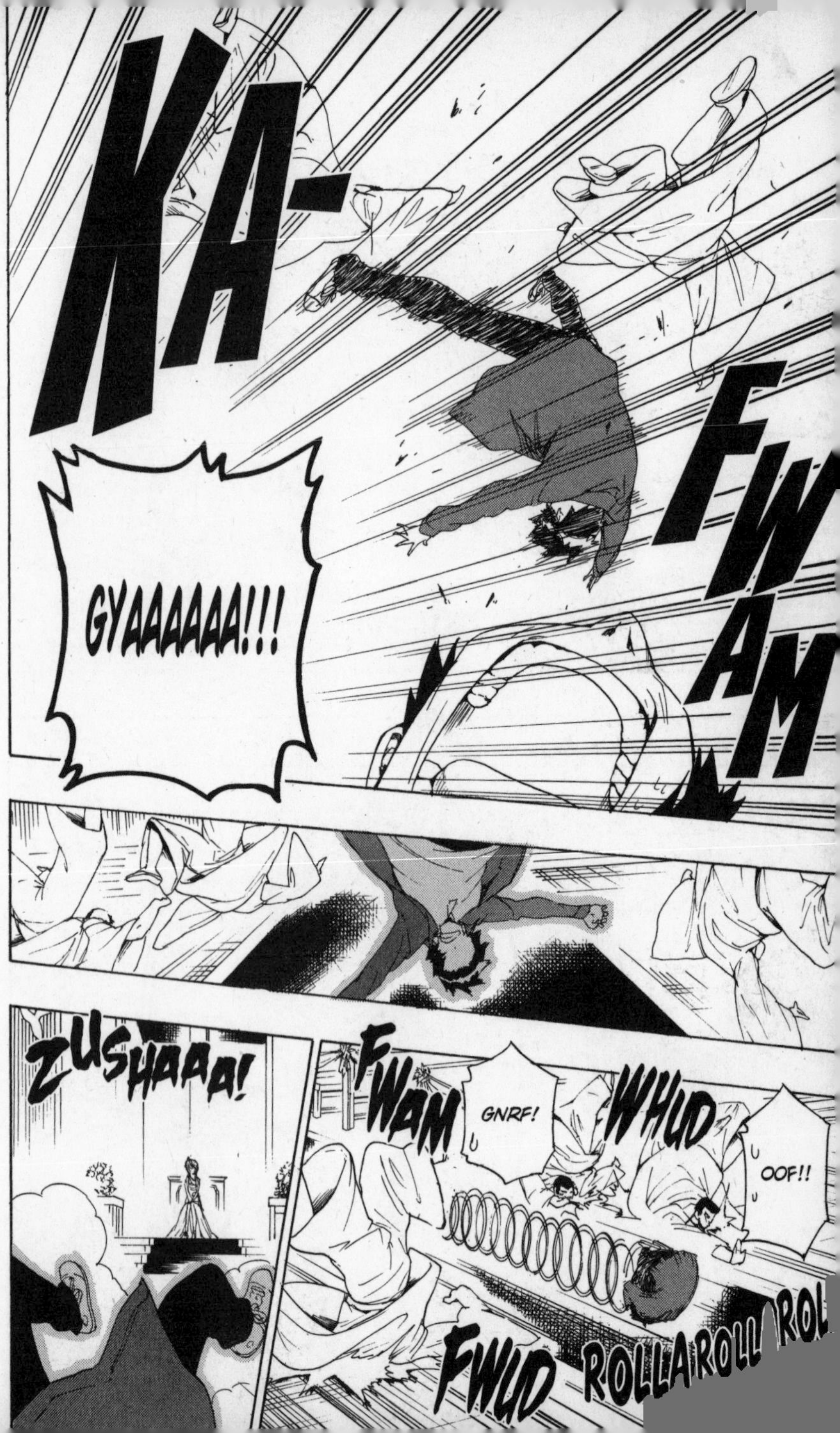
FWAM
KA-
GYAAAAAA!!!
WHUD
OOF!!
GNRF!
FWAM
ROLLAROLL ROL
FWUD
ZUSHAAA!

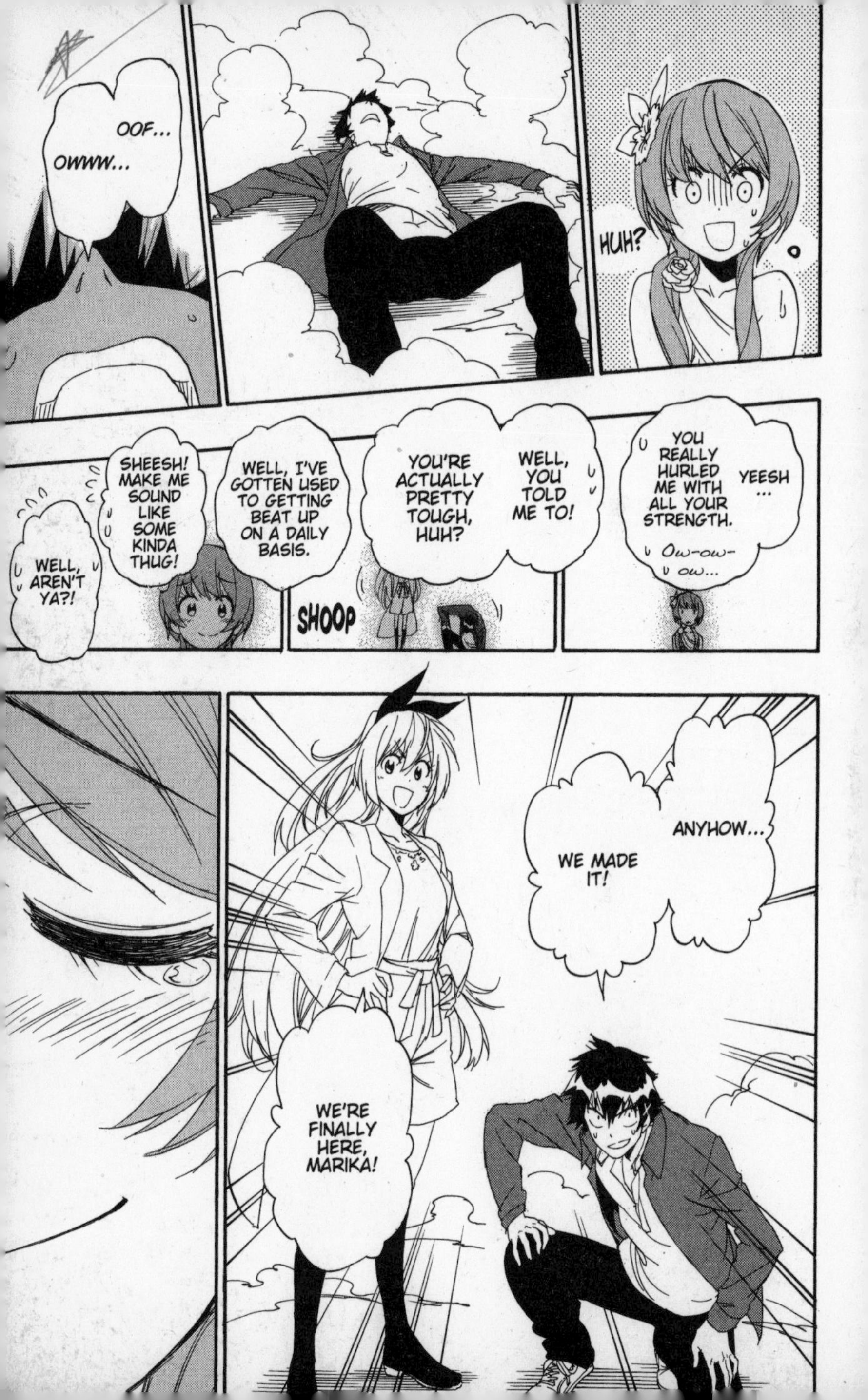
HUH?
OOF... OWWW...
YEESH...
YOU REALLY HURLED ME WITH ALL YOUR STRENGTH.
Ow-ow-ow...
WELL, YOU TOLD ME TO!
YOU'RE ACTUALLY PRETTY TOUGH, HUH?
SHOOP
WELL, I'VE GOTTEN USED TO GETTING BEAT UP ON A DAILY BASIS.
SHEESH! MAKE ME SOUND LIKE SOME KINDA THUG!
WELL, AREN'T YA?!
ANYHOW...
WE MADE IT!
WE'RE FINALLY HERE, MARIKA!

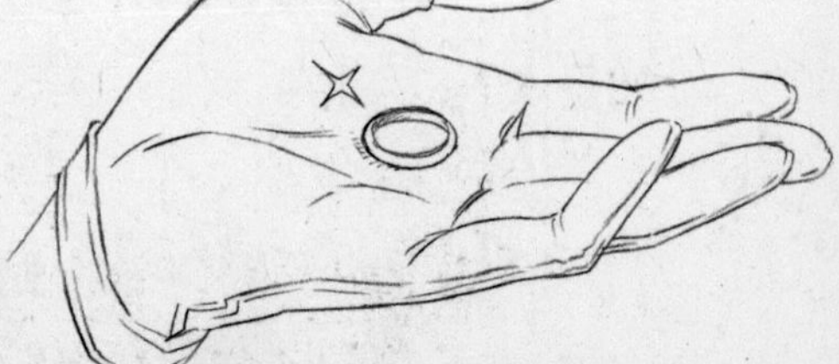

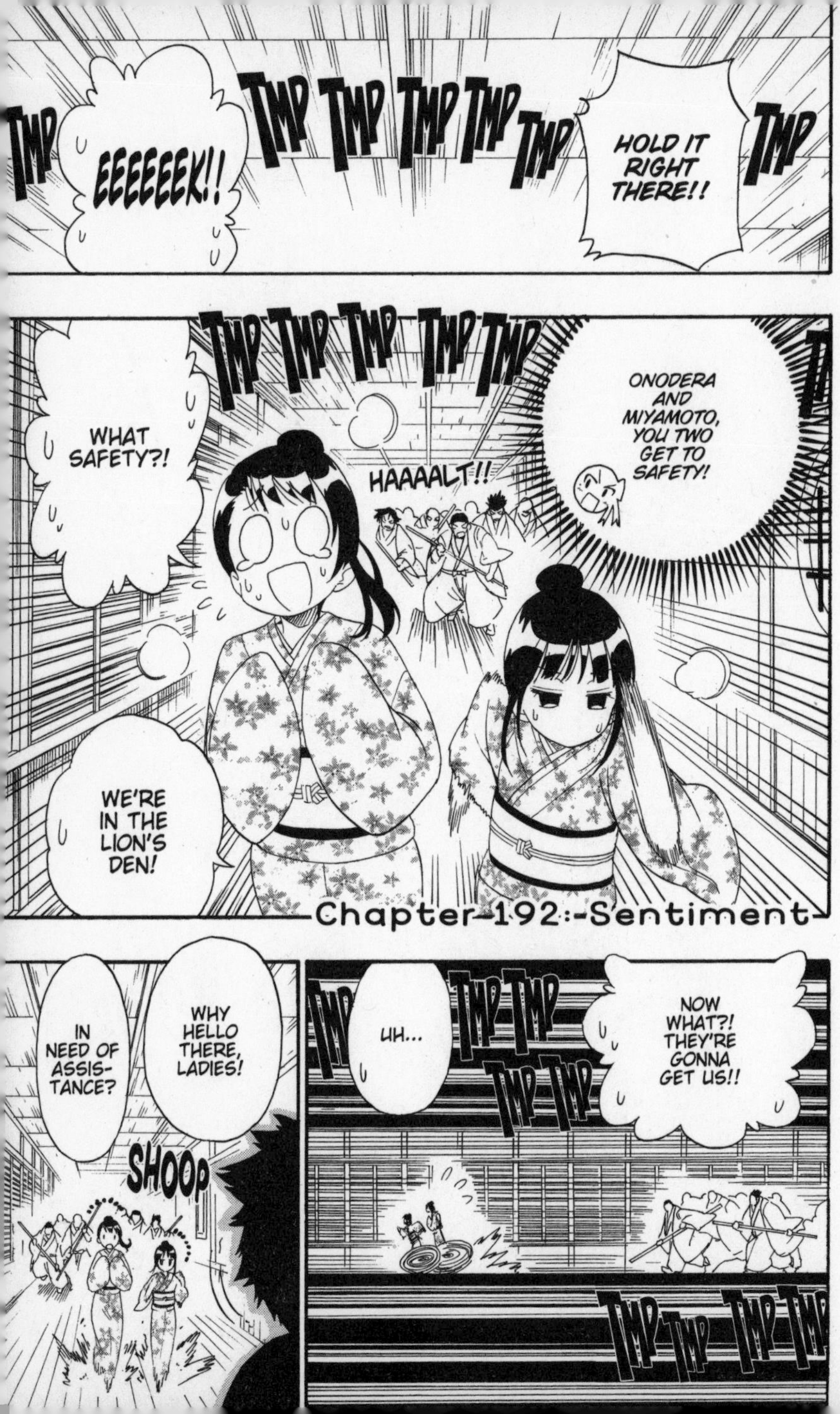
TMP
HOLD IT RIGHT THERE!!
TMP TMP TMP TMP TMP
EEEEEEK!!
TMP
TMP
ONODERA AND MIYAMOTO, YOU TWO GET TO SAFETY!
TMP TMP TMP TMP TMP
HAAAALT!!
WHAT SAFETY?!
WE'RE IN THE LION'S DEN!
Chapter 192: Sentiment
NOW WHAT?! THEY'RE GONNA GET US!!
TMP TMP
TMP TMP
UH...
TMP
TMP TMP TMP TMP
WHY HELLO THERE, LADIES!
IN NEED OF ASSIS-TANCE?
SHOOP

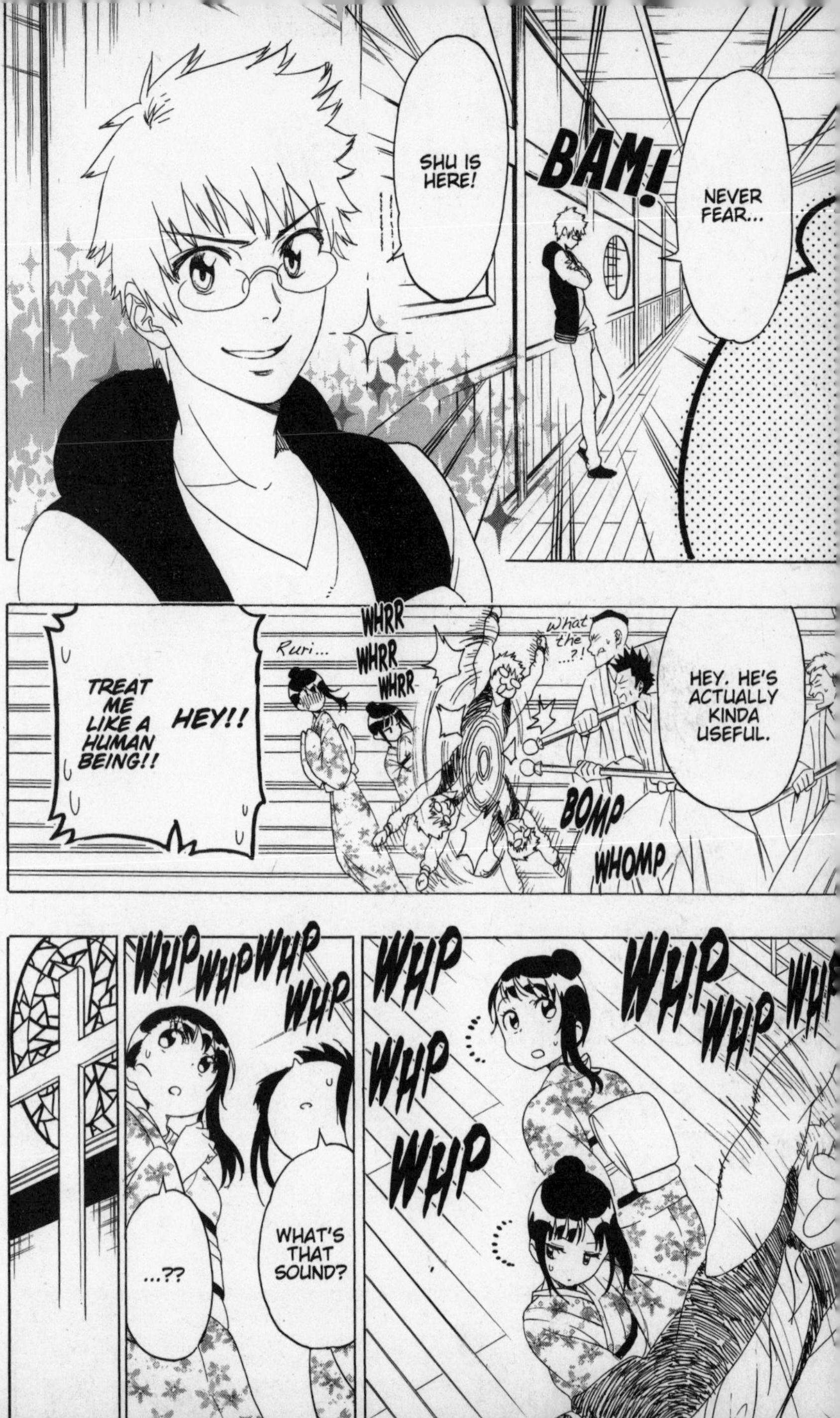
NEVER FEAR...
BAM!
SHU IS HERE!
HEY. HE'S ACTUALLY KINDA USEFUL.
What the ...?!
WHRR WHRR WHRR
Ruri...
BOMP
WHOMP
HEY!!
TREAT ME LIKE A HUMAN BEING!!
WHP WHP WHP
WHP WHP WHP WHP
WHP WHP WHP WHP
WHAT'S THAT SOUND?
...??

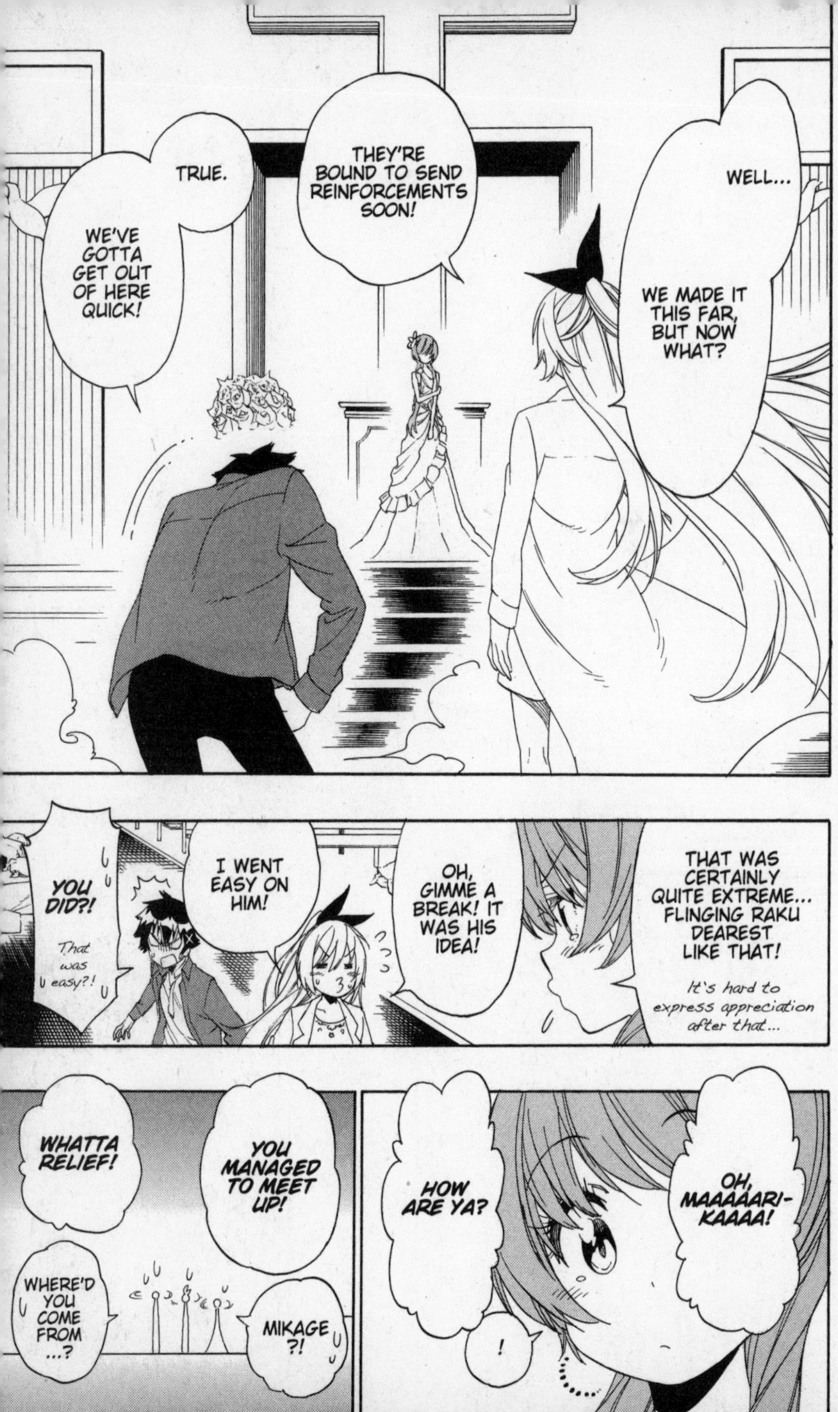
WELL...
WE MADE IT THIS FAR, BUT NOW WHAT?
THEY'RE BOUND TO SEND REINFORCEMENTS SOON!
TRUE.
WE'VE GOTTA GET OUT OF HERE QUICK!
THAT WAS CERTAINLY QUITE EXTREME... FLINGING RAKU DEAREST LIKE THAT!
It's hard to express appreciation after that...
OH, GIMME A BREAK! IT WAS HIS IDEA!
I WENT EASY ON HIM!
YOU DID?!
That was easy?!
OH, MAAAAARI-KAAAA!
HOW ARE YA?
!
YOU MANAGED TO MEET UP!
WHATTA RELIEF!
MIKAGE?!
WHERE'D YOU COME FROM ...?

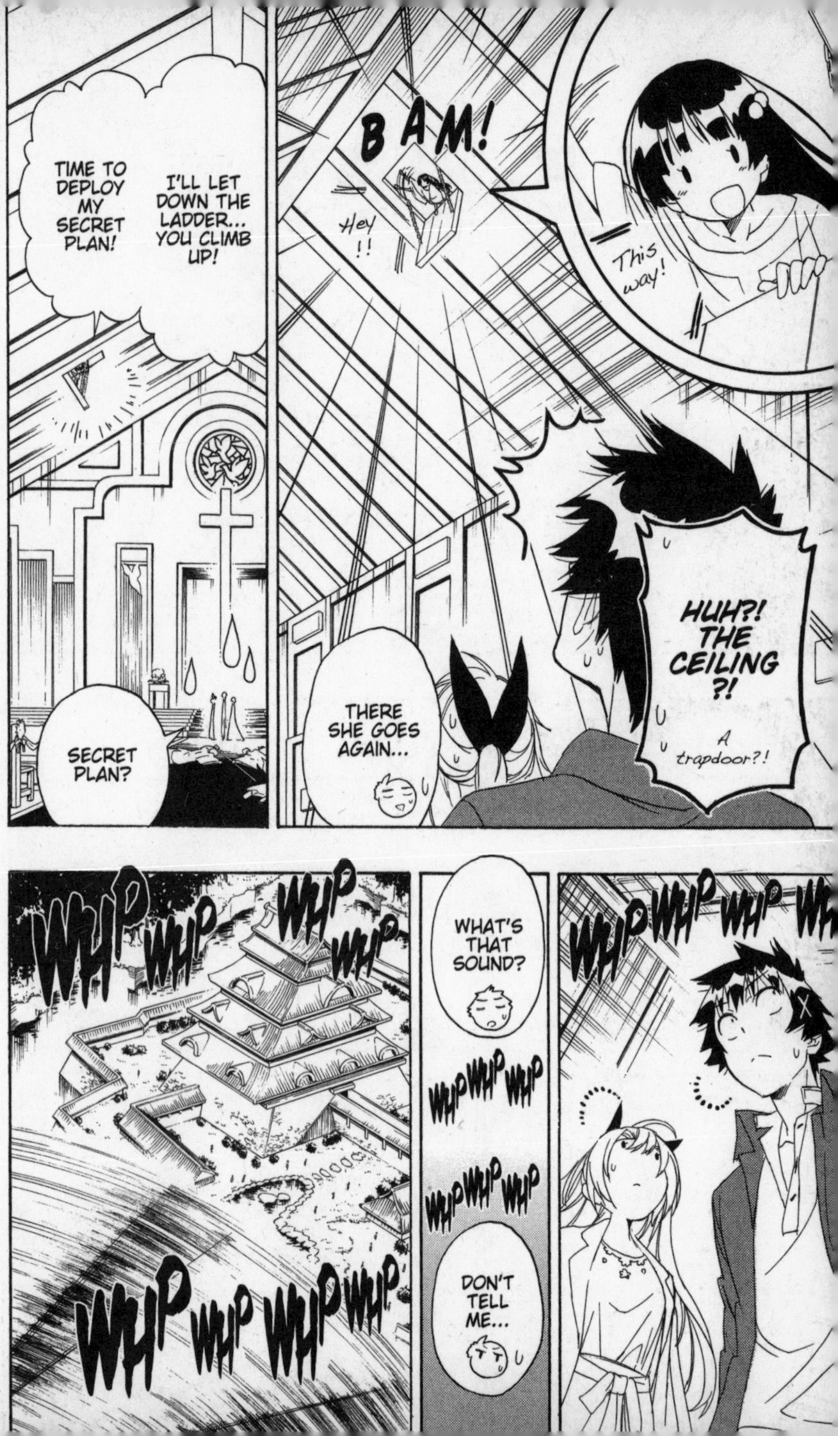

This way!
BAM!
Hey!!
HUH?! THE CEILING?!
A trapdoor?!
THERE SHE GOES AGAIN...
TIME TO DEPLOY MY SECRET PLAN! I'LL LET DOWN THE LADDER... YOU CLIMB UP!
SECRET PLAN?
WHP WHP WHP WHP
WHAT'S THAT SOUND?
WHP WHP WHP
WHP WHP WHP
DON'T TELL ME...
WHP WHP WHP WHP
WHP WHP WHP WHP

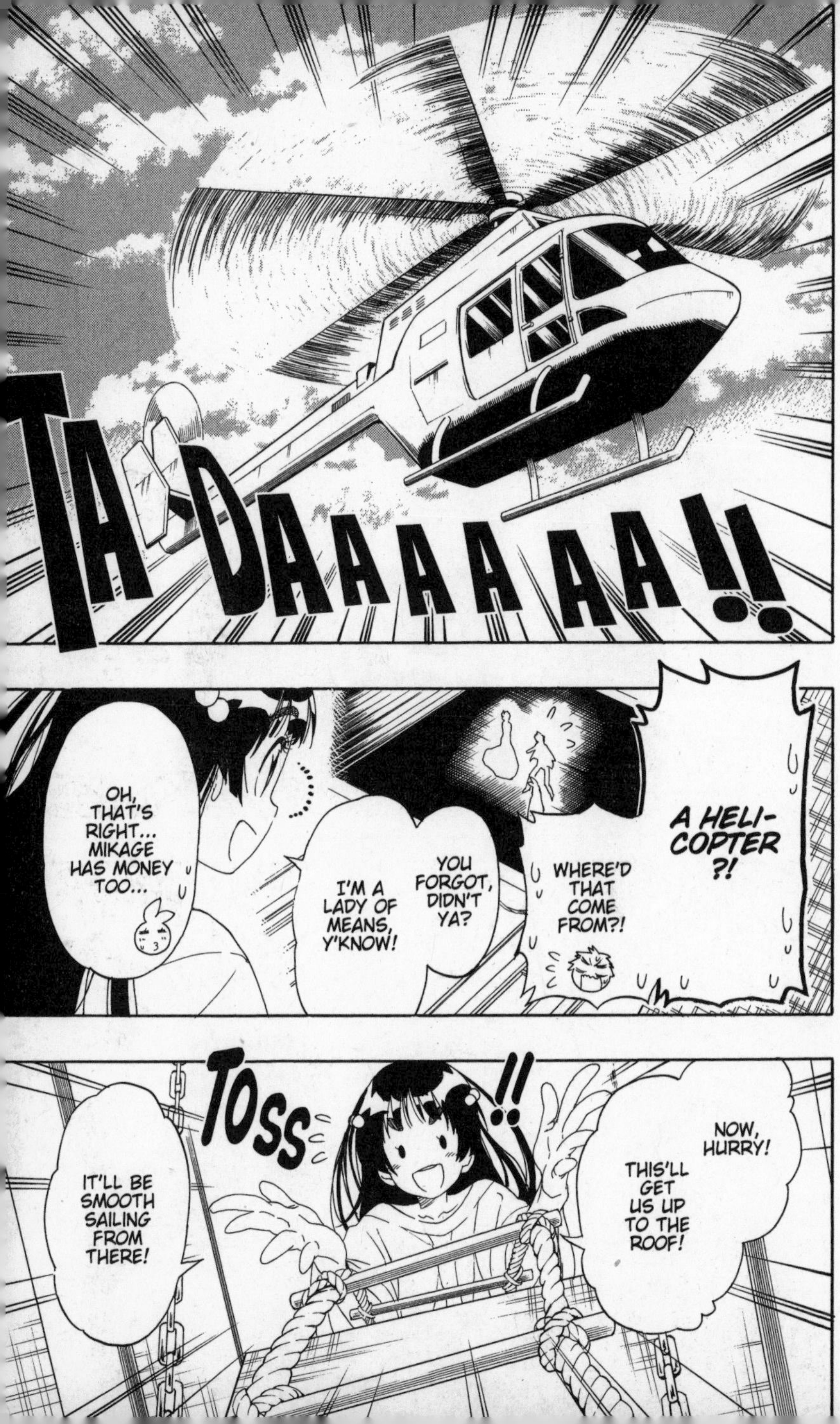
TA-DAAAAAA!!
A HELI-COPTER?!
WHERE'D THAT COME FROM?!
YOU FORGOT, DIDN'T YA?
I'M A LADY OF MEANS, Y'KNOW!
OH, THAT'S RIGHT... MIKAGE HAS MONEY TOO...
NOW, HURRY!
THIS'LL GET US UP TO THE ROOF!
TOSS!!
IT'LL BE SMOOTH SAILING FROM THERE!

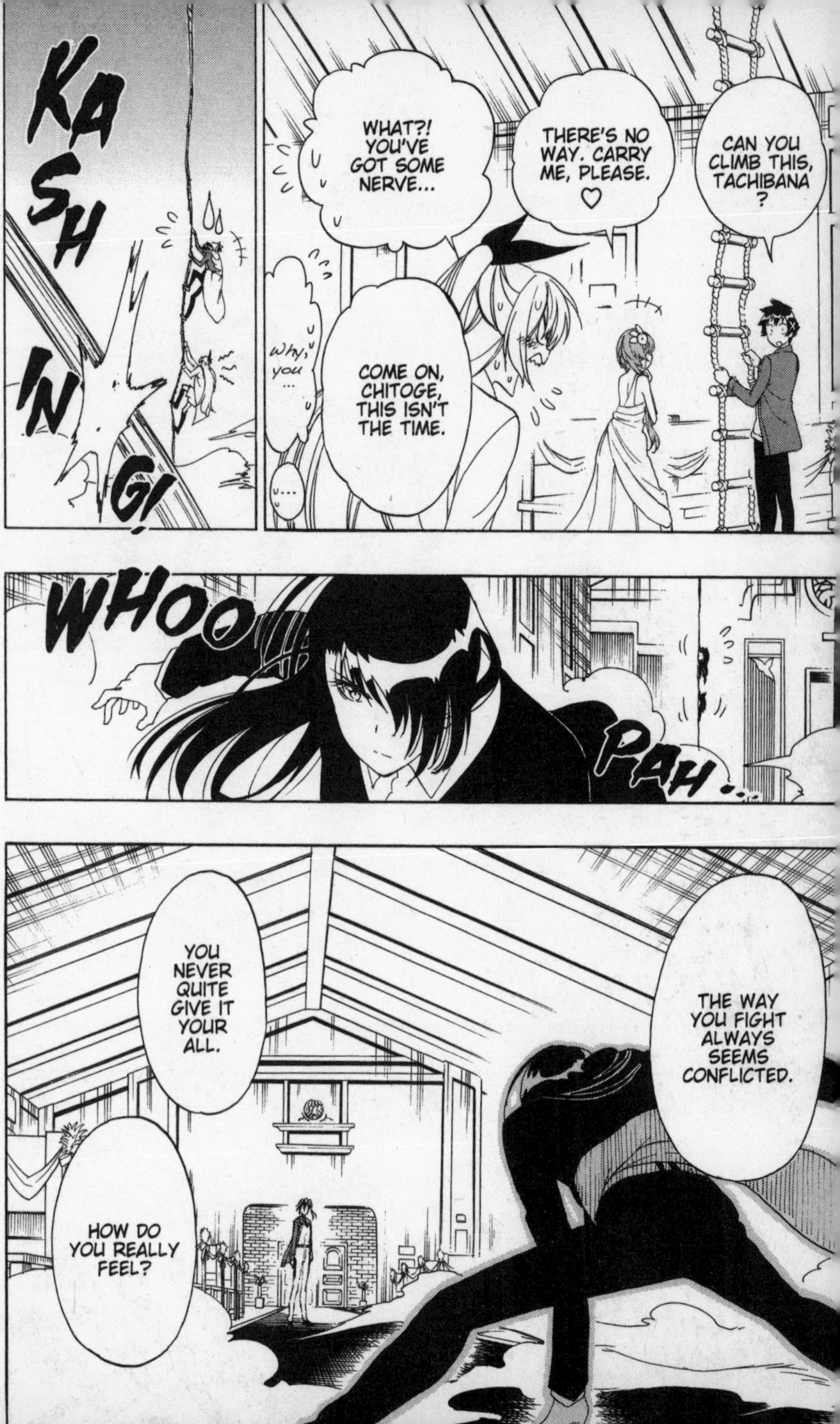
CAN YOU CLIMB THIS, TACHIBANA?
THERE'S NO WAY. CARRY ME, PLEASE. ♡
WHAT?! YOU'VE GOT SOME NERVE...
Why, you ...
COME ON, CHITOGE, THIS ISN'T THE TIME.
...
KASHING!
WHOO
PAH...
THE WAY YOU FIGHT ALWAYS SEEMS CONFLICTED.
YOU NEVER QUITE GIVE IT YOUR ALL.
HOW DO YOU REALLY FEEL?

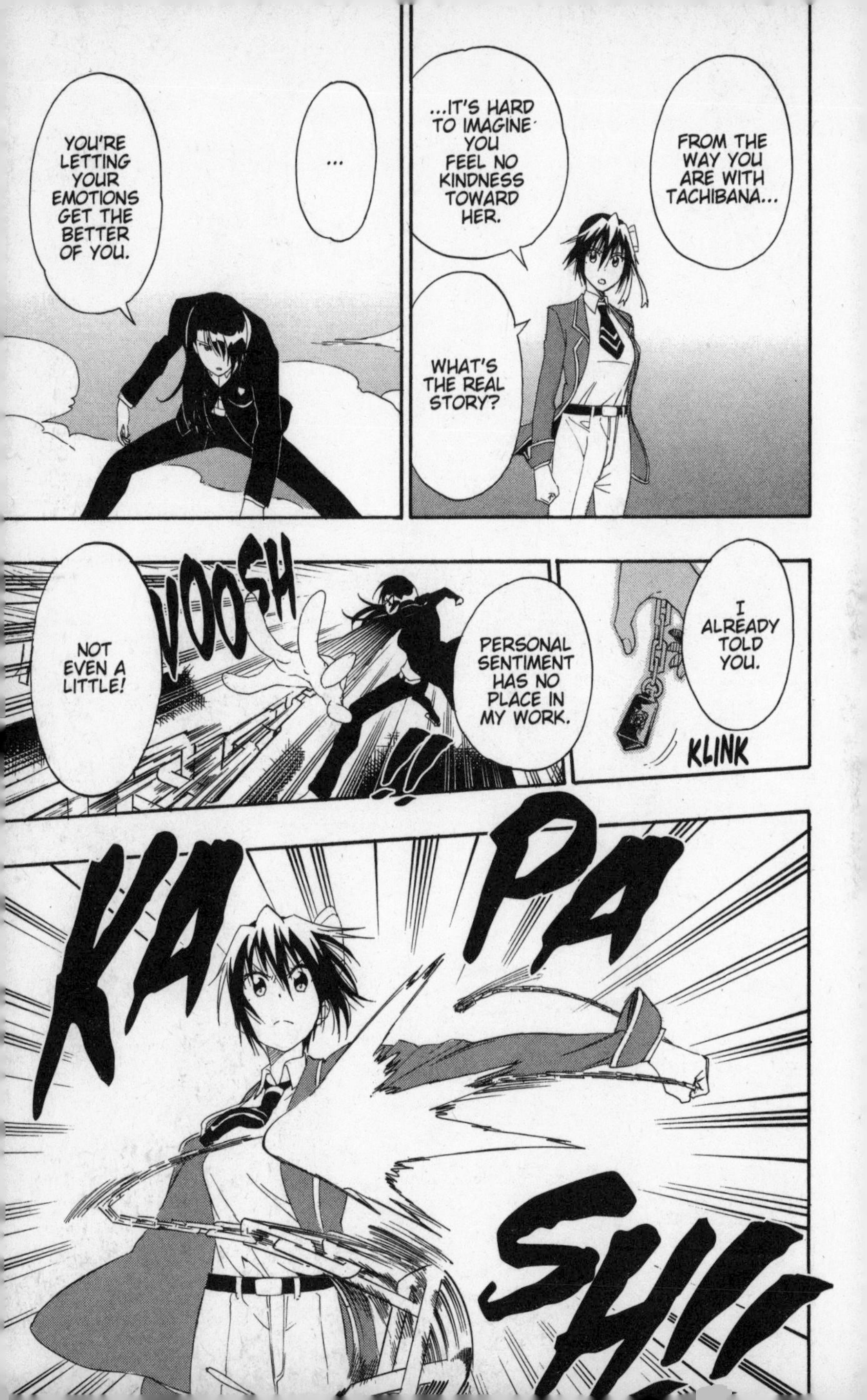
FROM THE WAY YOU ARE WITH TACHIBANA...
...IT'S HARD TO IMAGINE YOU FEEL NO KINDNESS TOWARD HER.
WHAT'S THE REAL STORY?
...
YOU'RE LETTING YOUR EMOTIONS GET THE BETTER OF YOU.
I ALREADY TOLD YOU.
KLINK
PERSONAL SENTIMENT HAS NO PLACE IN MY WORK.
VOOSH
NOT EVEN A LITTLE!
KA
PA
SHI!!

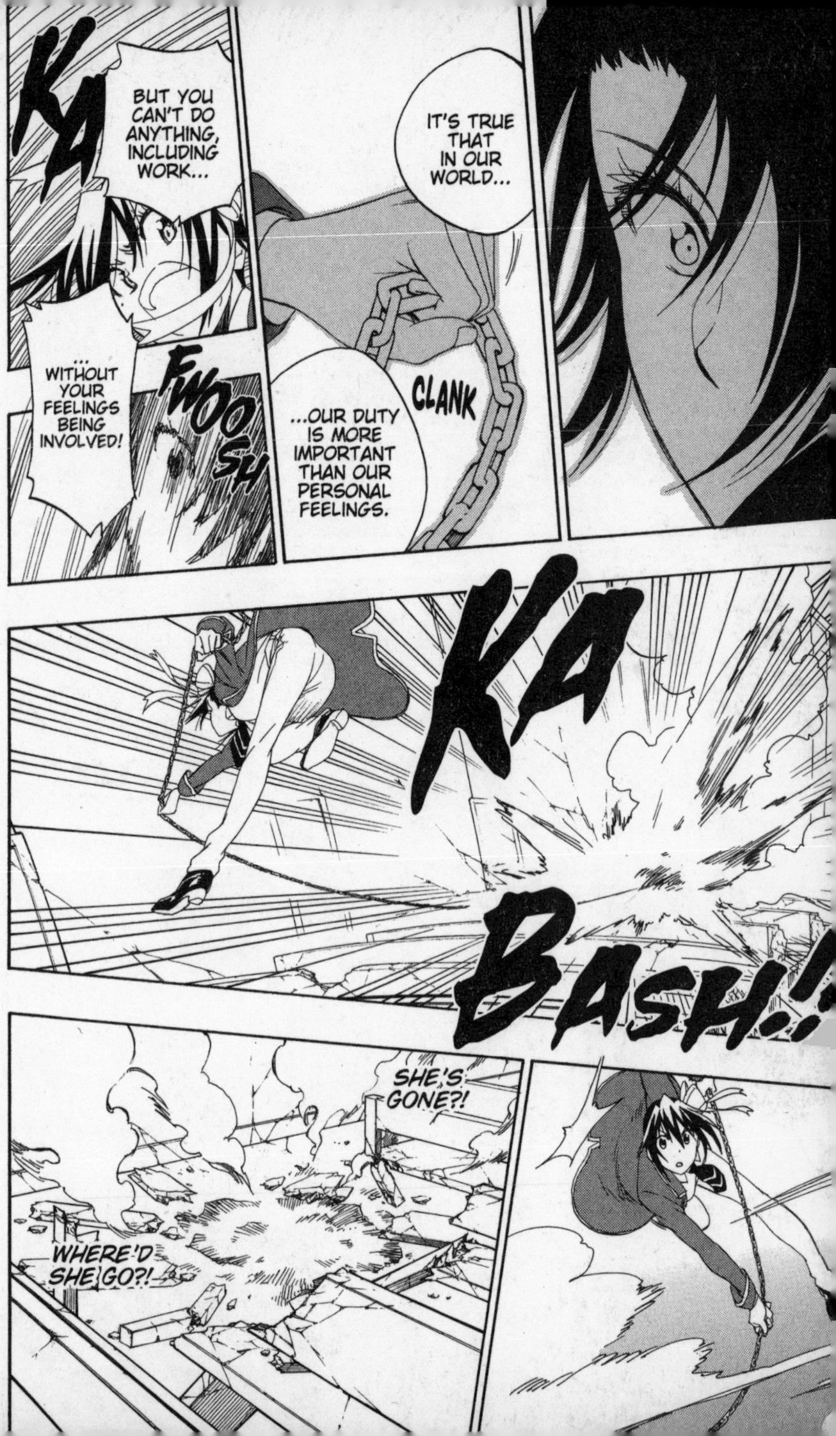
IT'S TRUE THAT IN OUR WORLD...
CLANK
...OUR DUTY IS MORE IMPORTANT THAN OUR PERSONAL FEELINGS.
KA
BUT YOU CAN'T DO ANYTHING, INCLUDING WORK...
FWOOSH
...WITHOUT YOUR FEELINGS BEING INVOLVED!
KA BASH!!
SHE'S GONE?!
...
WHERE'D SHE GO?!

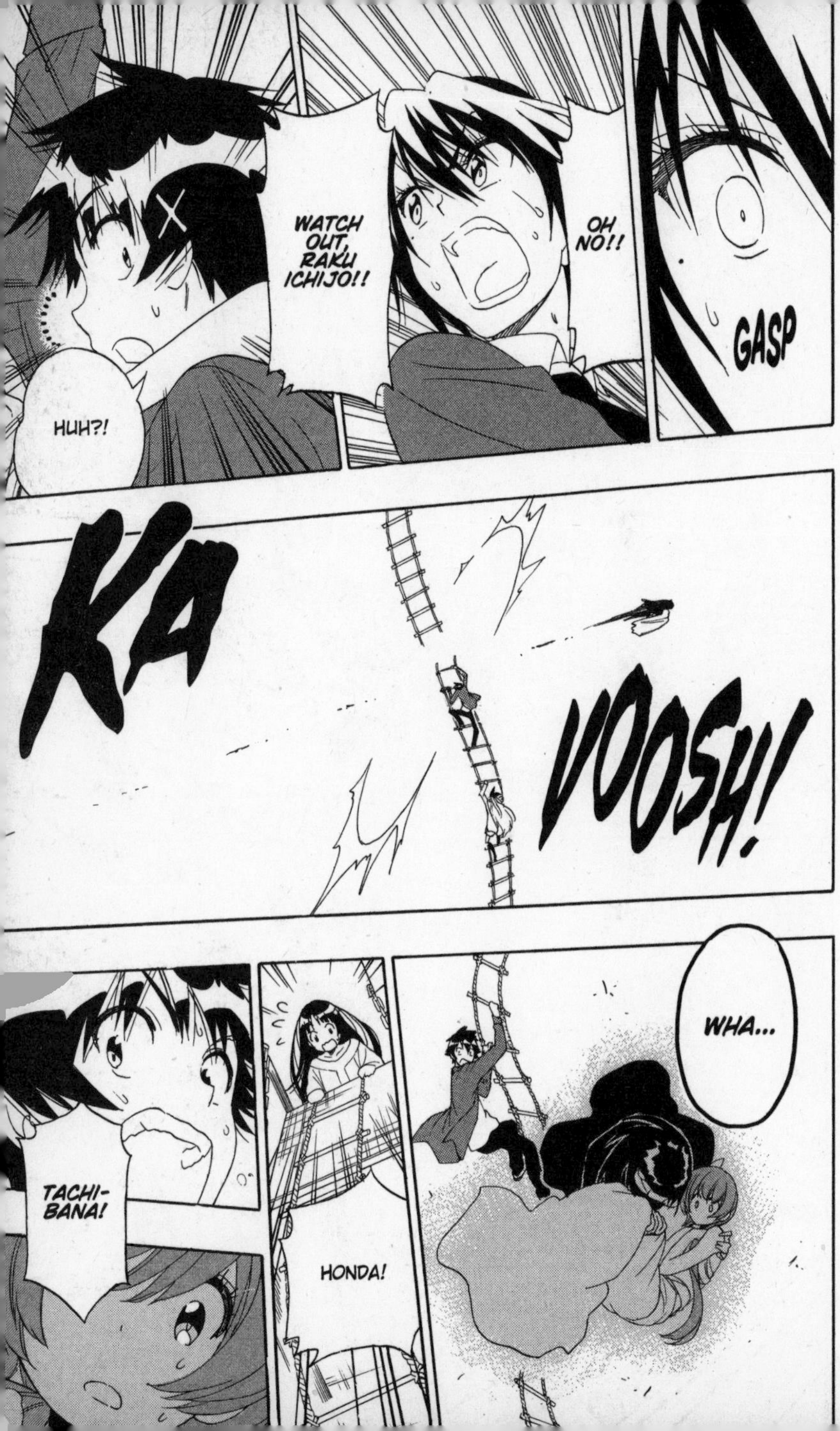
GASP
OH NO!!
WATCH OUT, RAKU ICHIJO!!
HUH?!
KA
VOOSH!
WHA...
HONDA!
TACHI-BANA!

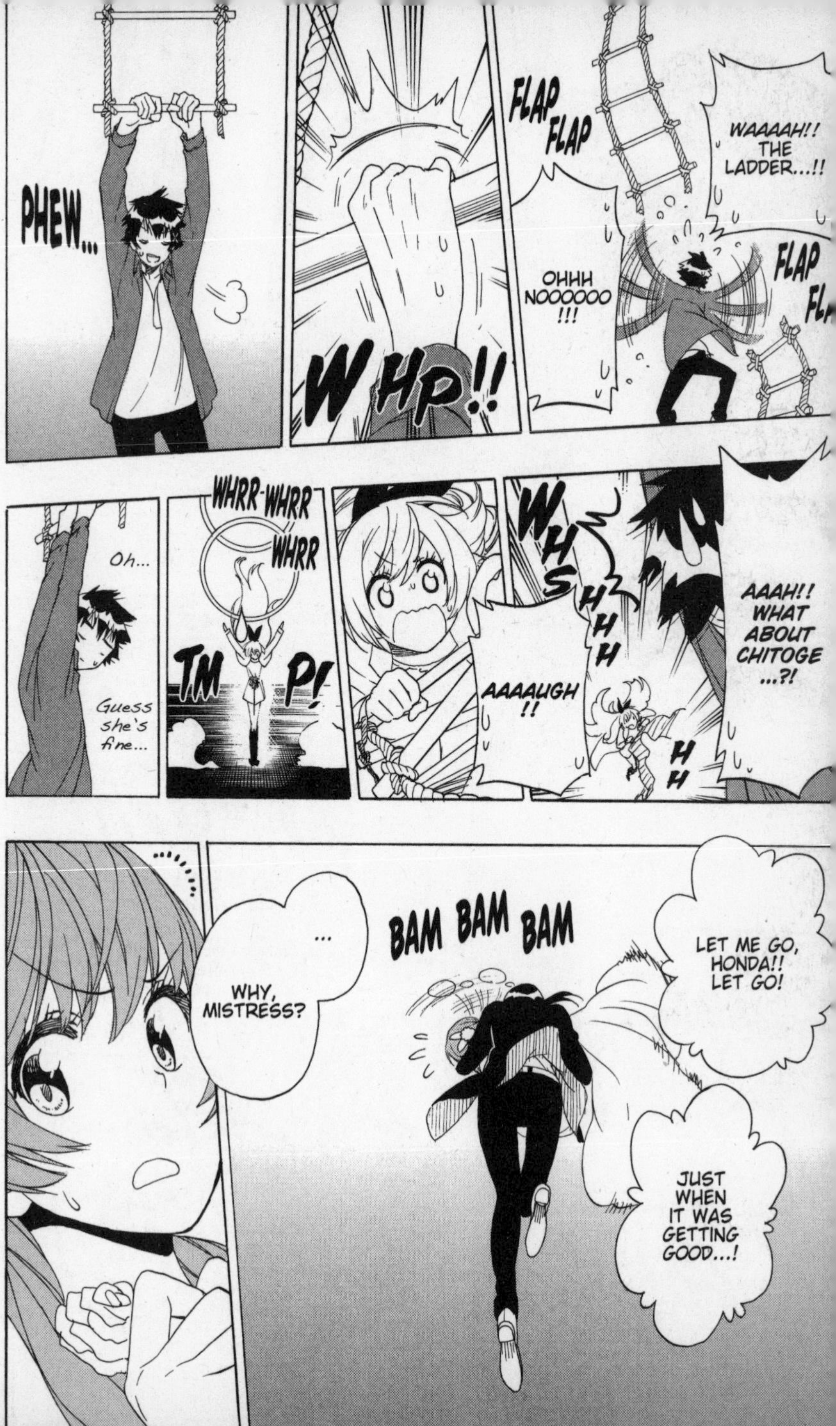
WAAAAH!! THE LADDER...!!
FLAP
FLAP FLAP
OHHH NOOOOOO!!!
WHP!!
PHEW...
AAAH!! WHAT ABOUT CHITOGE...?!
WHSHHHHH
AAAAUGH!!
WHRR-WHRR WHRR
TMP!
Oh...
Guess she's fine...
LET ME GO, HONDA!! LET GO!
JUST WHEN IT WAS GETTING GOOD...!
BAM BAM BAM
...
WHY, MISTRESS?
......

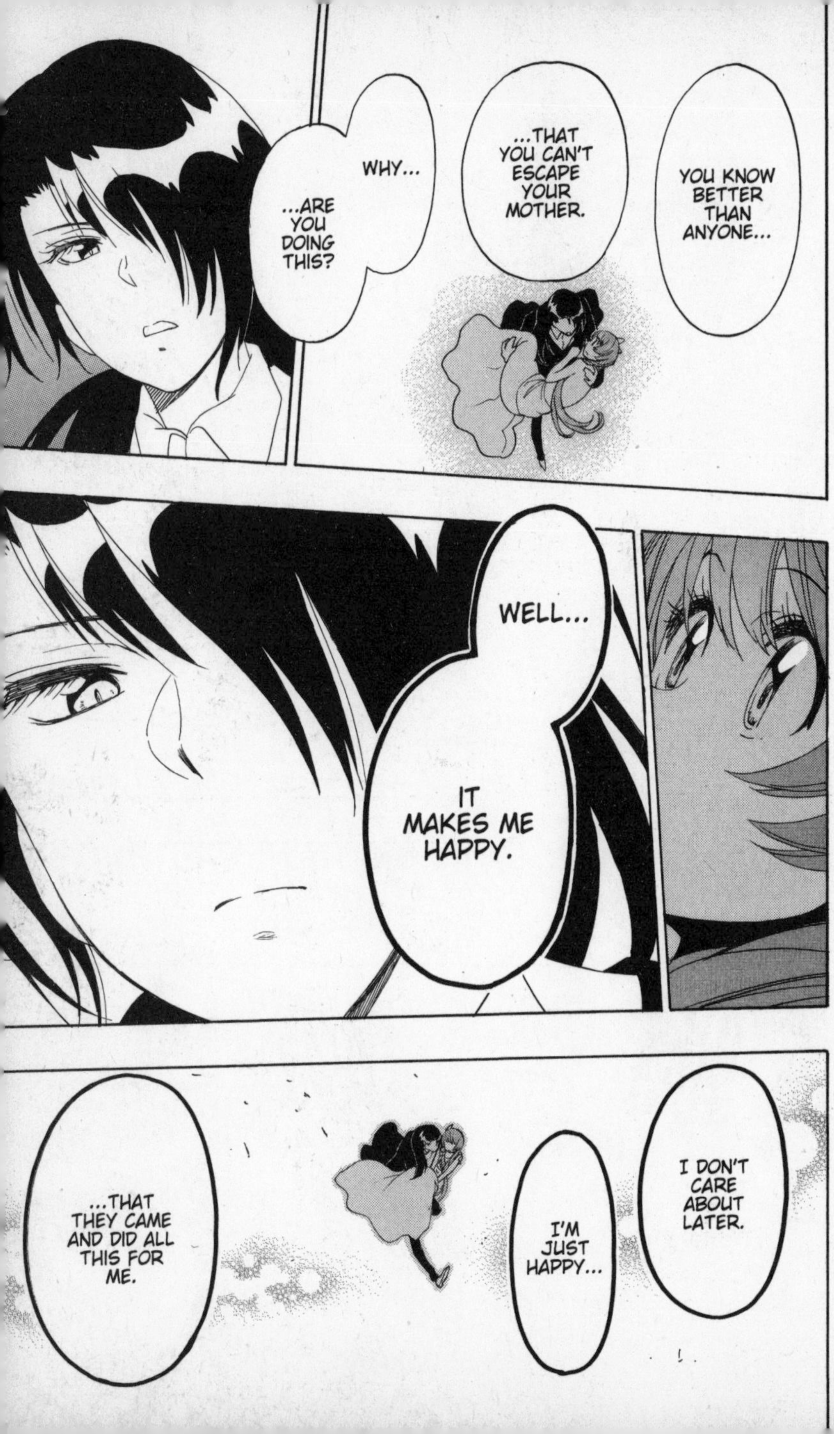
YOU KNOW BETTER THAN ANYONE...
...THAT YOU CAN'T ESCAPE YOUR MOTHER.
WHY...
...ARE YOU DOING THIS?
WELL...
IT MAKES ME HAPPY.
I DON'T CARE ABOUT LATER.
I'M JUST HAPPY...
...THAT THEY CAME AND DID ALL THIS FOR ME.

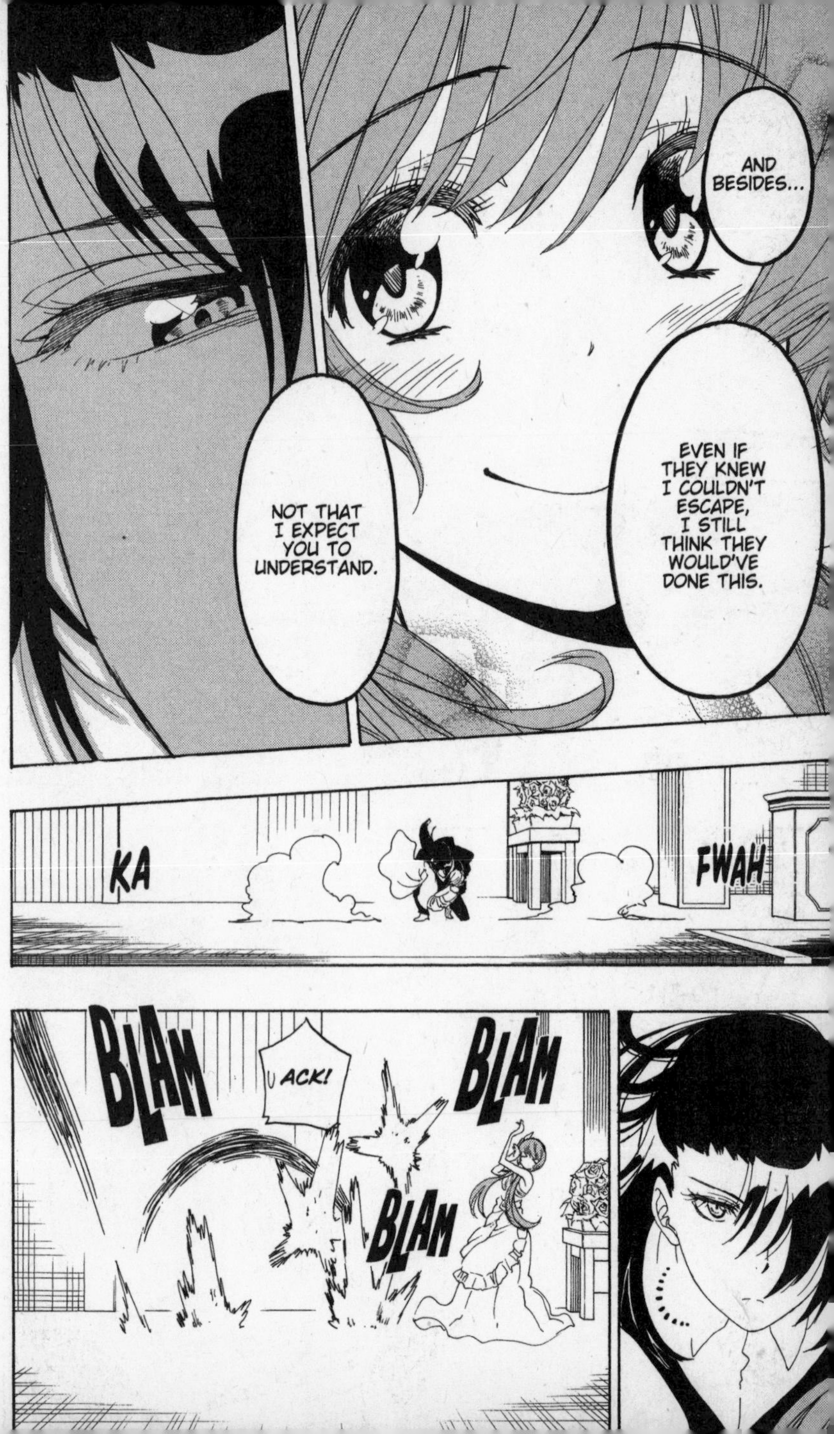
AND BESIDES...
EVEN IF THEY KNEW I COULDN'T ESCAPE, I STILL THINK THEY WOULD'VE DONE THIS.
NOT THAT I EXPECT YOU TO UNDERSTAND.
FWAH
KA
BLAM
BLAM
ACK!
BLAM

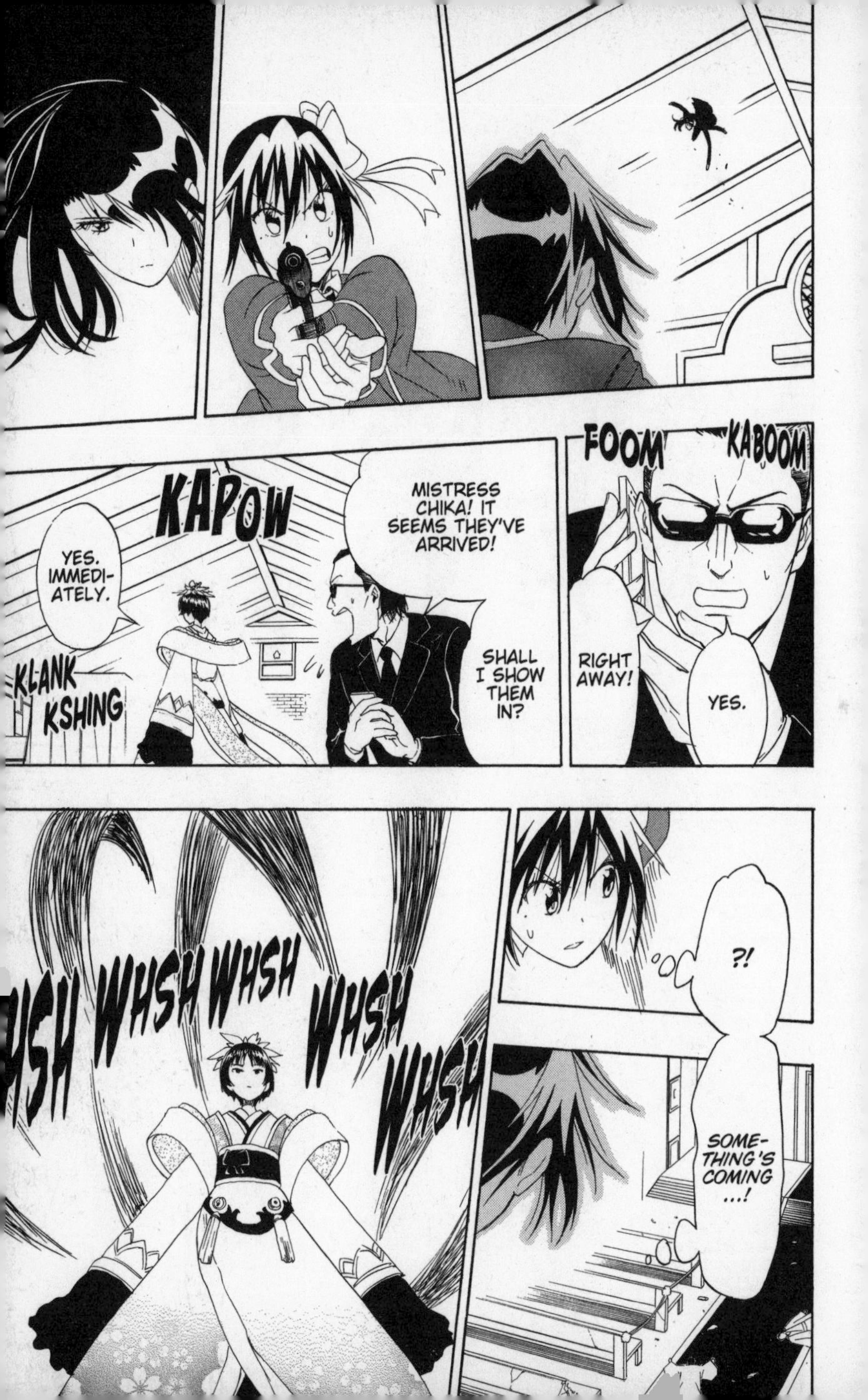
KABOOM
FOOM
YES.
RIGHT AWAY!
MISTRESS CHIKA! IT SEEMS THEY'VE ARRIVED!
SHALL I SHOW THEM IN?
KAPOW
YES. IMMEDIATELY.
KLANK KSHING
?!
SOMETHING'S COMING...!
WHSH WHSH WHSH WHSH WHSH

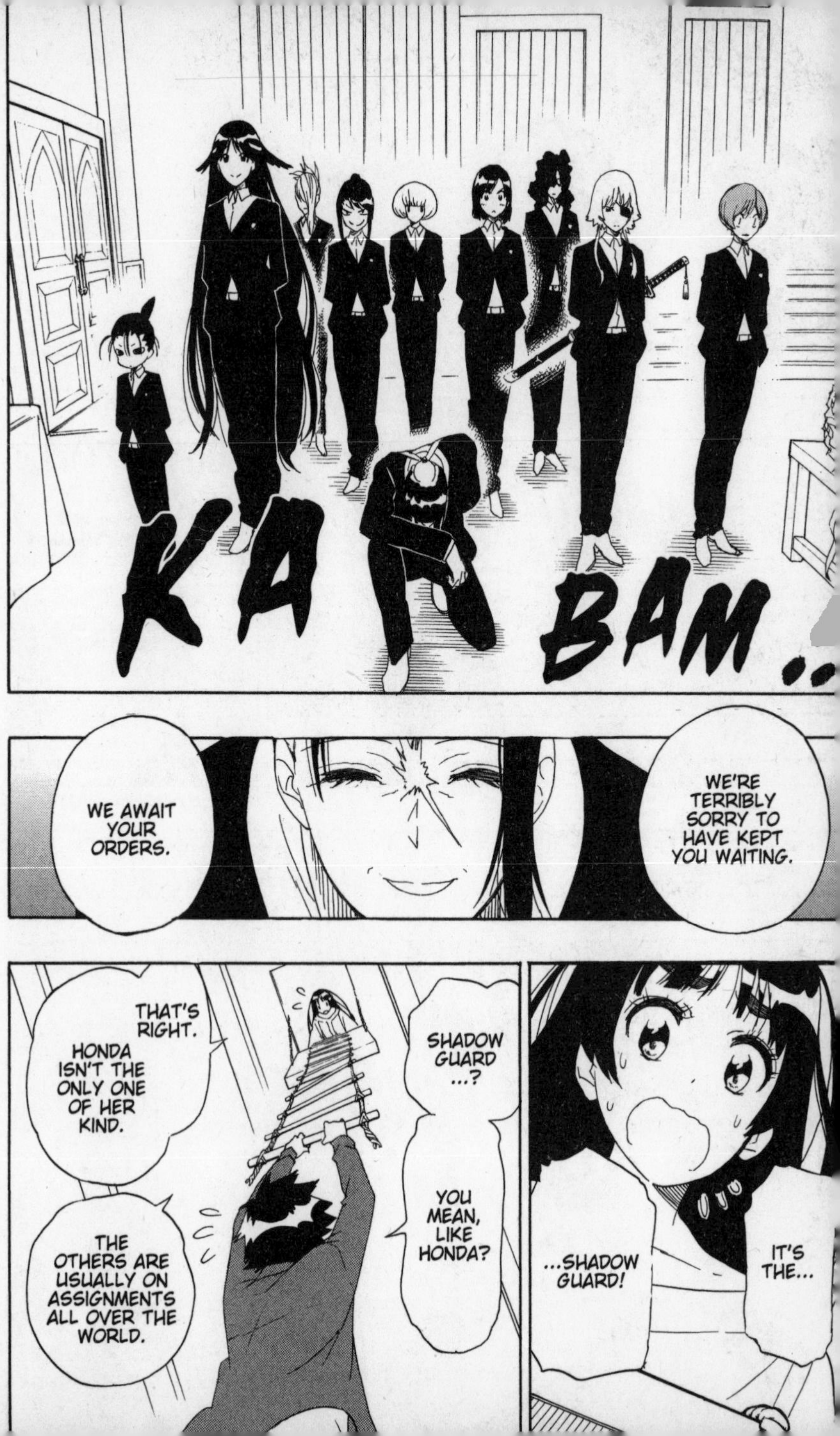
KA BAM...
WE'RE TERRIBLY SORRY TO HAVE KEPT YOU WAITING.
WE AWAIT YOUR ORDERS.
IT'S THE...
...SHADOW GUARD!
SHADOW GUARD ...?
YOU MEAN, LIKE HONDA?
THAT'S RIGHT. HONDA ISN'T THE ONLY ONE OF HER KIND.
THE OTHERS ARE USUALLY ON ASSIGNMENTS ALL OVER THE WORLD.

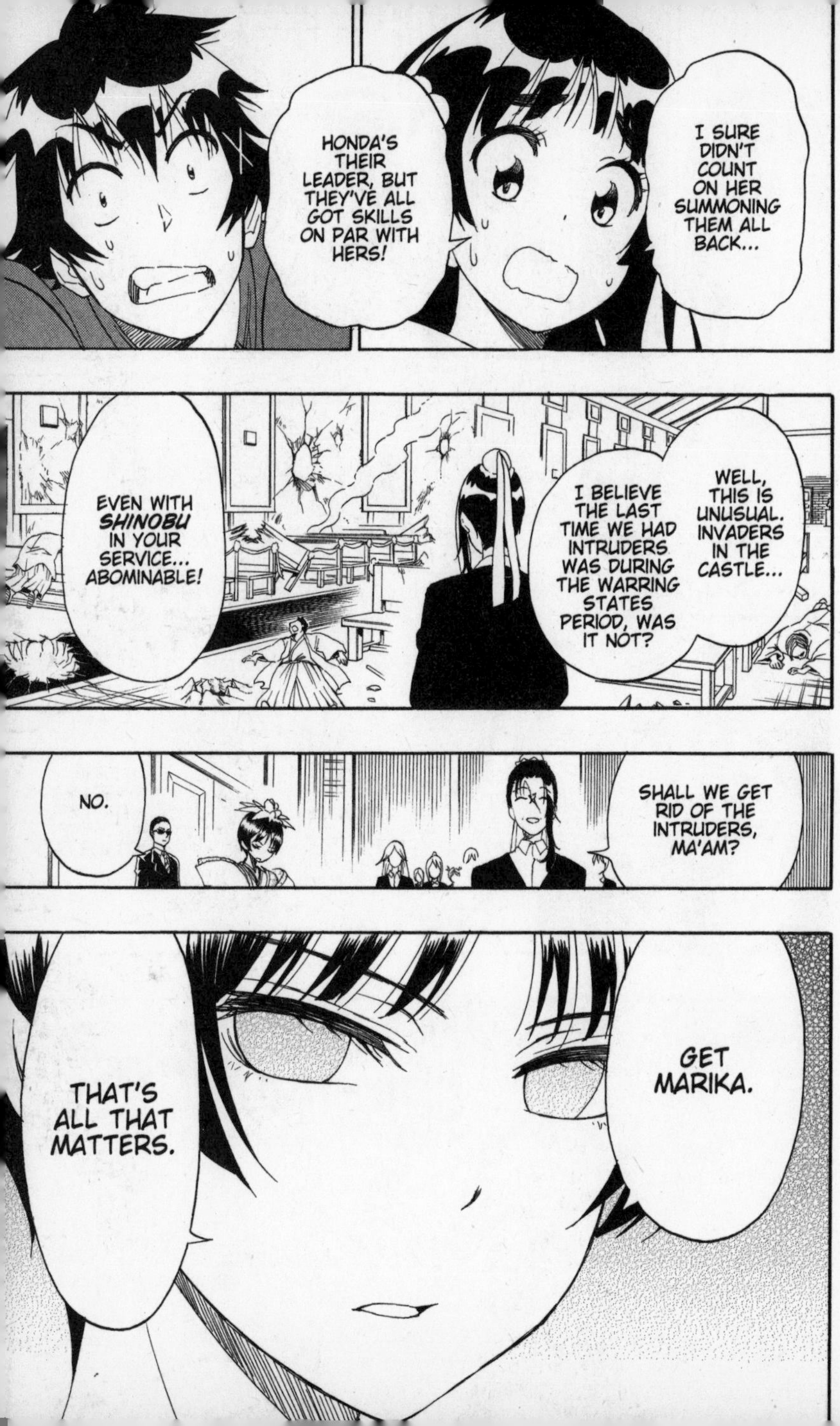
I SURE DIDN'T COUNT ON HER SUMMONING THEM ALL BACK...
HONDA'S THEIR LEADER, BUT THEY'VE ALL GOT SKILLS ON PAR WITH HERS!
WELL, THIS IS UNUSUAL. INVADERS IN THE CASTLE...
I BELIEVE THE LAST TIME WE HAD INTRUDERS WAS DURING THE WARRING STATES PERIOD, WAS IT NOT?
EVEN WITH *SHINOBU* IN YOUR SERVICE... ABOMINABLE!
SHALL WE GET RID OF THE INTRUDERS, MA'AM?
NO.
GET MARIKA.
THAT'S ALL THAT MATTERS.

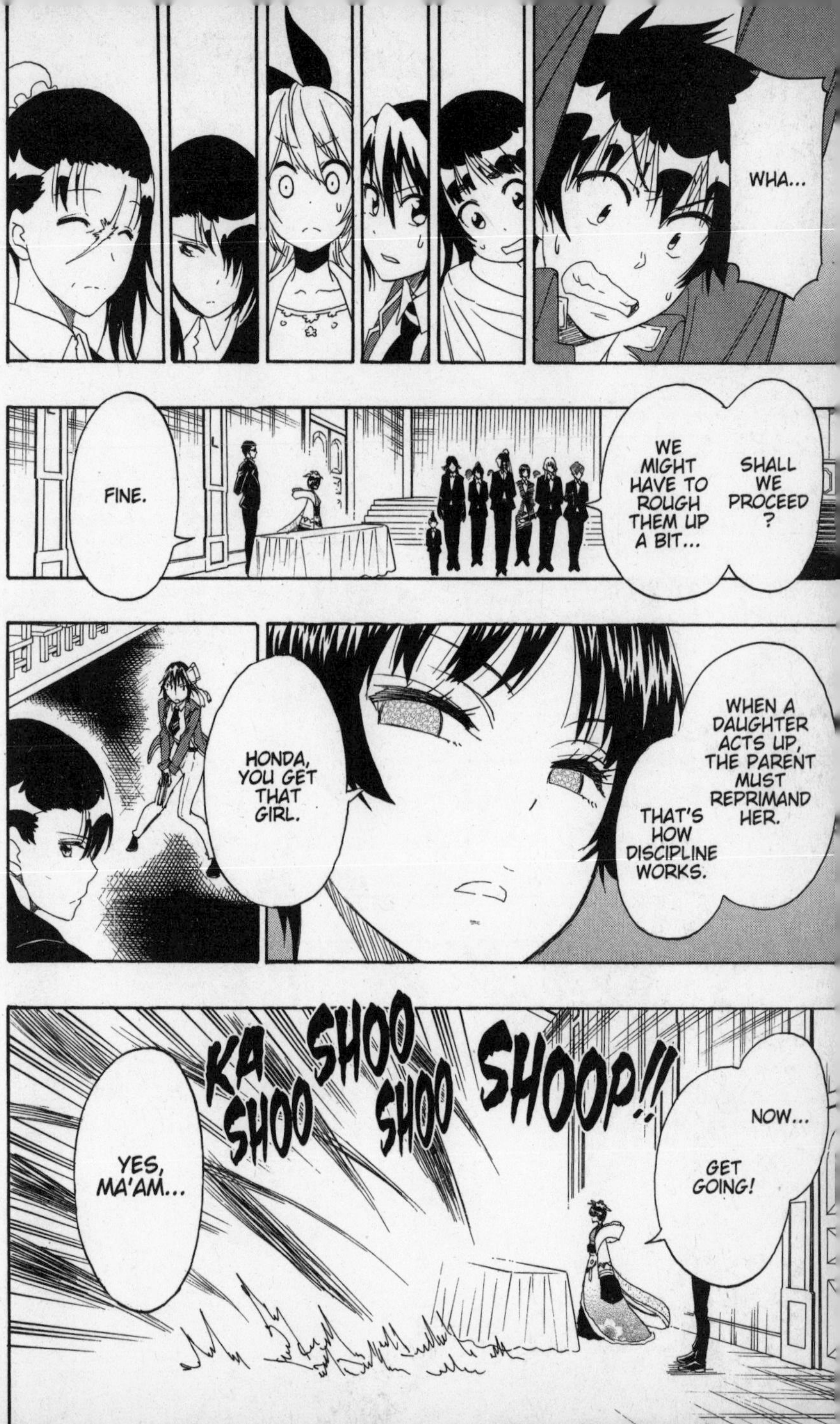
WHA...
SHALL WE PROCEED?
WE MIGHT HAVE TO ROUGH THEM UP A BIT...
FINE.
WHEN A DAUGHTER ACTS UP, THE PARENT MUST REPRIMAND HER.
THAT'S HOW DISCIPLINE WORKS.
HONDA, YOU GET THAT GIRL.
NOW...
GET GOING!
SHOOP!!
SHOO SHOO
SHOO SHOO
KA SHOO
YES, MA'AM...

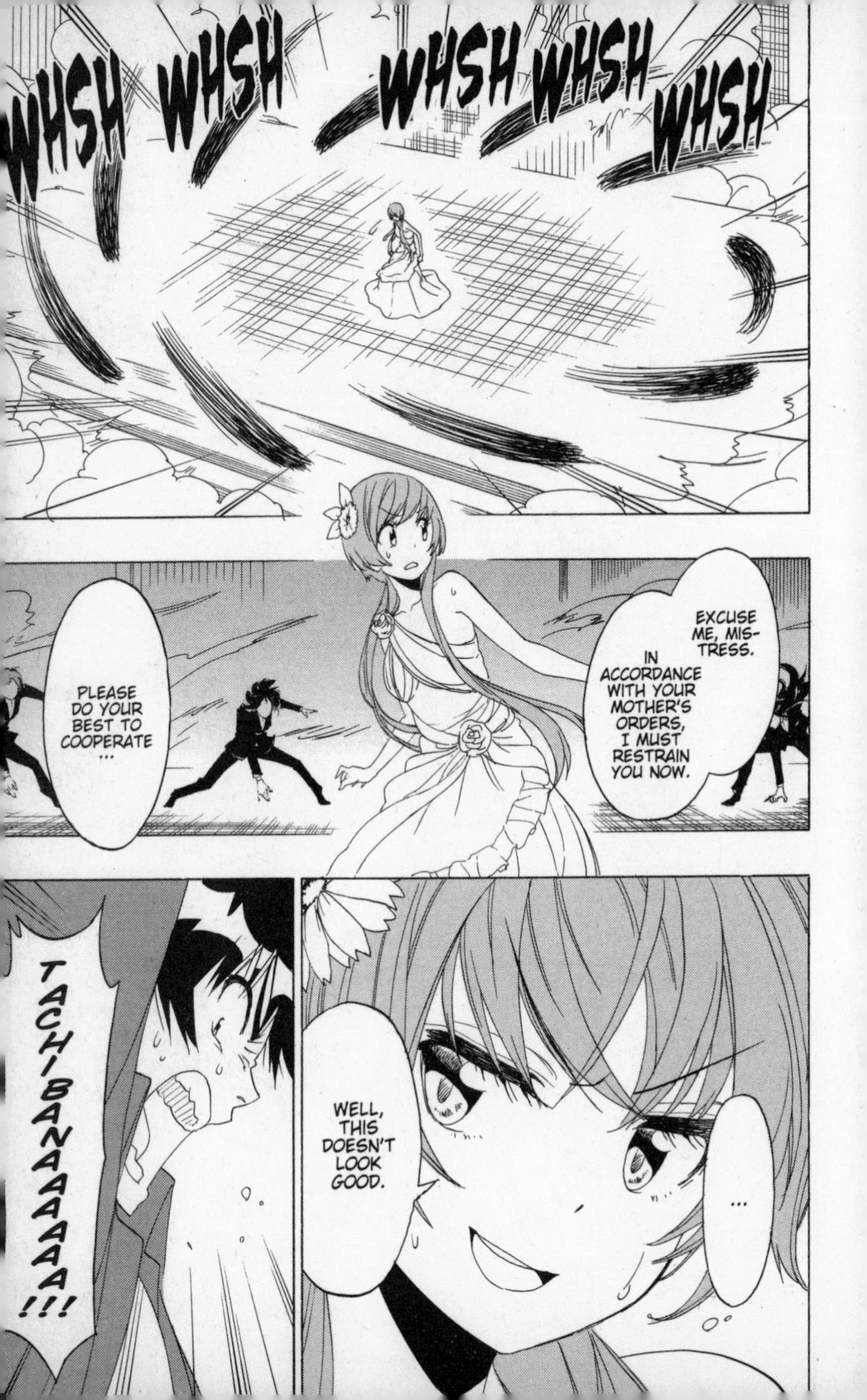
WHSH WHSH
WHSH WHSH
WHSH
EXCUSE ME, MIS-TRESS.
IN ACCORDANCE WITH YOUR MOTHER'S ORDERS, I MUST RESTRAIN YOU NOW.
PLEASE DO YOUR BEST TO COOPERATE ...
...
WELL, THIS DOESN'T LOOK GOOD.
TACHIBANAAAAAAA!!!

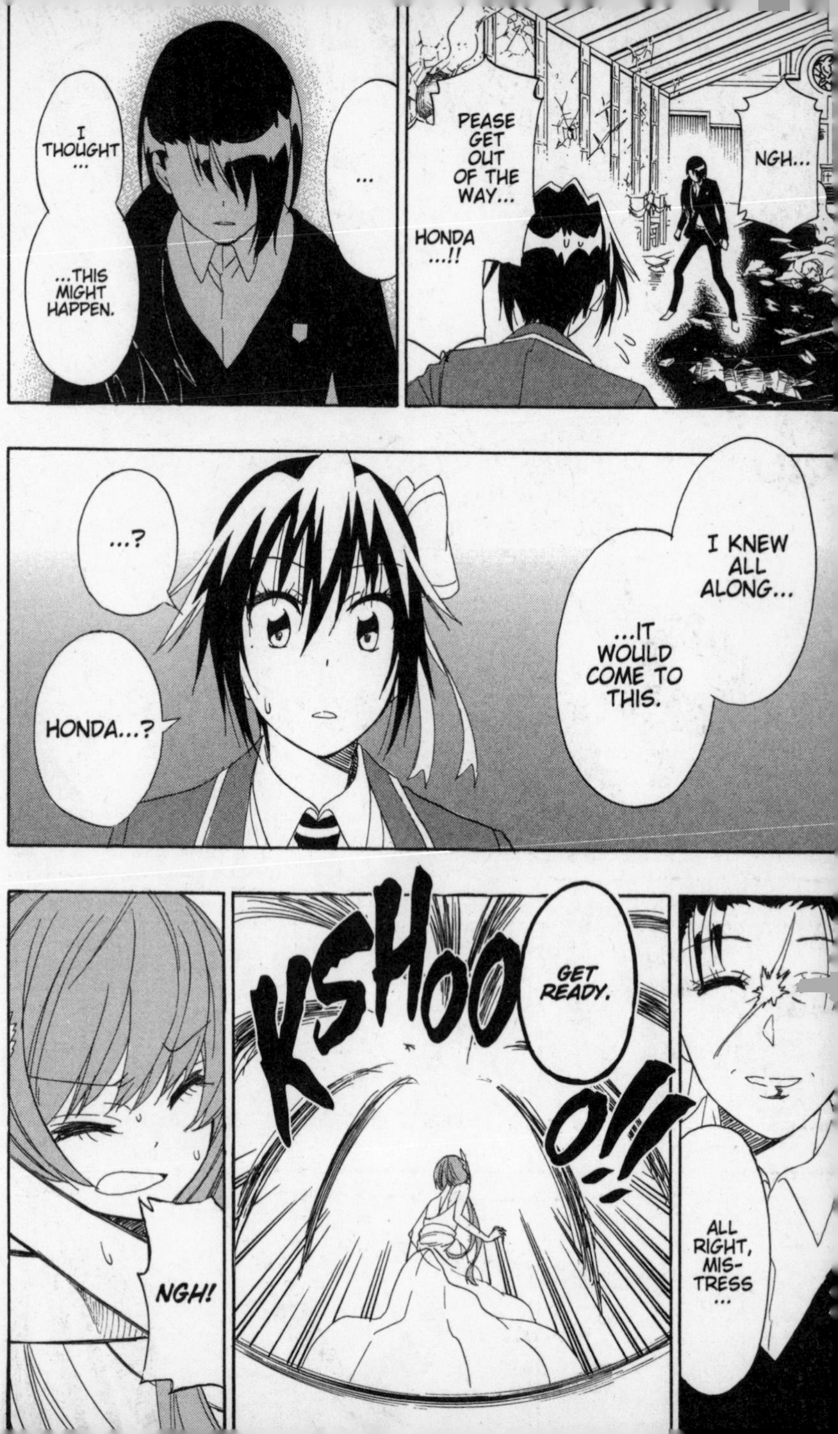
NGH...
PEASE GET OUT OF THE WAY...
HONDA ...!!
...
I THOUGHT ...
...THIS MIGHT HAPPEN.
I KNEW ALL ALONG...
...IT WOULD COME TO THIS.
...?
HONDA...?
ALL RIGHT, MIS- TRESS ...
GET READY.
KSHOOO!!
NGH!

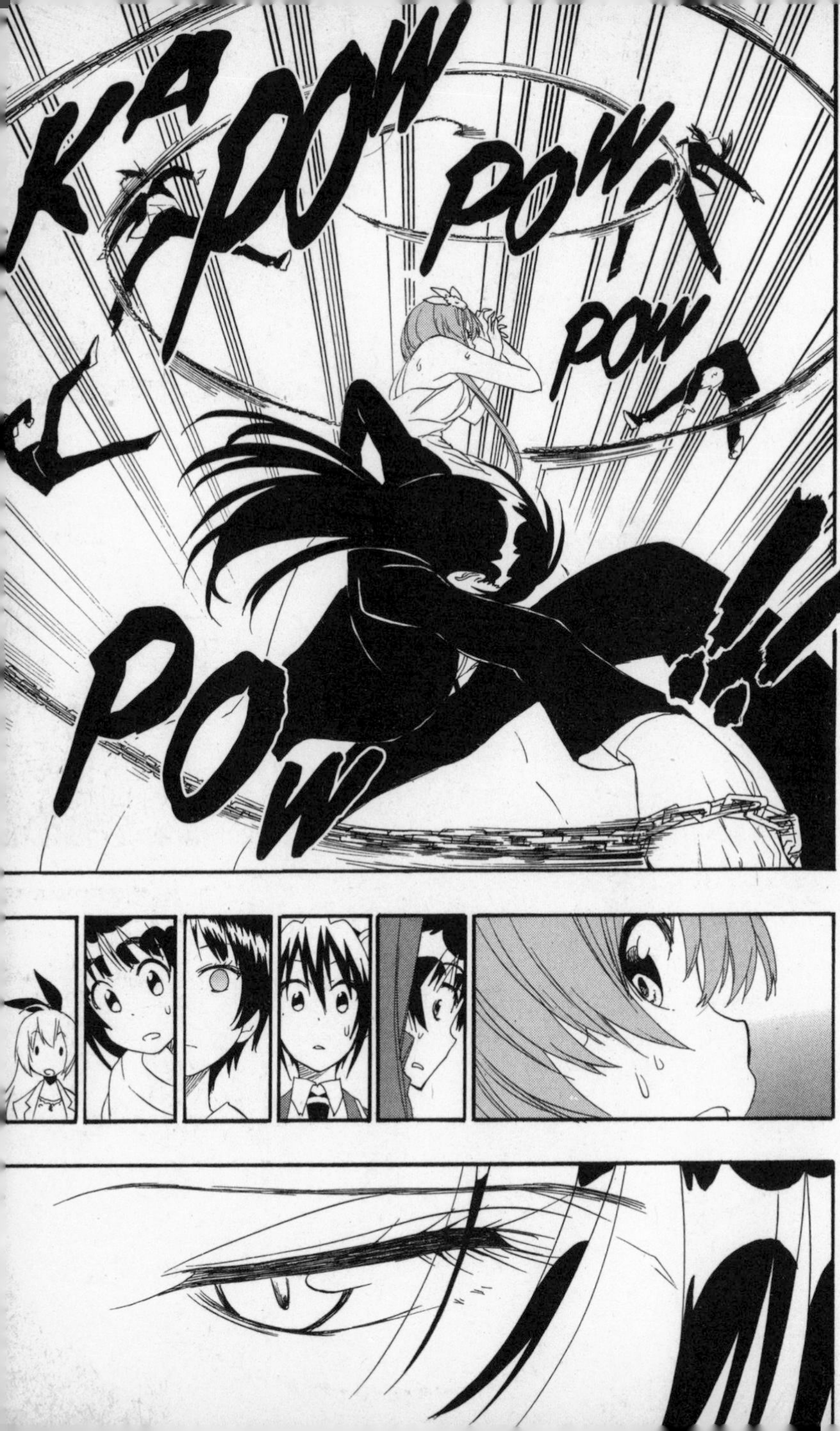
KAPOW
POW
POW
POW!!

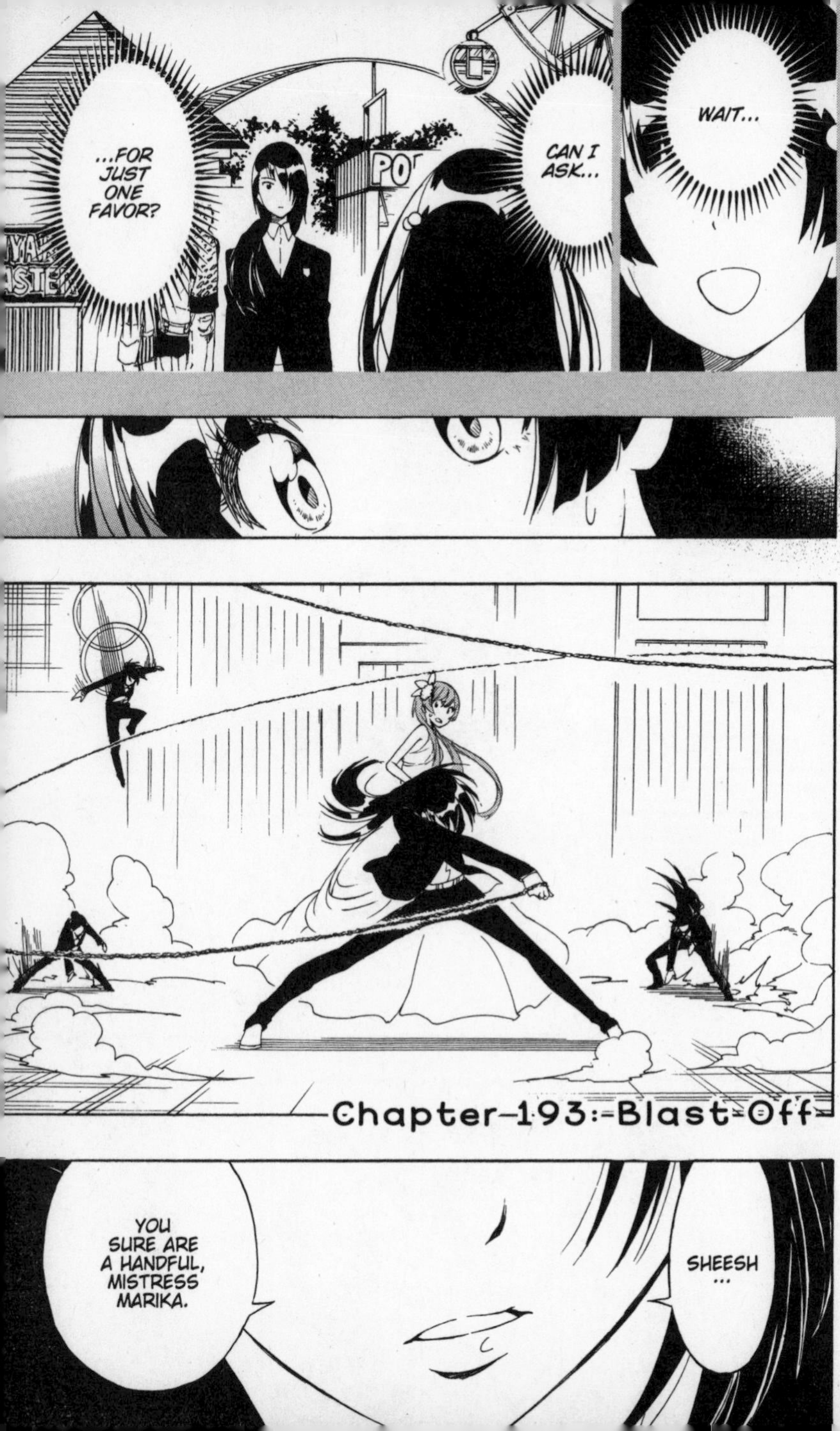
WAIT...
CAN I ASK...
...FOR JUST ONE FAVOR?
Chapter 193: Blast Off
SHEESH ...
YOU SURE ARE A HANDFUL, MISTRESS MARIKA.

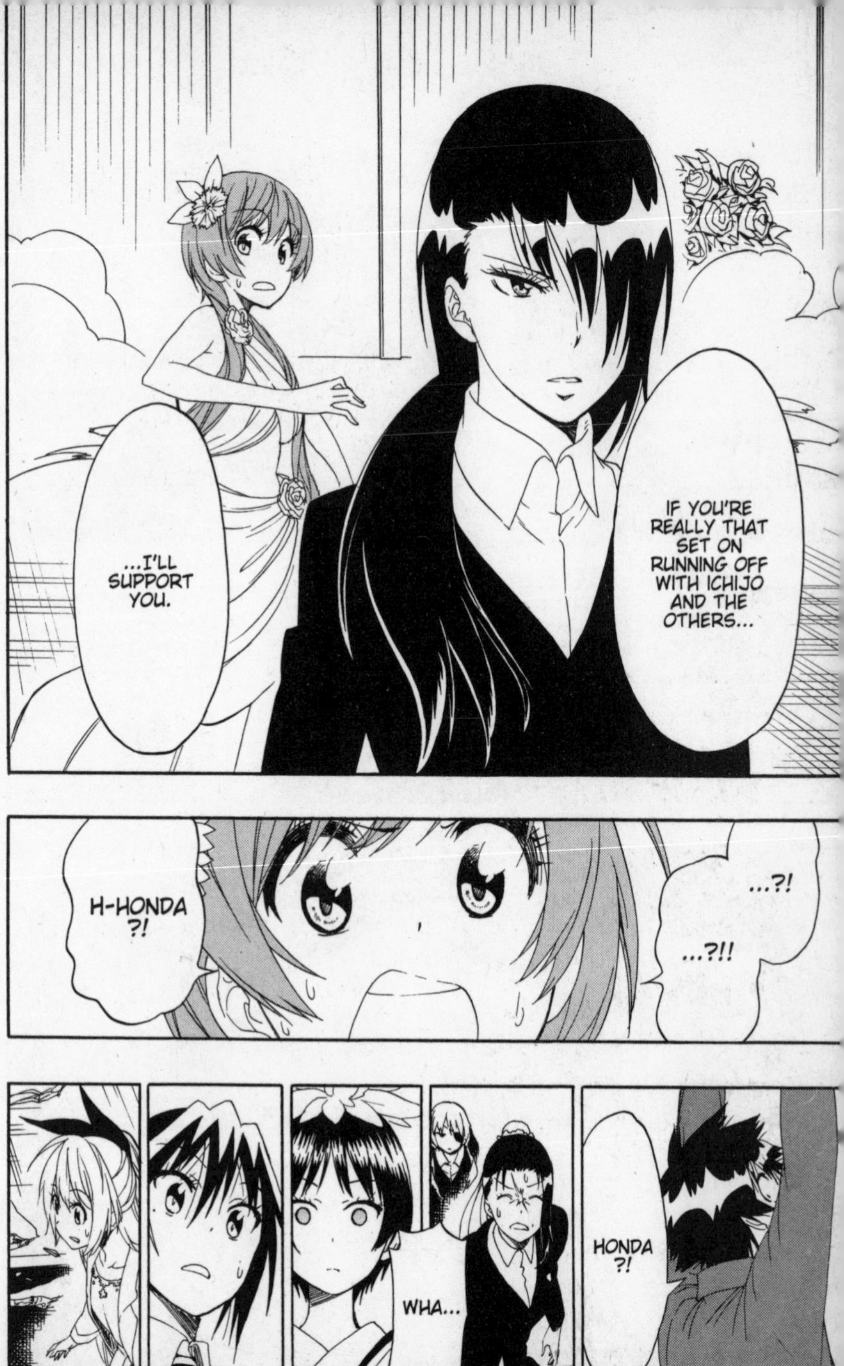
IF YOU'RE REALLY THAT SET ON RUNNING OFF WITH ICHIJO AND THE OTHERS...
...I'LL SUPPORT YOU.
...?!
...?!!
H-HONDA ?!
HONDA ?!
WHA...

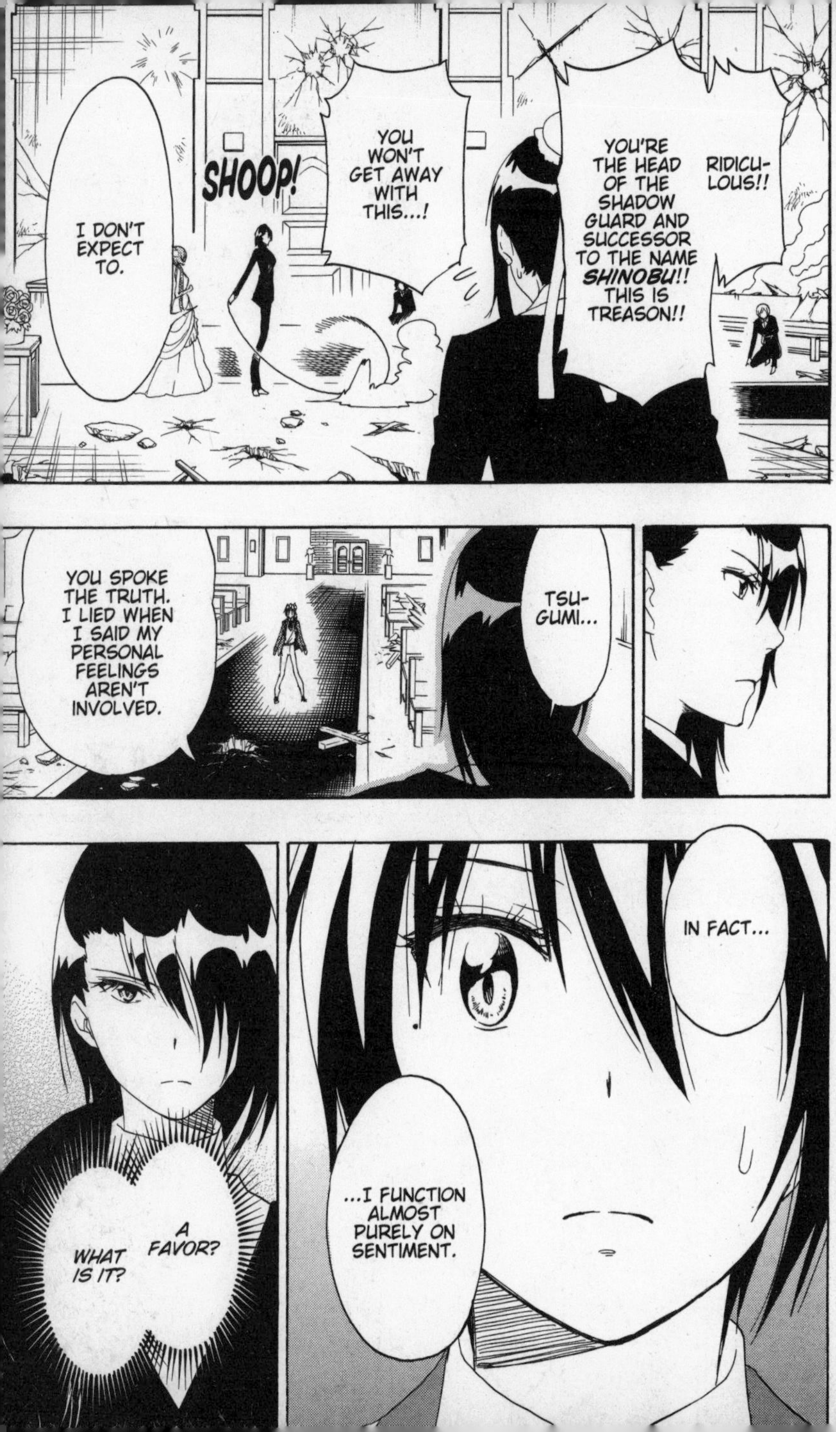
RIDICU-LOUS!!
YOU'RE THE HEAD OF THE SHADOW GUARD AND SUCCESSOR TO THE NAME *SHINOBU*!! THIS IS TREASON!!
YOU WON'T GET AWAY WITH THIS...!
SHOOP!
I DON'T EXPECT TO.
TSU-GUMI...
YOU SPOKE THE TRUTH. I LIED WHEN I SAID MY PERSONAL FEELINGS AREN'T INVOLVED.
IN FACT...
...I FUNCTION ALMOST PURELY ON SENTIMENT.
A FAVOR?
WHAT IS IT?

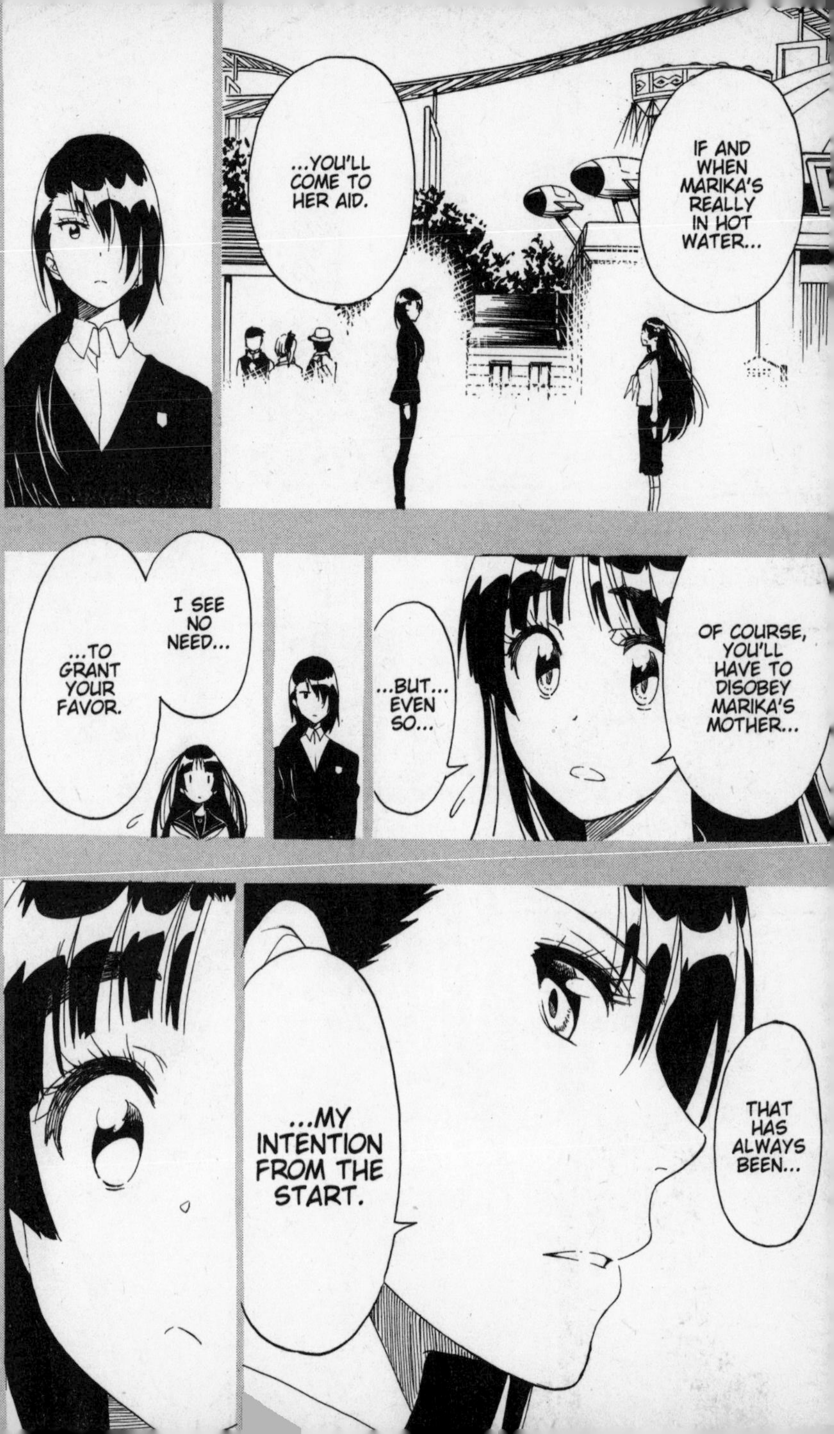
IF AND WHEN MARIKA'S REALLY IN HOT WATER...
...YOU'LL COME TO HER AID.
OF COURSE, YOU'LL HAVE TO DISOBEY MARIKA'S MOTHER...
...BUT... EVEN SO...
I SEE NO NEED...
...TO GRANT YOUR FAVOR.
THAT HAS ALWAYS BEEN...
...MY INTENTION FROM THE START.

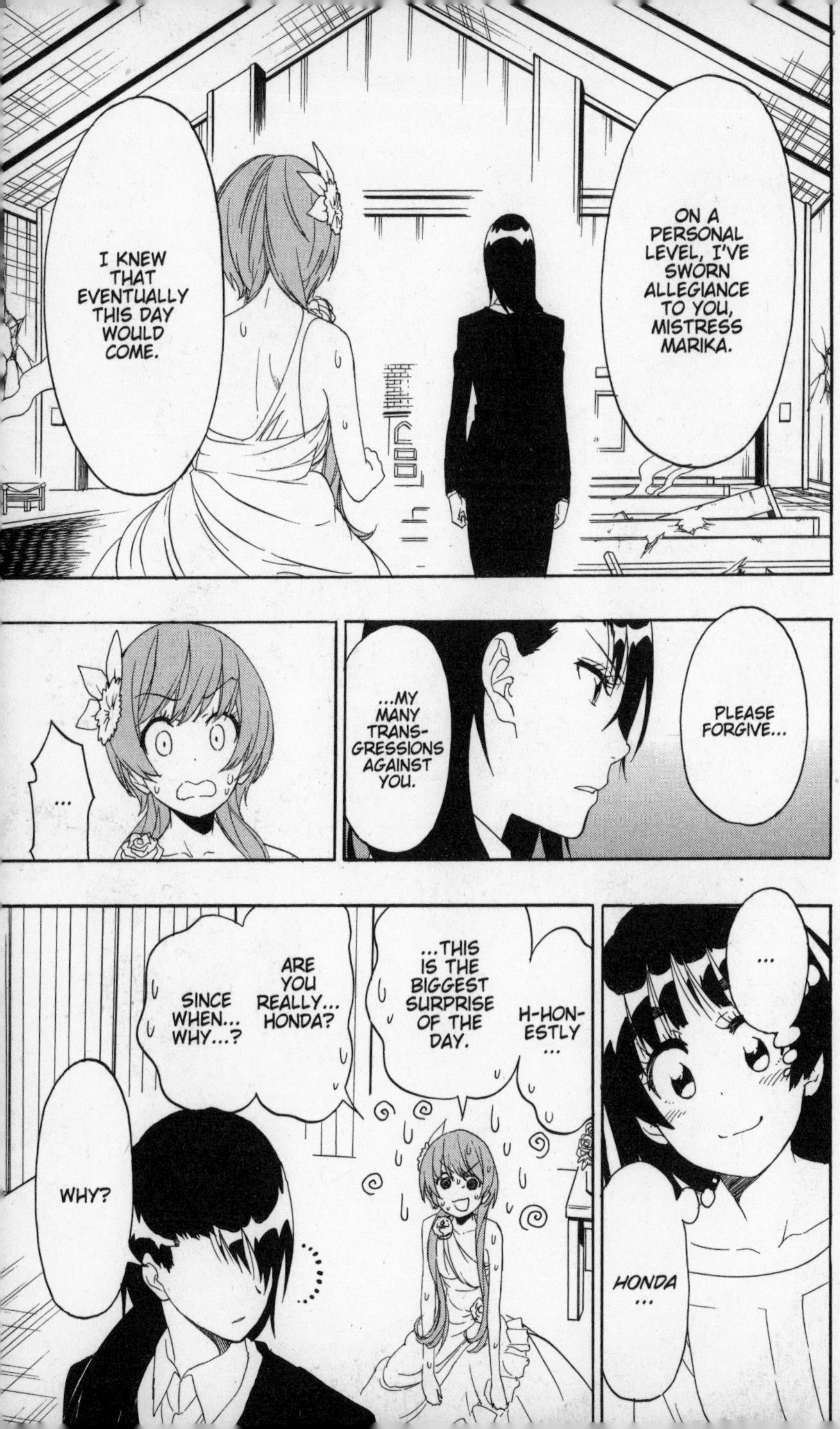
ON A PERSONAL LEVEL, I'VE SWORN ALLEGIANCE TO YOU, MISTRESS MARIKA.
I KNEW THAT EVENTUALLY THIS DAY WOULD COME.
PLEASE FORGIVE...
...MY MANY TRANS-GRESSIONS AGAINST YOU.
...
...
HONDA...
H-HON-ESTLY...
...THIS IS THE BIGGEST SURPRISE OF THE DAY.
ARE YOU REALLY... HONDA?
SINCE WHEN... WHY...?
WHY?

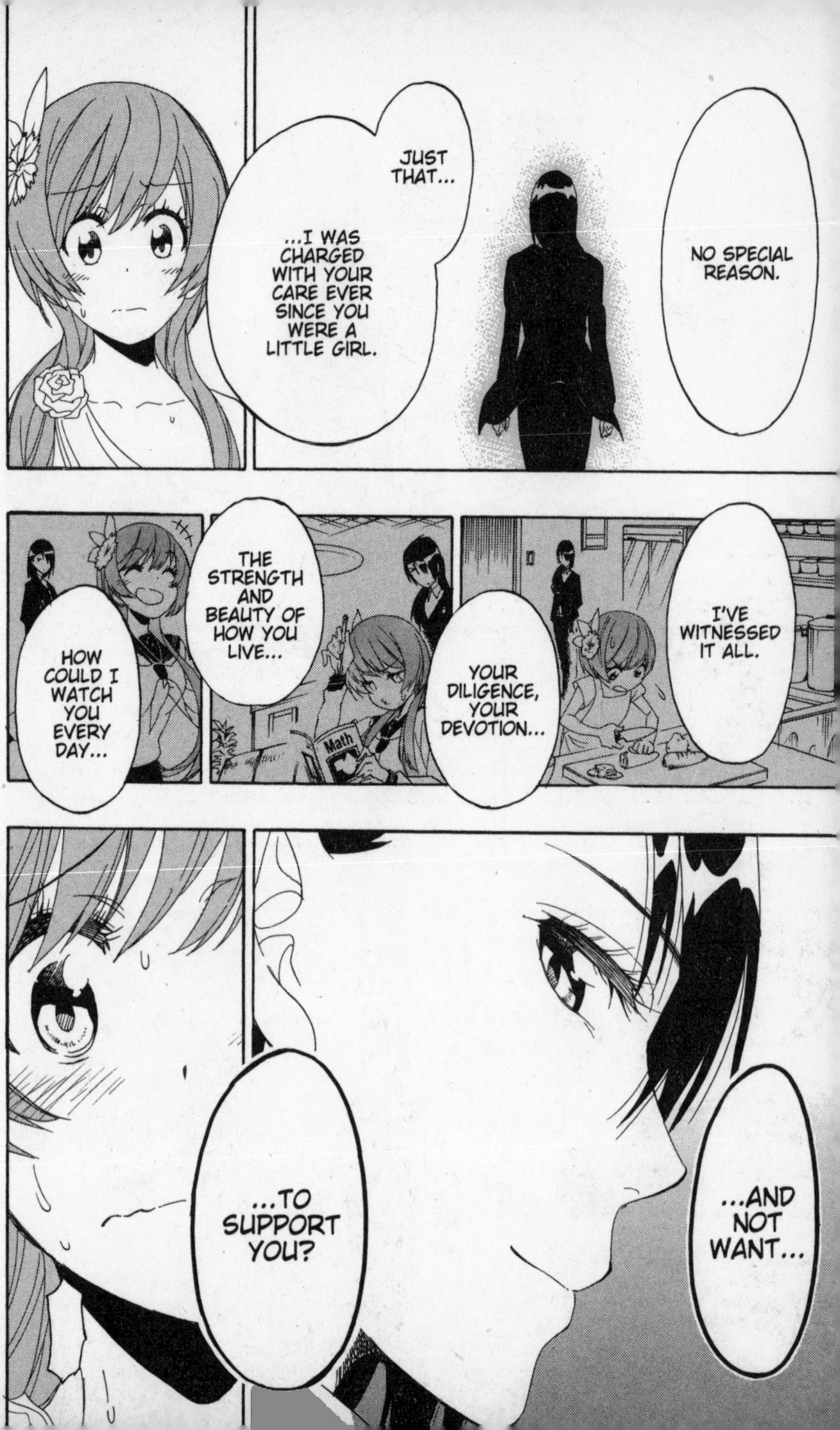
NO SPECIAL REASON.
JUST THAT...
...I WAS CHARGED WITH YOUR CARE EVER SINCE YOU WERE A LITTLE GIRL.
I'VE WITNESSED IT ALL.
YOUR DILIGENCE, YOUR DEVOTION...
THE STRENGTH AND BEAUTY OF HOW YOU LIVE...
Math
HOW COULD I WATCH YOU EVERY DAY...
...AND NOT WANT...
...TO SUPPORT YOU?

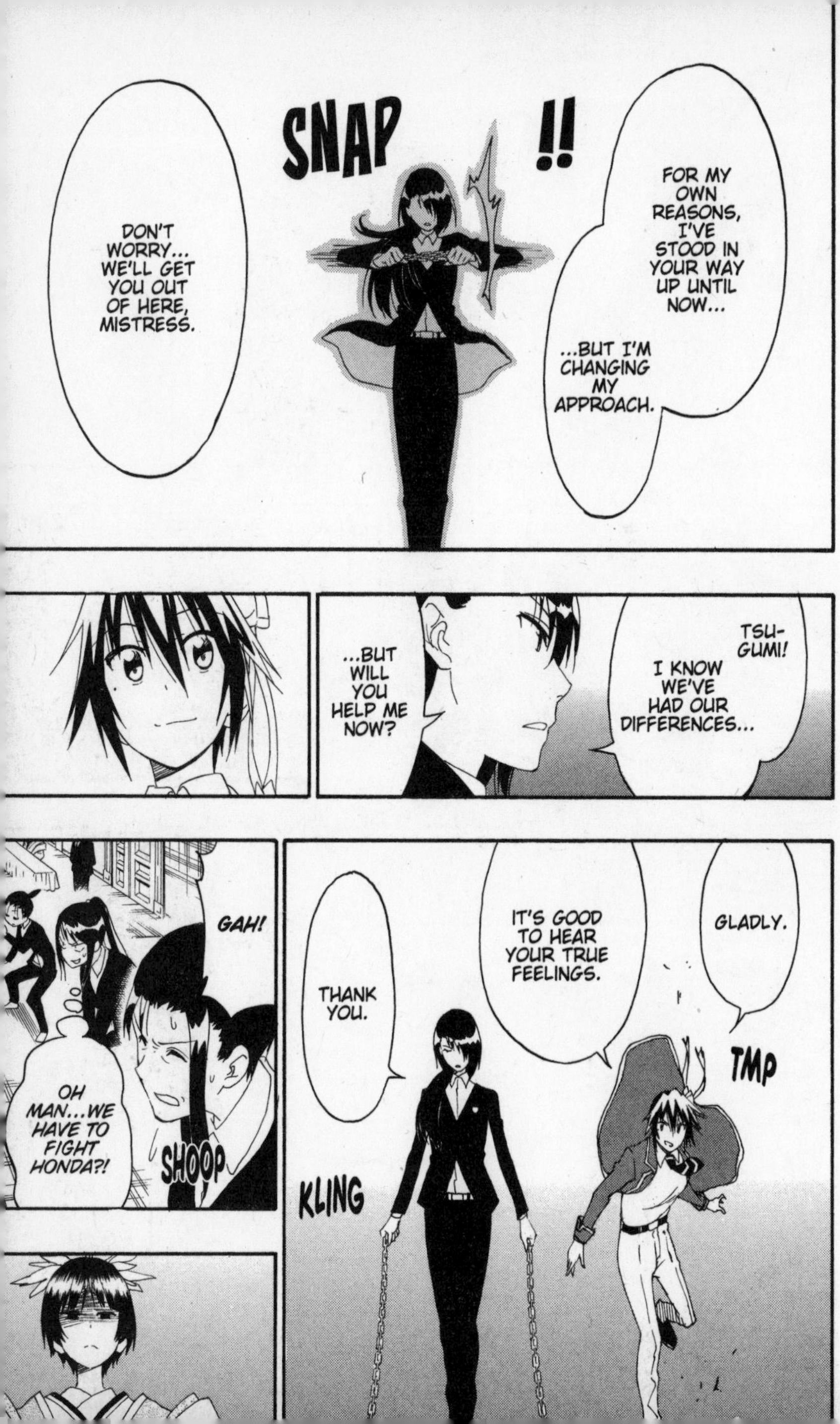
FOR MY OWN REASONS, I'VE STOOD IN YOUR WAY UP UNTIL NOW...
...BUT I'M CHANGING MY APPROACH.
SNAP!!
DON'T WORRY... WE'LL GET YOU OUT OF HERE, MISTRESS.
TSU-GUMI!
I KNOW WE'VE HAD OUR DIFFERENCES...
...BUT WILL YOU HELP ME NOW?
GLADLY.
IT'S GOOD TO HEAR YOUR TRUE FEELINGS.
TMP
THANK YOU.
KLING
GAH!
SHOOP
OH MAN...WE HAVE TO FIGHT HONDA?!

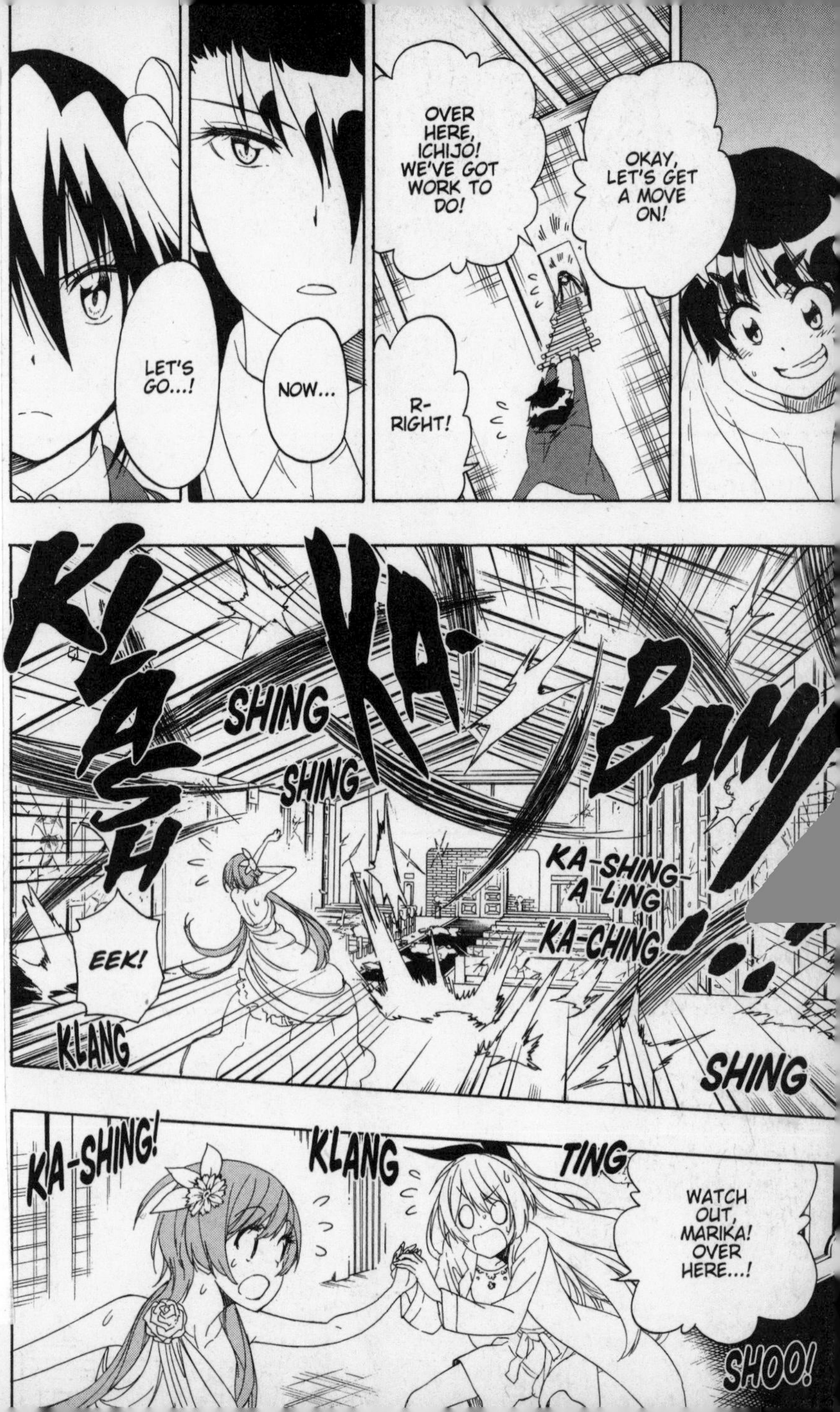
OKAY, LET'S GET A MOVE ON!
OVER HERE, ICHIJO! WE'VE GOT WORK TO DO!
R-RIGHT!
NOW...
LET'S GO...!
KA-BAM!!
KLASH
SHING
SHING
KA-SHING-A-LING
KA-CHING
SHING
EEK!
KLANG
WATCH OUT, MARIKA! OVER HERE...!
TING
KLANG
KA-SHING!
SHOO!

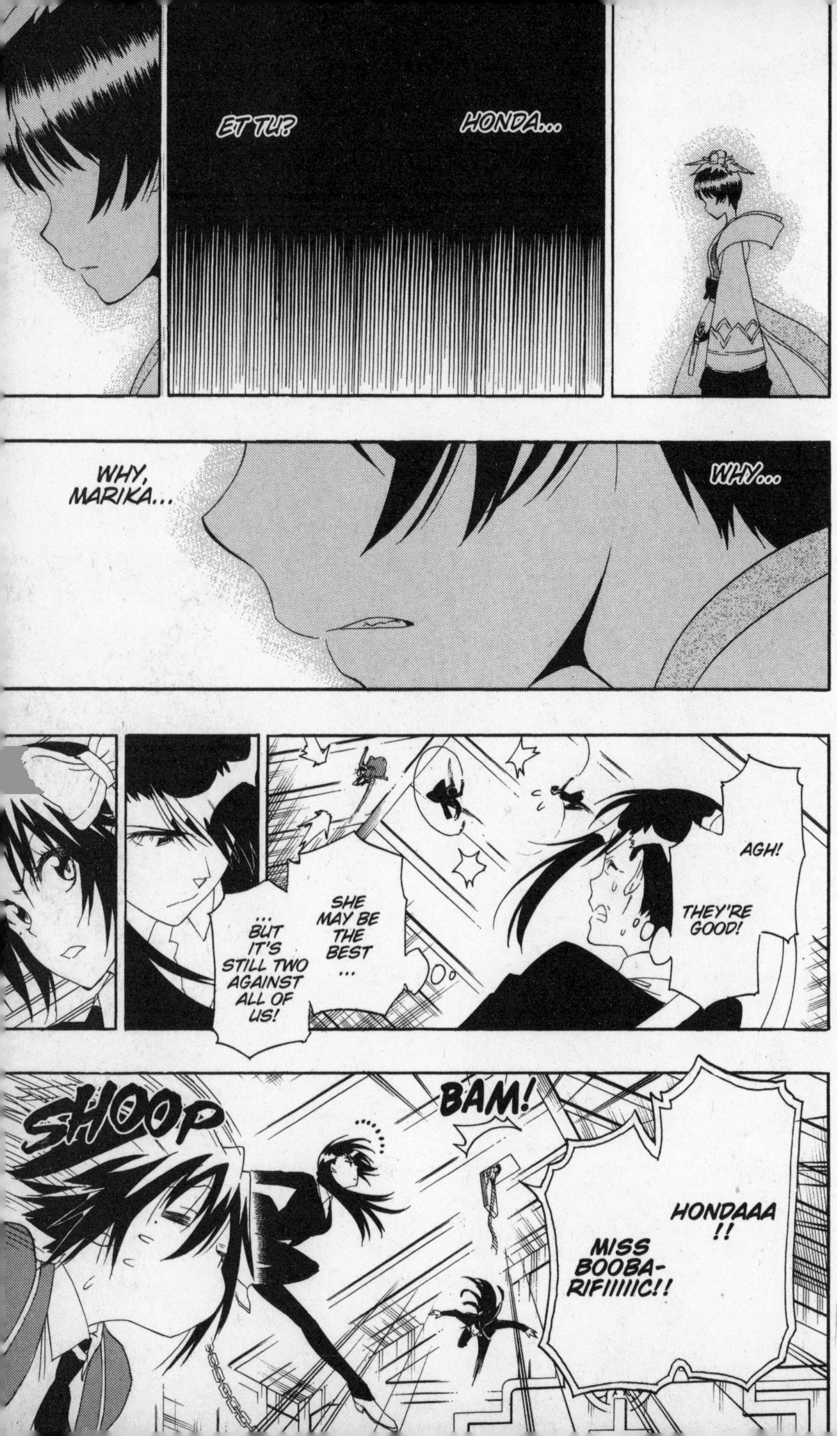
HONDA...
ET TU?
WHY...
WHY, MARIKA...
AGH!
THEY'RE GOOD!
SHE MAY BE THE BEST...
...BUT IT'S STILL TWO AGAINST ALL OF US!
HONDAAA!!
MISS BOOBA-RIFIIIIIIC!!
BAM!
SHOOP

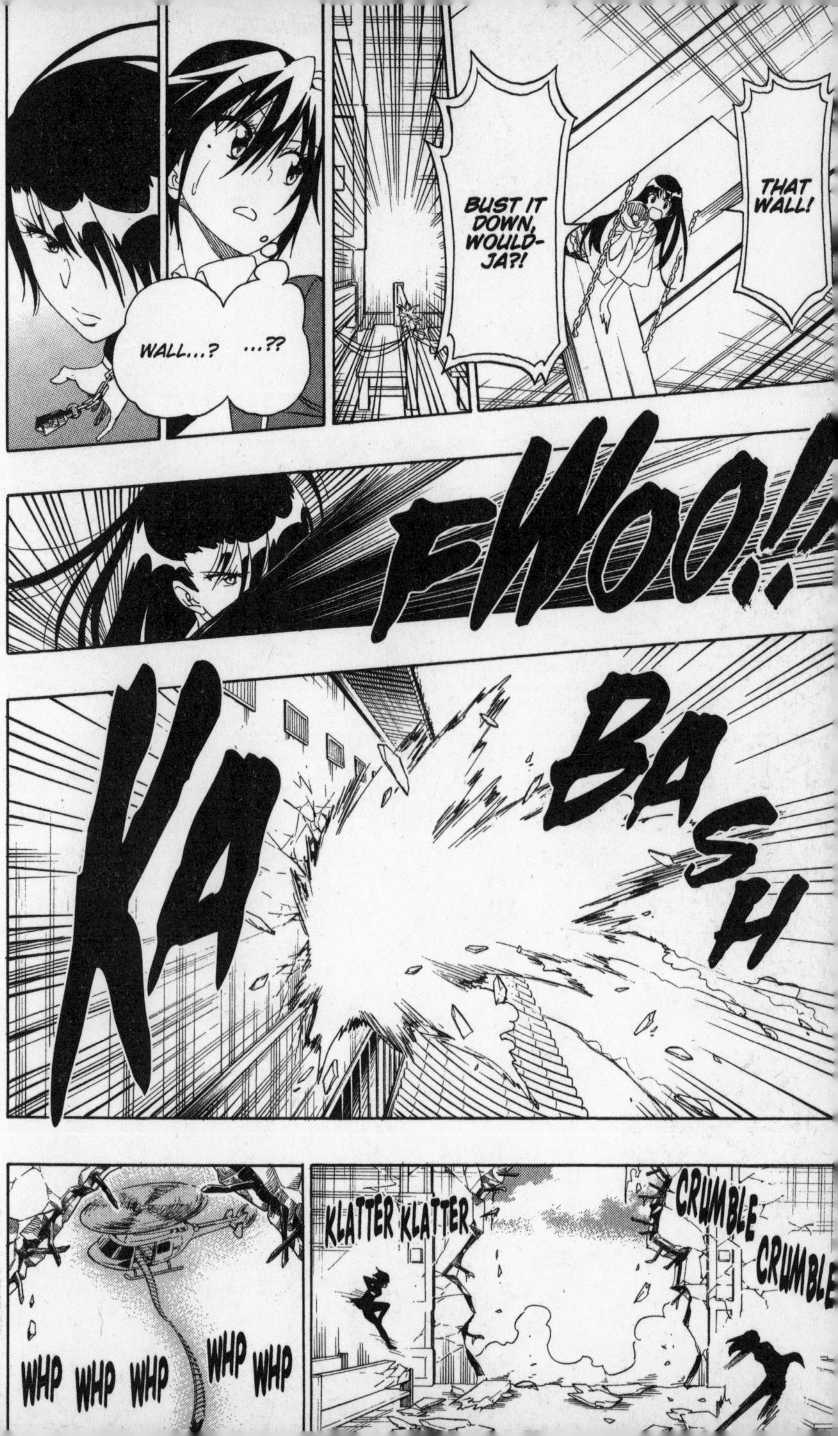
THAT WALL!
BUST IT DOWN, WOULD-JA?!
...??
WALL...?
FWOO!!
KA BASH
CRUMBLE CRUMBLE
KLATTER KLATTER
WHP WHP
WHP WHP WHP

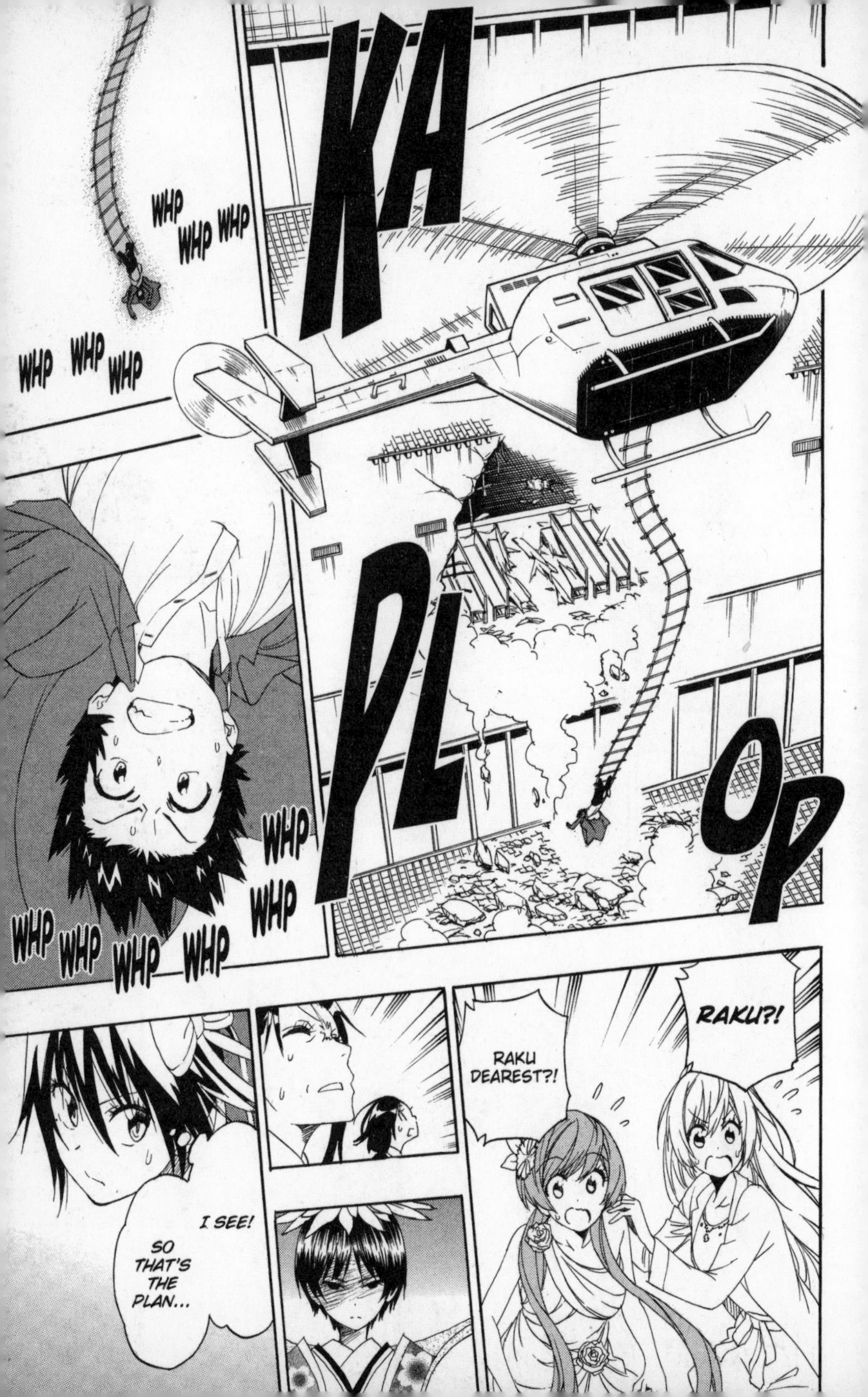
KA PL OP
WHP WHP WHP
WHP WHP WHP
WHP WHP WHP WHP WHP WHP WHP WHP
RAKU?!
RAKU DEAREST?!
I SEE!
SO THAT'S THE PLAN...

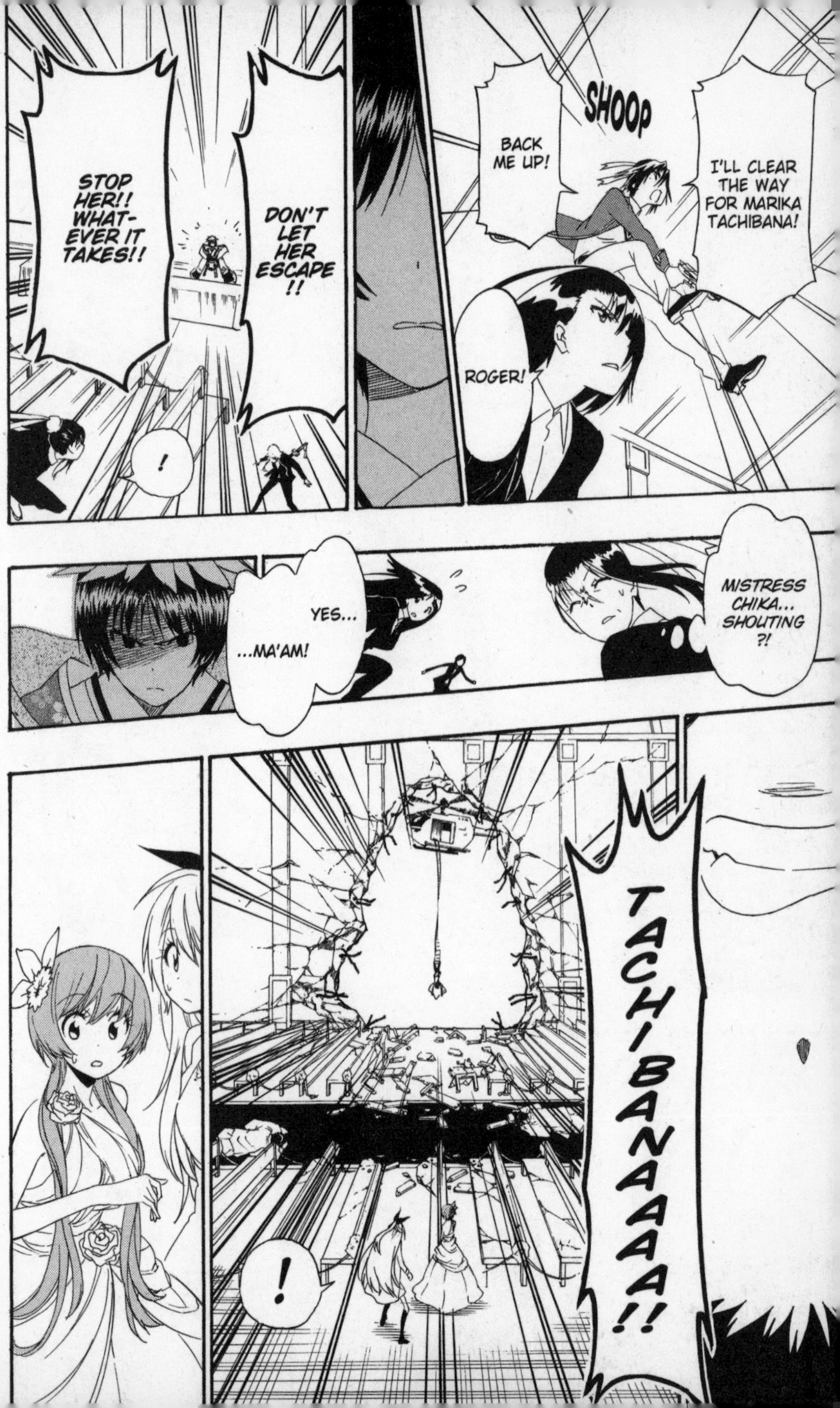
I'LL CLEAR THE WAY FOR MARIKA TACHIBANA!
SHOOP
BACK ME UP!
ROGER!
DON'T LET HER ESCAPE!!
STOP HER!! WHATEVER IT TAKES!!
!
MISTRESS CHIKA... SHOUTING?!
YES...
...MA'AM!
TACHIBANAAAAAA!!
!

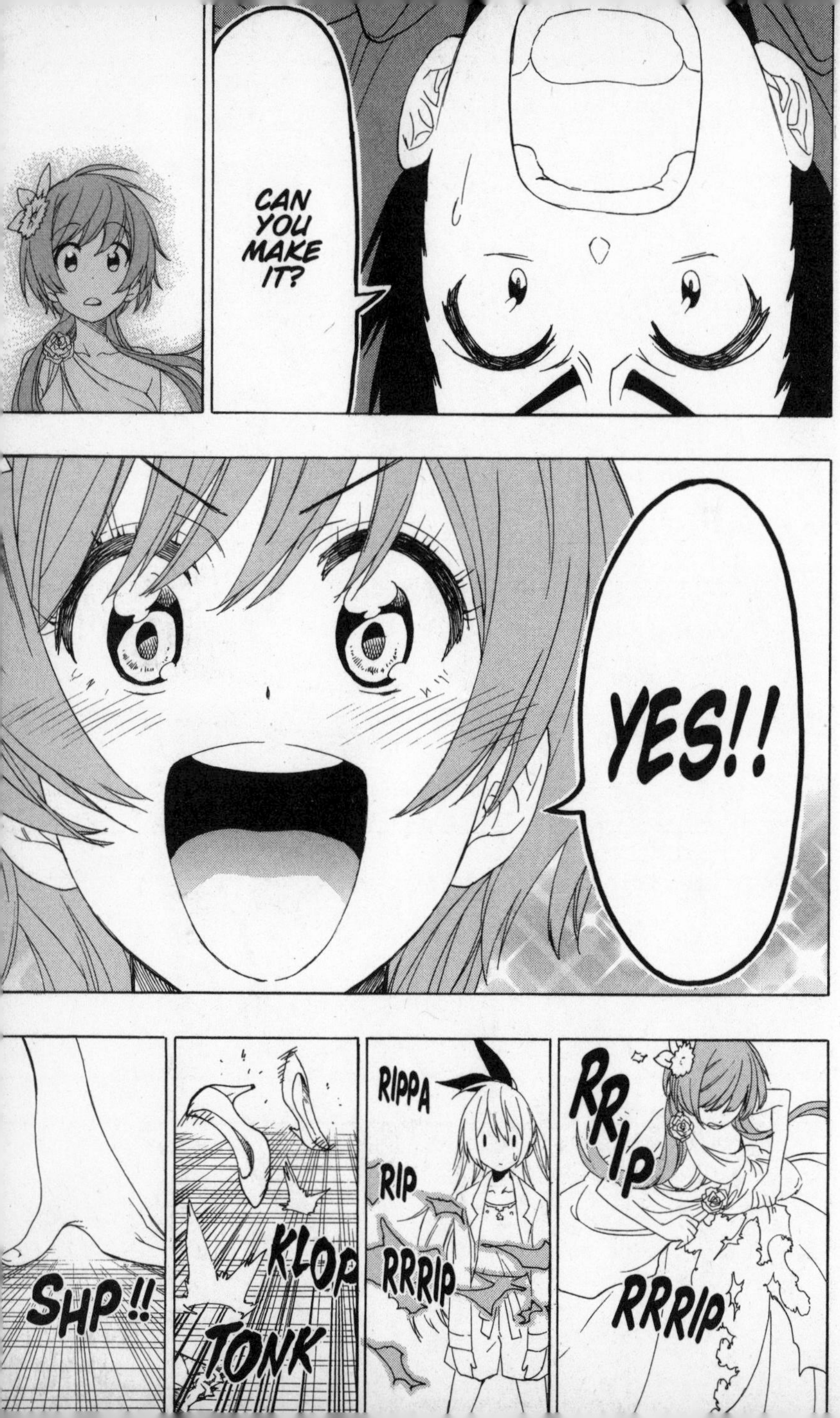
CAN YOU MAKE IT?
YES!!
RRIP
RRRIP
RIPPA
RIP
RRRIP
KLOP
TONK
SHP!!

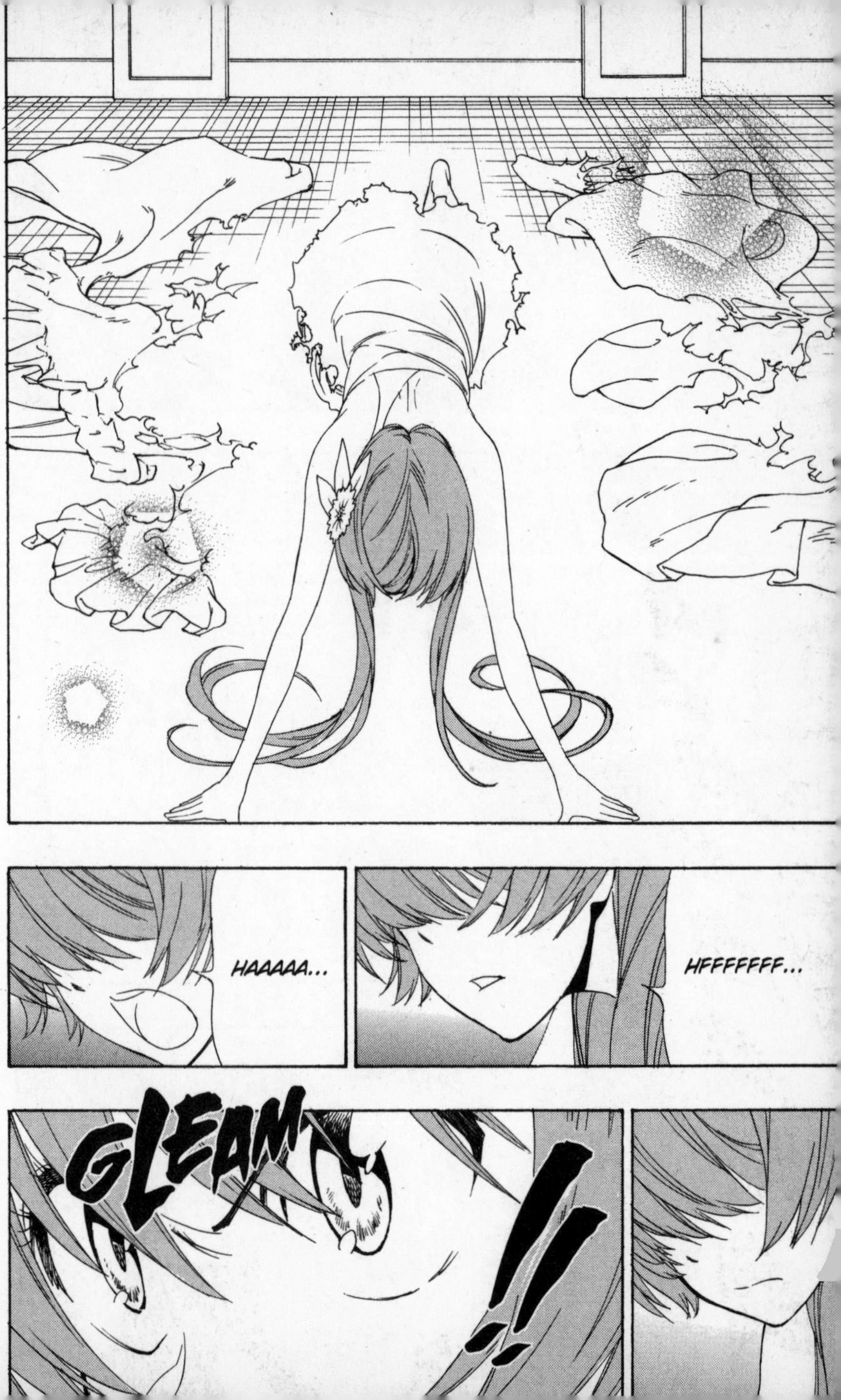
HFFFFFFF...
HAAAAA...
GLEAM
!!

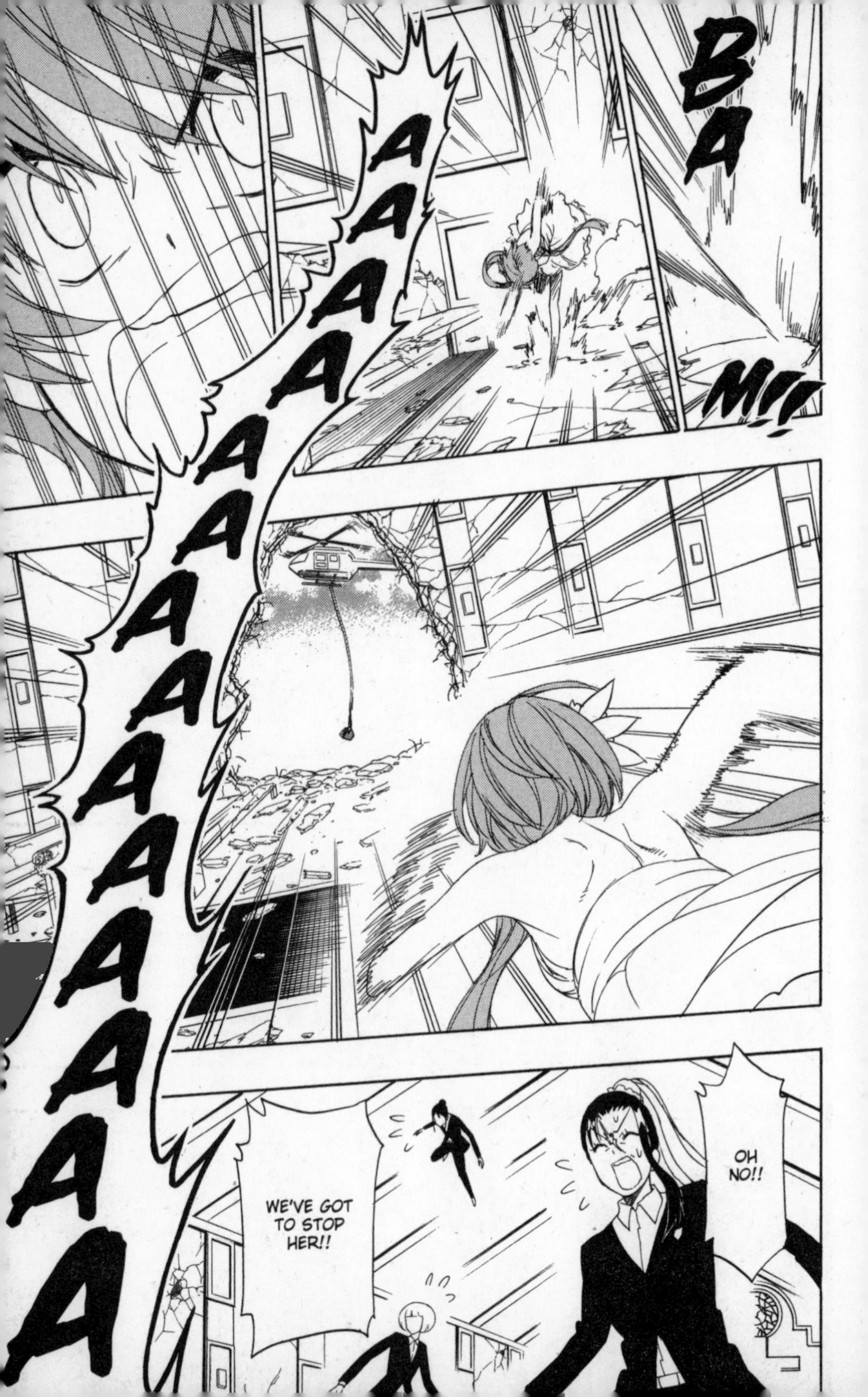
BAM!!
AAAAAAAAAAAAAAAAAA
OH NO!!
WE'VE GOT TO STOP HER!!

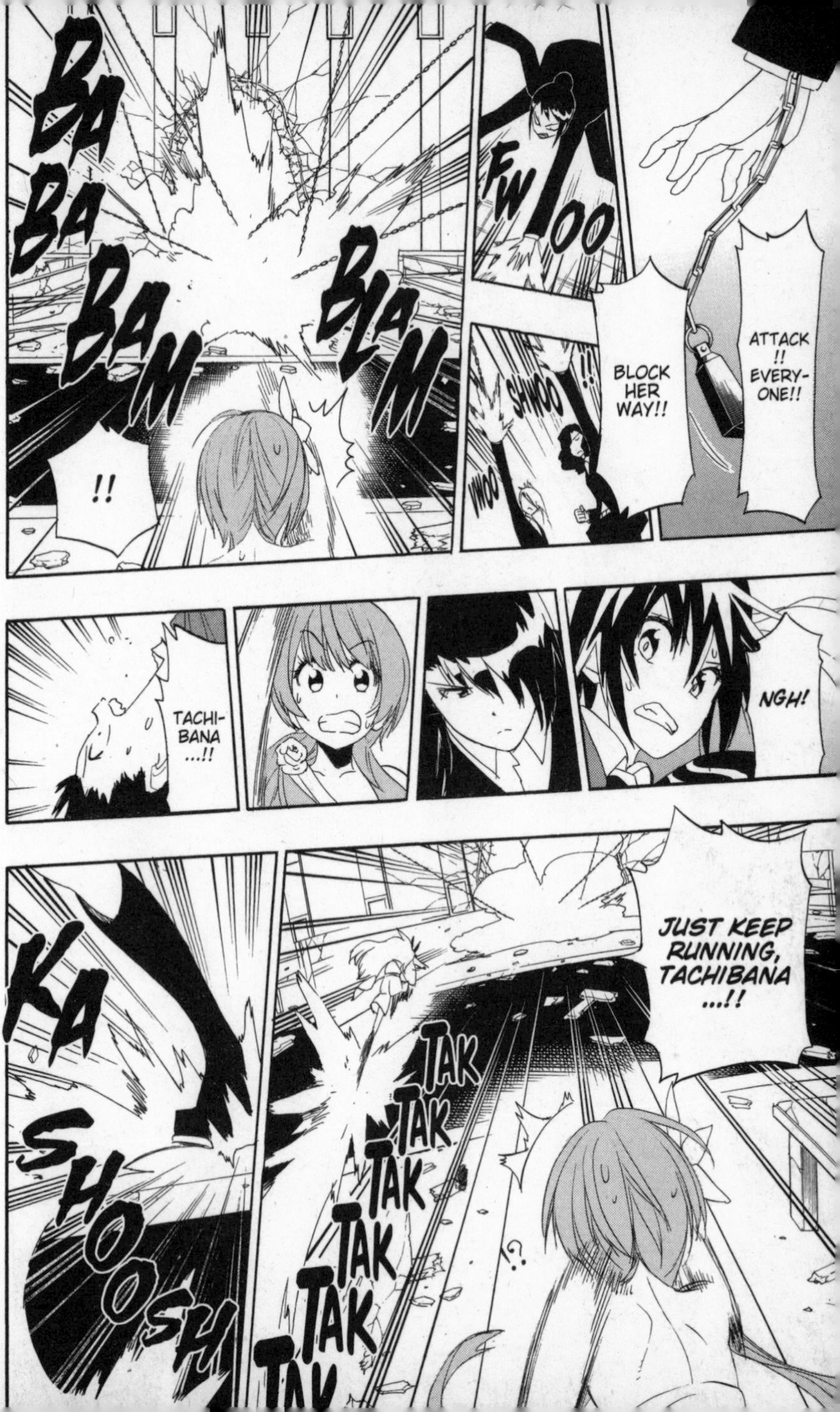
ATTACK!! EVERYONE!!
FWOO
BLOCK HER WAY!!
SHWOO
!!
WHOO
BA BA BA BAM
BLAM
!!
NGH!
TACHIBANA...!!
JUST KEEP RUNNING, TACHIBANA...!!
TAK TAK TAK TAK TAK
!?
KA
SHOOSH

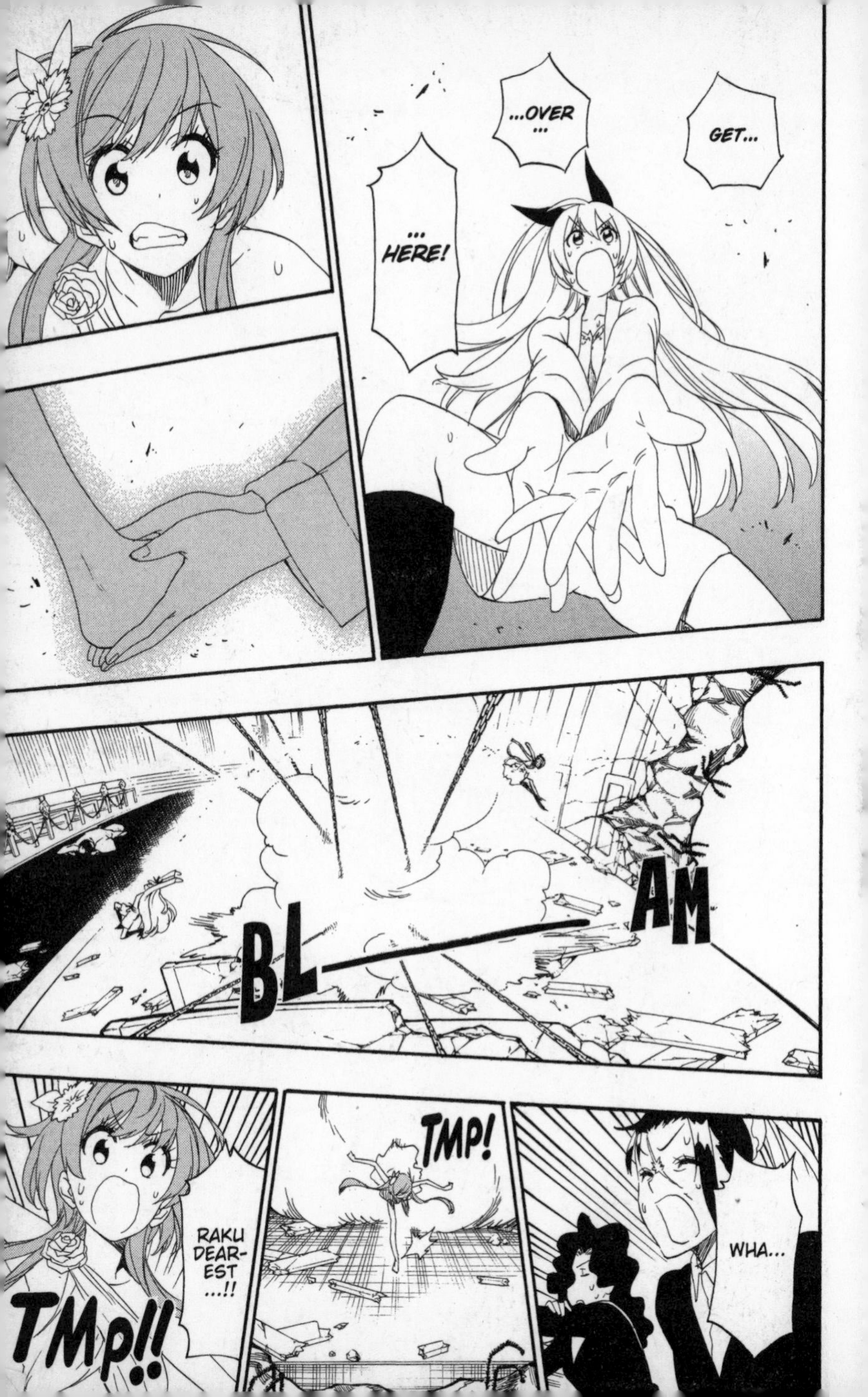
GET...
...OVER ...
... HERE!
BL——AM
WHA...
TMP!
RAKU DEAR-EST ...!!
TMp!!

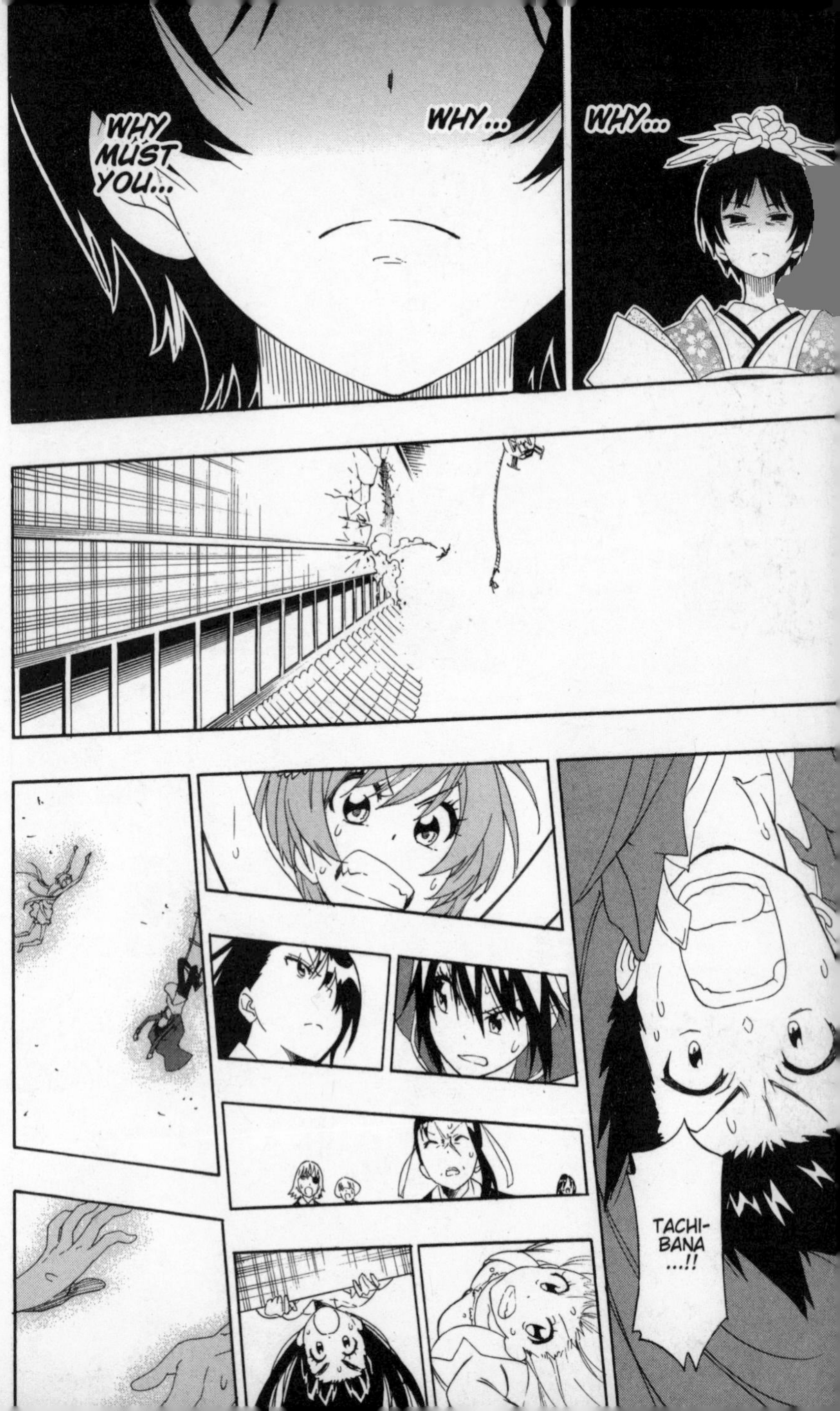
WHY...
WHY...
WHY MUST YOU...
TACHI-BANA ...!!

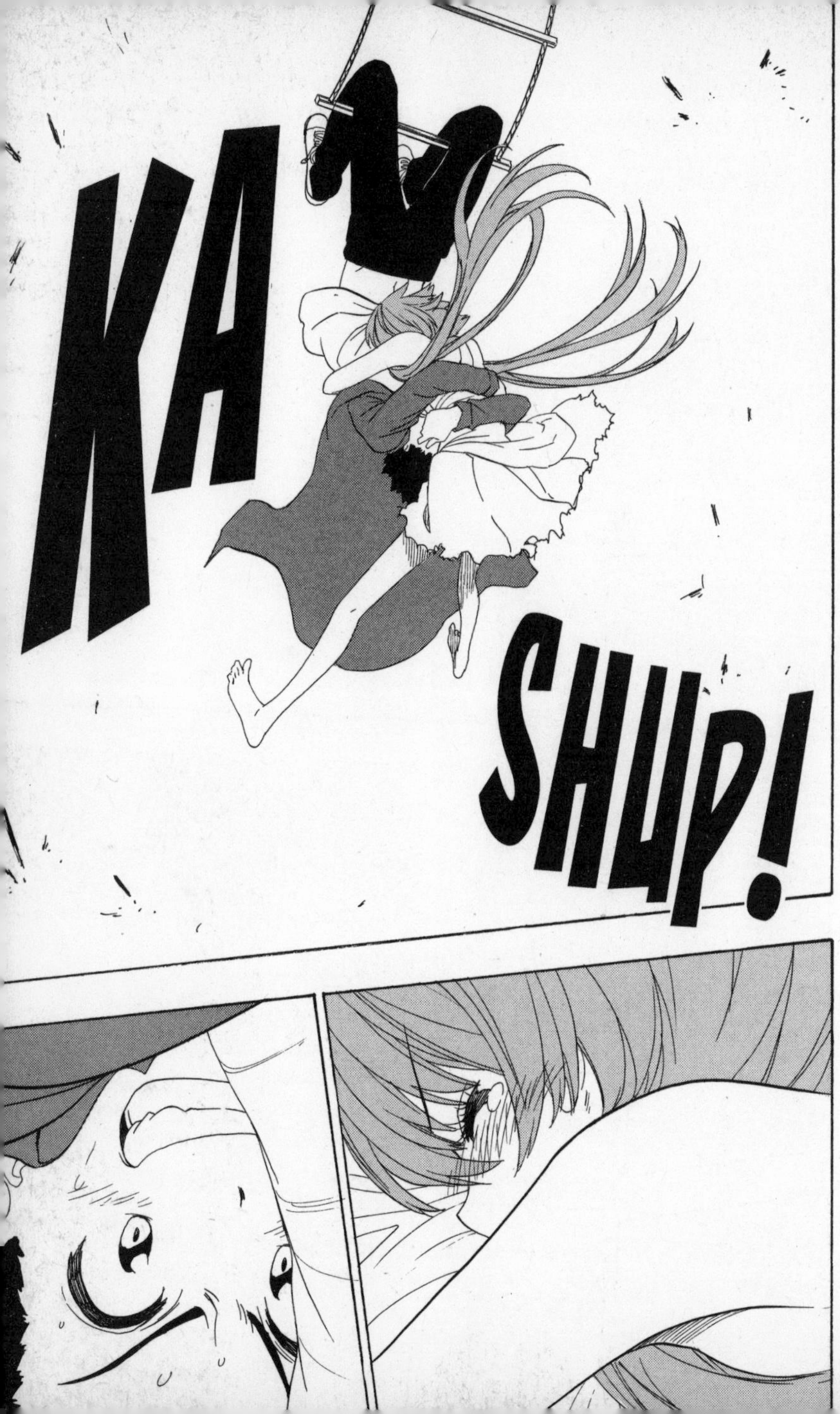
KA
SHUP!

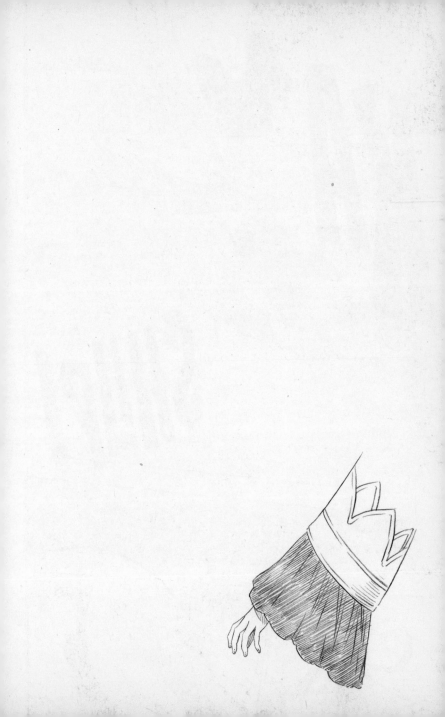

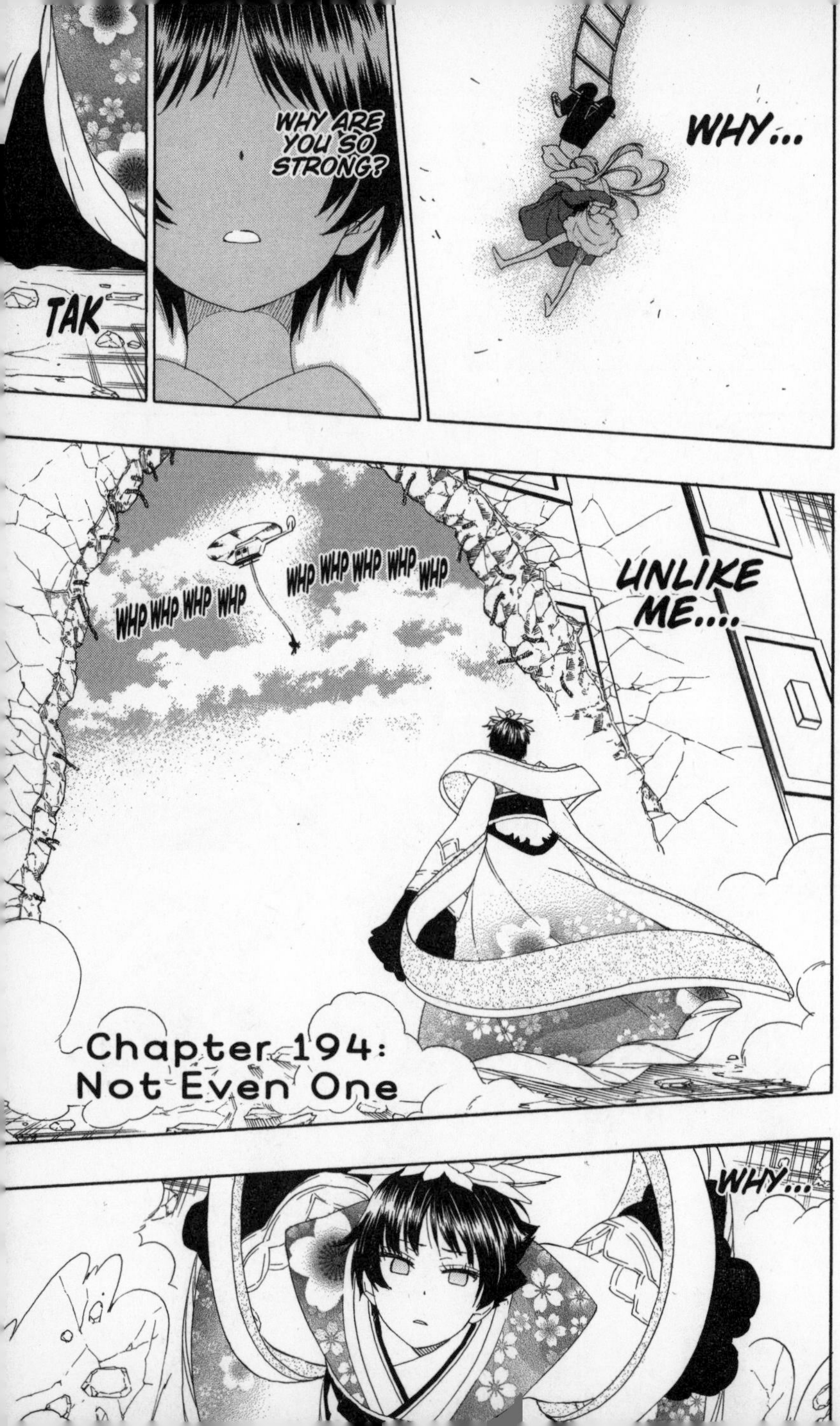
WHY...
WHY ARE YOU SO STRONG?
TAK
UNLIKE ME....
WHP WHP WHP WHP WHP
WHP WHP WHP WHP
WHY...

Chapter 194: Not Even One

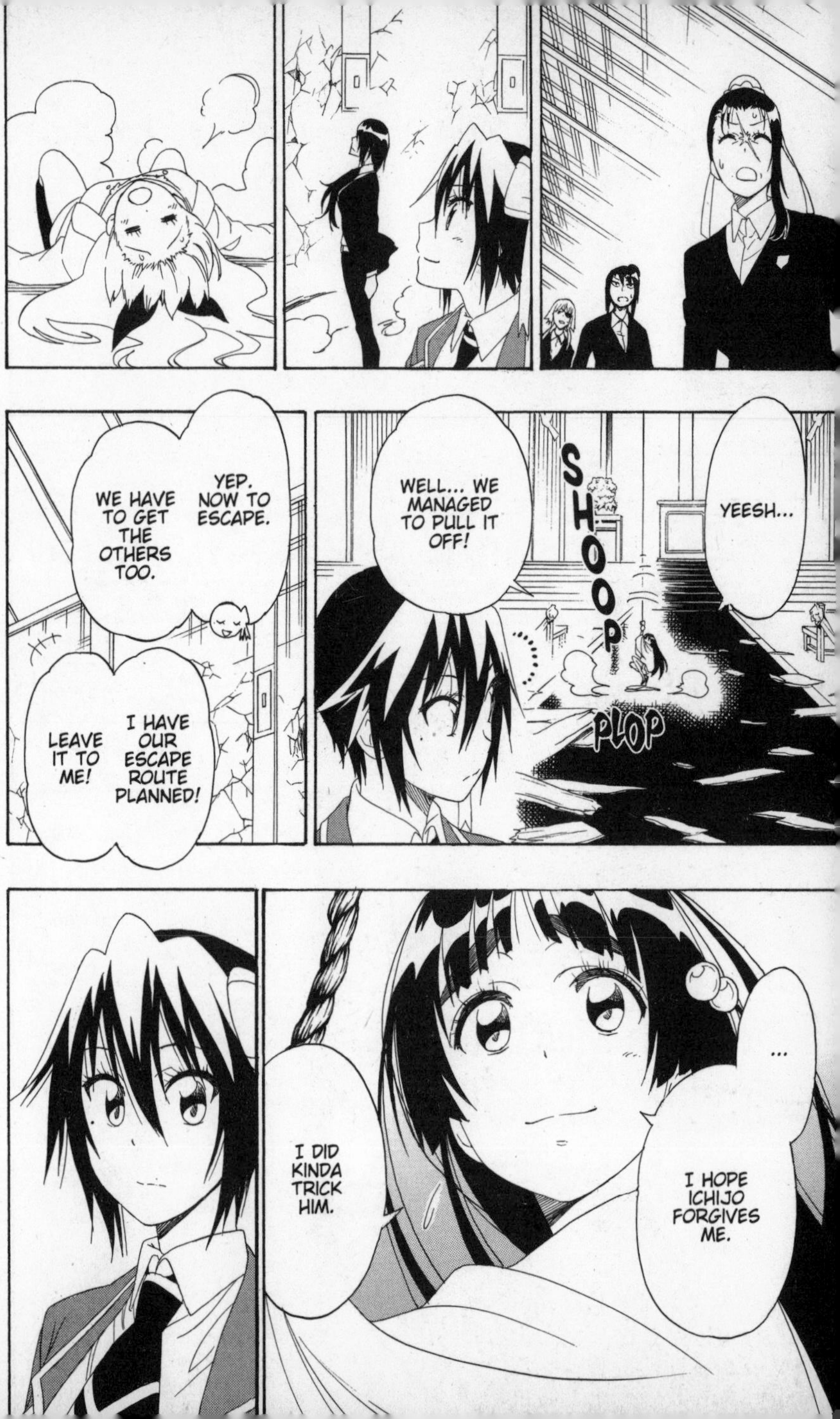
YEESH...
WELL... WE MANAGED TO PULL IT OFF!
SHOOP
PLOP
YEP. NOW TO ESCAPE.
WE HAVE TO GET THE OTHERS TOO.
I HAVE OUR ESCAPE ROUTE PLANNED!
LEAVE IT TO ME!
...
I HOPE ICHIJO FORGIVES ME.
I DID KINDA TRICK HIM.

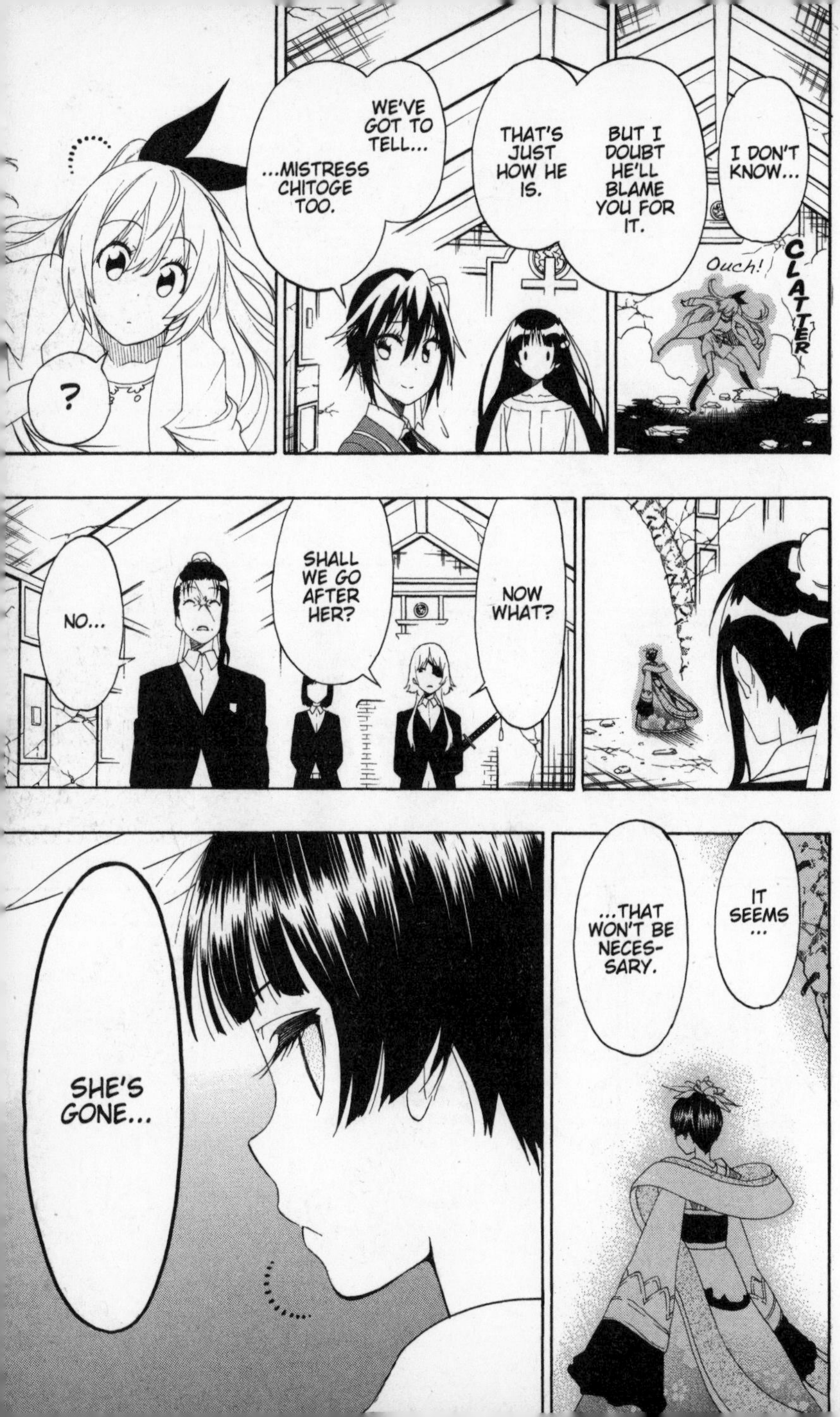
I DON'T KNOW...
Ouch!
CLATTER
BUT I DOUBT HE'LL BLAME YOU FOR IT.
THAT'S JUST HOW HE IS.
WE'VE GOT TO TELL...
...MISTRESS CHITOGE TOO.
?
NOW WHAT?
SHALL WE GO AFTER HER?
NO...
IT SEEMS...
...THAT WON'T BE NECES-SARY.
SHE'S GONE...

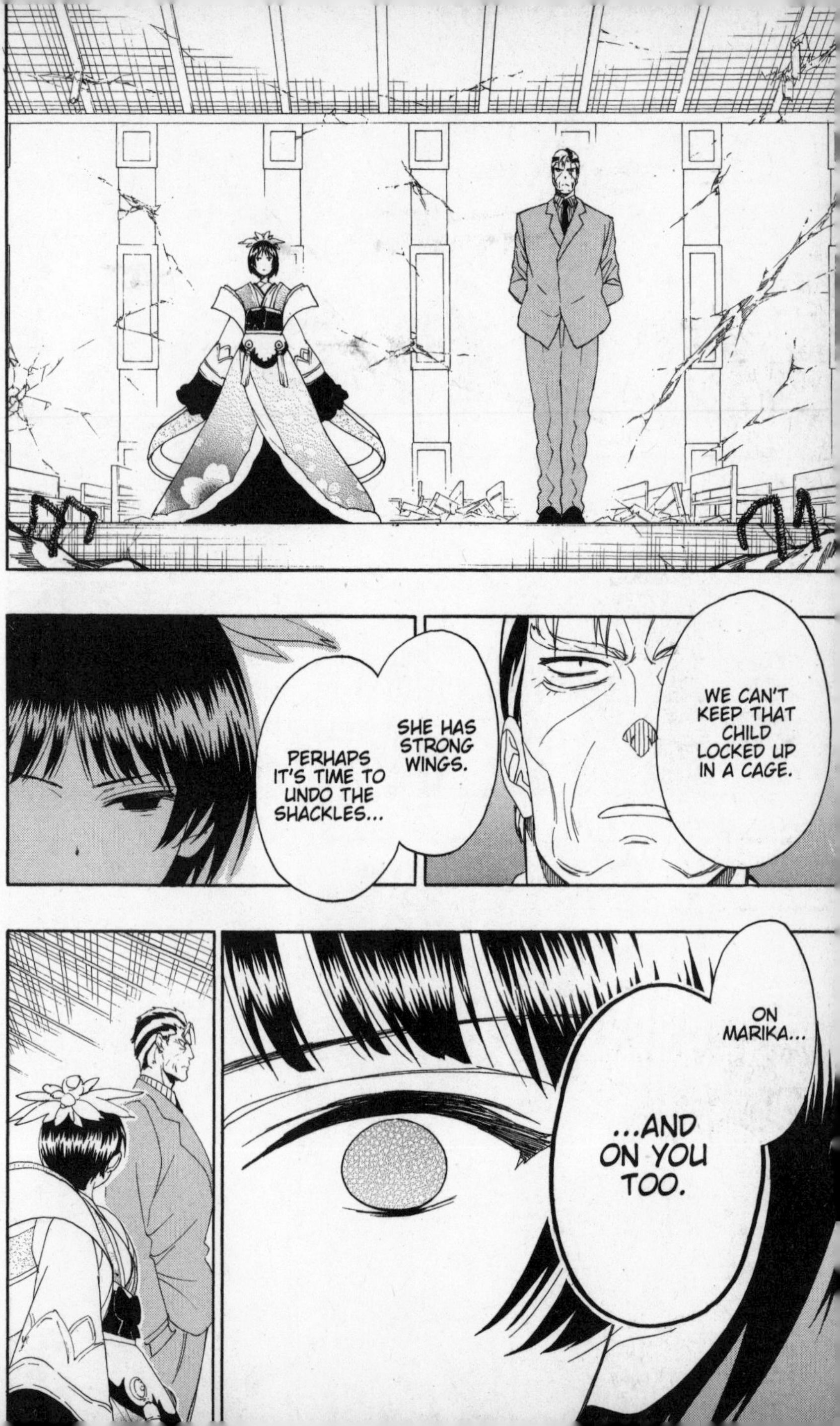
WE CAN'T KEEP THAT CHILD LOCKED UP IN A CAGE.
SHE HAS STRONG WINGS.
PERHAPS IT'S TIME TO UNDO THE SHACKLES...
ON MARIKA...
...AND ON YOU TOO.

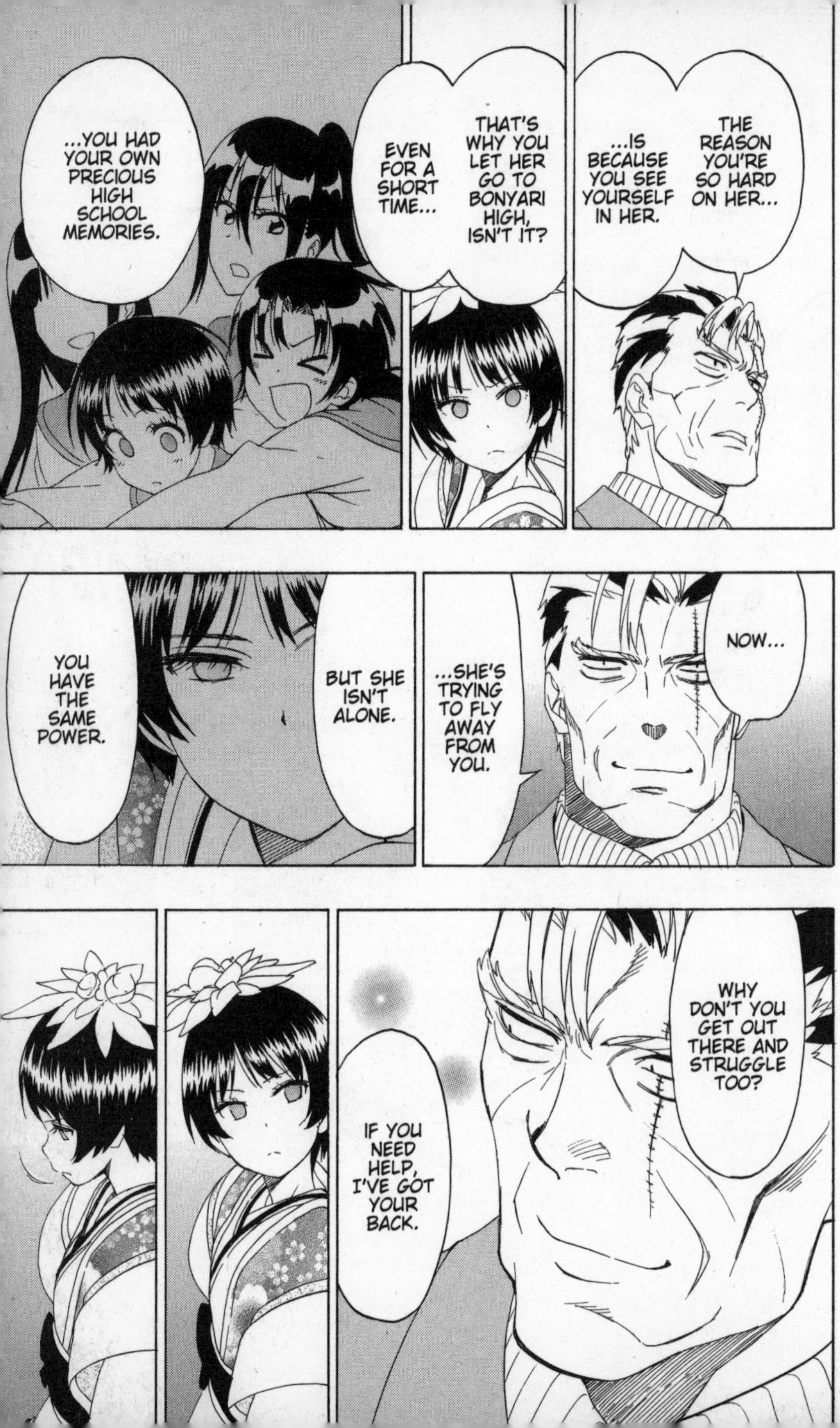
THE REASON YOU'RE SO HARD ON HER...
...IS BECAUSE YOU SEE YOURSELF IN HER.
THAT'S WHY YOU LET HER GO TO BONYARI HIGH, ISN'T IT?
EVEN FOR A SHORT TIME...
...YOU HAD YOUR OWN PRECIOUS HIGH SCHOOL MEMORIES.
NOW...
...SHE'S TRYING TO FLY AWAY FROM YOU.
BUT SHE ISN'T ALONE.
YOU HAVE THE SAME POWER.
WHY DON'T YOU GET OUT THERE AND STRUGGLE TOO?
IF YOU NEED HELP, I'VE GOT YOUR BACK.

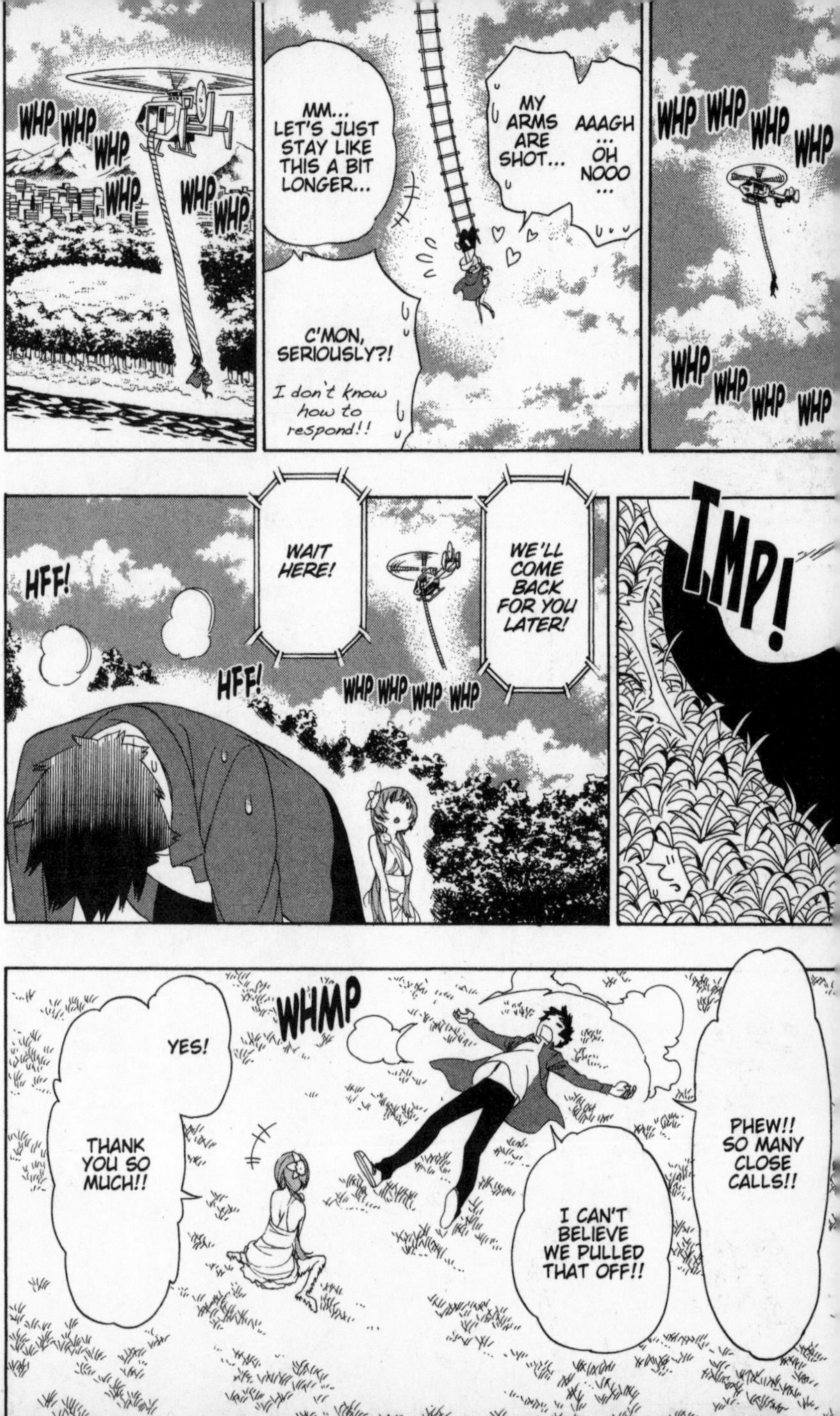
WHP WHP WHP WHP
WHP WHP WHP WHP
MY ARMS ARE SHOT... AAAGH... OH NOOO...
MM... LET'S JUST STAY LIKE THIS A BIT LONGER...
C'MON, SERIOUSLY?!
I don't know how to respond!!
WHP WHP WHP WHP WHP WHP
TMP!
WE'LL COME BACK FOR YOU LATER!
WAIT HERE!
WHP WHP WHP WHP
HFF!
HFF!
PHEW!! SO MANY CLOSE CALLS!!
I CAN'T BELIEVE WE PULLED THAT OFF!!
WHMP
YES!
THANK YOU SO MUCH!!

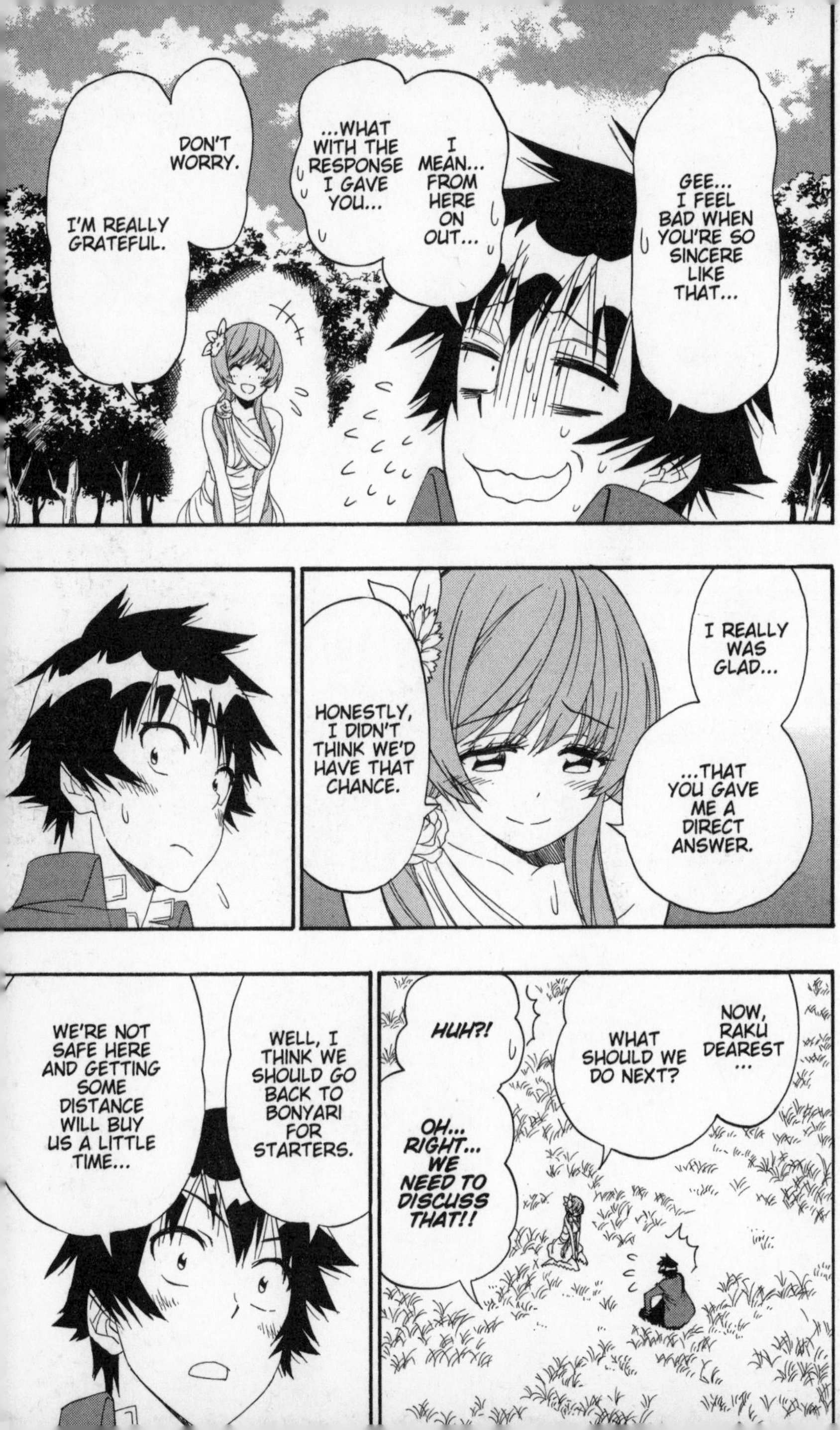
GEE... I FEEL BAD WHEN YOU'RE SO SINCERE LIKE THAT...
I MEAN... FROM HERE ON OUT...
...WHAT WITH THE RESPONSE I GAVE YOU...
DON'T WORRY.
I'M REALLY GRATEFUL.
I REALLY WAS GLAD...
...THAT YOU GAVE ME A DIRECT ANSWER.
HONESTLY, I DIDN'T THINK WE'D HAVE THAT CHANCE.
NOW, RAKU DEAREST ...
WHAT SHOULD WE DO NEXT?
HUH?!
OH... RIGHT... WE NEED TO DISCUSS THAT!!
WELL, I THINK WE SHOULD GO BACK TO BONYARI FOR STARTERS.
WE'RE NOT SAFE HERE AND GETTING SOME DISTANCE WILL BUY US A LITTLE TIME...

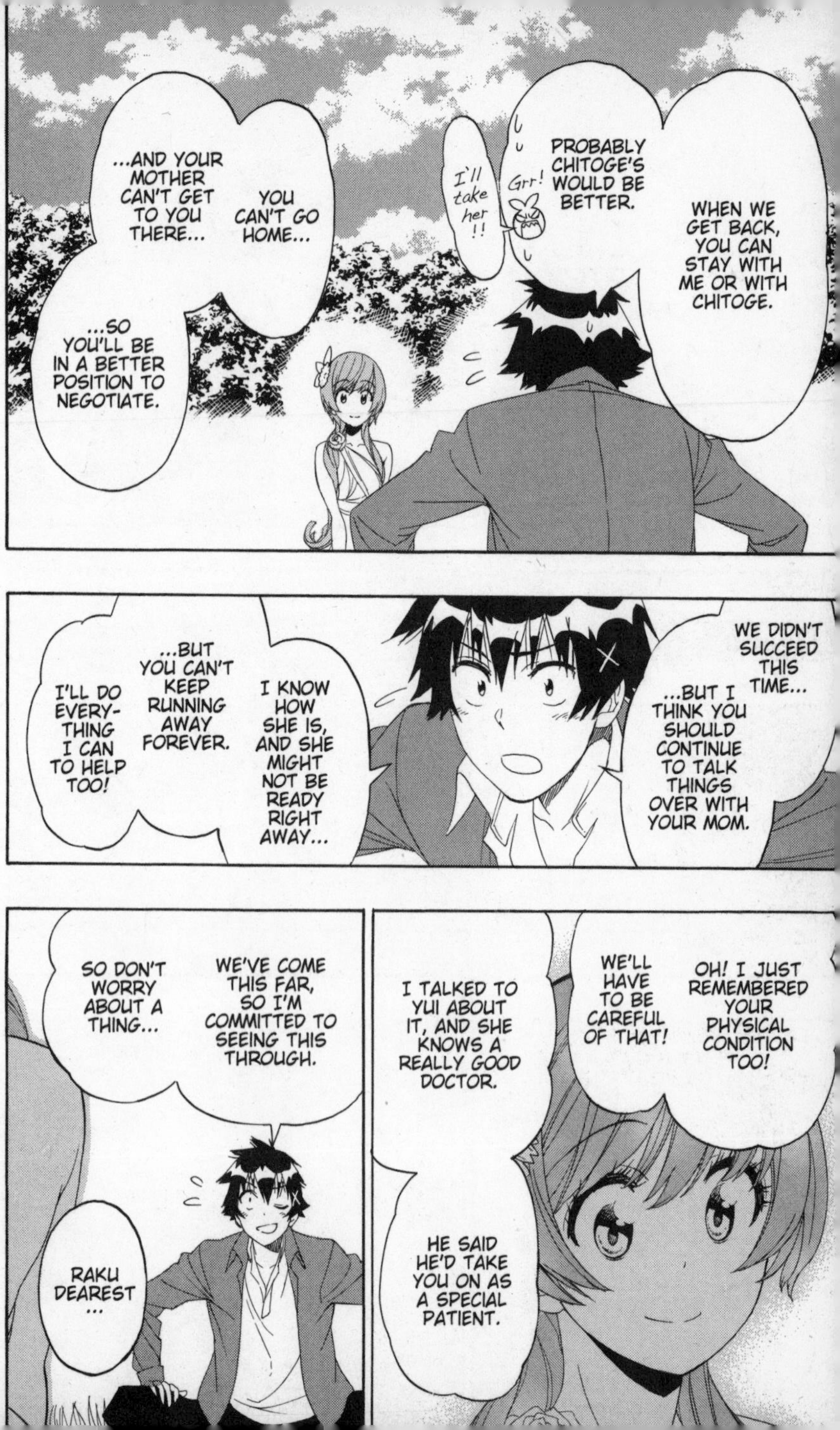
WHEN WE GET BACK, YOU CAN STAY WITH ME OR WITH CHITOGE.
PROBABLY CHITOGE'S WOULD BE BETTER.
Grr!
I'll take her!!
YOU CAN'T GO HOME...
...AND YOUR MOTHER CAN'T GET TO YOU THERE...
...SO YOU'LL BE IN A BETTER POSITION TO NEGOTIATE.
WE DIDN'T SUCCEED THIS TIME...
...BUT I THINK YOU SHOULD CONTINUE TO TALK THINGS OVER WITH YOUR MOM.
I KNOW HOW SHE IS, AND SHE MIGHT NOT BE READY RIGHT AWAY...
...BUT YOU CAN'T KEEP RUNNING AWAY FOREVER.
I'LL DO EVERY-THING I CAN TO HELP TOO!
OH! I JUST REMEMBERED YOUR PHYSICAL CONDITION TOO!
WE'LL HAVE TO BE CAREFUL OF THAT!
I TALKED TO YUI ABOUT IT, AND SHE KNOWS A REALLY GOOD DOCTOR.
HE SAID HE'D TAKE YOU ON AS A SPECIAL PATIENT.
WE'VE COME THIS FAR, SO I'M COMMITTED TO SEEING THIS THROUGH.
SO DON'T WORRY ABOUT A THING...
RAKU DEAREST ...

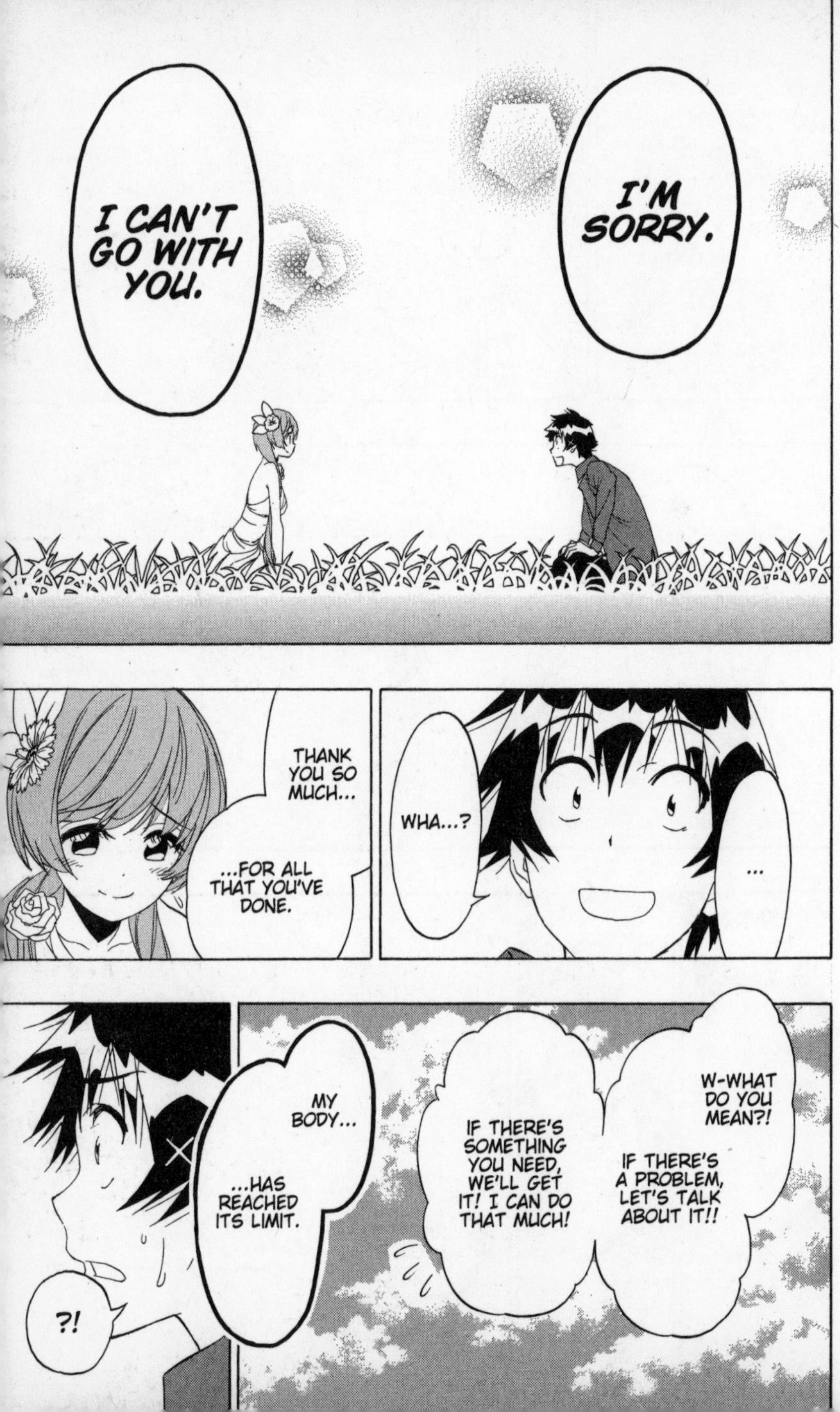
I'M SORRY.
I CAN'T GO WITH YOU.
...
WHA...?
THANK YOU SO MUCH...
...FOR ALL THAT YOU'VE DONE.
W-WHAT DO YOU MEAN?!
IF THERE'S A PROBLEM, LET'S TALK ABOUT IT!!
IF THERE'S SOMETHING YOU NEED, WE'LL GET IT! I CAN DO THAT MUCH!
MY BODY...
...HAS REACHED ITS LIMIT.
?!

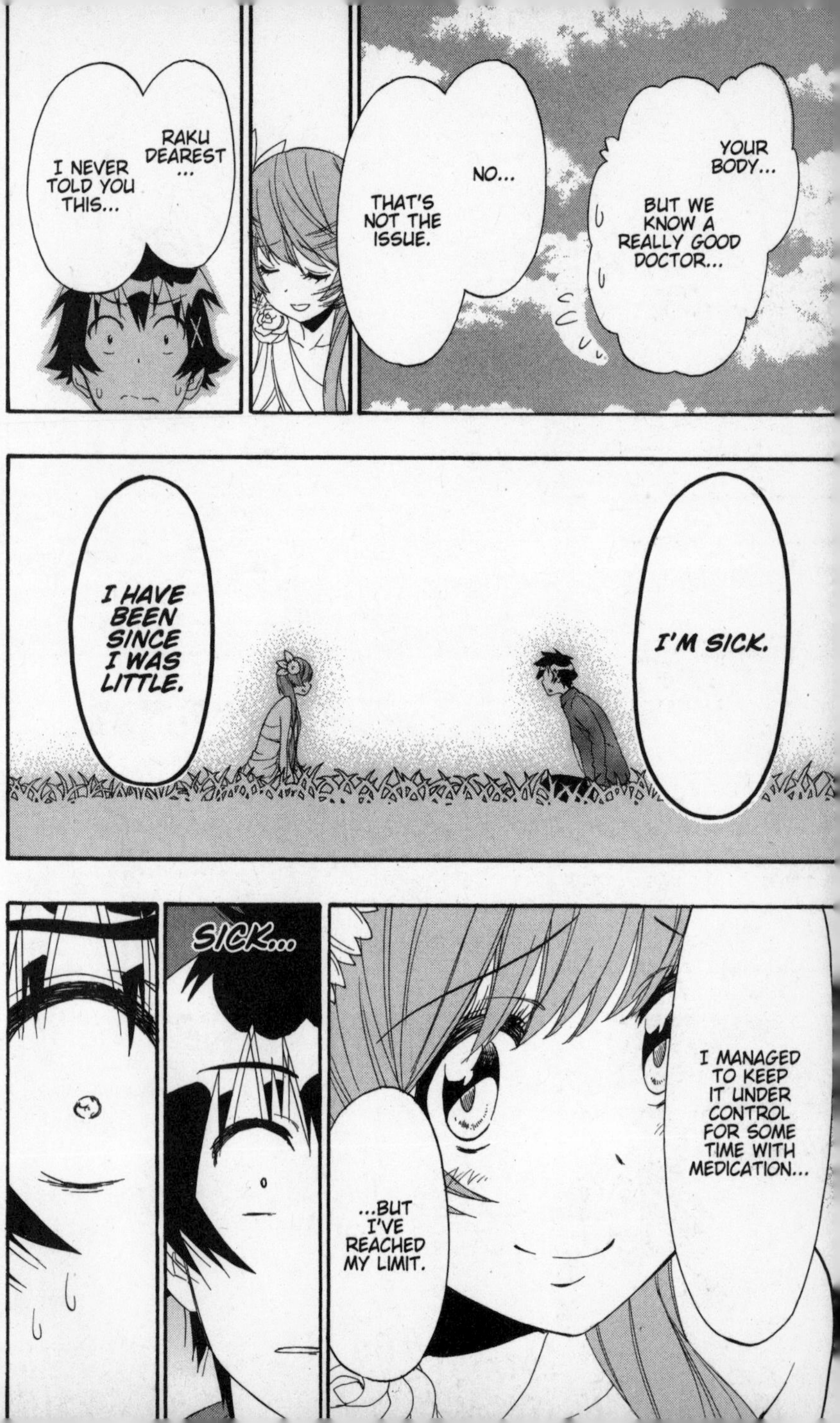
YOUR BODY...
BUT WE KNOW A REALLY GOOD DOCTOR...
NO...
THAT'S NOT THE ISSUE.
RAKU DEAREST ...
I NEVER TOLD YOU THIS...
I'M SICK.
I HAVE BEEN SINCE I WAS LITTLE.
I MANAGED TO KEEP IT UNDER CONTROL FOR SOME TIME WITH MEDICATION...
...BUT I'VE REACHED MY LIMIT.
SICK...

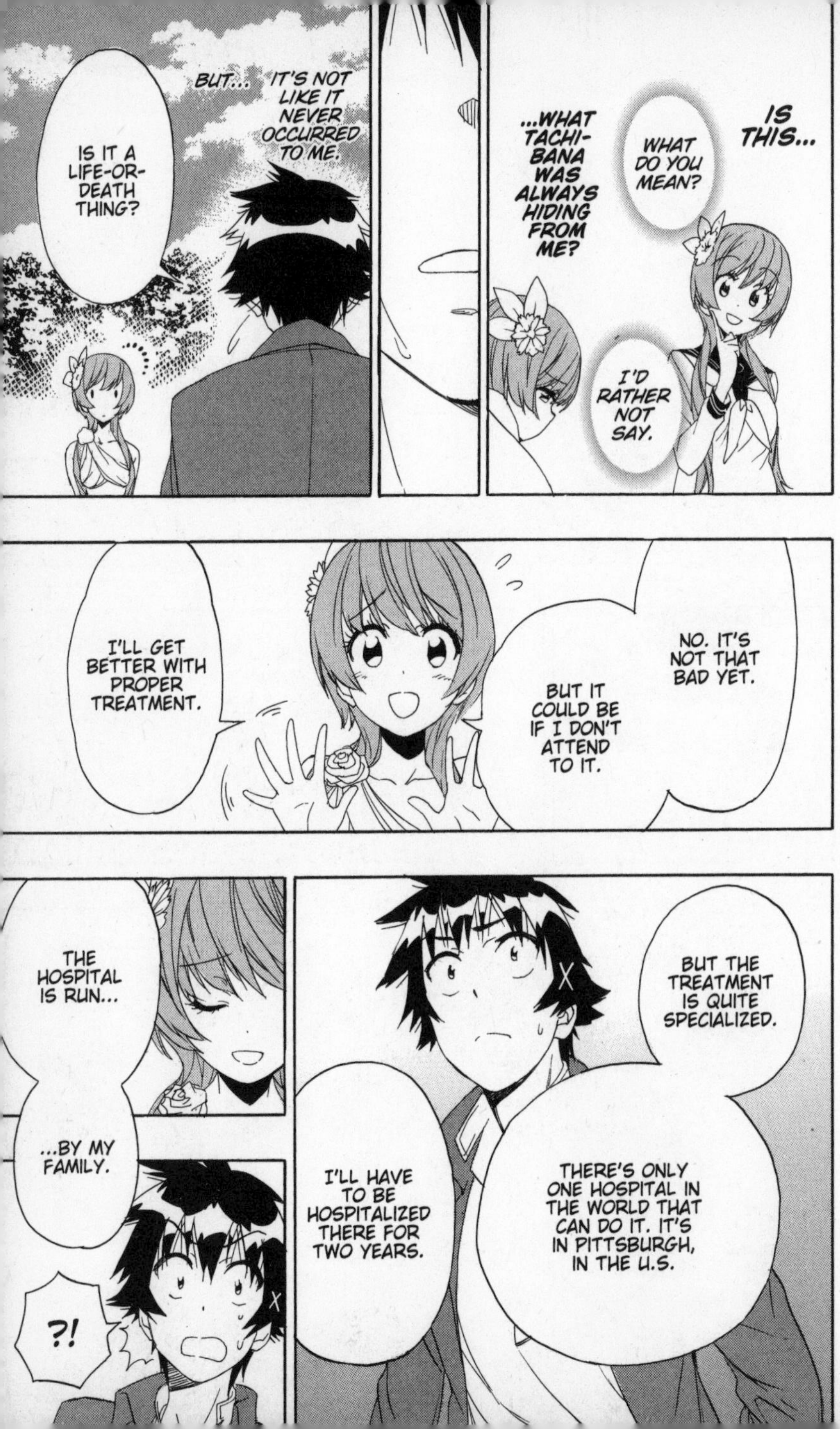
IS THIS...
WHAT DO YOU MEAN?
...WHAT TACHIBANA WAS ALWAYS HIDING FROM ME?
I'D RATHER NOT SAY.
BUT...
IT'S NOT LIKE IT NEVER OCCURRED TO ME.
IS IT A LIFE-OR-DEATH THING?
NO. IT'S NOT THAT BAD YET.
BUT IT COULD BE IF I DON'T ATTEND TO IT.
I'LL GET BETTER WITH PROPER TREATMENT.
BUT THE TREATMENT IS QUITE SPECIALIZED.
THERE'S ONLY ONE HOSPITAL IN THE WORLD THAT CAN DO IT. IT'S IN PITTSBURGH, IN THE U.S.
I'LL HAVE TO BE HOSPITALIZED THERE FOR TWO YEARS.
THE HOSPITAL IS RUN...
...BY MY FAMILY.
?!

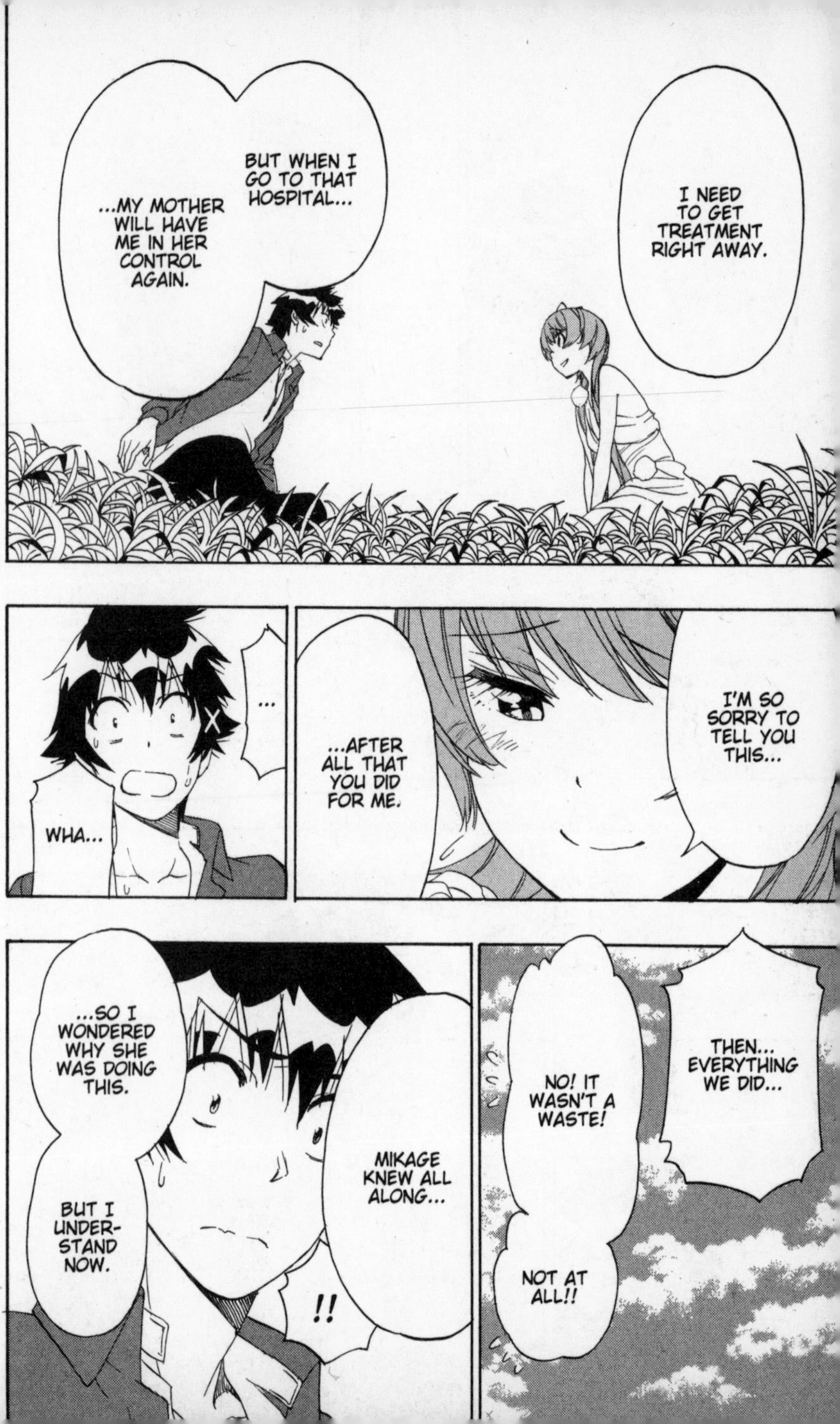
I NEED TO GET TREATMENT RIGHT AWAY.
BUT WHEN I GO TO THAT HOSPITAL...
...MY MOTHER WILL HAVE ME IN HER CONTROL AGAIN.
I'M SO SORRY TO TELL YOU THIS...
...AFTER ALL THAT YOU DID FOR ME.
...
WHA...
THEN... EVERYTHING WE DID...
NO! IT WASN'T A WASTE!
NOT AT ALL!!
MIKAGE KNEW ALL ALONG...
...SO I WONDERED WHY SHE WAS DOING THIS.
BUT I UNDER-STAND NOW.
!!

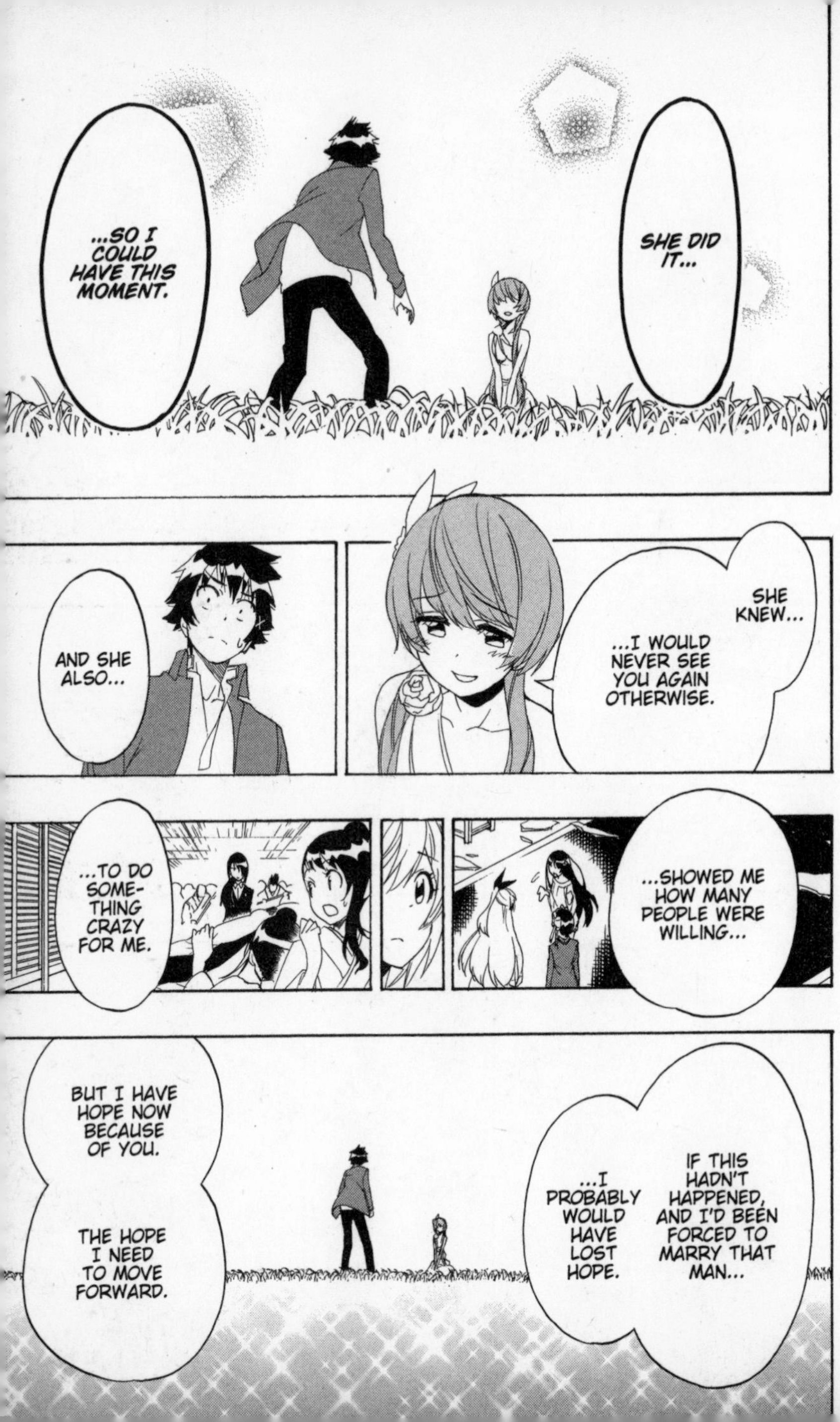
SHE DID IT...
...SO I COULD HAVE THIS MOMENT.
SHE KNEW...
...I WOULD NEVER SEE YOU AGAIN OTHERWISE.
AND SHE ALSO...
...SHOWED ME HOW MANY PEOPLE WERE WILLING...
...TO DO SOME-THING CRAZY FOR ME.
IF THIS HADN'T HAPPENED, AND I'D BEEN FORCED TO MARRY THAT MAN...
...I PROBABLY WOULD HAVE LOST HOPE.
BUT I HAVE HOPE NOW BECAUSE OF YOU.
THE HOPE I NEED TO MOVE FORWARD.

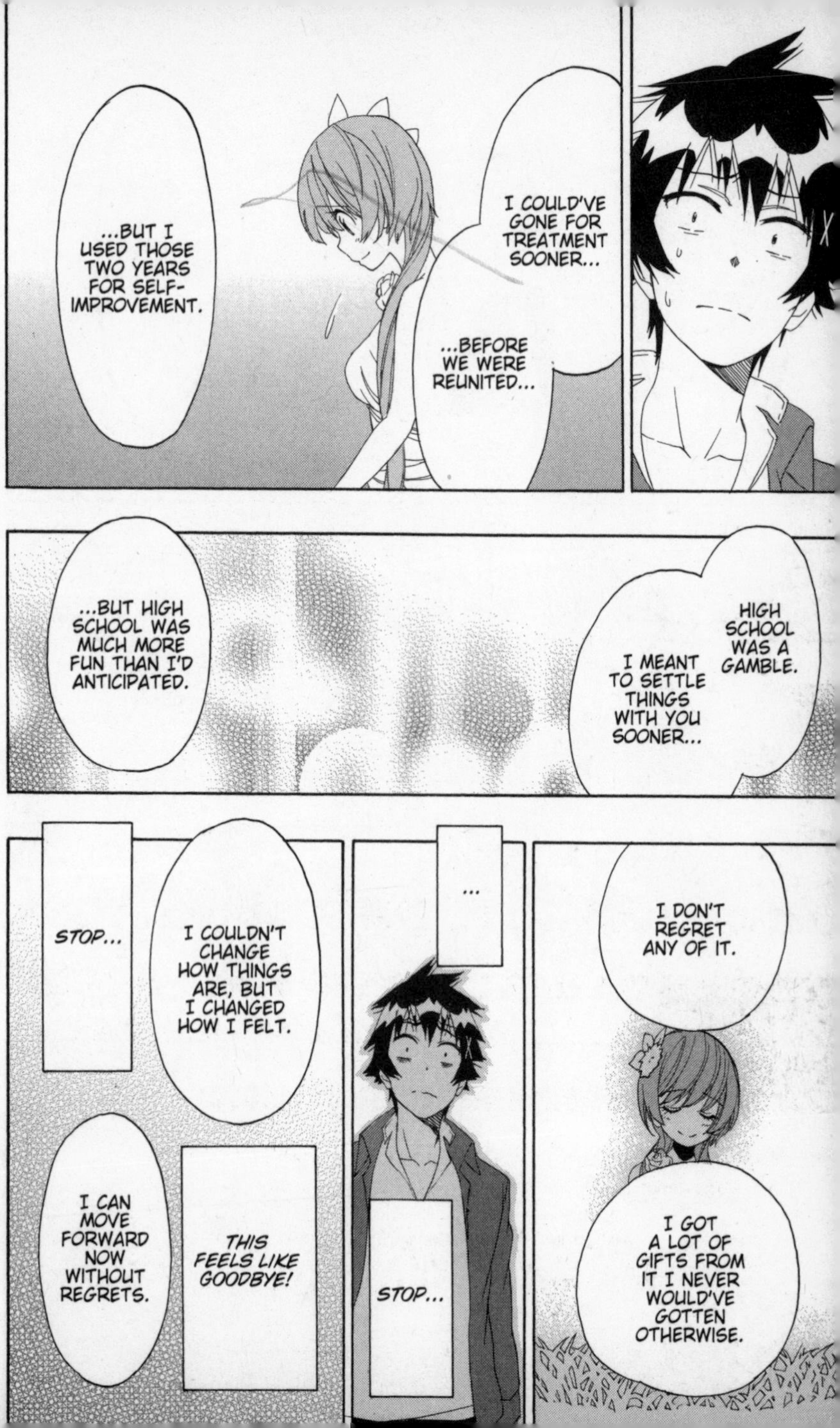
I COULD'VE GONE FOR TREATMENT SOONER...
...BEFORE WE WERE REUNITED...
...BUT I USED THOSE TWO YEARS FOR SELF-IMPROVEMENT.
HIGH SCHOOL WAS A GAMBLE.
I MEANT TO SETTLE THINGS WITH YOU SOONER...
...BUT HIGH SCHOOL WAS MUCH MORE FUN THAN I'D ANTICIPATED.
I DON'T REGRET ANY OF IT.
I GOT A LOT OF GIFTS FROM IT I NEVER WOULD'VE GOTTEN OTHERWISE.
...
STOP...
I COULDN'T CHANGE HOW THINGS ARE, BUT I CHANGED HOW I FELT.
STOP...
THIS FEELS LIKE GOODBYE!
I CAN MOVE FORWARD NOW WITHOUT REGRETS.

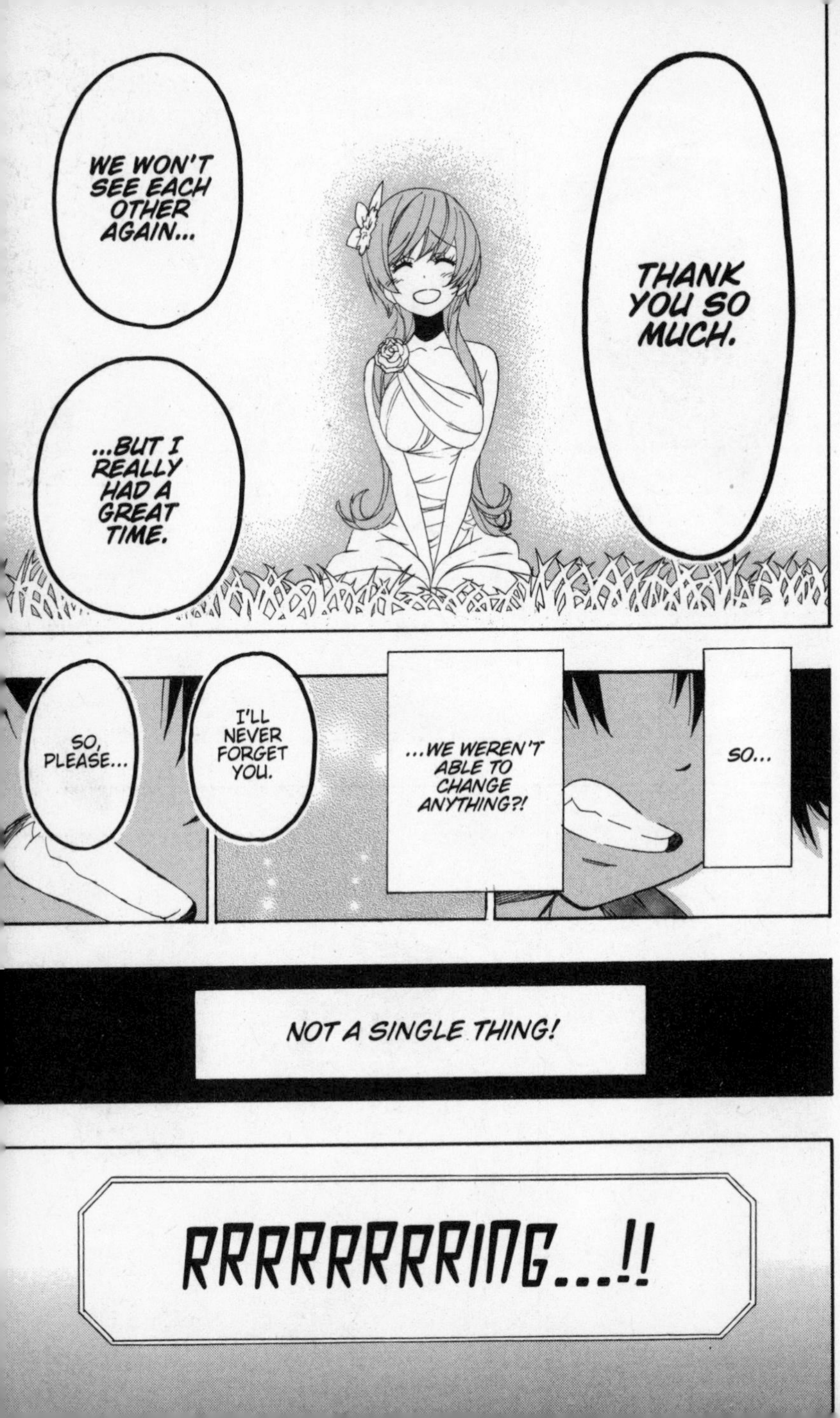
THANK YOU SO MUCH.
WE WON'T SEE EACH OTHER AGAIN...
...BUT I REALLY HAD A GREAT TIME.
SO...
...WE WEREN'T ABLE TO CHANGE ANYTHING?!
I'LL NEVER FORGET YOU.
SO, PLEASE...
NOT A SINGLE THING!
RRRRRRRRING...!!

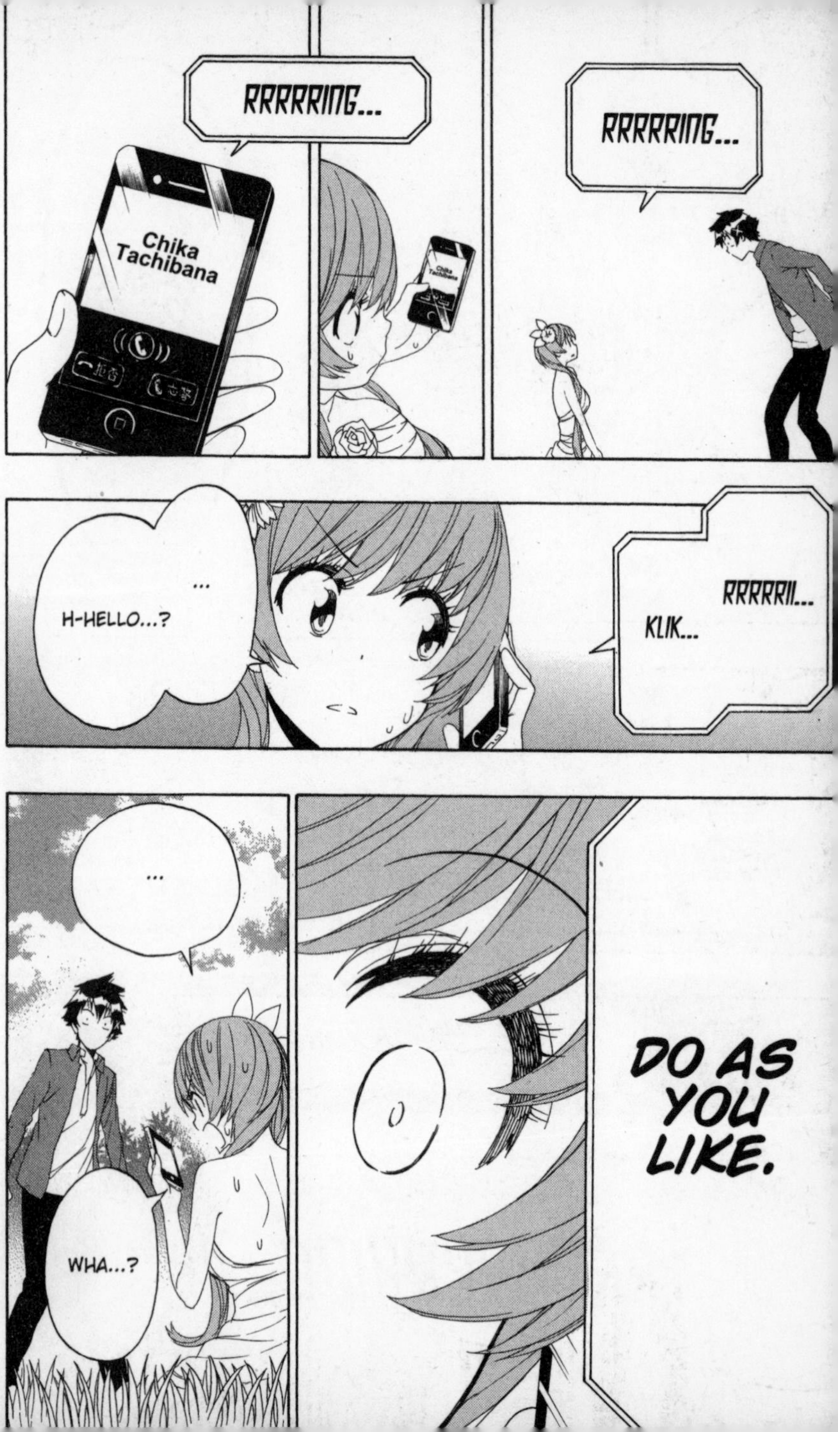
RRRRRING...
Chika Tachibana
RRRRRING...
Chika Tachibana
RRRRRII...
KLIK...
...
H-HELLO...?
DO AS YOU LIKE.
...
WHA...?

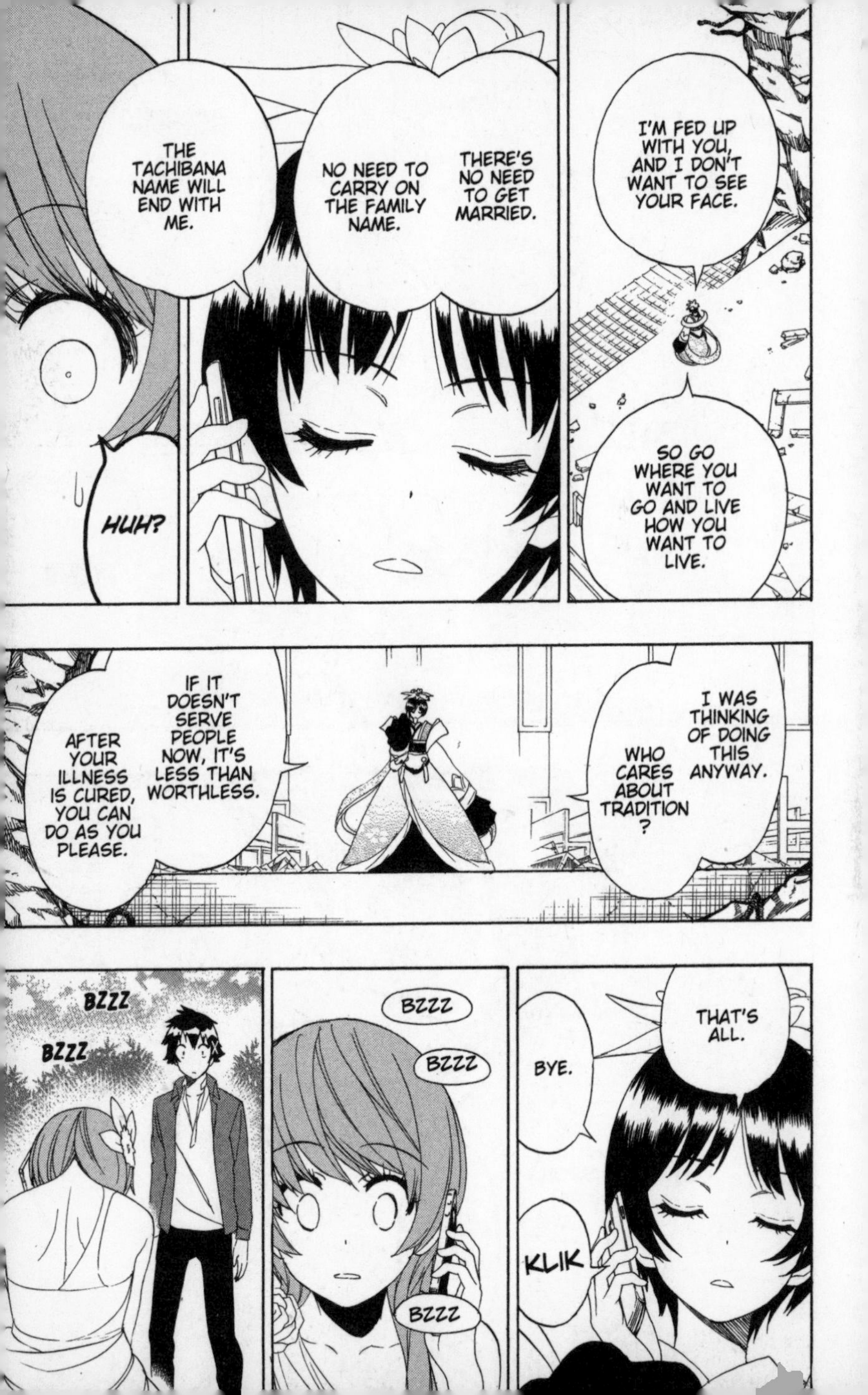

I'M FED UP WITH YOU, AND I DON'T WANT TO SEE YOUR FACE.
SO GO WHERE YOU WANT TO GO AND LIVE HOW YOU WANT TO LIVE.
THERE'S NO NEED TO GET MARRIED.
NO NEED TO CARRY ON THE FAMILY NAME.
THE TACHIBANA NAME WILL END WITH ME.
HUH?
I WAS THINKING OF DOING THIS ANYWAY.
WHO CARES ABOUT TRADITION?
IF IT DOESN'T SERVE PEOPLE NOW, IT'S LESS THAN WORTHLESS.
AFTER YOUR ILLNESS IS CURED, YOU CAN DO AS YOU PLEASE.
THAT'S ALL.
BYE.
KLIK
BZZZ
BZZZ
BZZZ
BZZZ
BZZZ

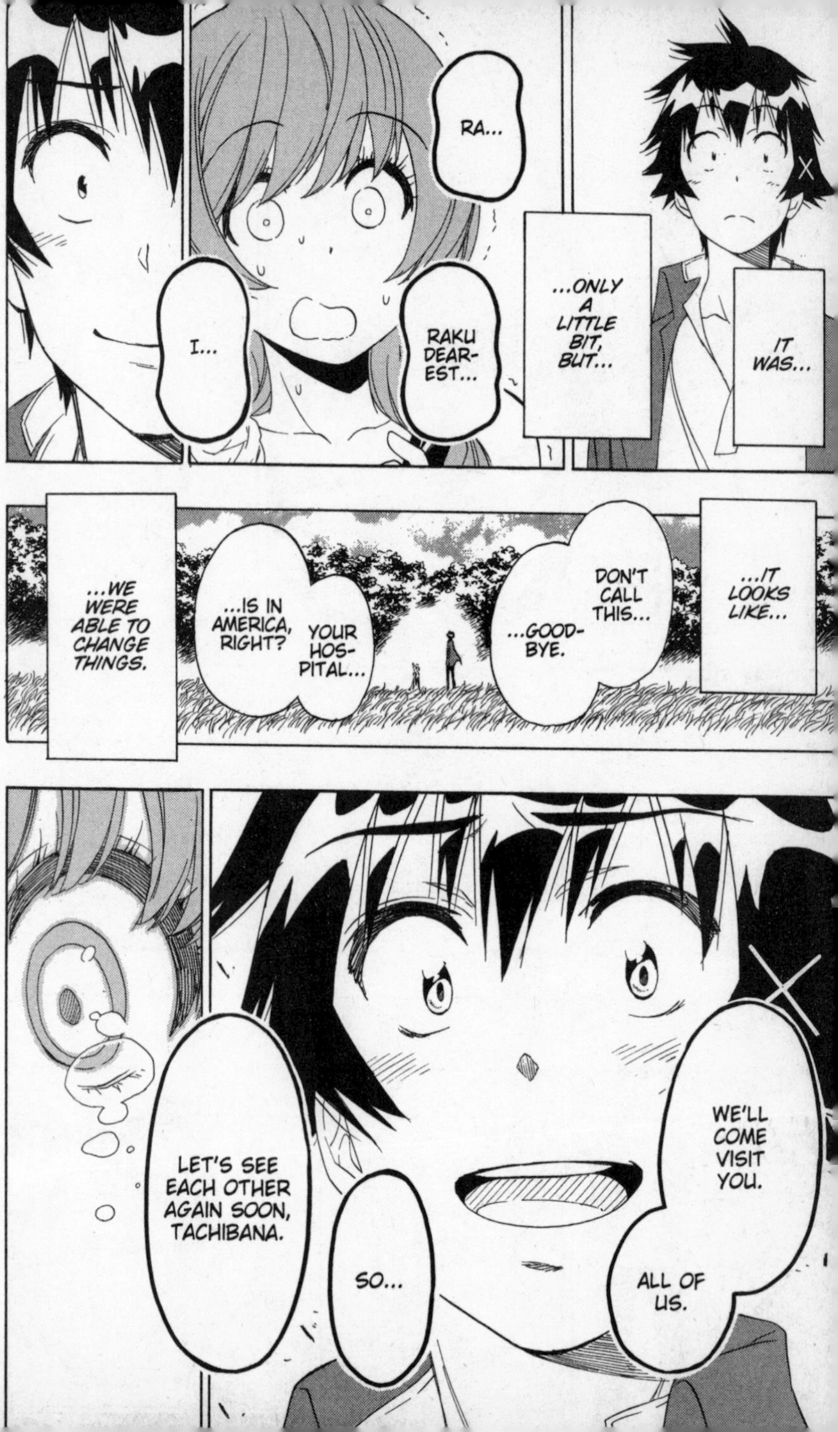
IT WAS...
...ONLY A LITTLE BIT, BUT...
RA...
RAKU DEAREST...
I...
...IT LOOKS LIKE...
DON'T CALL THIS...
...GOOD-BYE.
YOUR HOSPITAL...
...IS IN AMERICA, RIGHT?
...WE WERE ABLE TO CHANGE THINGS.
WE'LL COME VISIT YOU.
ALL OF US.
SO...
LET'S SEE EACH OTHER AGAIN SOON, TACHIBANA.

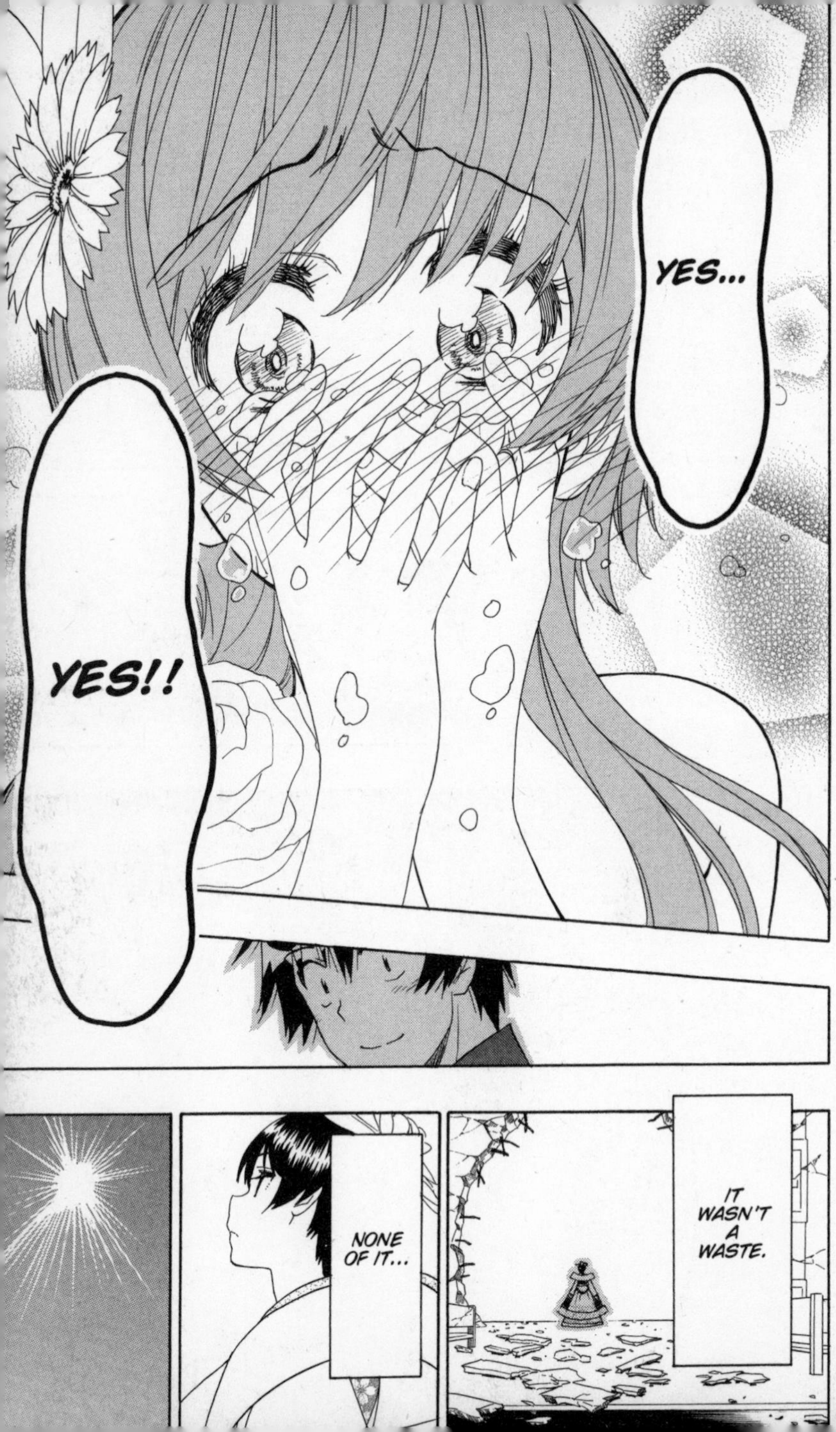
YES...
YES!!
IT WASN'T A WASTE.
NONE OF IT...

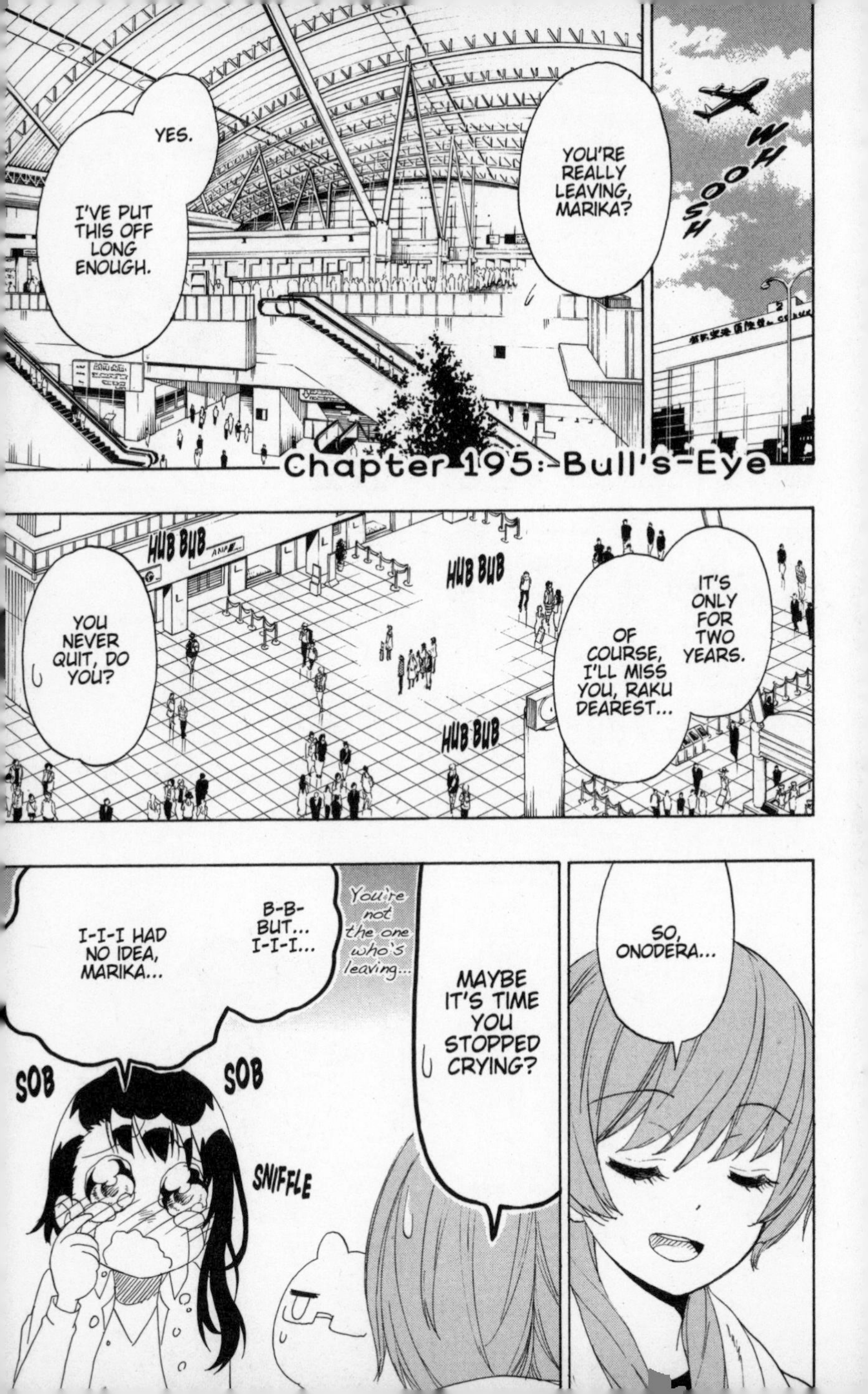
WHOOOSH
YOU'RE REALLY LEAVING, MARIKA?
YES.
I'VE PUT THIS OFF LONG ENOUGH.
Chapter 195: Bull's-Eye
IT'S ONLY FOR TWO YEARS.
OF COURSE, I'LL MISS YOU, RAKU DEAREST...
HUB BUB
HUB BUB
HUB BUB
YOU NEVER QUIT, DO YOU?
SO, ONODERA...
MAYBE IT'S TIME YOU STOPPED CRYING?
You're not the one who's leaving...
B-B-BUT... I-I-I...
I-I-I HAD NO IDEA, MARIKA...
SOB
SOB
SNIFFLE

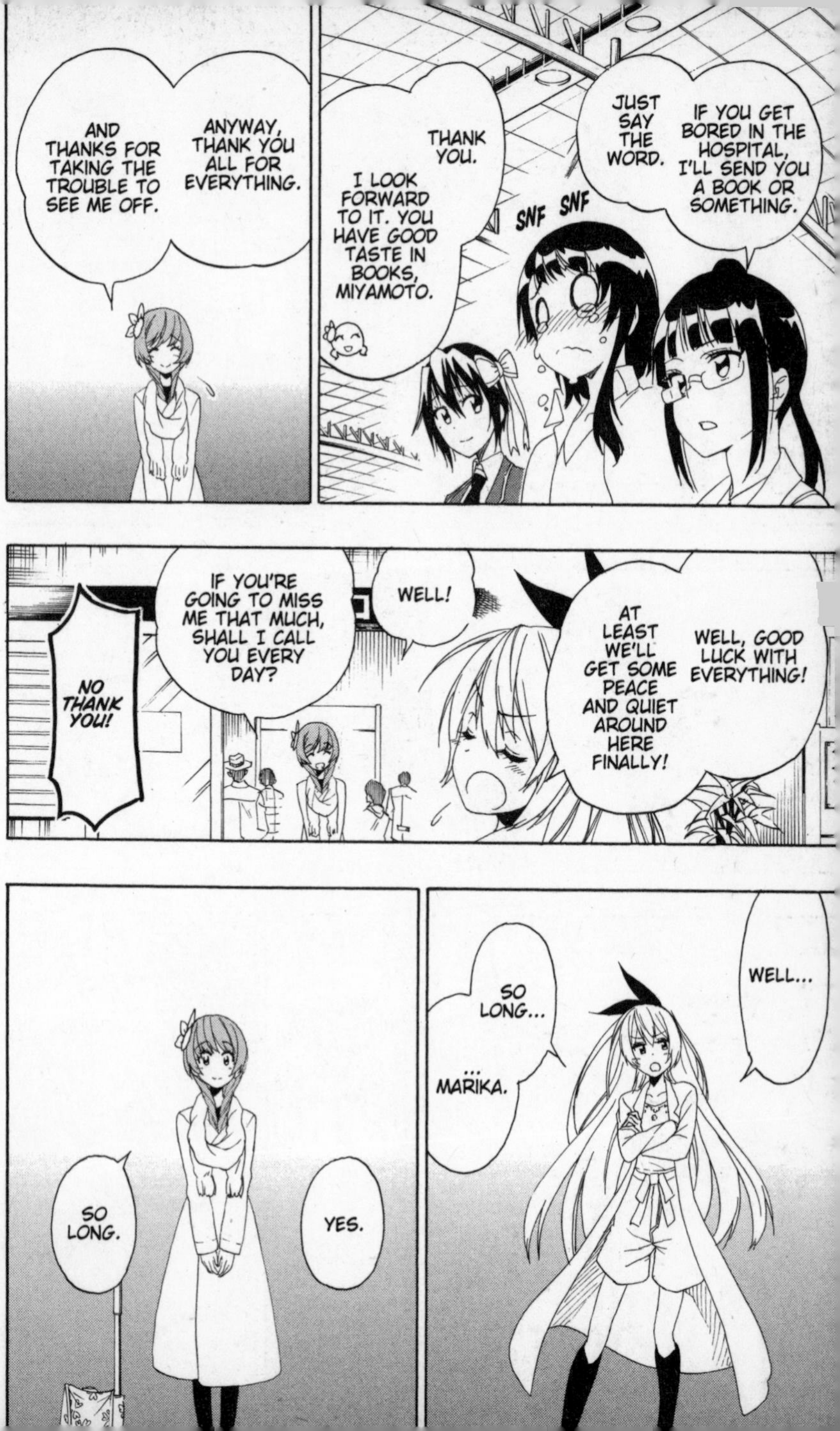
IF YOU GET BORED IN THE HOSPITAL, I'LL SEND YOU A BOOK OR SOMETHING.
JUST SAY THE WORD.
SNF SNF
THANK YOU.
I LOOK FORWARD TO IT. YOU HAVE GOOD TASTE IN BOOKS, MIYAMOTO.
ANYWAY, THANK YOU ALL FOR EVERYTHING.
AND THANKS FOR TAKING THE TROUBLE TO SEE ME OFF.
WELL, GOOD LUCK WITH EVERYTHING!
AT LEAST WE'LL GET SOME PEACE AND QUIET AROUND HERE FINALLY!
WELL!
IF YOU'RE GOING TO MISS ME THAT MUCH, SHALL I CALL YOU EVERY DAY?
NO THANK YOU!
WELL...
SO LONG...
...MARIKA.
YES.
SO LONG.

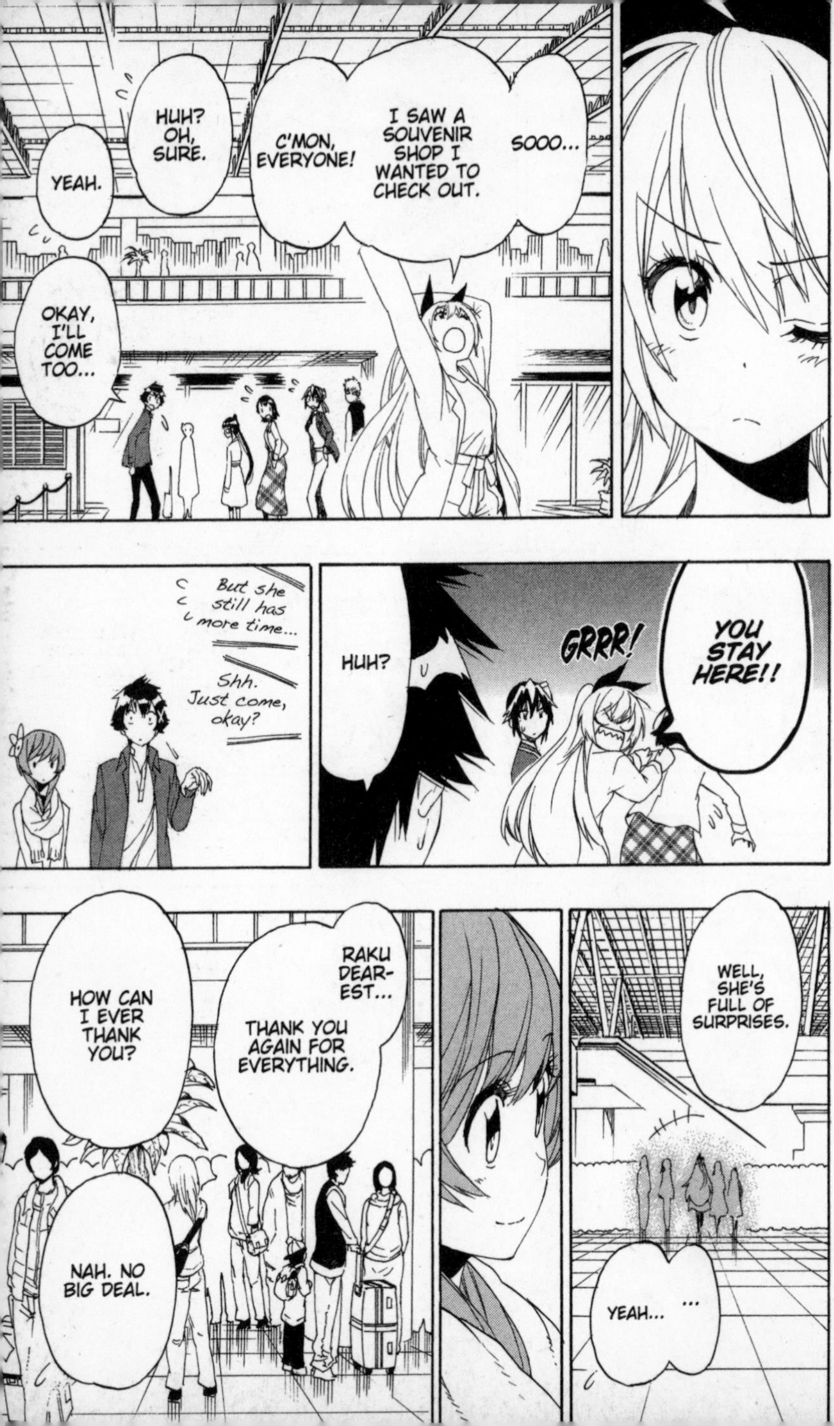
SOOO...
I SAW A SOUVENIR SHOP I WANTED TO CHECK OUT.
C'MON, EVERYONE!
HUH? OH, SURE.
YEAH.
OKAY, I'LL COME TOO...
YOU STAY HERE!!
GRRR!
HUH?
But she still has more time...
Shh. Just come, okay?
WELL, SHE'S FULL OF SURPRISES.
...
YEAH...
RAKU DEAREST...
THANK YOU AGAIN FOR EVERYTHING.
HOW CAN I EVER THANK YOU?
NAH. NO BIG DEAL.

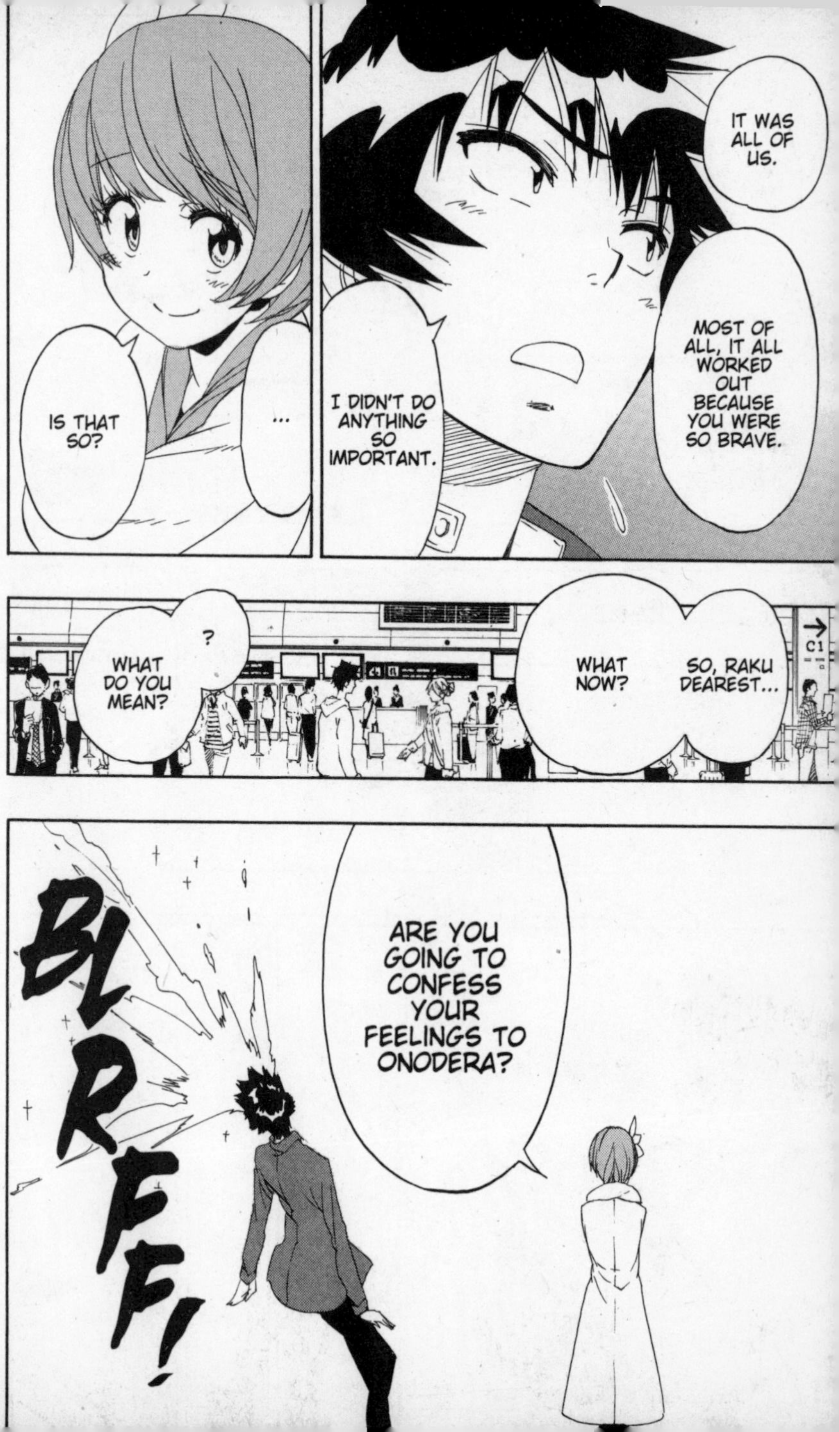
IT WAS ALL OF US.
MOST OF ALL, IT ALL WORKED OUT BECAUSE YOU WERE SO BRAVE.
I DIDN'T DO ANYTHING SO IMPORTANT.
...
IS THAT SO?
C1
SO, RAKU DEAREST...
WHAT NOW?
?
WHAT DO YOU MEAN?
ARE YOU GOING TO CONFESS YOUR FEELINGS TO ONODERA?
BLRFF!

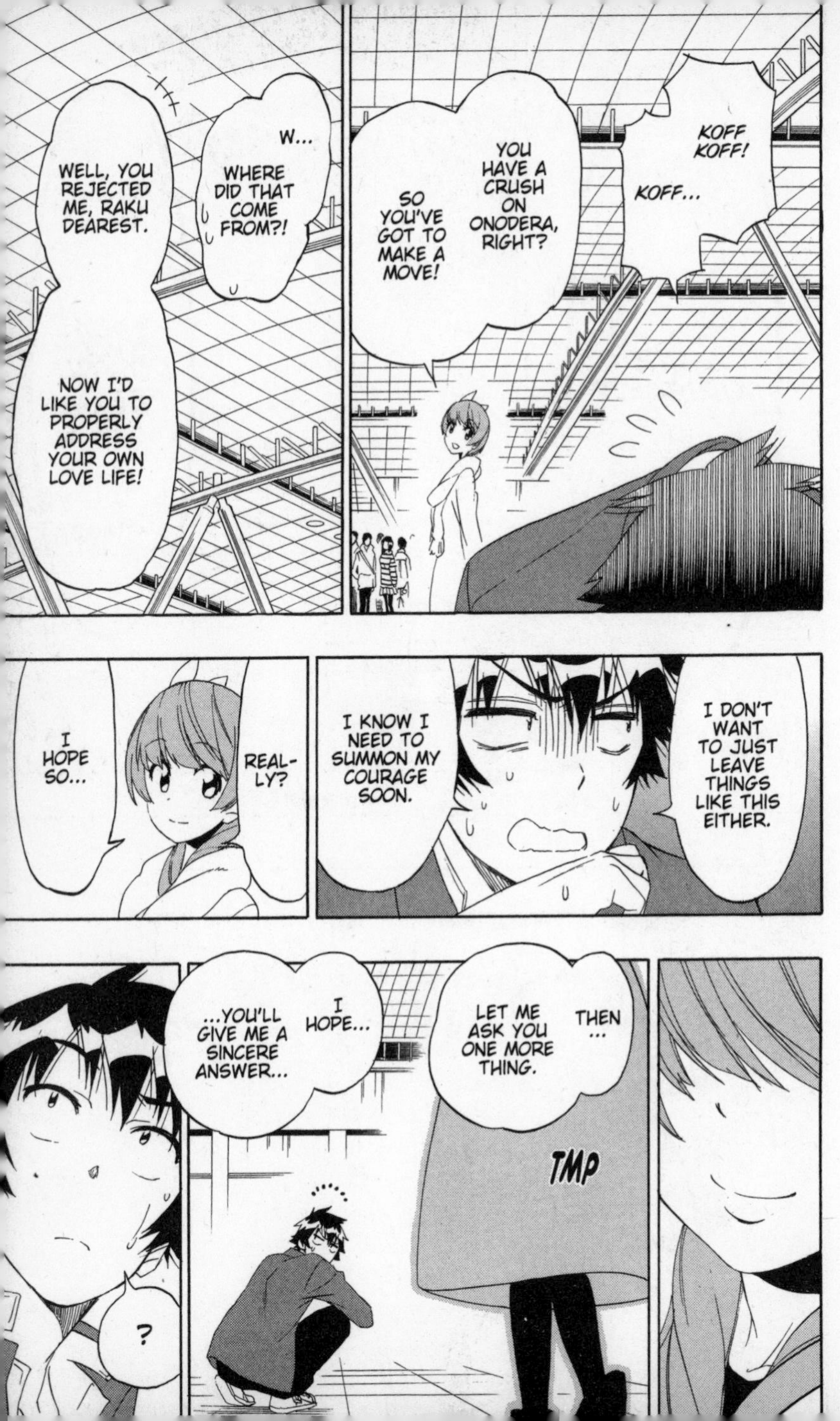

KOFF KOFF!
KOFF...
YOU HAVE A CRUSH ON ONODERA, RIGHT?
SO YOU'VE GOT TO MAKE A MOVE!
W...
WHERE DID THAT COME FROM?!
WELL, YOU REJECTED ME, RAKU DEAREST.
NOW I'D LIKE YOU TO PROPERLY ADDRESS YOUR OWN LOVE LIFE!
I DON'T WANT TO JUST LEAVE THINGS LIKE THIS EITHER.
I KNOW I NEED TO SUMMON MY COURAGE SOON.
REAL-LY?
I HOPE SO...
THEN ...
LET ME ASK YOU ONE MORE THING.
TMP
I HOPE...
...YOU'LL GIVE ME A SINCERE ANSWER...
?

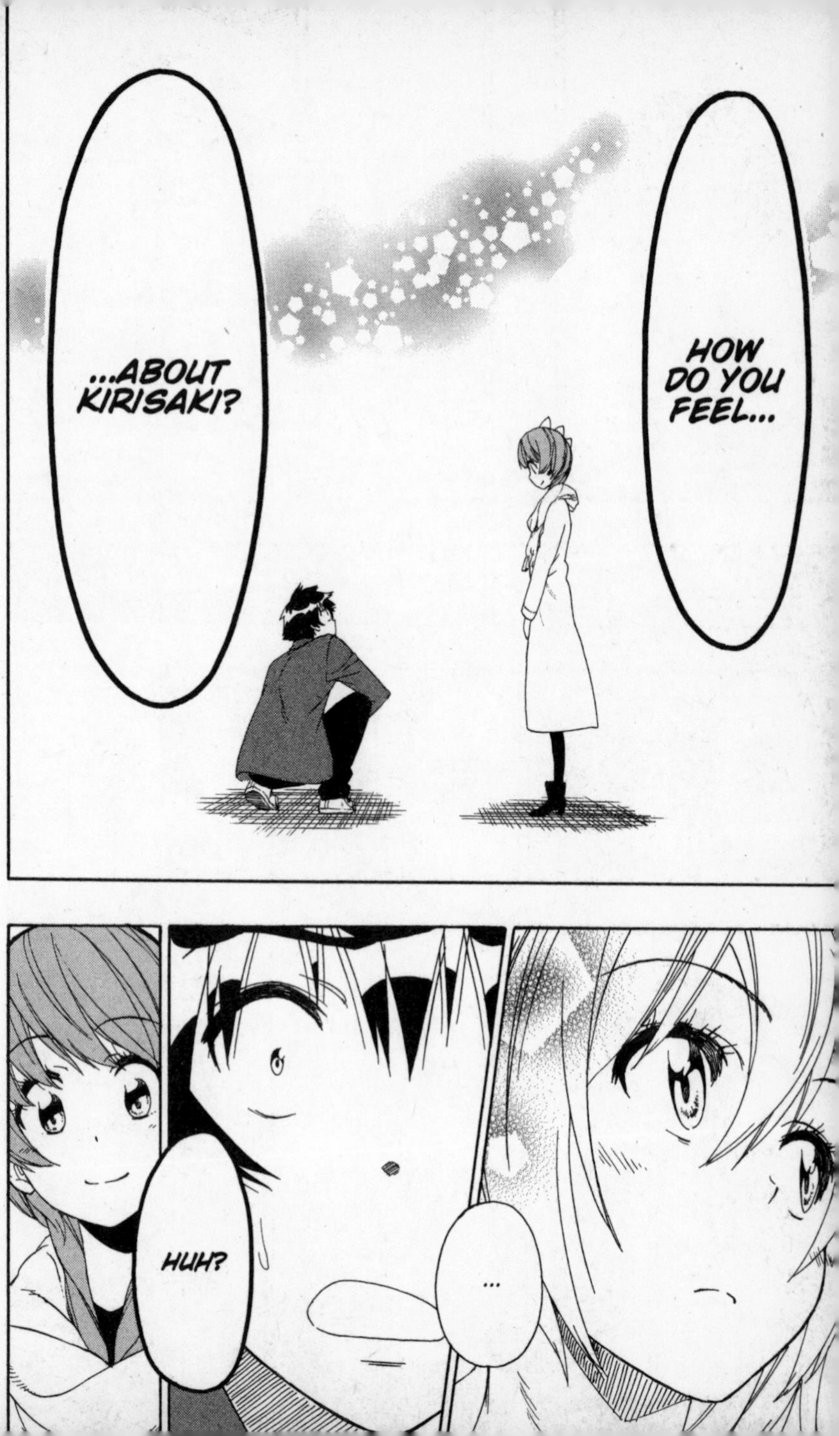
HOW DO YOU FEEL...
...ABOUT KIRISAKI?
...
HUH?

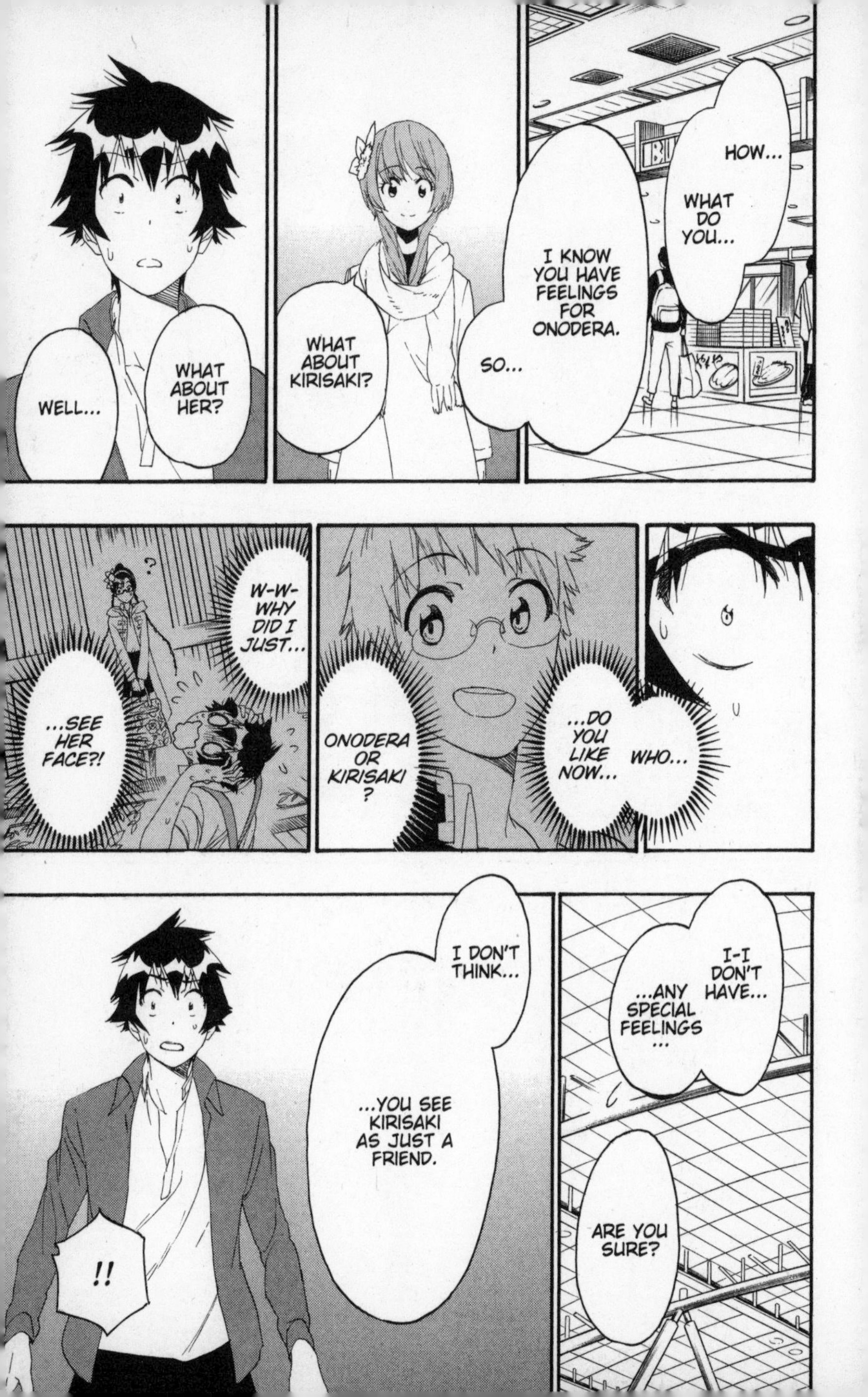
HOW...
WHAT DO YOU...
I KNOW YOU HAVE FEELINGS FOR ONODERA.
SO...
WHAT ABOUT KIRISAKI?
WHAT ABOUT HER?
WELL...
WHO...
...DO YOU LIKE NOW...
ONODERA OR KIRISAKI?
W-W-WHY DID I JUST...
...SEE HER FACE?!
I-I DON'T HAVE...
...ANY SPECIAL FEELINGS...
ARE YOU SURE?
I DON'T THINK...
...YOU SEE KIRISAKI AS JUST A FRIEND.
!!

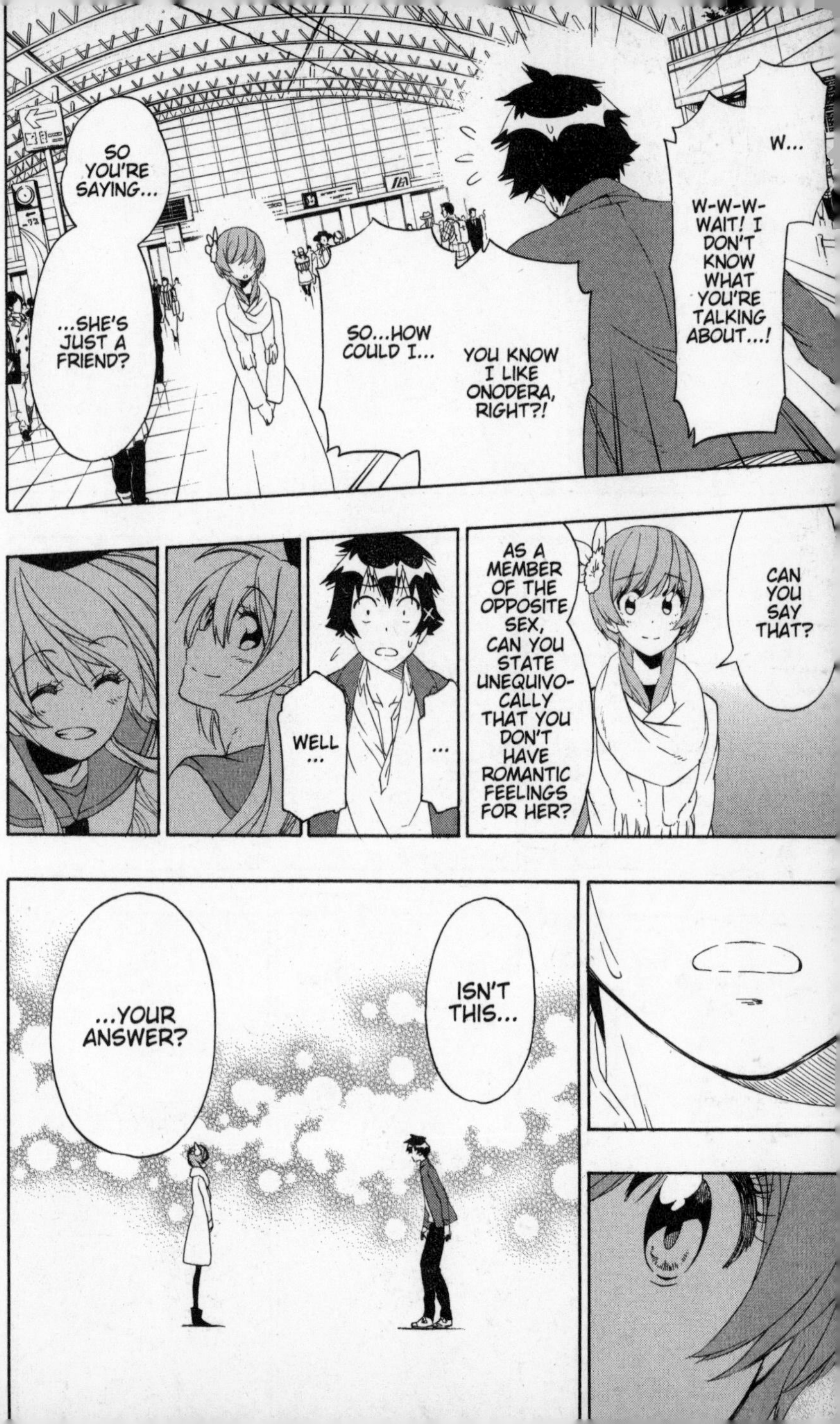
W...
W-W-W-WAIT! I DON'T KNOW WHAT YOU'RE TALKING ABOUT...!
YOU KNOW I LIKE ONODERA, RIGHT?!
SO...HOW COULD I...
SO YOU'RE SAYING...
...SHE'S JUST A FRIEND?
AS A MEMBER OF THE OPPOSITE SEX, CAN YOU STATE UNEQUIVO-CALLY THAT YOU DON'T HAVE ROMANTIC FEELINGS FOR HER?
CAN YOU SAY THAT?
...
WELL...
ISN'T THIS...
...YOUR ANSWER?

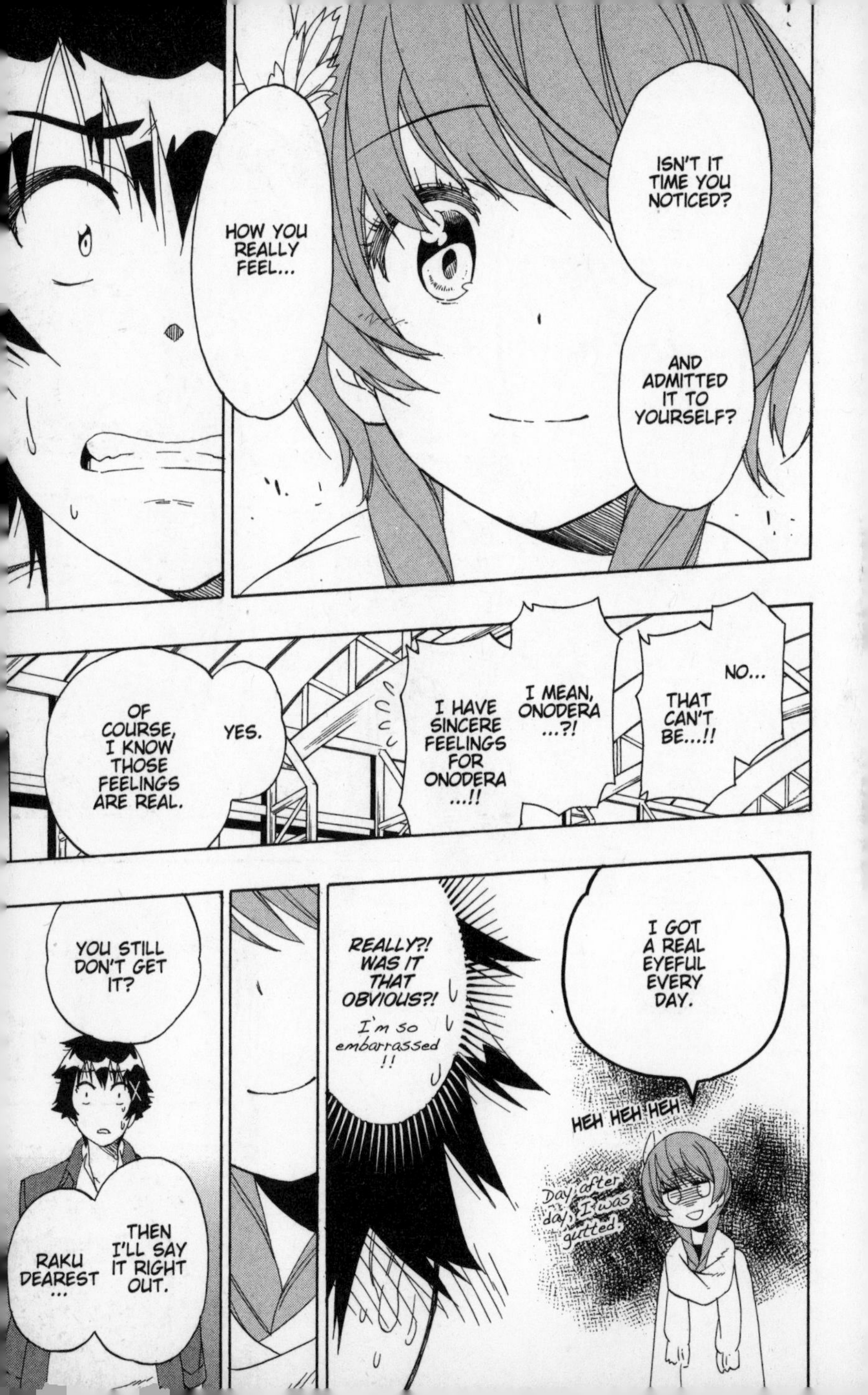
ISN'T IT TIME YOU NOTICED?
HOW YOU REALLY FEEL...
AND ADMITTED IT TO YOURSELF?
NO... THAT CAN'T BE...!!
I MEAN, ONODERA...?!
I HAVE SINCERE FEELINGS FOR ONODERA...!!
YES.
OF COURSE, I KNOW THOSE FEELINGS ARE REAL.
I GOT A REAL EYEFUL EVERY DAY.
HEH HEH HEH
Day after day, I was gutted.
REALLY?! WAS IT THAT OBVIOUS?!
I'm so embarrassed!!
YOU STILL DON'T GET IT?
THEN I'LL SAY IT RIGHT OUT.
RAKU DEAREST...

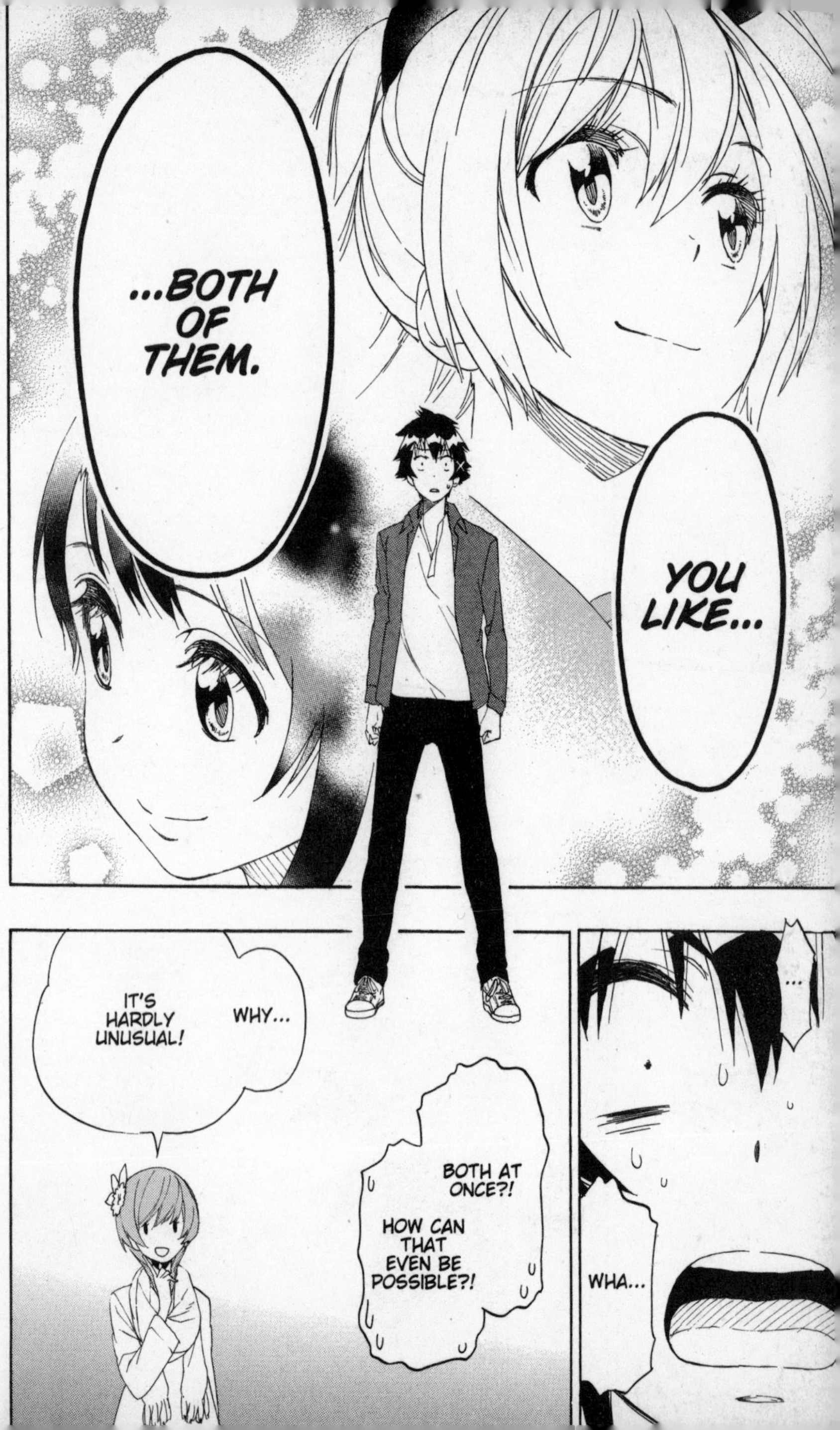
YOU LIKE...
...BOTH OF THEM.
...
WHA...
BOTH AT ONCE?!
HOW CAN THAT EVEN BE POSSIBLE?!
WHY...
IT'S HARDLY UNUSUAL!

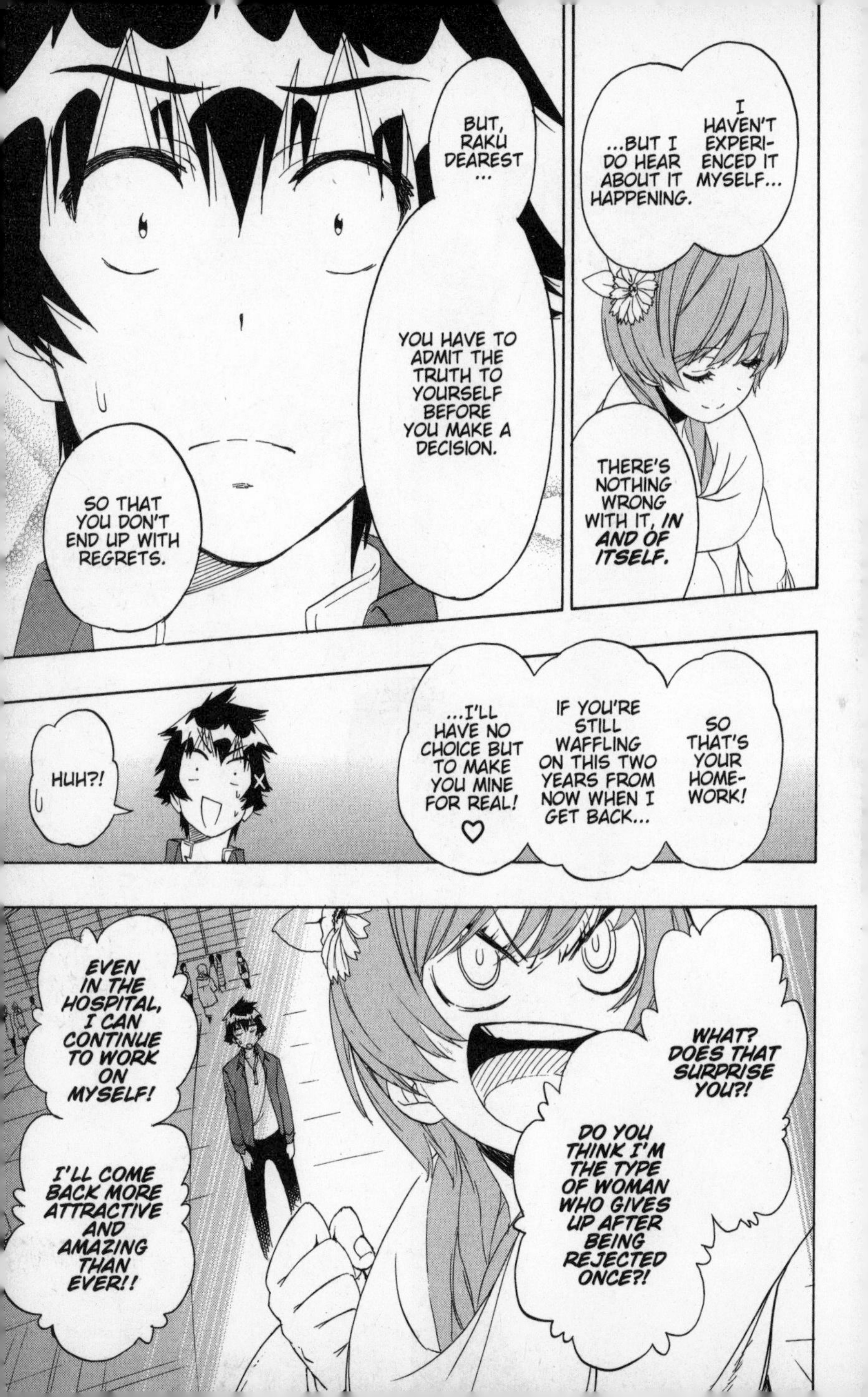
I HAVEN'T EXPERIENCED IT MYSELF...
...BUT I DO HEAR ABOUT IT HAPPENING.
THERE'S NOTHING WRONG WITH IT, *IN AND OF ITSELF.*
BUT, RAKU DEAREST...
YOU HAVE TO ADMIT THE TRUTH TO YOURSELF BEFORE YOU MAKE A DECISION.
SO THAT YOU DON'T END UP WITH REGRETS.
SO THAT'S YOUR HOMEWORK!
IF YOU'RE STILL WAFFLING ON THIS TWO YEARS FROM NOW WHEN I GET BACK...
...I'LL HAVE NO CHOICE BUT TO MAKE YOU MINE FOR REAL! ♡
HUH?!
WHAT? DOES THAT SURPRISE YOU?!
DO YOU THINK I'M THE TYPE OF WOMAN WHO GIVES UP AFTER BEING REJECTED ONCE?!
EVEN IN THE HOSPITAL, I CAN CONTINUE TO WORK ON MYSELF!
I'LL COME BACK MORE ATTRACTIVE AND AMAZING THAN EVER!!

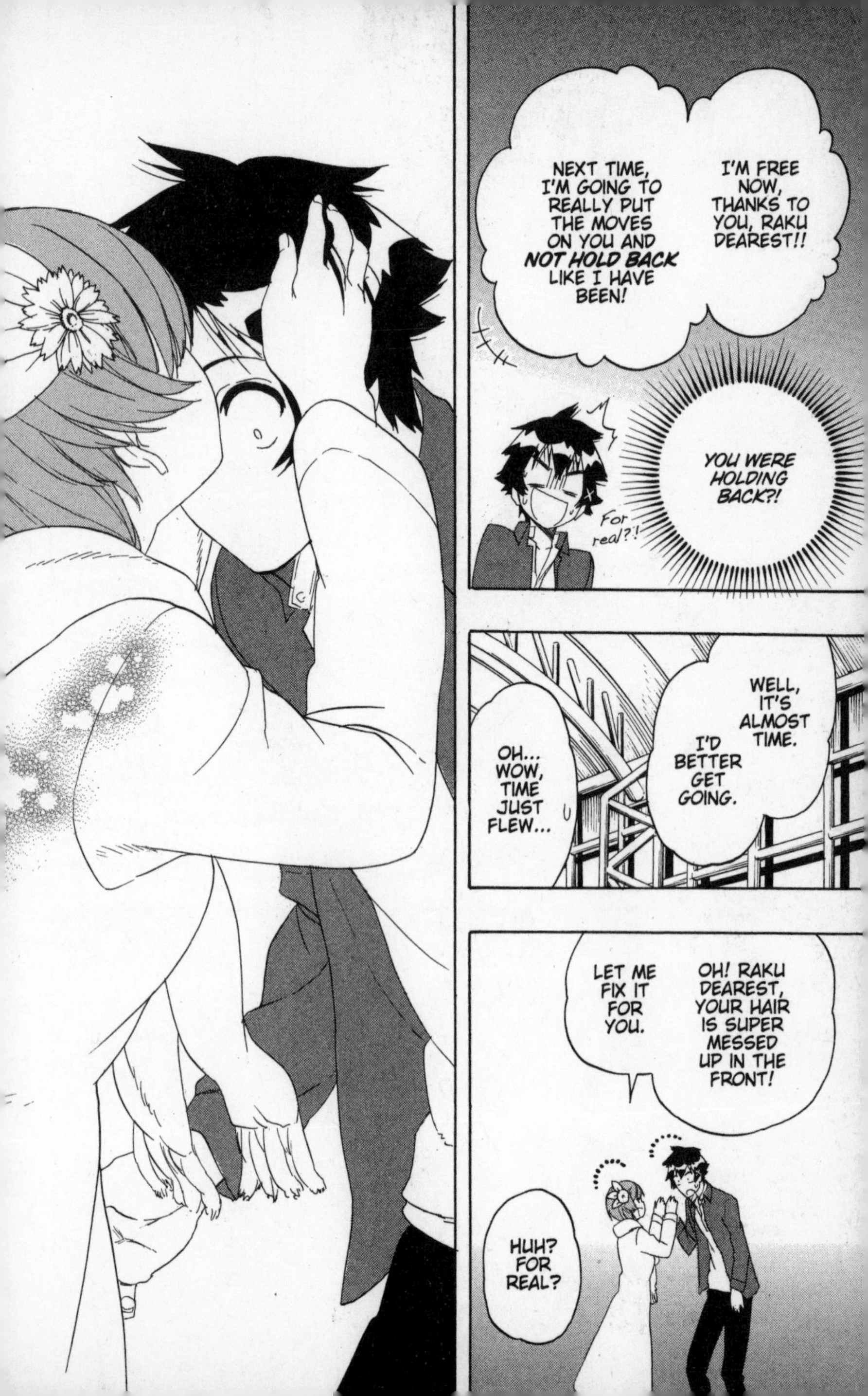
I'M FREE NOW, THANKS TO YOU, RAKU DEAREST!!
NEXT TIME, I'M GOING TO REALLY PUT THE MOVES ON YOU AND ***NOT HOLD BACK*** LIKE I HAVE BEEN!
YOU WERE HOLDING BACK?!
For real?!
WELL, IT'S ALMOST TIME.
I'D BETTER GET GOING.
OH... WOW, TIME JUST FLEW...
OH! RAKU DEAREST, YOUR HAIR IS SUPER MESSED UP IN THE FRONT!
LET ME FIX IT FOR YOU.
HUH? FOR REAL?

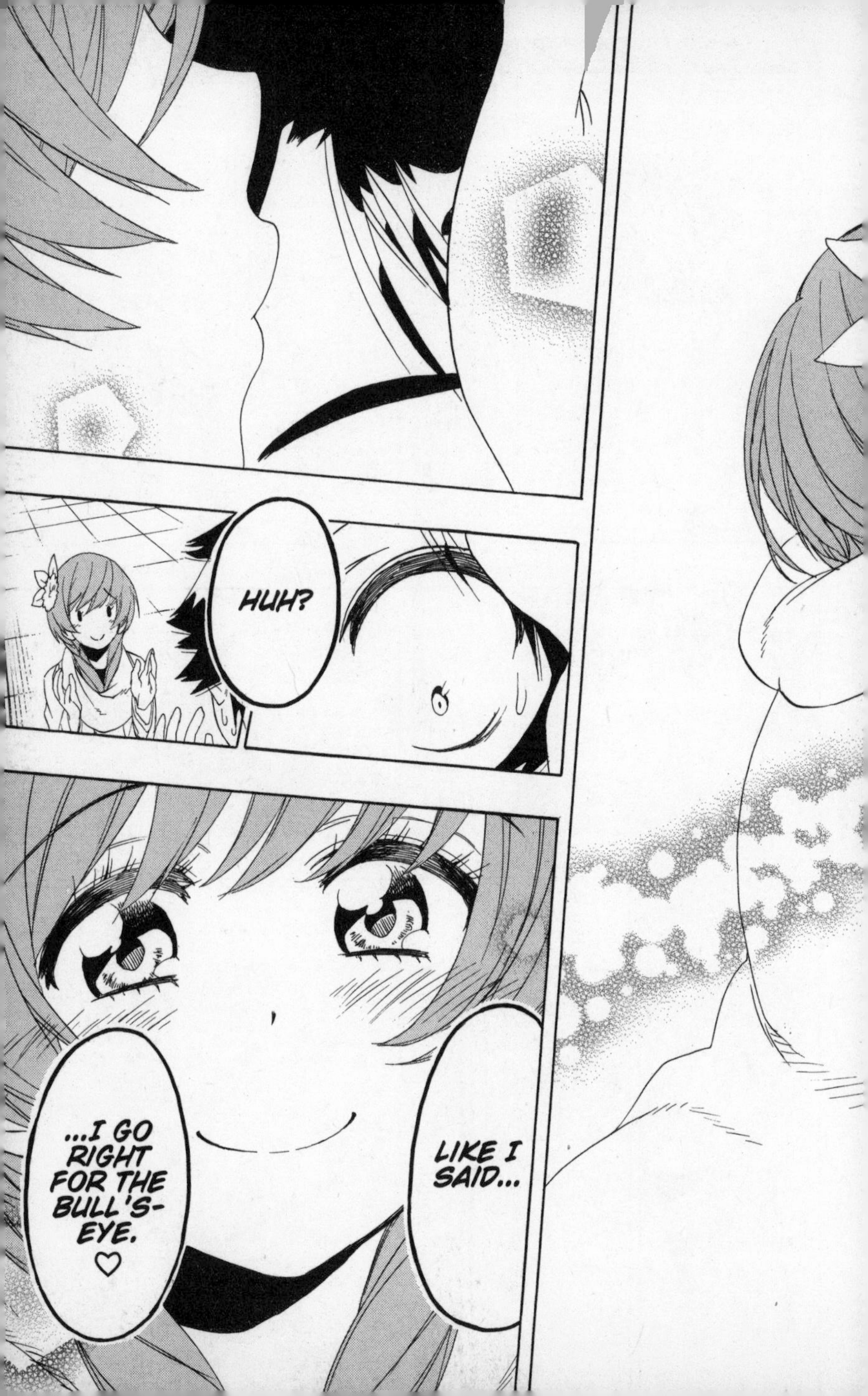
HUH?
LIKE I SAID...
...I GO RIGHT FOR THE BULL'S-EYE. ♡

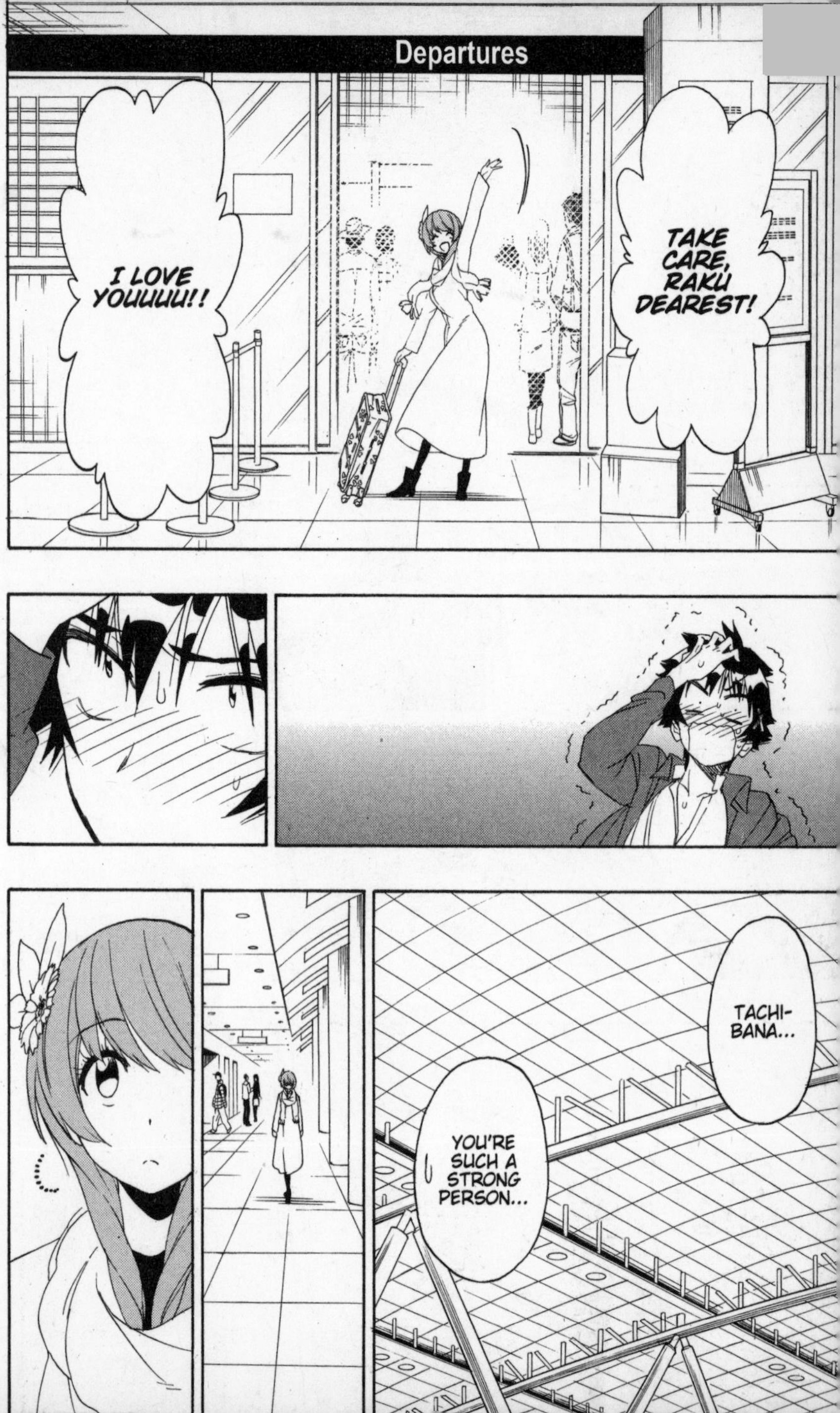
Departures
TAKE CARE, RAKU DEAREST!
I LOVE YOUUUU!!
TACHI-BANA...
YOU'RE SUCH A STRONG PERSON...

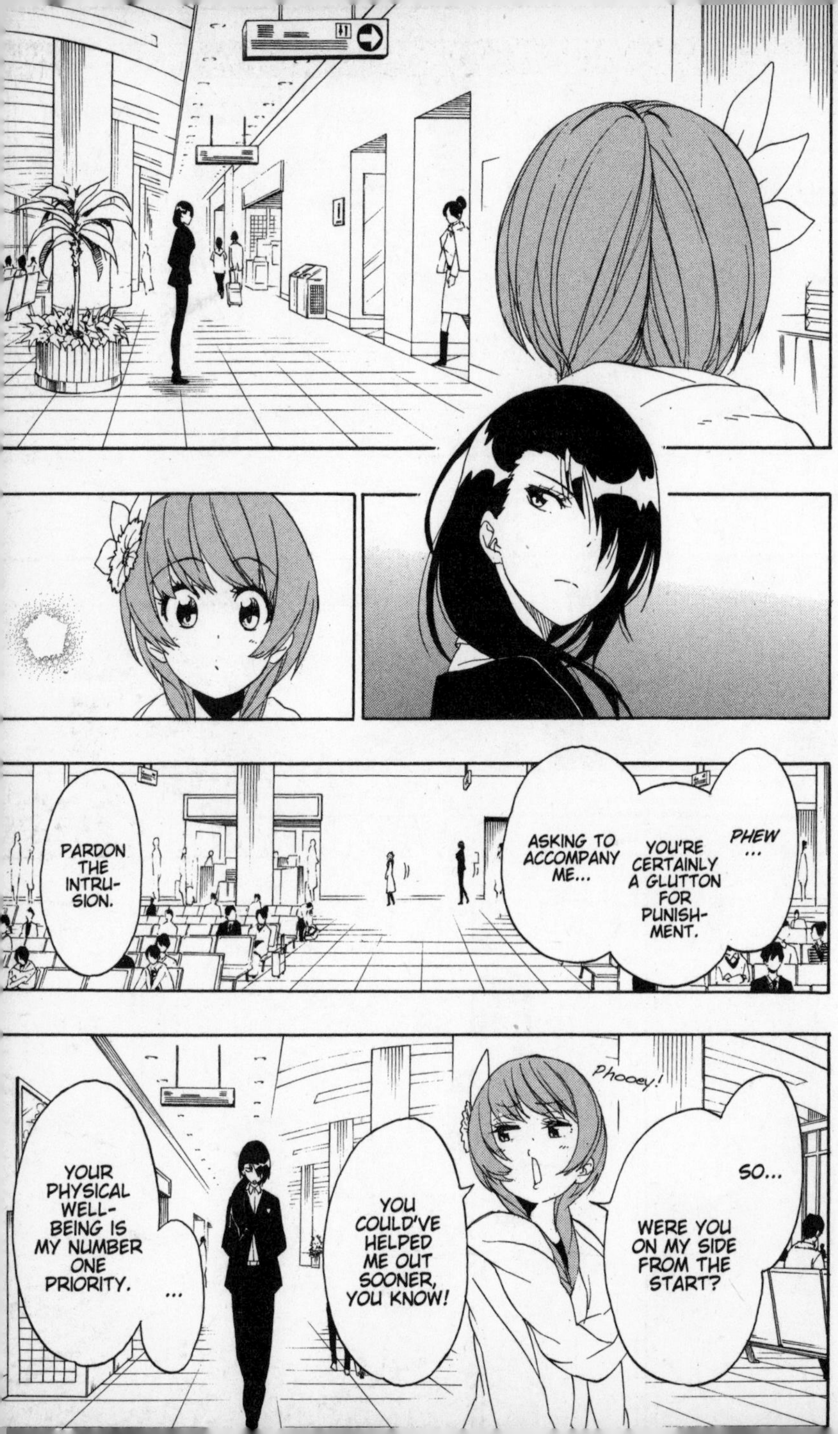
PHEW ...
YOU'RE CERTAINLY A GLUTTON FOR PUNISHMENT.
ASKING TO ACCOMPANY ME...
PARDON THE INTRUSION.
Phooey!
SO...
WERE YOU ON MY SIDE FROM THE START?
YOU COULD'VE HELPED ME OUT SOONER, YOU KNOW!
...
YOUR PHYSICAL WELL-BEING IS MY NUMBER ONE PRIORITY.

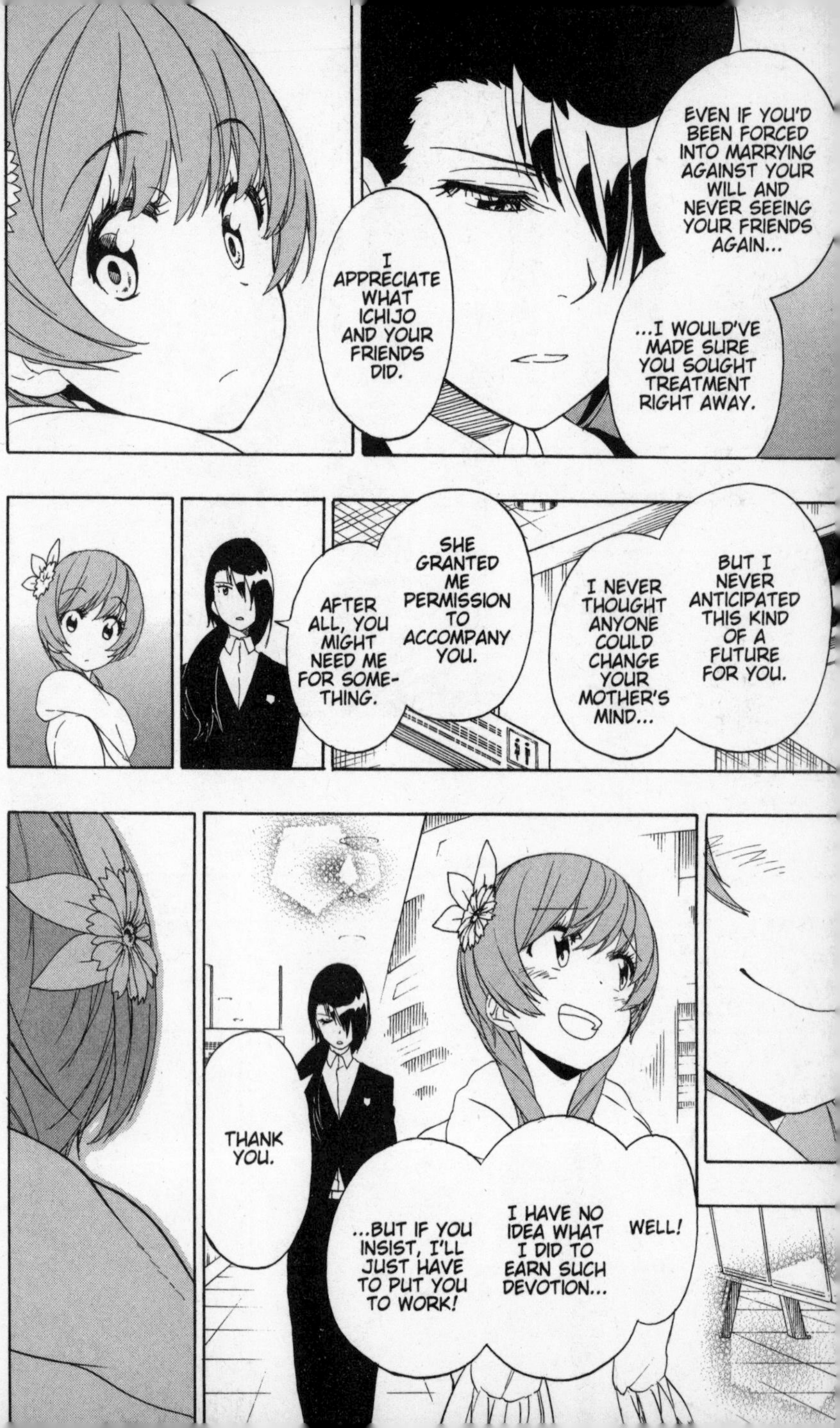
EVEN IF YOU'D BEEN FORCED INTO MARRYING AGAINST YOUR WILL AND NEVER SEEING YOUR FRIENDS AGAIN...
...I WOULD'VE MADE SURE YOU SOUGHT TREATMENT RIGHT AWAY.
I APPRECIATE WHAT ICHIJO AND YOUR FRIENDS DID.
BUT I NEVER ANTICIPATED THIS KIND OF A FUTURE FOR YOU.
I NEVER THOUGHT ANYONE COULD CHANGE YOUR MOTHER'S MIND...
SHE GRANTED ME PERMISSION TO ACCOMPANY YOU.
AFTER ALL, YOU MIGHT NEED ME FOR SOME-THING.
WELL!
I HAVE NO IDEA WHAT I DID TO EARN SUCH DEVOTION...
...BUT IF YOU INSIST, I'LL JUST HAVE TO PUT YOU TO WORK!
THANK YOU.

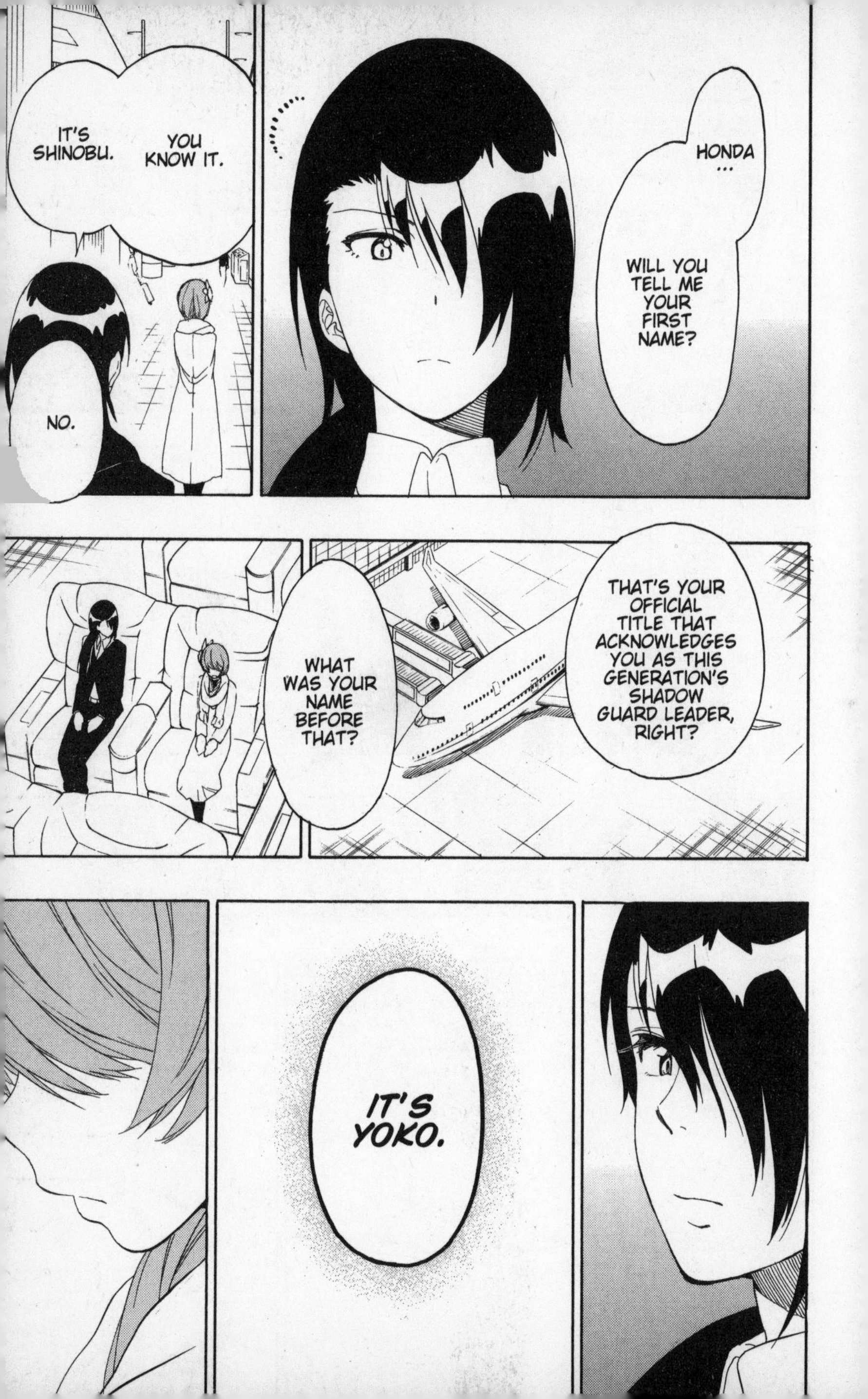
HONDA ... WILL YOU TELL ME YOUR FIRST NAME?
......
IT'S SHINOBU. YOU KNOW IT.
NO.
THAT'S YOUR OFFICIAL TITLE THAT ACKNOWLEDGES YOU AS THIS GENERATION'S SHADOW GUARD LEADER, RIGHT?
WHAT WAS YOUR NAME BEFORE THAT?
IT'S YOKO.

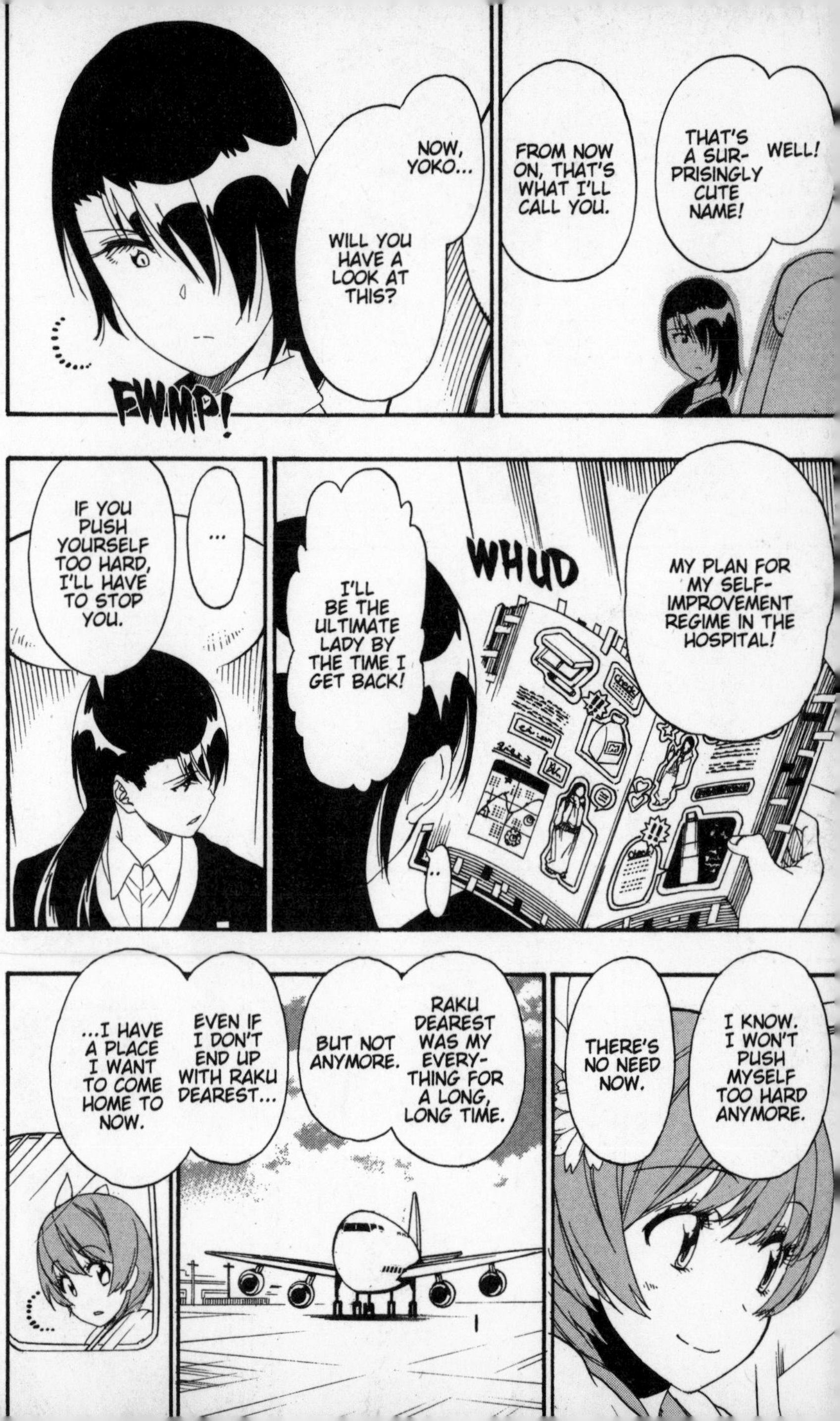
WELL!
THAT'S A SURPRISINGLY CUTE NAME!
FROM NOW ON, THAT'S WHAT I'LL CALL YOU.
NOW, YOKO...
WILL YOU HAVE A LOOK AT THIS?
......
FWMP!
MY PLAN FOR MY SELF-IMPROVEMENT REGIME IN THE HOSPITAL!
WHUD
I'LL BE THE ULTIMATE LADY BY THE TIME I GET BACK!
...
...
IF YOU PUSH YOURSELF TOO HARD, I'LL HAVE TO STOP YOU.
I KNOW. I WON'T PUSH MYSELF TOO HARD ANYMORE.
THERE'S NO NEED NOW.
RAKU DEAREST WAS MY EVERYTHING FOR A LONG, LONG TIME.
BUT NOT ANYMORE.
EVEN IF I DON'T END UP WITH RAKU DEAREST...
...I HAVE A PLACE I WANT TO COME HOME TO NOW.
......

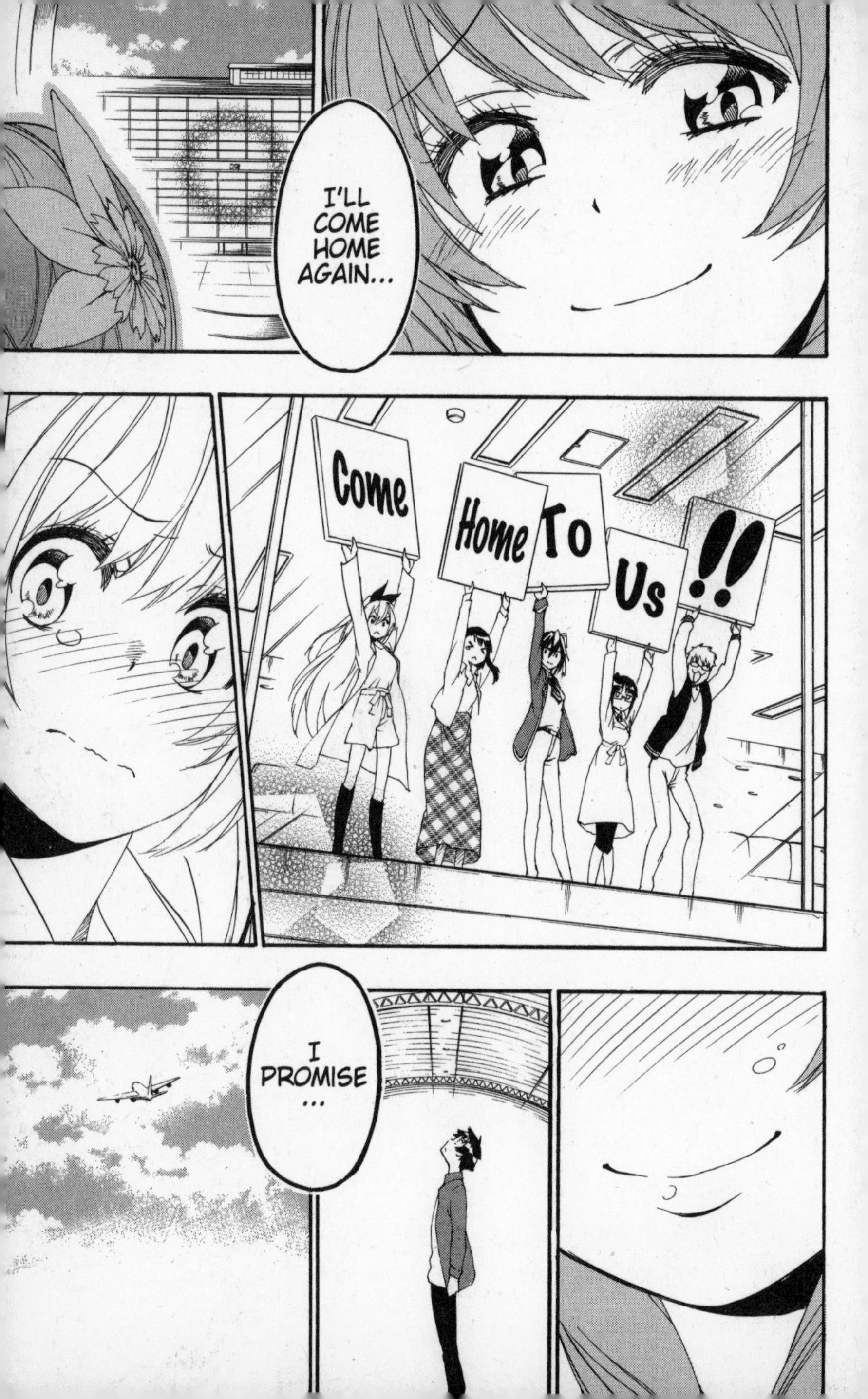
I'LL COME HOME AGAIN...
Come Home To Us!!
I PROMISE ...

Yoko...
Please face the other way for a little while.
SNIFFLE
Of course.

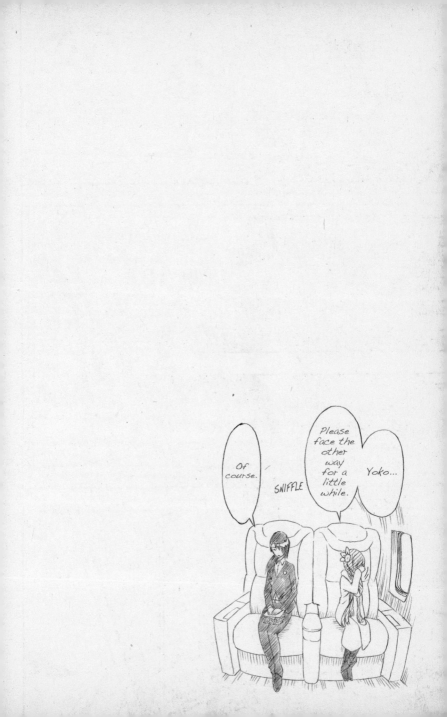

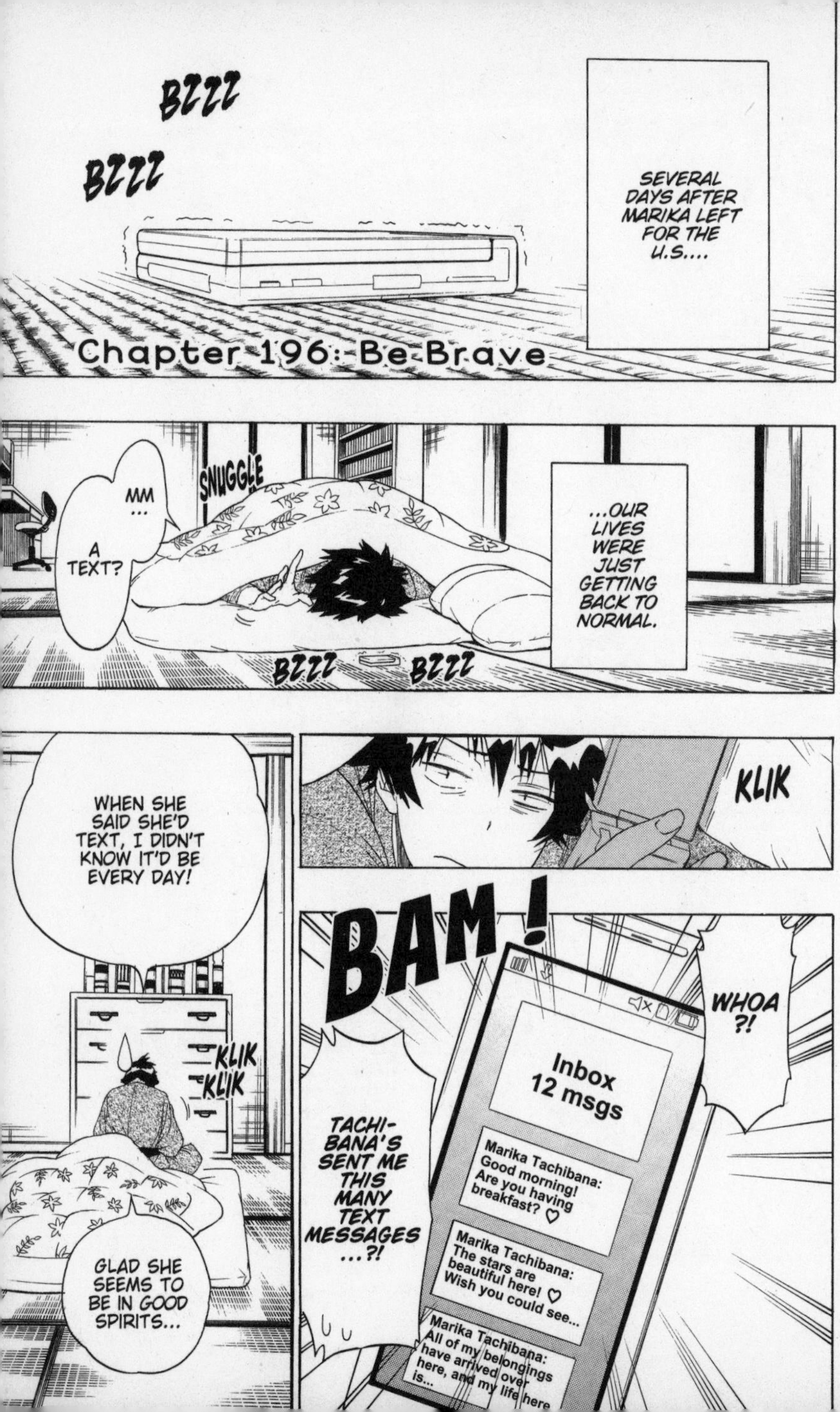
SEVERAL DAYS AFTER MARIKA LEFT FOR THE U.S....
BZZZ
BZZZ
Chapter 196: Be Brave
...OUR LIVES WERE JUST GETTING BACK TO NORMAL.
BZZZ
BZZZ
SNUGGLE
MM... A TEXT?
KLIK
WHOA?!
BAM!
Inbox 12 msgs
Marika Tachibana: Good morning! Are you having breakfast? ♡
Marika Tachibana: The stars are beautiful here! ♡ Wish you could see...
Marika Tachibana: All of my belongings have arrived over here, and my life here is...
TACHIBANA'S SENT ME THIS MANY TEXT MESSAGES...?!
WHEN SHE SAID SHE'D TEXT, I DIDN'T KNOW IT'D BE EVERY DAY!
KLIK
KLIK
GLAD SHE SEEMS TO BE IN GOOD SPIRITS...

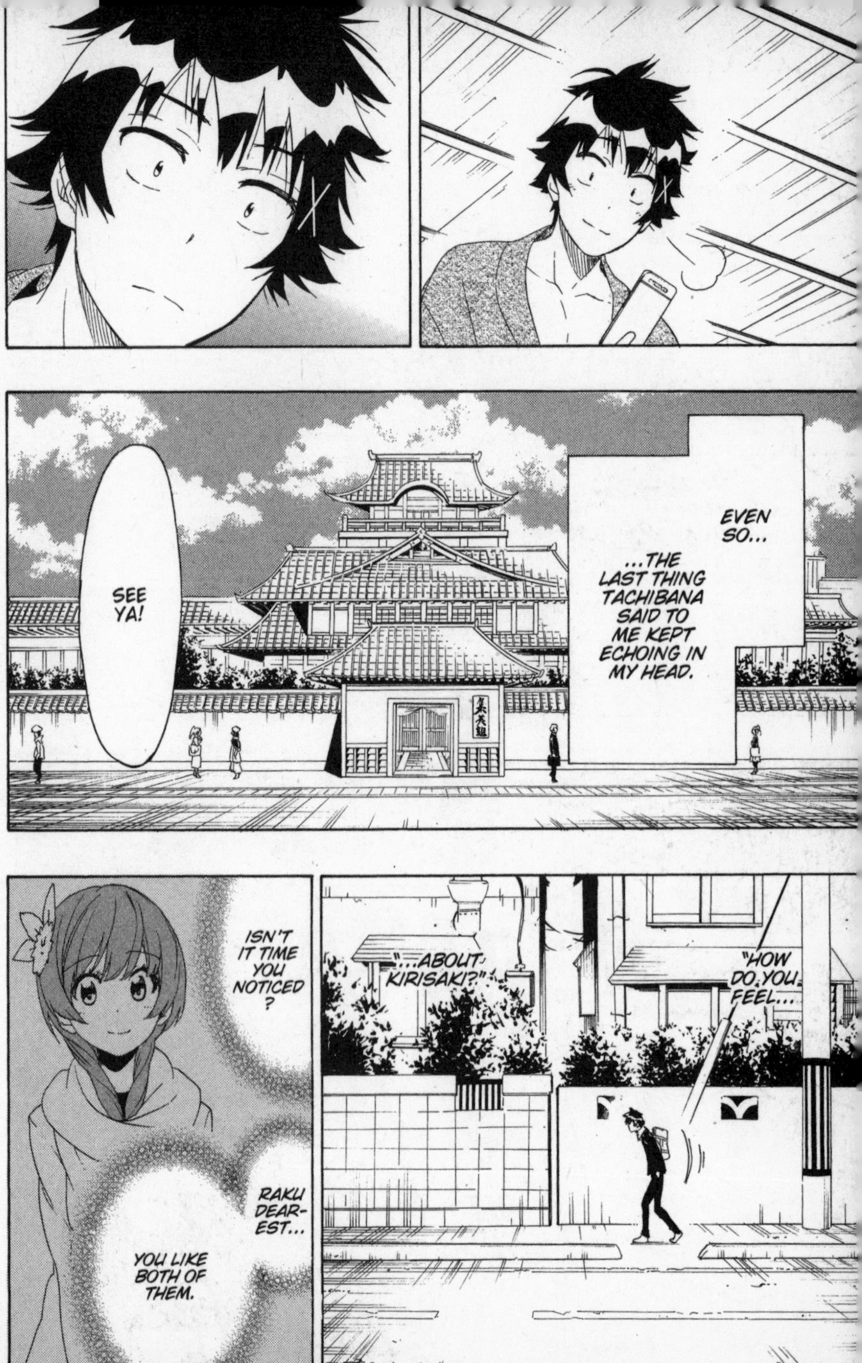
EVEN SO...
...THE LAST THING TACHIBANA SAID TO ME KEPT ECHOING IN MY HEAD.
SEE YA!
"HOW DO YOU FEEL...
"...ABOUT KIRISAKI?"
ISN'T IT TIME YOU NOTICED?
RAKU DEAREST...
YOU LIKE BOTH OF THEM.

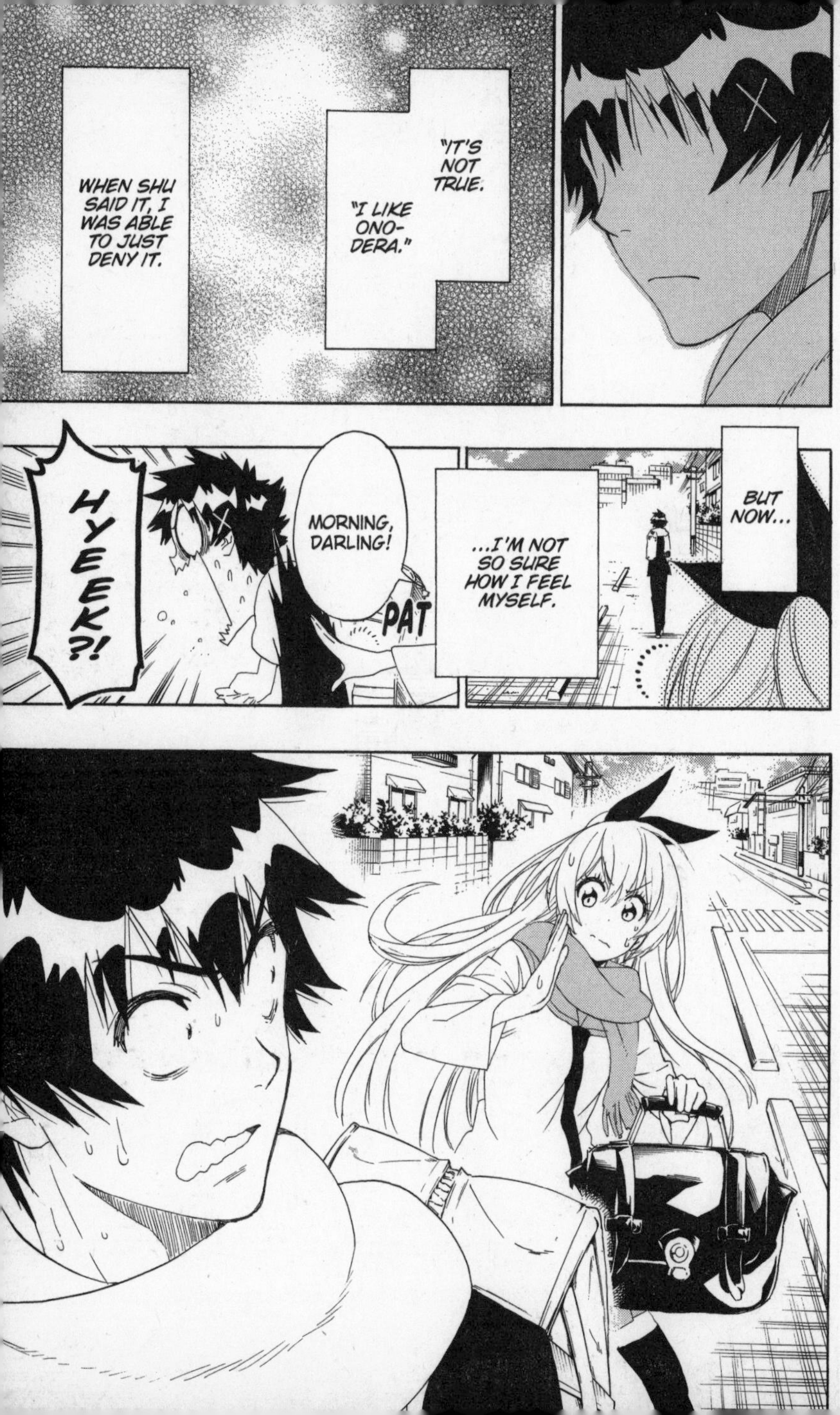
"IT'S NOT TRUE.
"I LIKE ONO-DERA."
WHEN SHU SAID IT, I WAS ABLE TO JUST DENY IT.
BUT NOW...
...I'M NOT SO SURE HOW I FEEL MYSELF.
MORNING, DARLING!
PAT
HYEEEK?!

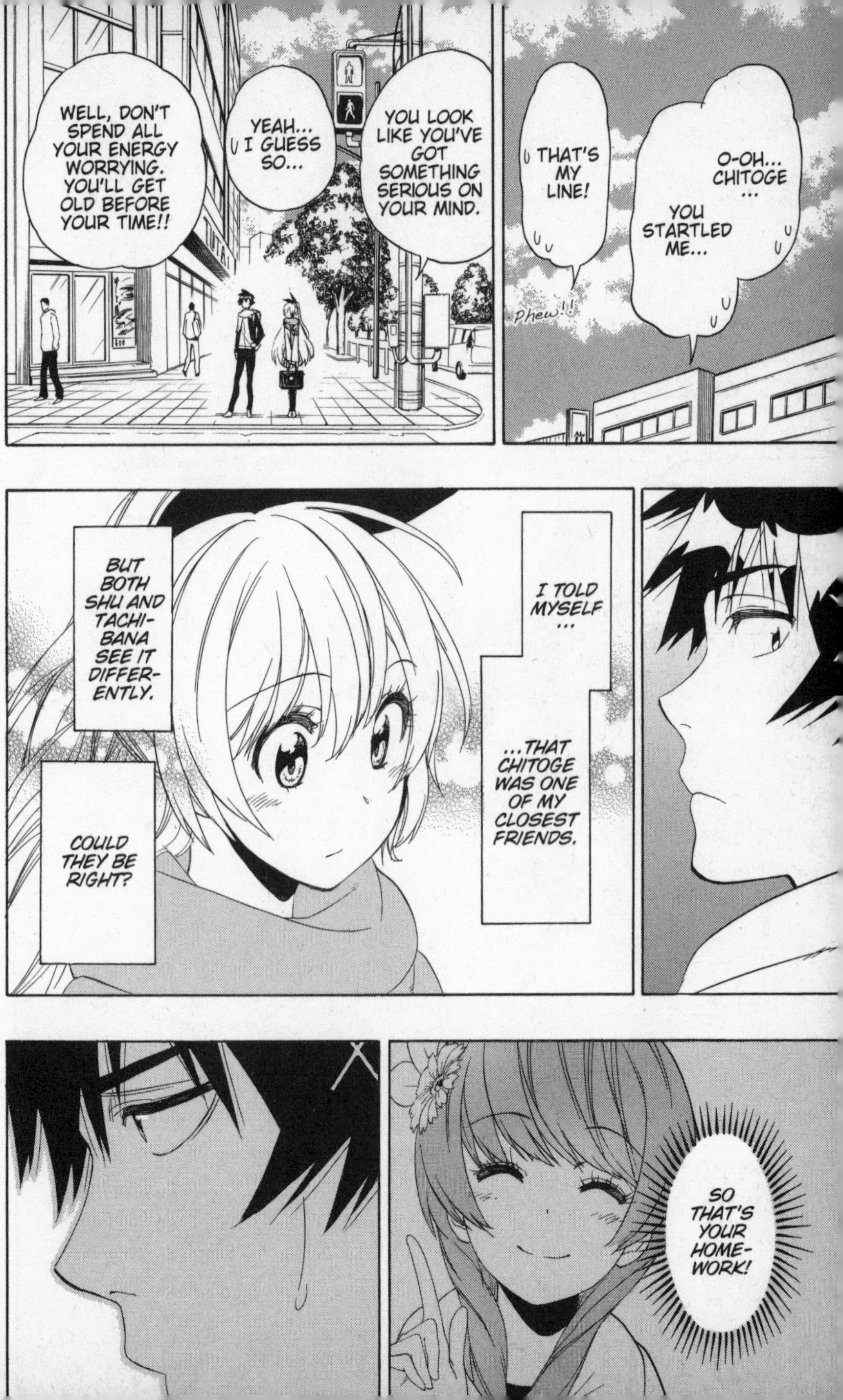
O-OH... CHITOGE... YOU STARTLED ME...
THAT'S MY LINE!
Phew!!
YOU LOOK LIKE YOU'VE GOT SOMETHING SERIOUS ON YOUR MIND.
YEAH... I GUESS SO...
WELL, DON'T SPEND ALL YOUR ENERGY WORRYING. YOU'LL GET OLD BEFORE YOUR TIME!!
I TOLD MYSELF...
...THAT CHITOGE WAS ONE OF MY CLOSEST FRIENDS.
BUT BOTH SHU AND TACHI-BANA SEE IT DIFFER-ENTLY.
COULD THEY BE RIGHT?
SO THAT'S YOUR HOME-WORK!

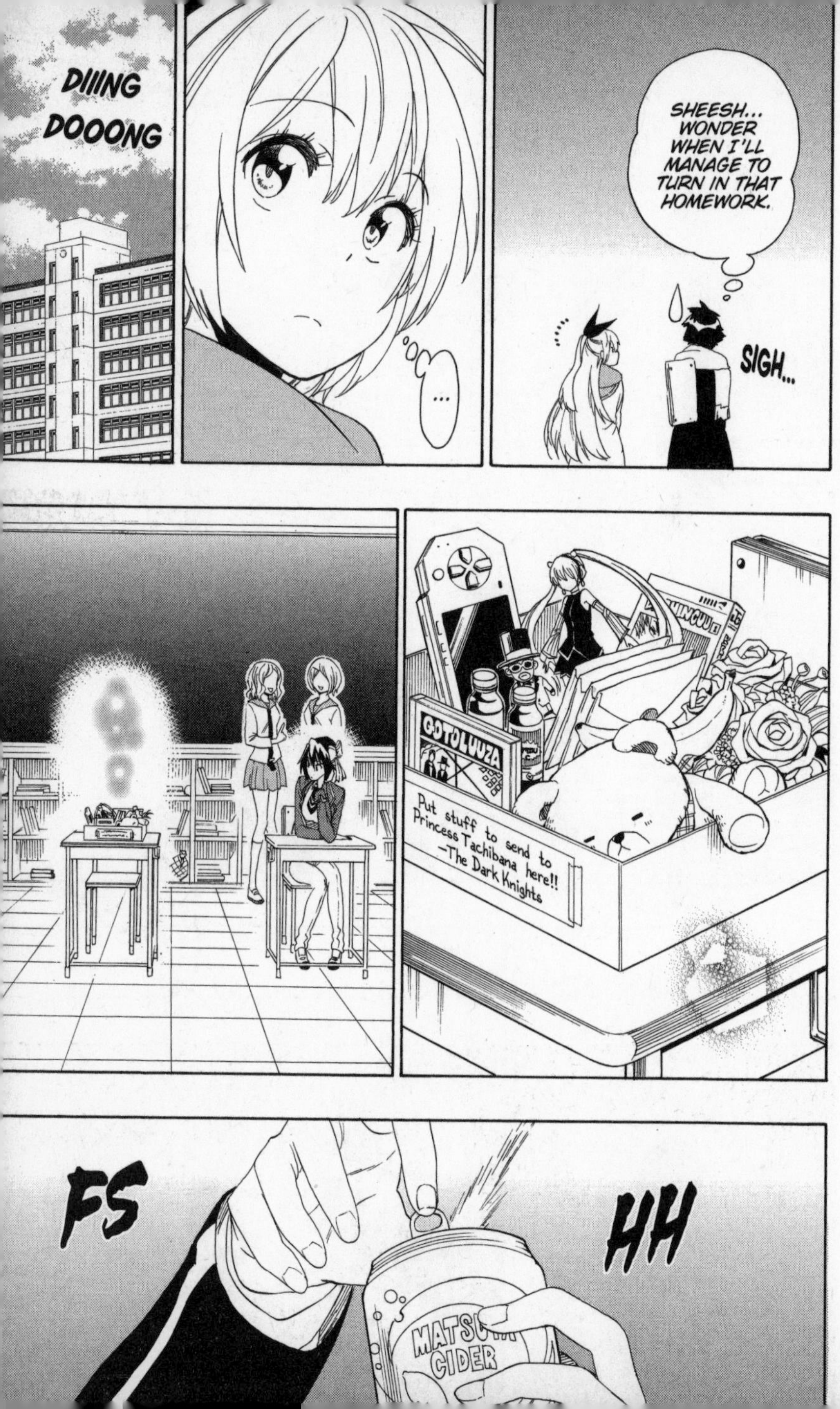
SHEESH... WONDER WHEN I'LL MANAGE TO TURN IN THAT HOMEWORK.
SIGH...
...
DIIING DOOONG
GOTOLUUZA
Put stuff to send to Princess Tachibana here!! —The Dark Knights
FS
HH
CIDER

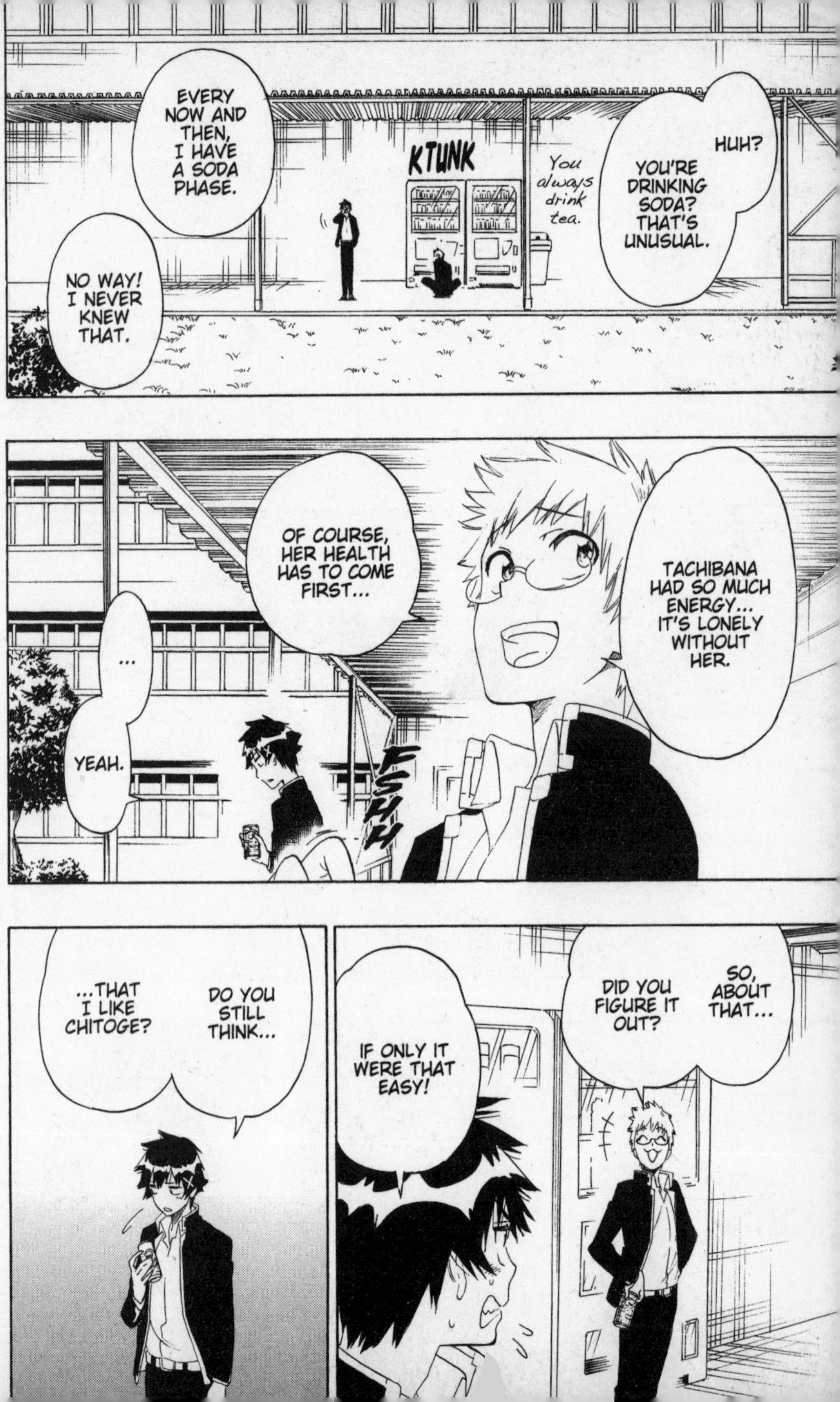
HUH?
YOU'RE DRINKING SODA? THAT'S UNUSUAL.
You always drink tea.
KTUNK
EVERY NOW AND THEN, I HAVE A SODA PHASE.
NO WAY! I NEVER KNEW THAT.
TACHIBANA HAD SO MUCH ENERGY... IT'S LONELY WITHOUT HER.
OF COURSE, HER HEALTH HAS TO COME FIRST...
...
YEAH.
FSHH
SO, ABOUT THAT...
DID YOU FIGURE IT OUT?
IF ONLY IT WERE THAT EASY!
DO YOU STILL THINK...
...THAT I LIKE CHITOGE?

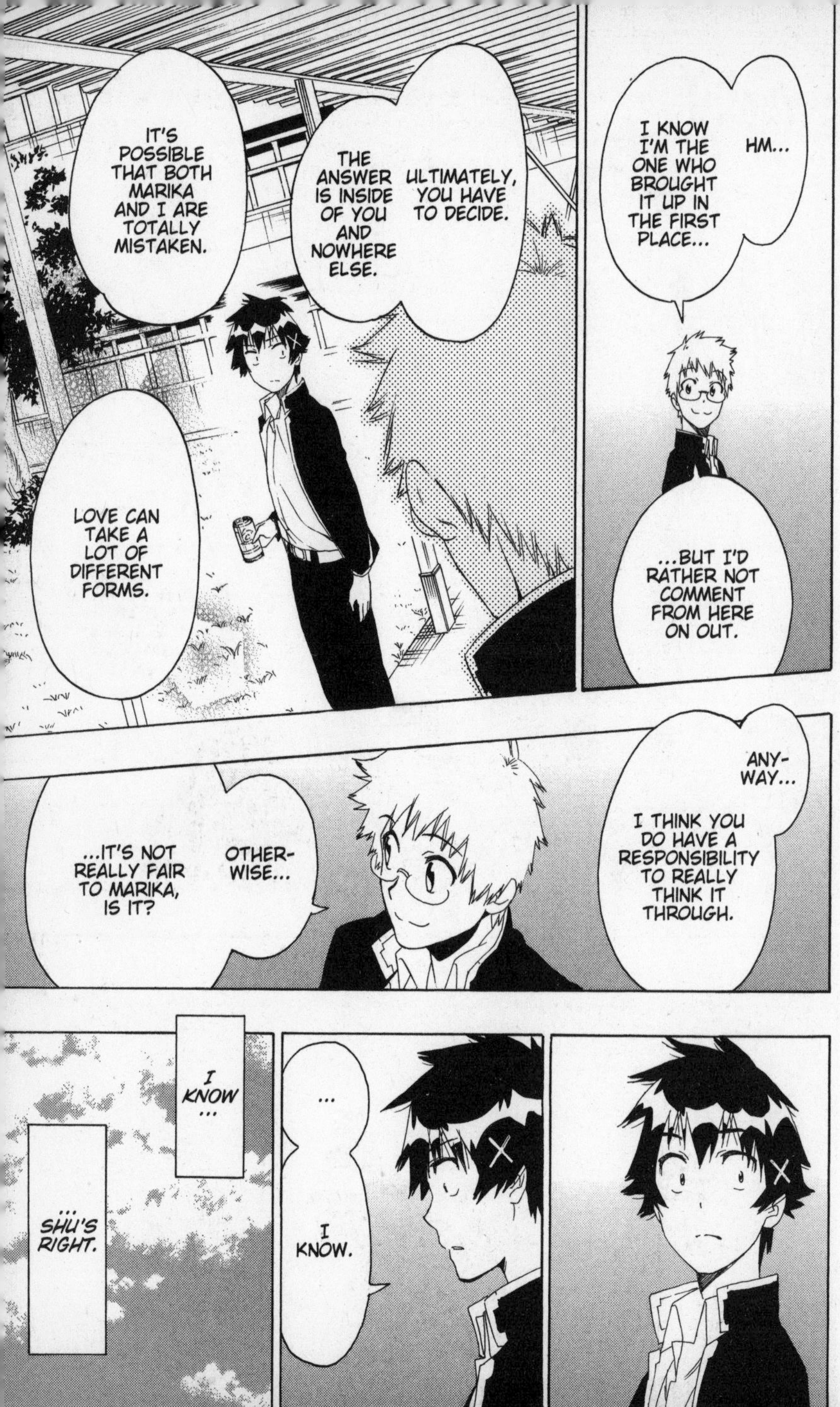
HM...
I KNOW I'M THE ONE WHO BROUGHT IT UP IN THE FIRST PLACE...
...BUT I'D RATHER NOT COMMENT FROM HERE ON OUT.
ULTIMATELY, YOU HAVE TO DECIDE.
THE ANSWER IS INSIDE OF YOU AND NOWHERE ELSE.
IT'S POSSIBLE THAT BOTH MARIKA AND I ARE TOTALLY MISTAKEN.
LOVE CAN TAKE A LOT OF DIFFERENT FORMS.
ANY-WAY...
I THINK YOU DO HAVE A RESPONSIBILITY TO REALLY THINK IT THROUGH.
OTHER-WISE...
...IT'S NOT REALLY FAIR TO MARIKA, IS IT?
...
I KNOW.
I KNOW...
...SHŪ'S RIGHT.

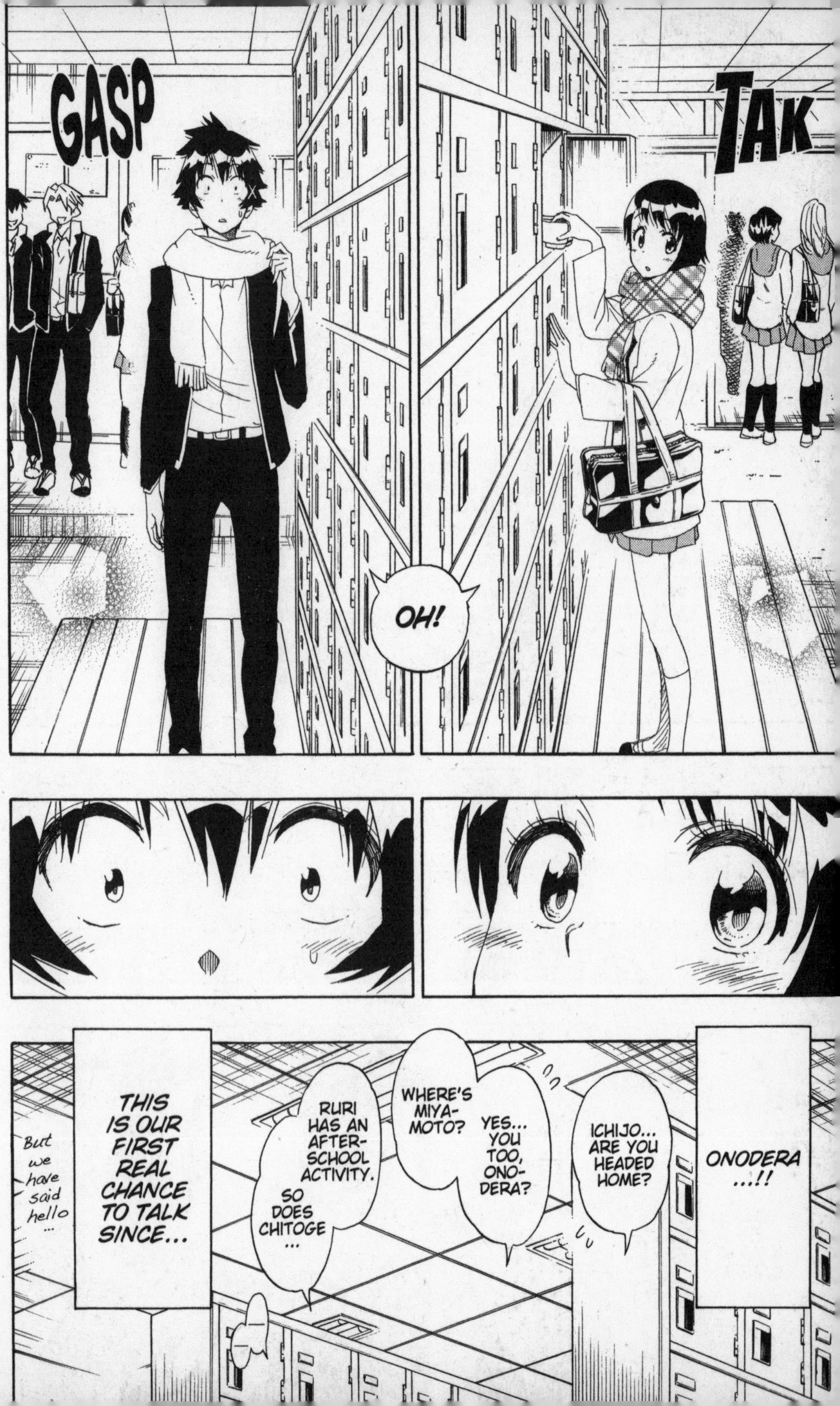
TAK
OH!
GASP
ONODERA ...!!
ICHIJO... ARE YOU HEADED HOME?
YES... YOU TOO, ONO-DERA?
WHERE'S MIYA-MOTO?
RURI HAS AN AFTER-SCHOOL ACTIVITY.
SO DOES CHITOGE ...
THIS IS OUR FIRST REAL CHANCE TO TALK SINCE...
But we have said hello ...

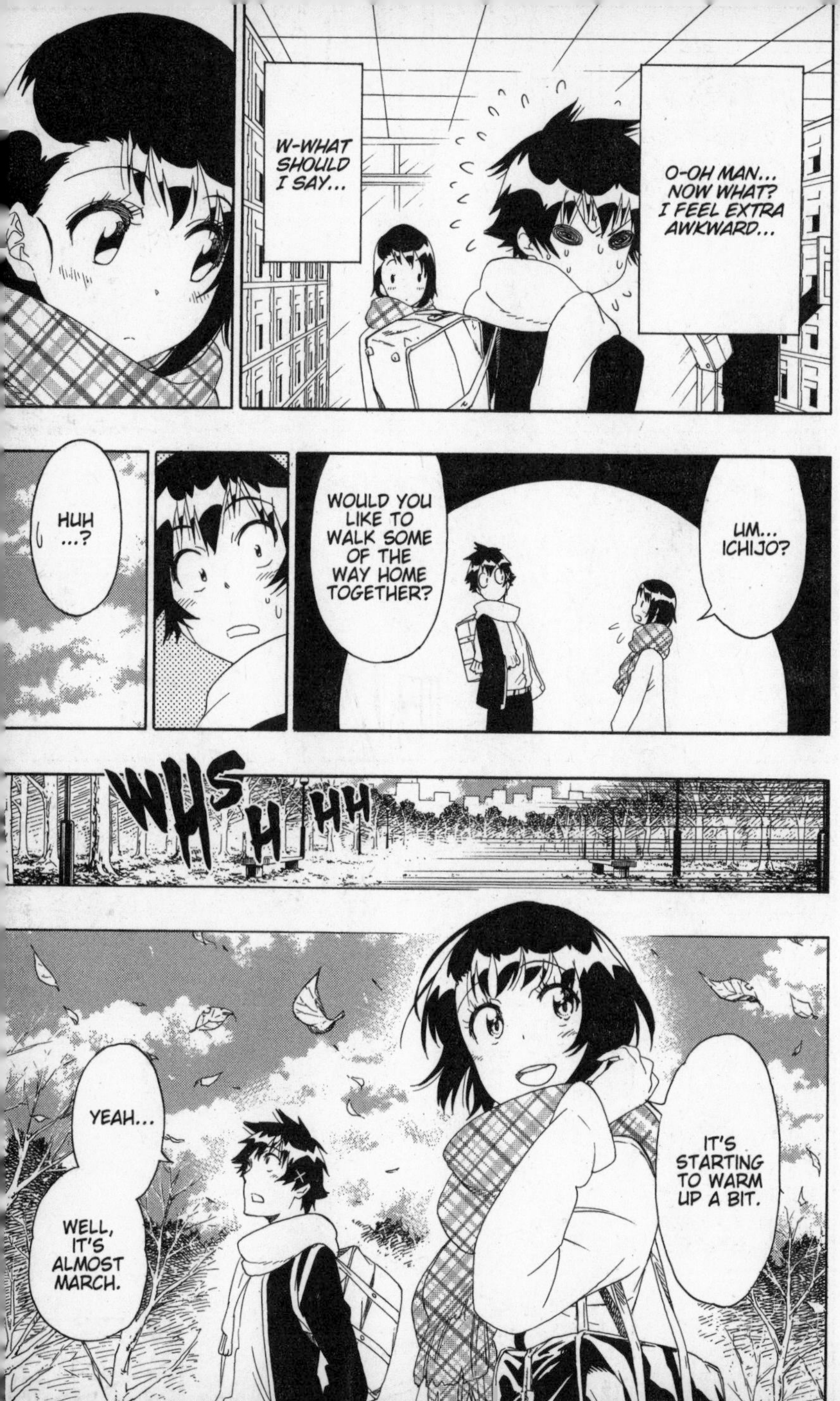
O-OH MAN... NOW WHAT? I FEEL EXTRA AWKWARD...
W-WHAT SHOULD I SAY...
UM... ICHIJO?
WOULD YOU LIKE TO WALK SOME OF THE WAY HOME TOGETHER?
HUH ...?
WHSHHH
IT'S STARTING TO WARM UP A BIT.
YEAH...
WELL, IT'S ALMOST MARCH.

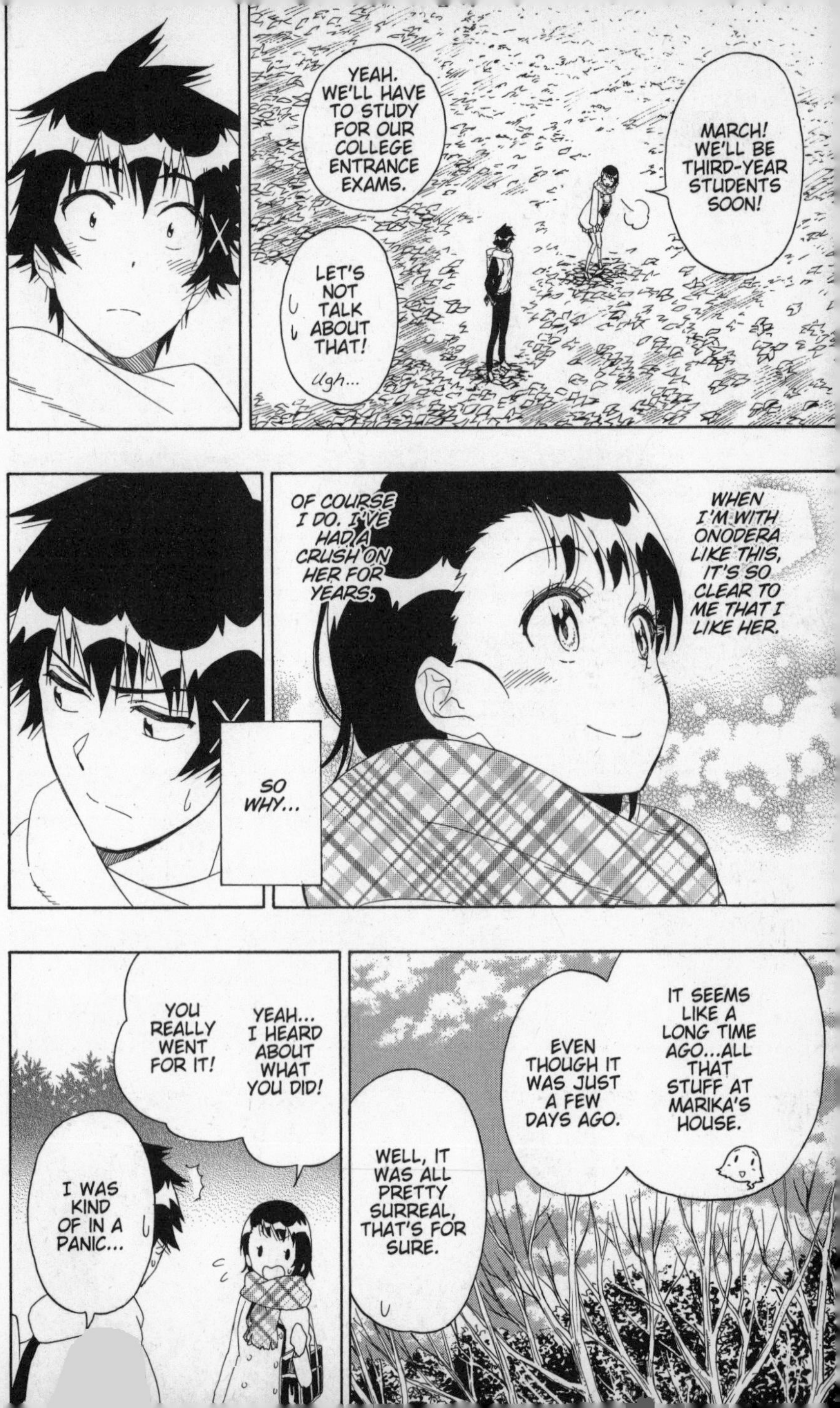
MARCH! WE'LL BE THIRD-YEAR STUDENTS SOON!
YEAH. WE'LL HAVE TO STUDY FOR OUR COLLEGE ENTRANCE EXAMS.
LET'S NOT TALK ABOUT THAT!
Ugh...
WHEN I'M WITH ONODERA LIKE THIS, IT'S SO CLEAR TO ME THAT I LIKE HER.
OF COURSE I DO. I'VE HAD A CRUSH ON HER FOR YEARS.
SO WHY...
IT SEEMS LIKE A LONG TIME AGO...ALL THAT STUFF AT MARIKA'S HOUSE.
EVEN THOUGH IT WAS JUST A FEW DAYS AGO.
WELL, IT WAS ALL PRETTY SURREAL, THAT'S FOR SURE.
YEAH... I HEARD ABOUT WHAT YOU DID!
YOU REALLY WENT FOR IT!
I WAS KIND OF IN A PANIC...

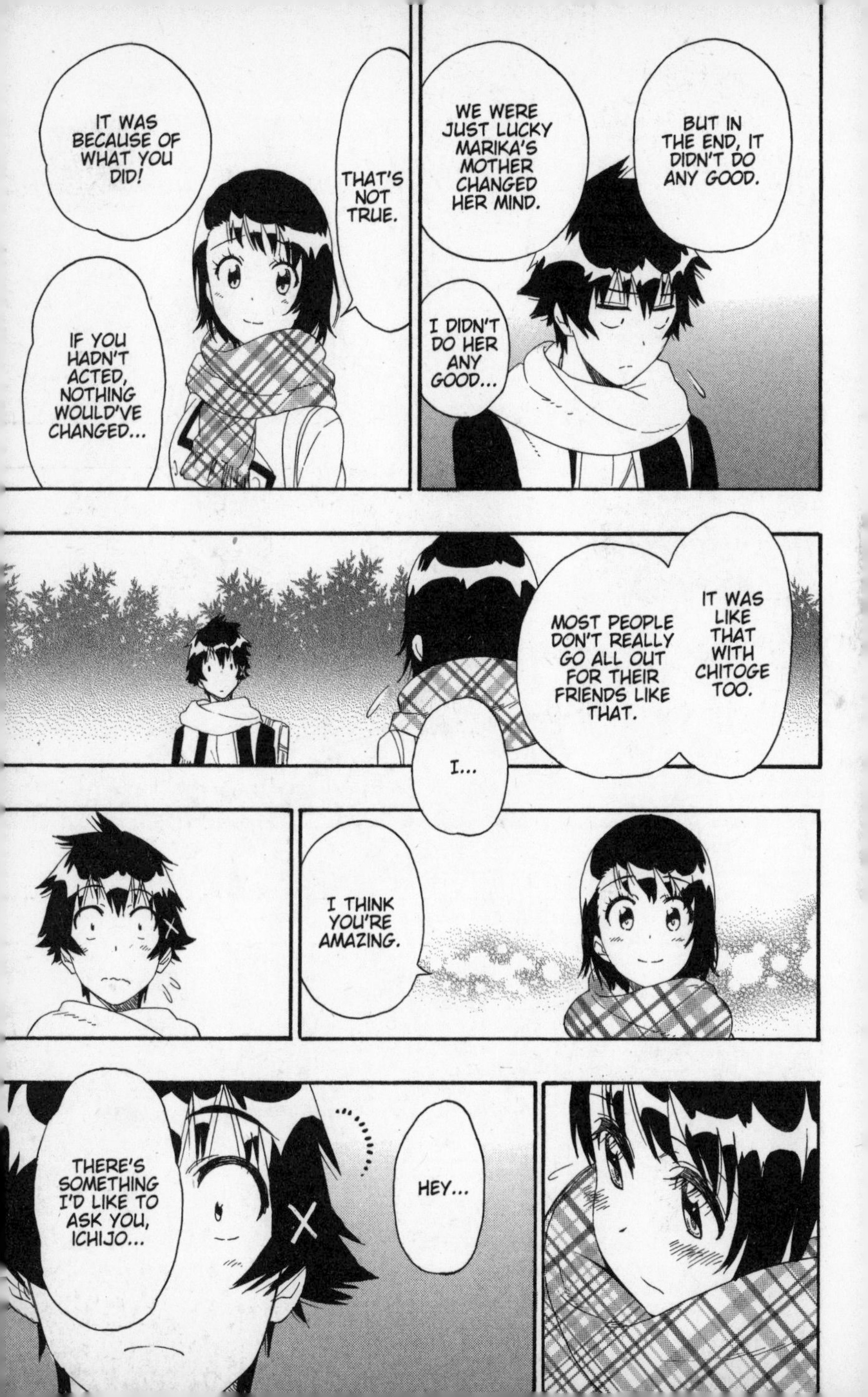
BUT IN THE END, IT DIDN'T DO ANY GOOD.
WE WERE JUST LUCKY MARIKA'S MOTHER CHANGED HER MIND.
I DIDN'T DO HER ANY GOOD...
THAT'S NOT TRUE.
IT WAS BECAUSE OF WHAT YOU DID!
IF YOU HADN'T ACTED, NOTHING WOULD'VE CHANGED...
IT WAS LIKE THAT WITH CHITOGE TOO.
MOST PEOPLE DON'T REALLY GO ALL OUT FOR THEIR FRIENDS LIKE THAT.
I...
I THINK YOU'RE AMAZING.
HEY...
THERE'S SOMETHING I'D LIKE TO ASK YOU, ICHIJO...

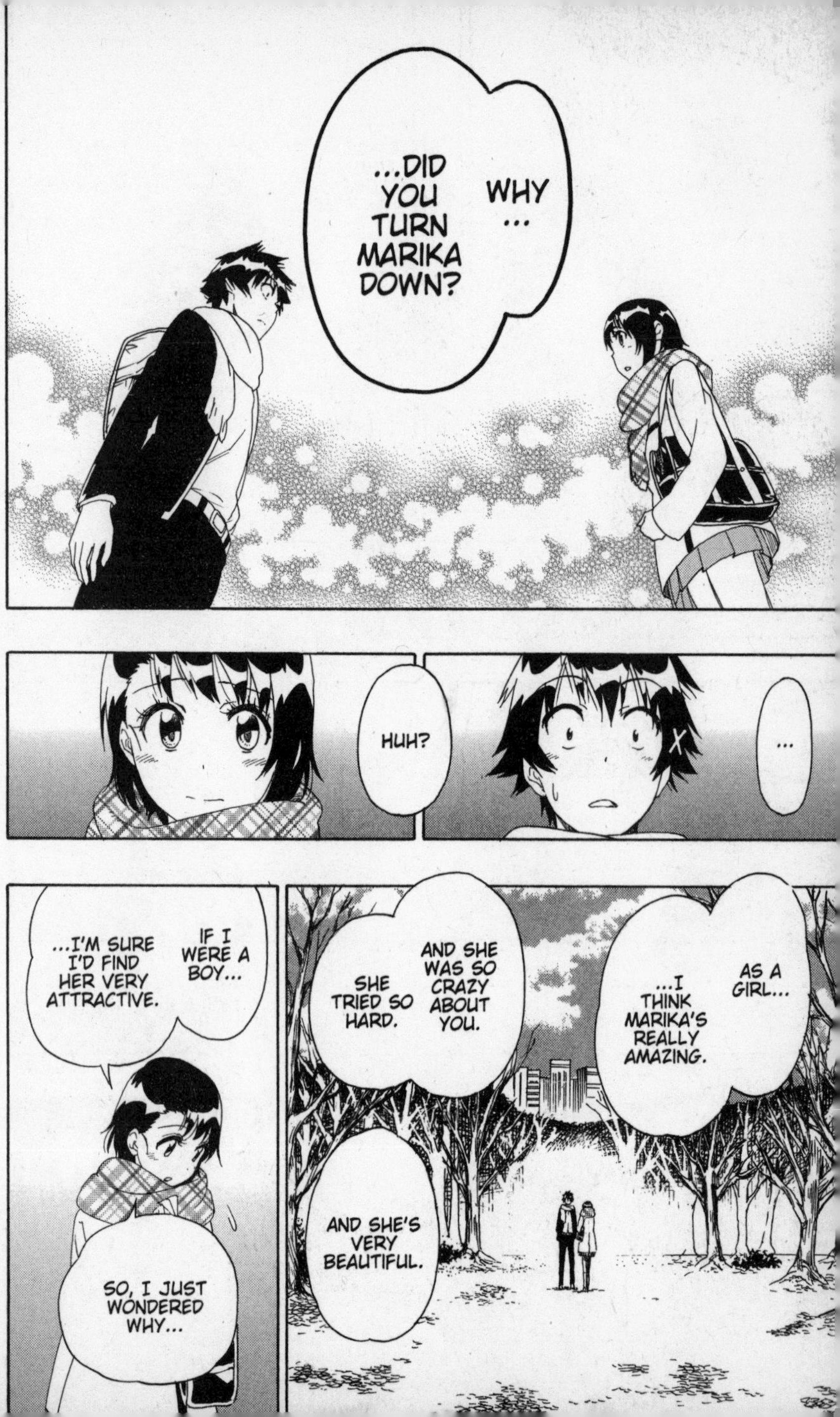
WHY... ...DID YOU TURN MARIKA DOWN?
...
HUH?
AS A GIRL... ...I THINK MARIKA'S REALLY AMAZING.
AND SHE WAS SO CRAZY ABOUT YOU. SHE TRIED SO HARD.
AND SHE'S VERY BEAUTIFUL.
IF I WERE A BOY... ...I'M SURE I'D FIND HER VERY ATTRACTIVE.
SO, I JUST WONDERED WHY...

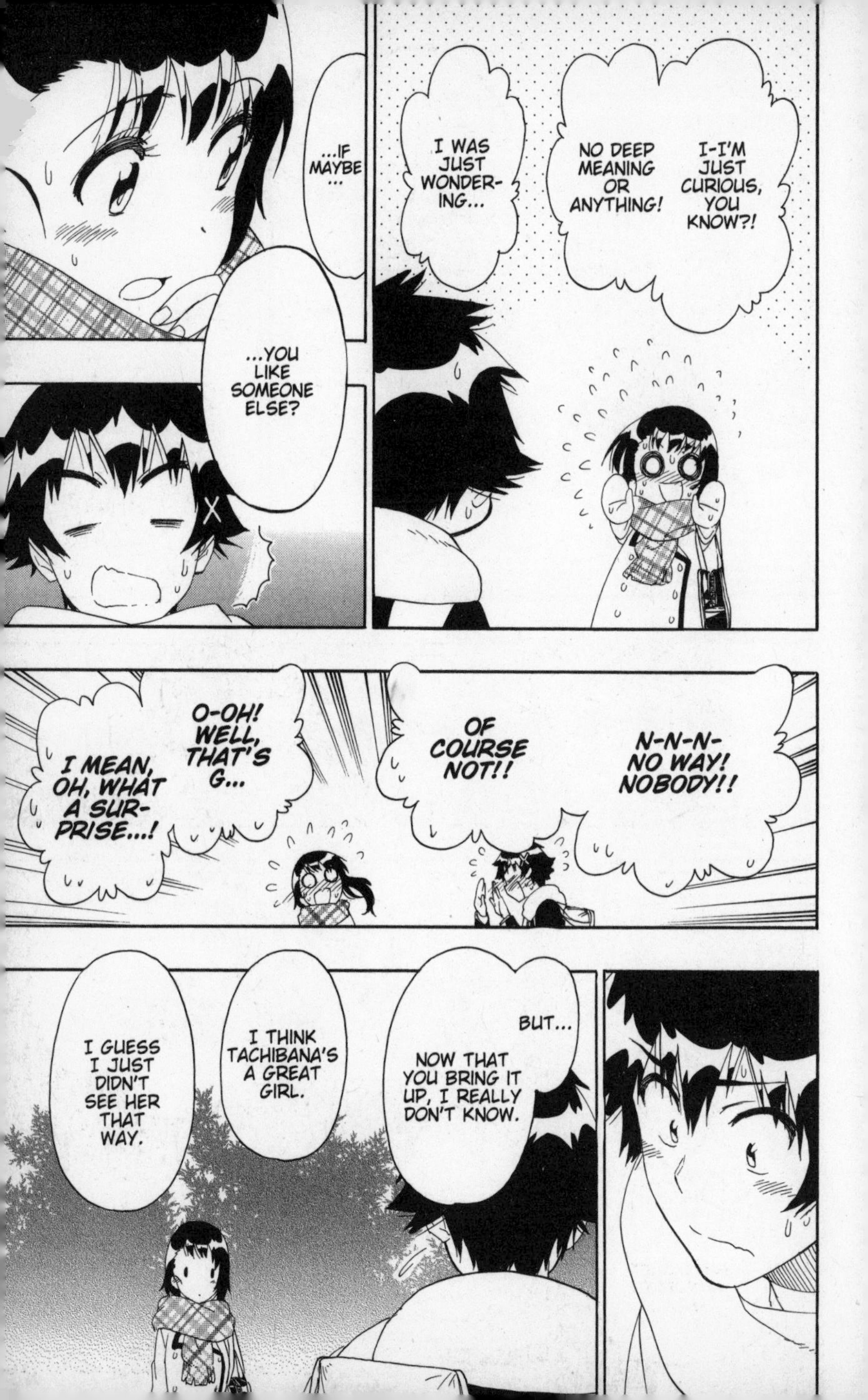
I-I'M JUST CURIOUS, YOU KNOW?!
NO DEEP MEANING OR ANYTHING!
I WAS JUST WONDER-ING...
...IF MAYBE...
...YOU LIKE SOMEONE ELSE?
N-N-N-NO WAY! NOBODY!!
OF COURSE NOT!!
O-OH! WELL, THAT'S G...
I MEAN, OH, WHAT A SUR-PRISE...!
BUT...
NOW THAT YOU BRING IT UP, I REALLY DON'T KNOW.
I THINK TACHIBANA'S A GREAT GIRL.
I GUESS I JUST DIDN'T SEE HER THAT WAY.

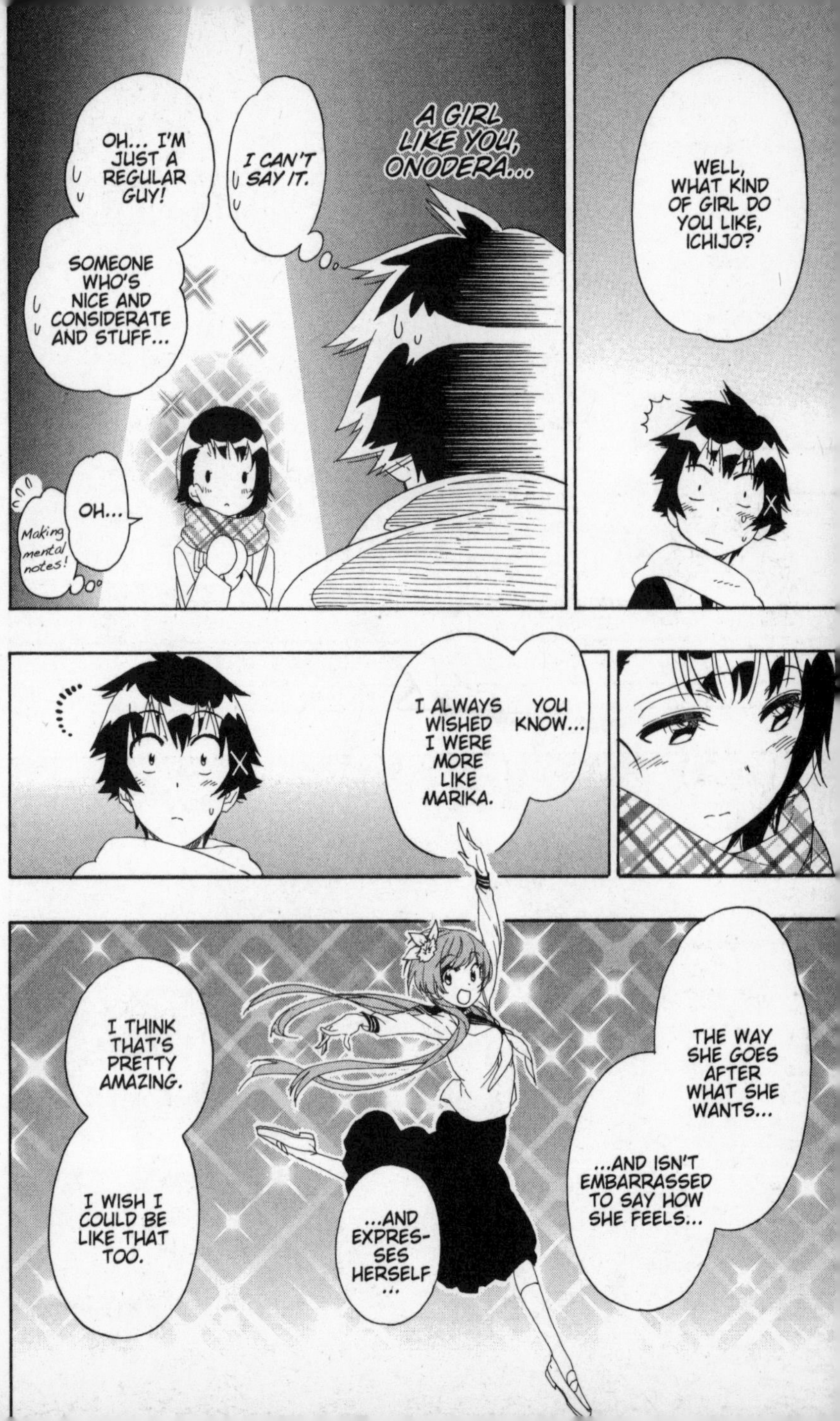
WELL, WHAT KIND OF GIRL DO YOU LIKE, ICHIJO?
A GIRL LIKE YOU, ONODERA...
I CAN'T SAY IT.
OH... I'M JUST A REGULAR GUY!
SOMEONE WHO'S NICE AND CONSIDERATE AND STUFF...
OH...
Making mental notes!
YOU KNOW...
I ALWAYS WISHED I WERE MORE LIKE MARIKA.
THE WAY SHE GOES AFTER WHAT SHE WANTS...
...AND ISN'T EMBARRASSED TO SAY HOW SHE FEELS...
...AND EXPRES-SES HERSELF...
I THINK THAT'S PRETTY AMAZING.
I WISH I COULD BE LIKE THAT TOO.

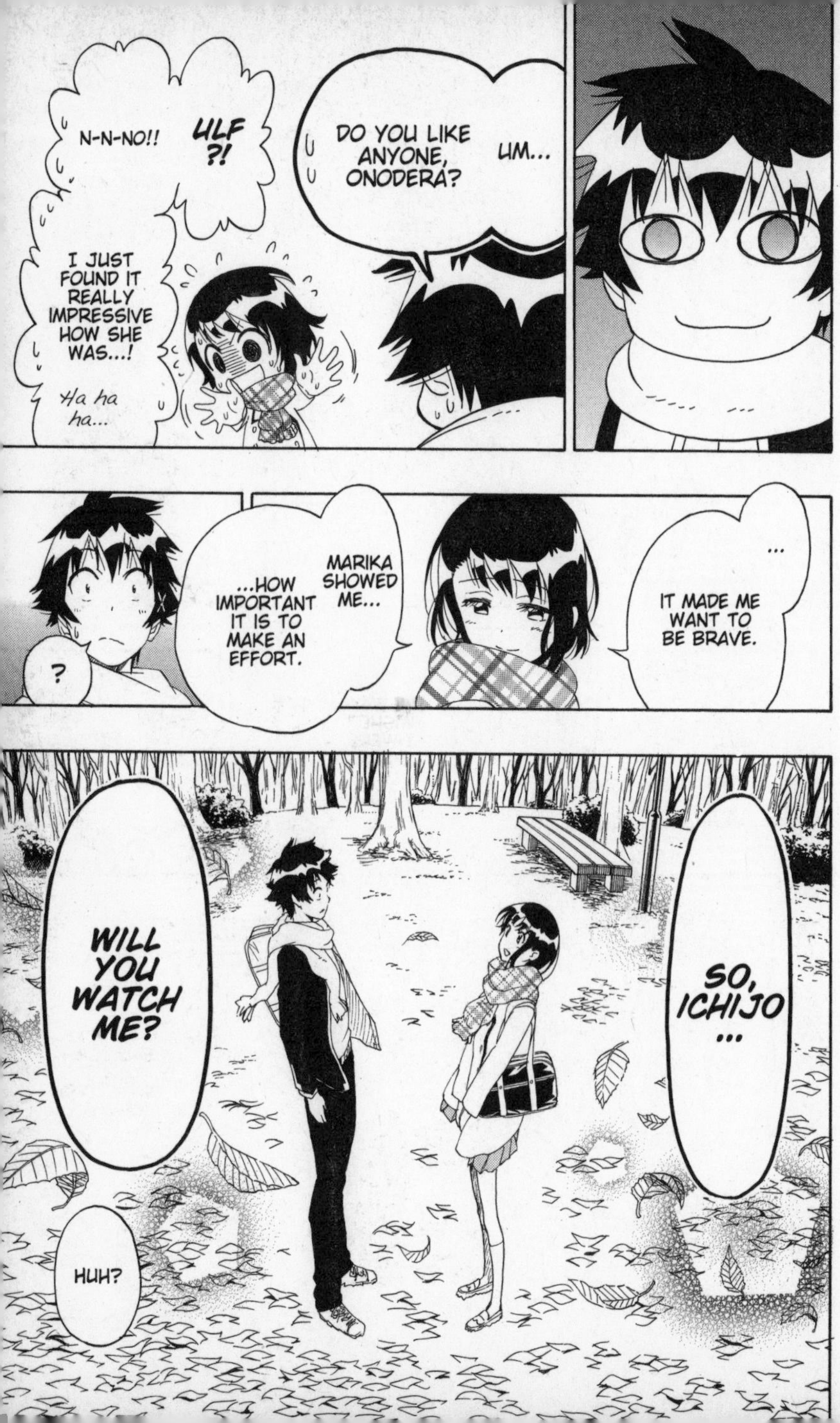
UM...
DO YOU LIKE ANYONE, ONODERA?
ULF ?!
N-N-NO!!
I JUST FOUND IT REALLY IMPRESSIVE HOW SHE WAS...!
Ha ha ha...
MARIKA SHOWED ME...
...HOW IMPORTANT IT IS TO MAKE AN EFFORT.
...
IT MADE ME WANT TO BE BRAVE.
?
SO, ICHIJO ...
WILL YOU WATCH ME?
HUH?

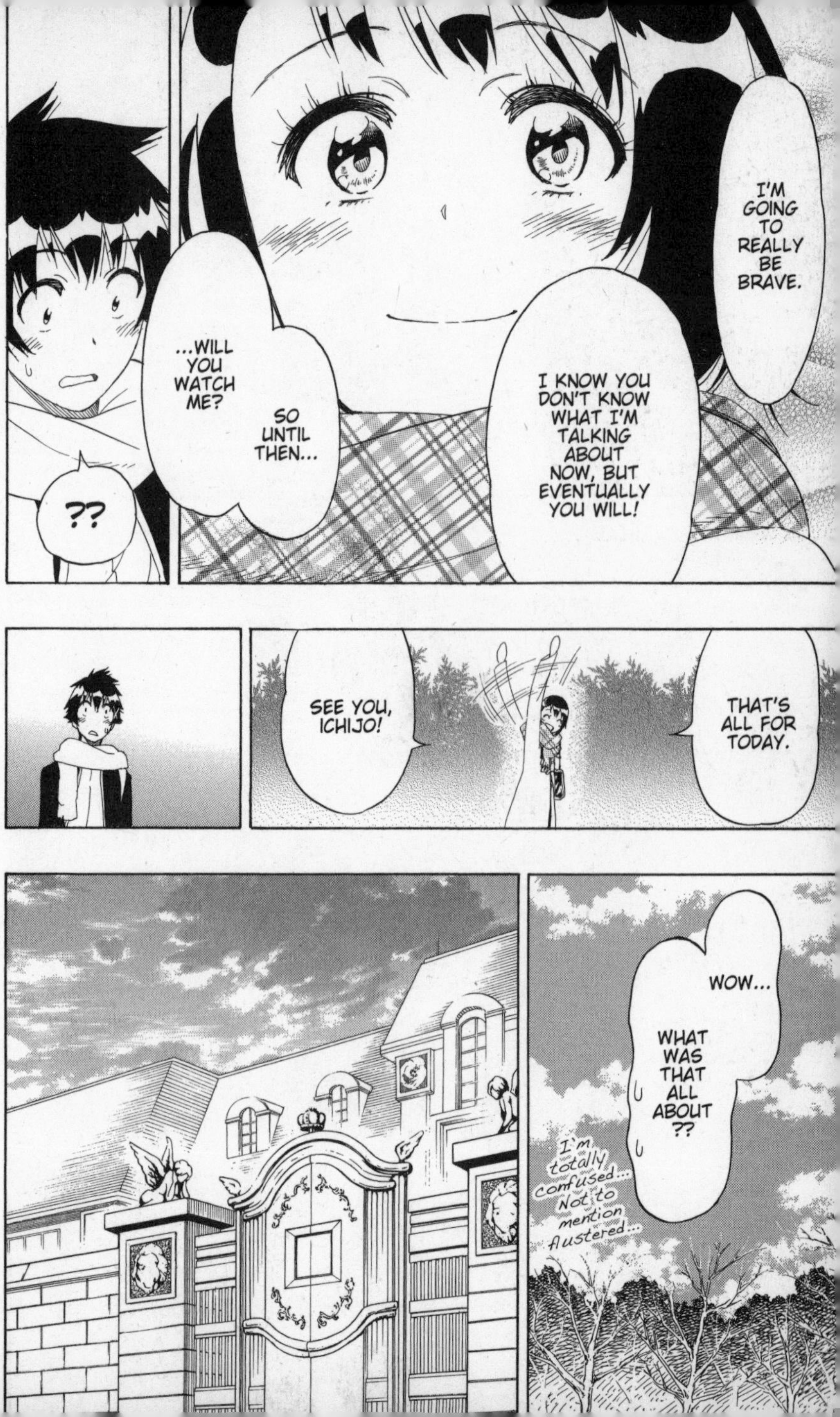
I'M GOING TO REALLY BE BRAVE.
I KNOW YOU DON'T KNOW WHAT I'M TALKING ABOUT NOW, BUT EVENTUALLY YOU WILL!
SO UNTIL THEN...
...WILL YOU WATCH ME?
??
THAT'S ALL FOR TODAY.
SEE YOU, ICHIJO!
WOW...
WHAT WAS THAT ALL ABOUT??
I'm totally confused... Not to mention flustered...

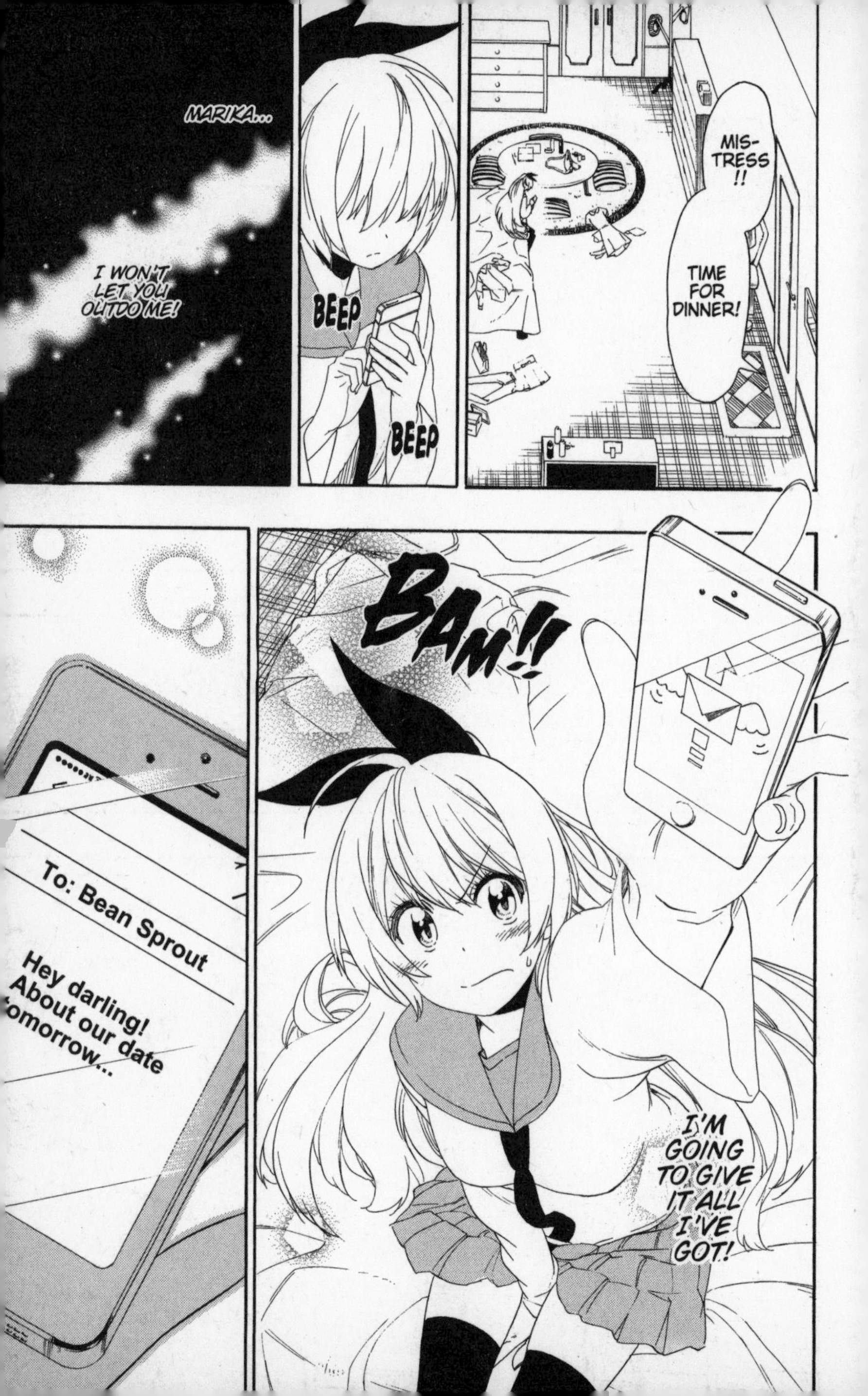
MIS-TRESS!!
TIME FOR DINNER!
BEEP
BEEP
MARIKA...
I WON'T LET YOU OUTDO ME!
BAM!!
I'M GOING TO GIVE IT ALL I'VE GOT!
To: Bean Sprout
Hey darling! About our date tomorrow...

Hey darling! About our date tomorrow...

Hmm... What should I write next?

Your presence is cordially requested at...

No, that's not right! I forgot how to write a normal text!

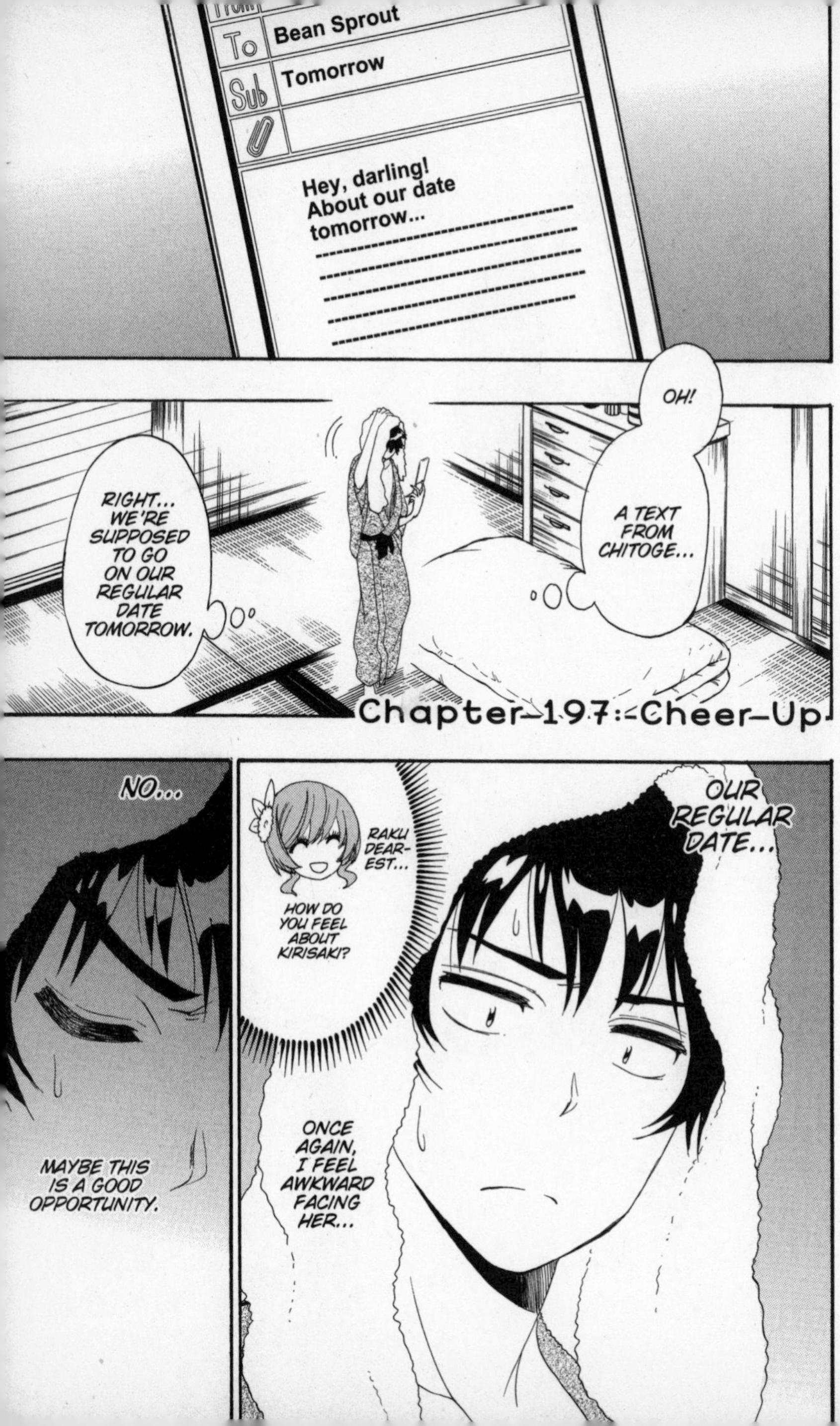
To
Bean Sprout
Sub
Tomorrow
Hey, darling! About our date tomorrow...
OH!
A TEXT FROM CHITOGE...
RIGHT... WE'RE SUPPOSED TO GO ON OUR REGULAR DATE TOMORROW.
Chapter 197: Cheer-Up
OUR REGULAR DATE...
RAKU DEAREST...
HOW DO YOU FEEL ABOUT KIRISAKI?
ONCE AGAIN, I FEEL AWKWARD FACING HER...
NO...
MAYBE THIS IS A GOOD OPPORTUNITY.

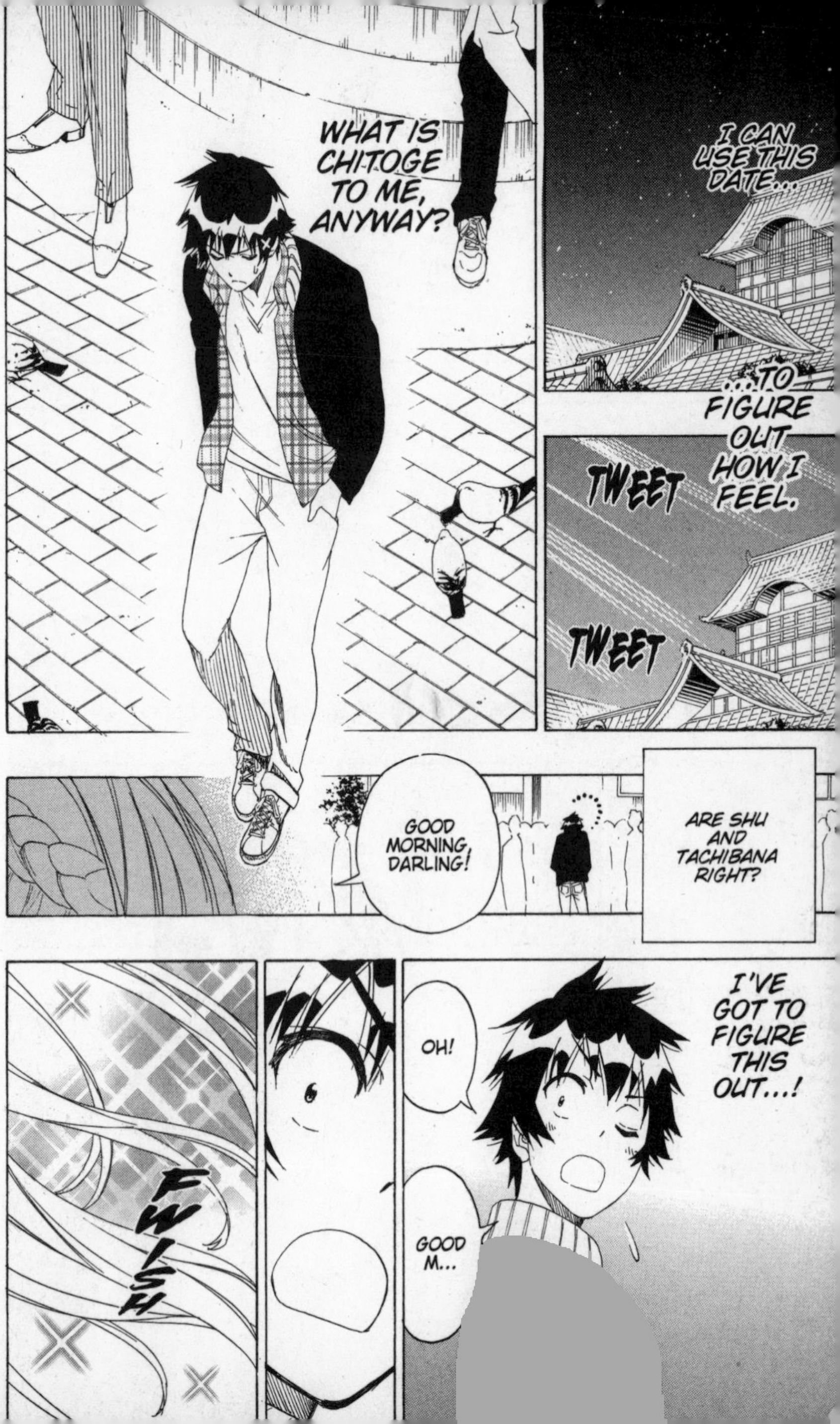
I CAN USE THIS DATE...
...TO FIGURE OUT HOW I FEEL.
TWEET
TWEET
WHAT IS CHITOGE TO ME, ANYWAY?
ARE SHU AND TACHIBANA RIGHT?
GOOD MORNING DARLING!
I'VE GOT TO FIGURE THIS OUT...!
OH!
GOOD M...
FWISH

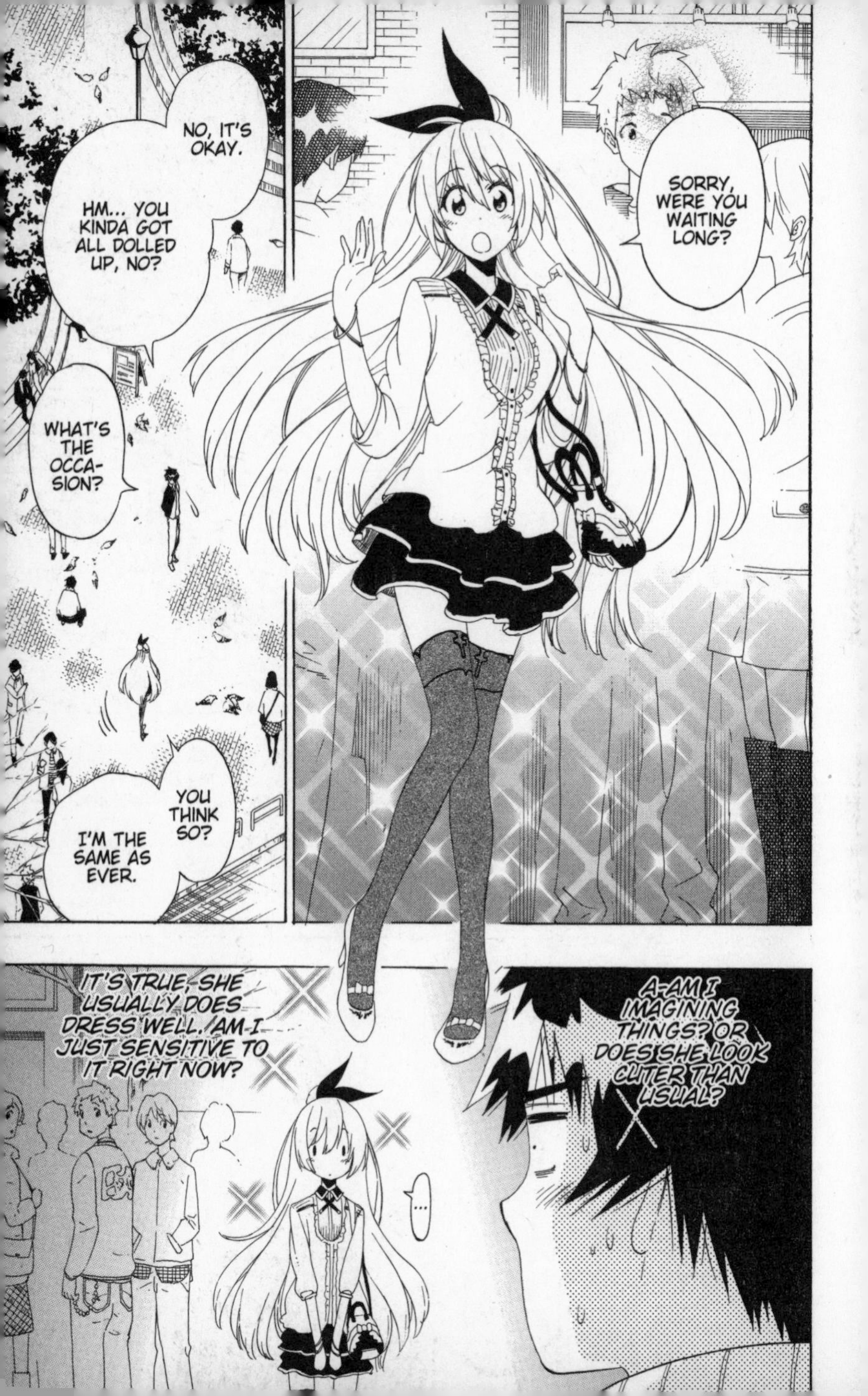
SORRY, WERE YOU WAITING LONG?
NO, IT'S OKAY.
HM... YOU KINDA GOT ALL DOLLED UP, NO?
WHAT'S THE OCCASION?
YOU THINK SO?
I'M THE SAME AS EVER.
A-AM I IMAGINING THINGS? OR DOES SHE LOOK CUTER THAN USUAL?
IT'S TRUE, SHE USUALLY DOES DRESS WELL. AM I JUST SENSITIVE TO IT RIGHT NOW?
...

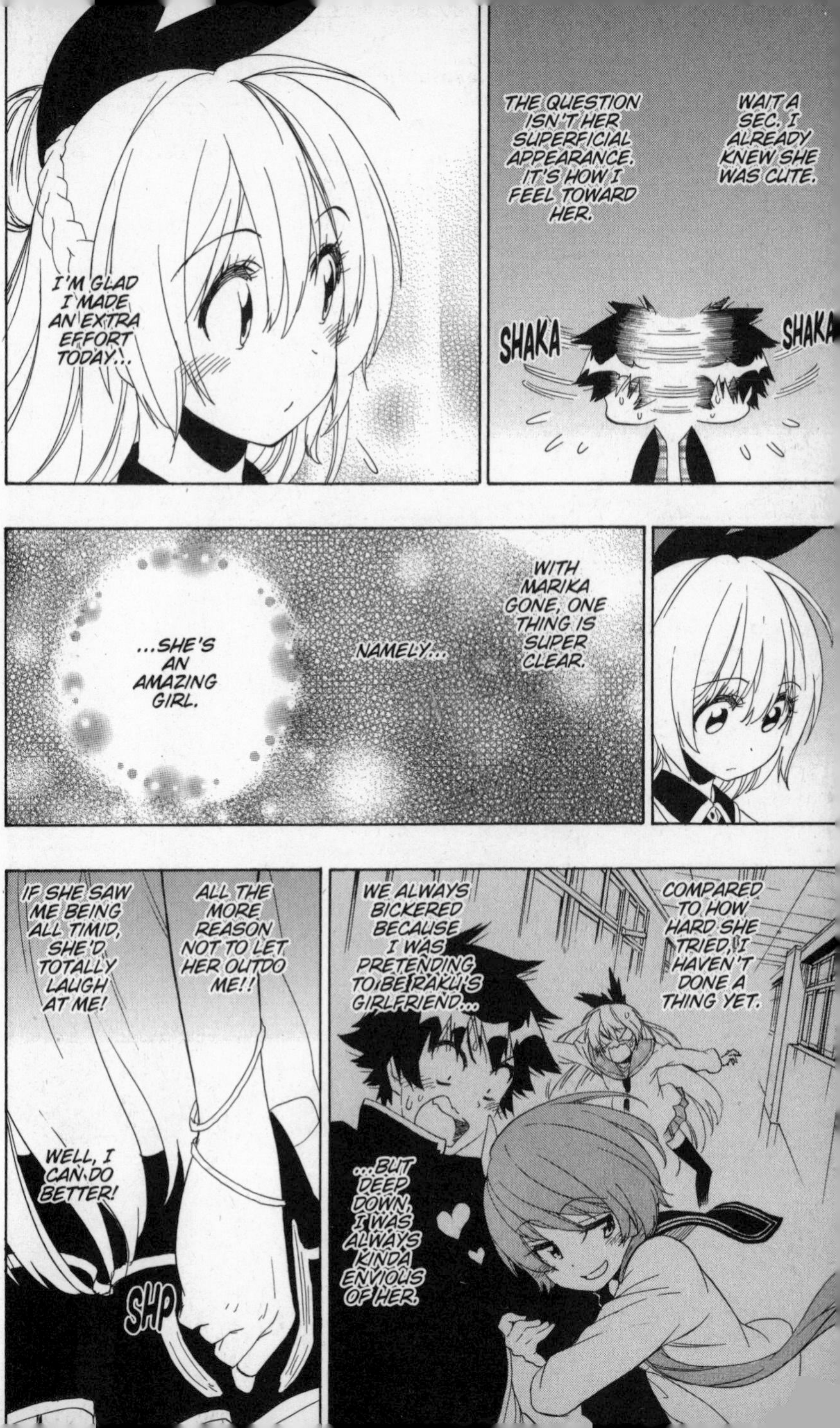
WAIT A SEC. I ALREADY KNEW SHE WAS CUTE.
THE QUESTION ISN'T HER SUPERFICIAL APPEARANCE. IT'S HOW I FEEL TOWARD HER.
SHAKA
SHAKA
I'M GLAD I MADE AN EXTRA EFFORT TODAY...
WITH MARIKA GONE, ONE THING IS SUPER CLEAR.
NAMELY...
...SHE'S AN AMAZING GIRL.
COMPARED TO HOW HARD SHE TRIED, I HAVEN'T DONE A THING YET.
WE ALWAYS BICKERED BECAUSE I WAS PRETENDING TO BE RAKU'S GIRLFRIEND...
...BUT DEEP DOWN, I WAS ALWAYS KINDA ENVIOUS OF HER.
ALL THE MORE REASON NOT TO LET HER OUTDO ME!!
IF SHE SAW ME BEING ALL TIMID, SHE'D TOTALLY LAUGH AT ME!
WELL, I CAN DO BETTER!
SHP

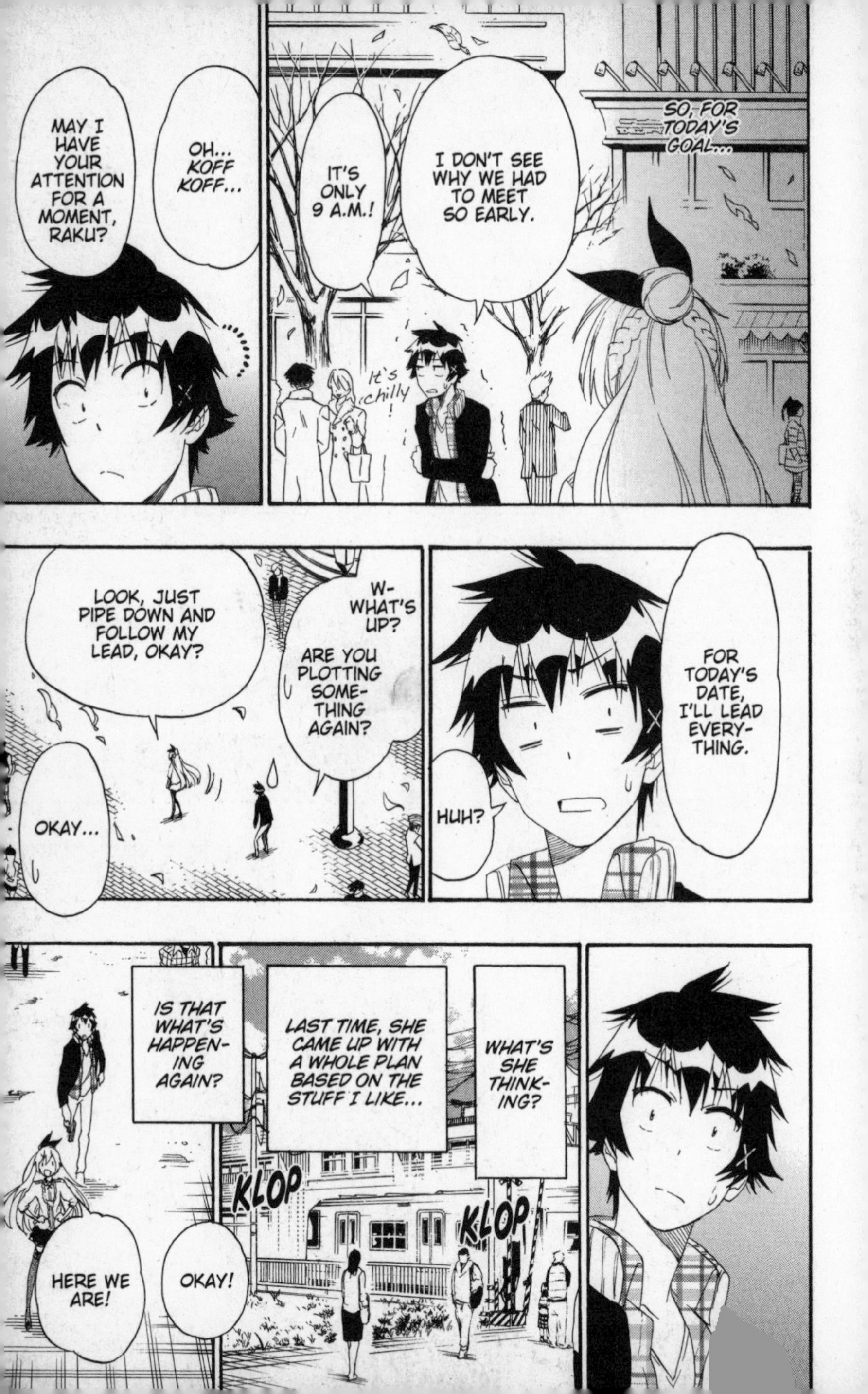
SO, FOR TODAY'S GOAL...
I DON'T SEE WHY WE HAD TO MEET SO EARLY.
IT'S ONLY 9 A.M.!
It's chilly!
OH... KOFF KOFF...
MAY I HAVE YOUR ATTENTION FOR A MOMENT, RAKU?
FOR TODAY'S DATE, I'LL LEAD EVERYTHING.
HUH?
W-WHAT'S UP?
ARE YOU PLOTTING SOMETHING AGAIN?
LOOK, JUST PIPE DOWN AND FOLLOW MY LEAD, OKAY?
OKAY...
WHAT'S SHE THINKING?
LAST TIME, SHE CAME UP WITH A WHOLE PLAN BASED ON THE STUFF I LIKE...
KLOP
KLOP
IS THAT WHAT'S HAPPENING AGAIN?
OKAY!
HERE WE ARE!

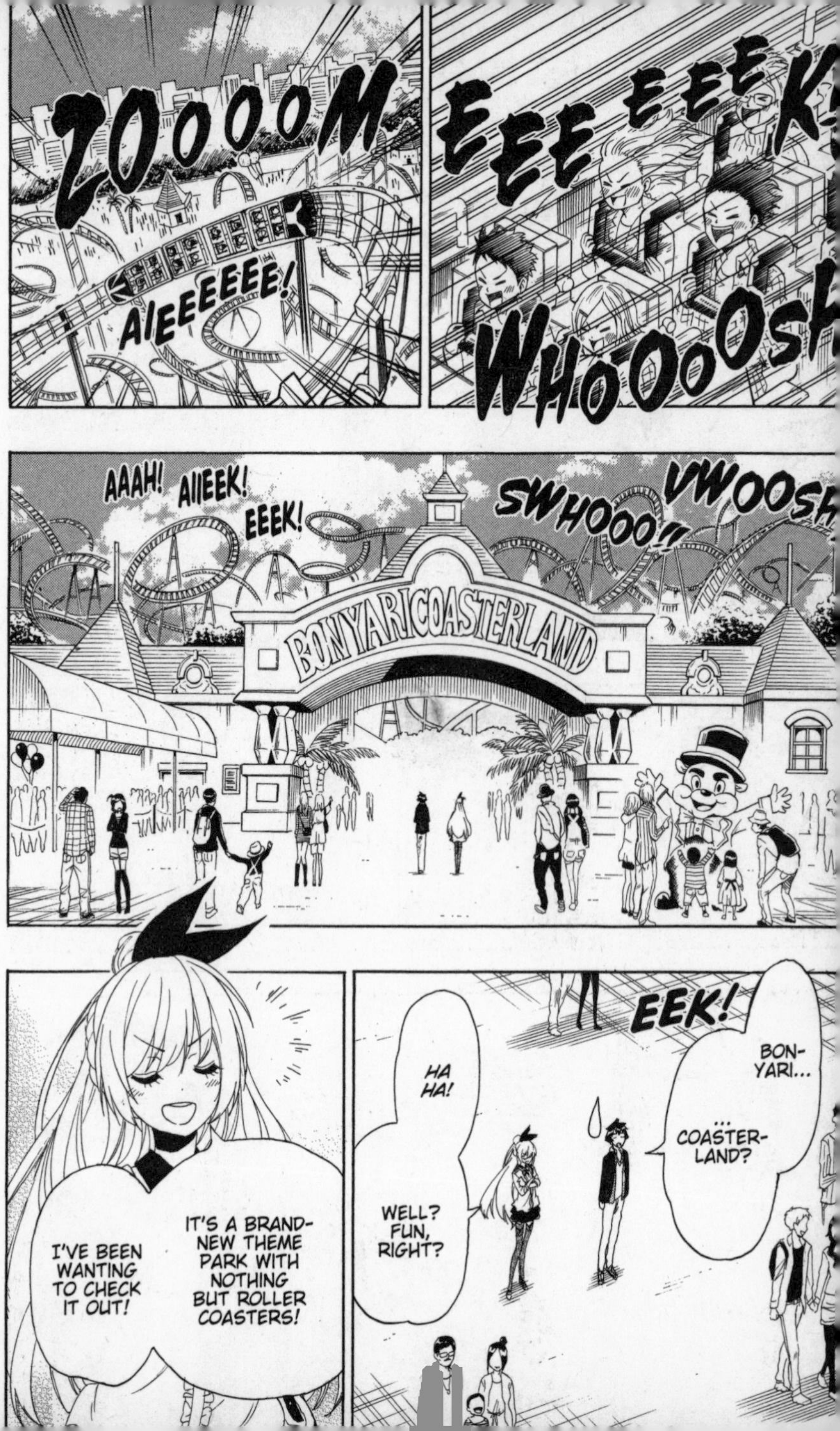
EEEEEEK
WHOOOOOSH
ZOOOOM
AIEEEEEE!
VWOOSH
SWHOOO!!
BONYARI COASTERLAND
AAAH!
AIIEEK!
EEEK!
EEK!
BON-YARI...
...COASTER-LAND?
HA HA!
WELL? FUN, RIGHT?
IT'S A BRAND-NEW THEME PARK WITH NOTHING BUT ROLLER COASTERS!
I'VE BEEN WANTING TO CHECK IT OUT!

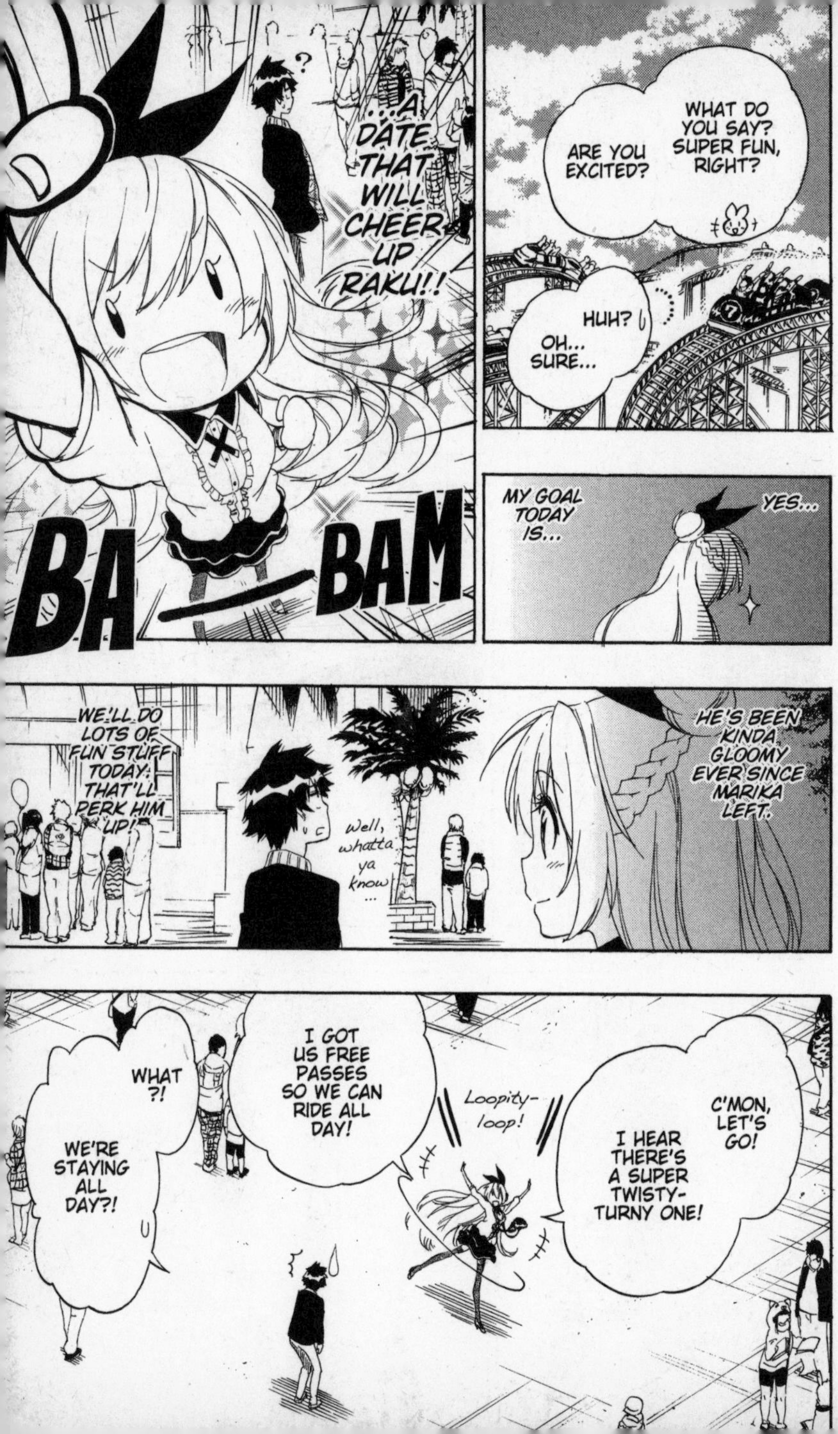
WHAT DO YOU SAY? SUPER FUN, RIGHT?
ARE YOU EXCITED?
HUH?
OH... SURE...
YES...
MY GOAL TODAY IS...
...A DATE THAT WILL CHEER UP RAKU!!
BA-BAM
HE'S BEEN KINDA GLOOMY EVER SINCE MARIKA LEFT.
Well, whatta ya know...
WE'LL DO LOTS OF FUN STUFF TODAY. THAT'LL PERK HIM UP!
C'MON, LET'S GO!
I HEAR THERE'S A SUPER TWISTY-TURNY ONE!
Loopity-loop!
I GOT US FREE PASSES SO WE CAN RIDE ALL DAY!
WHAT?!
WE'RE STAYING ALL DAY?!

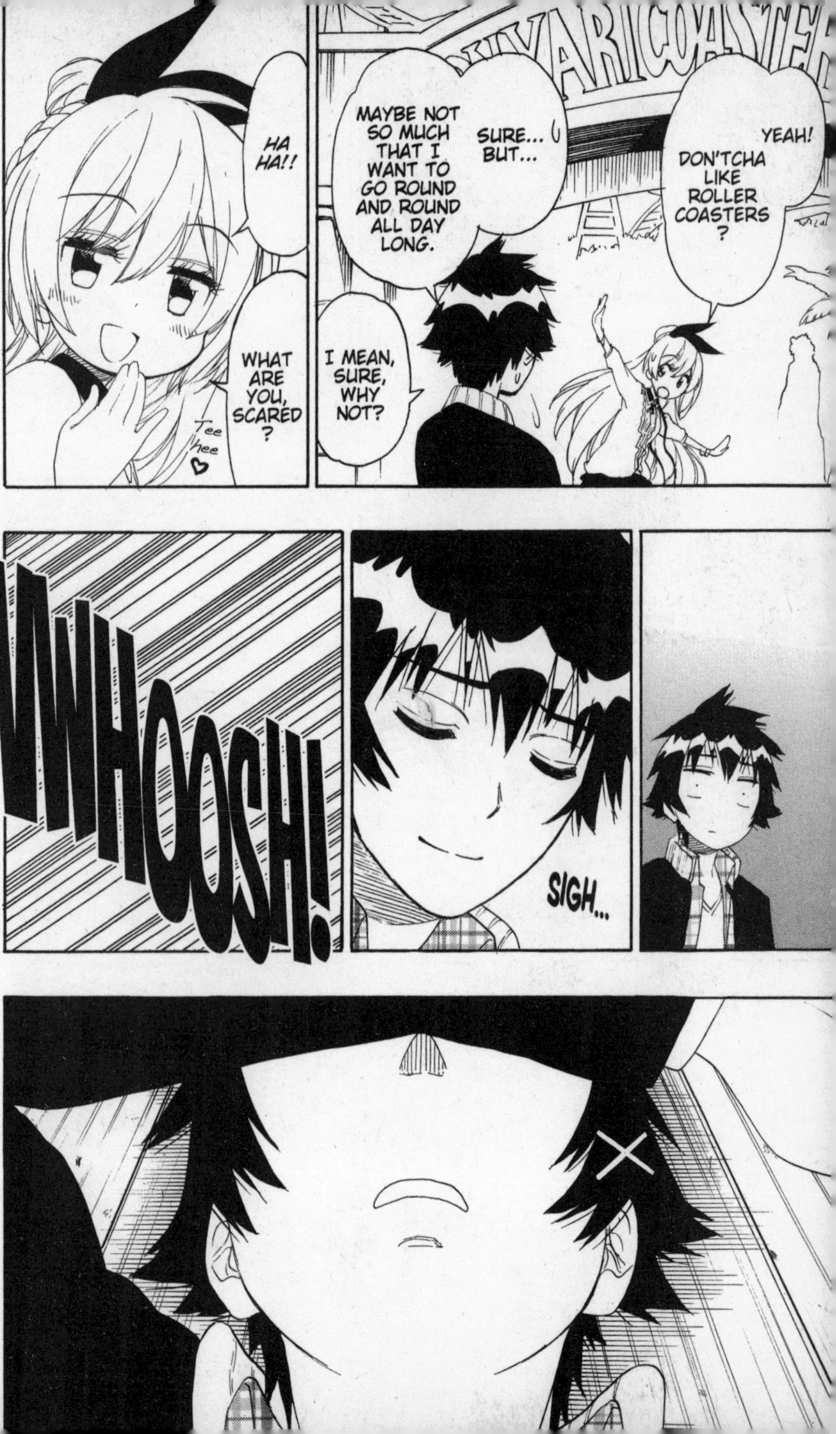
YEAH!
DON'TCHA LIKE ROLLER COASTERS?
SURE... BUT...
MAYBE NOT SO MUCH THAT I WANT TO GO ROUND AND ROUND ALL DAY LONG.
I MEAN, SURE, WHY NOT?
HA HA!!
WHAT ARE YOU, SCARED?
Tee hee ♡
SIGH...
WHOOSH!

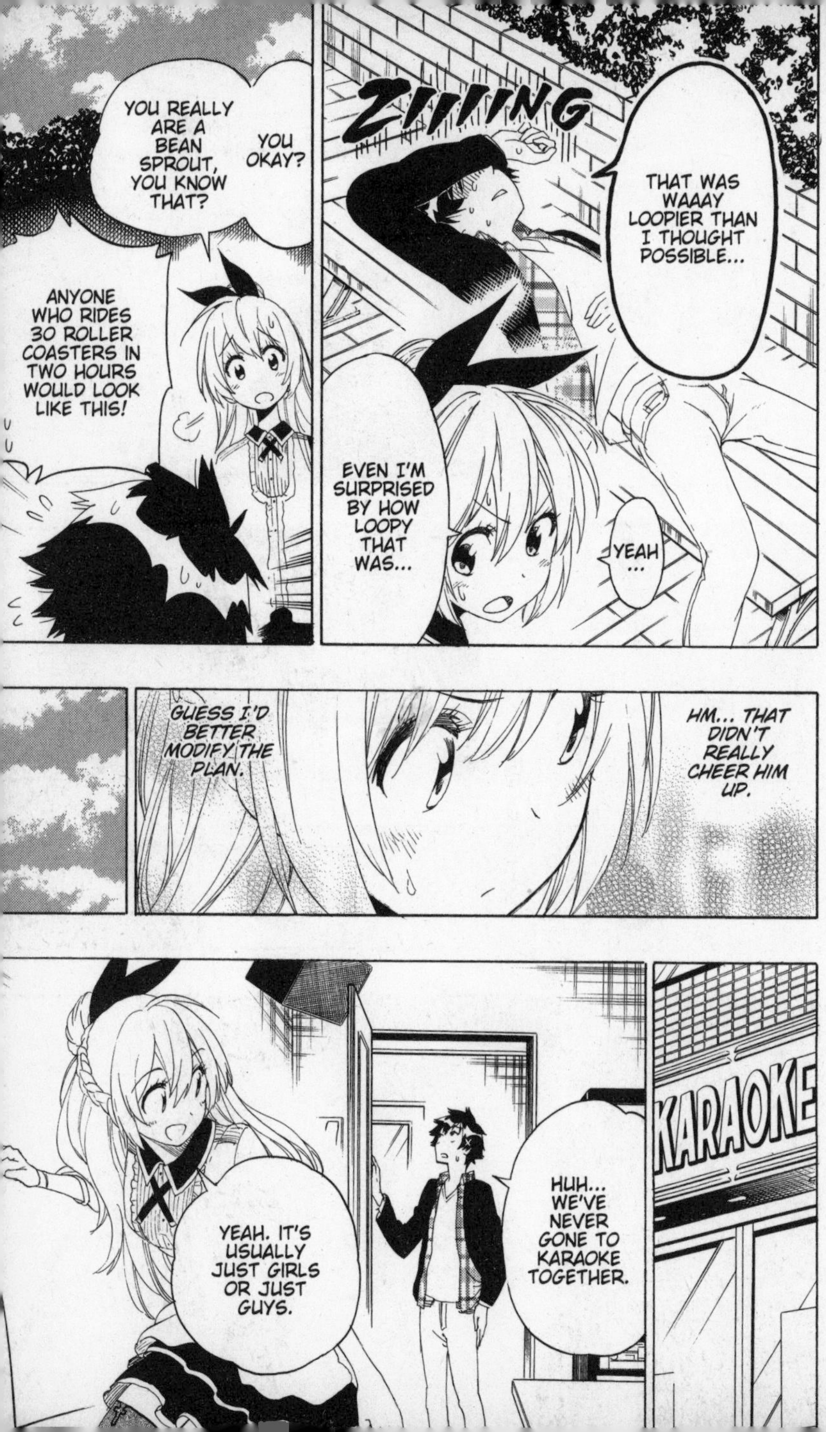
ZIIIING
THAT WAS WAAAY LOOPIER THAN I THOUGHT POSSIBLE...
YEAH...
EVEN I'M SURPRISED BY HOW LOOPY THAT WAS...
YOU OKAY?
YOU REALLY ARE A BEAN SPROUT, YOU KNOW THAT?
ANYONE WHO RIDES 30 ROLLER COASTERS IN TWO HOURS WOULD LOOK LIKE THIS!
HM... THAT DIDN'T REALLY CHEER HIM UP.
GUESS I'D BETTER MODIFY THE PLAN.
KARAOKE
HUH... WE'VE NEVER GONE TO KARAOKE TOGETHER.
YEAH. IT'S USUALLY JUST GIRLS OR JUST GUYS.

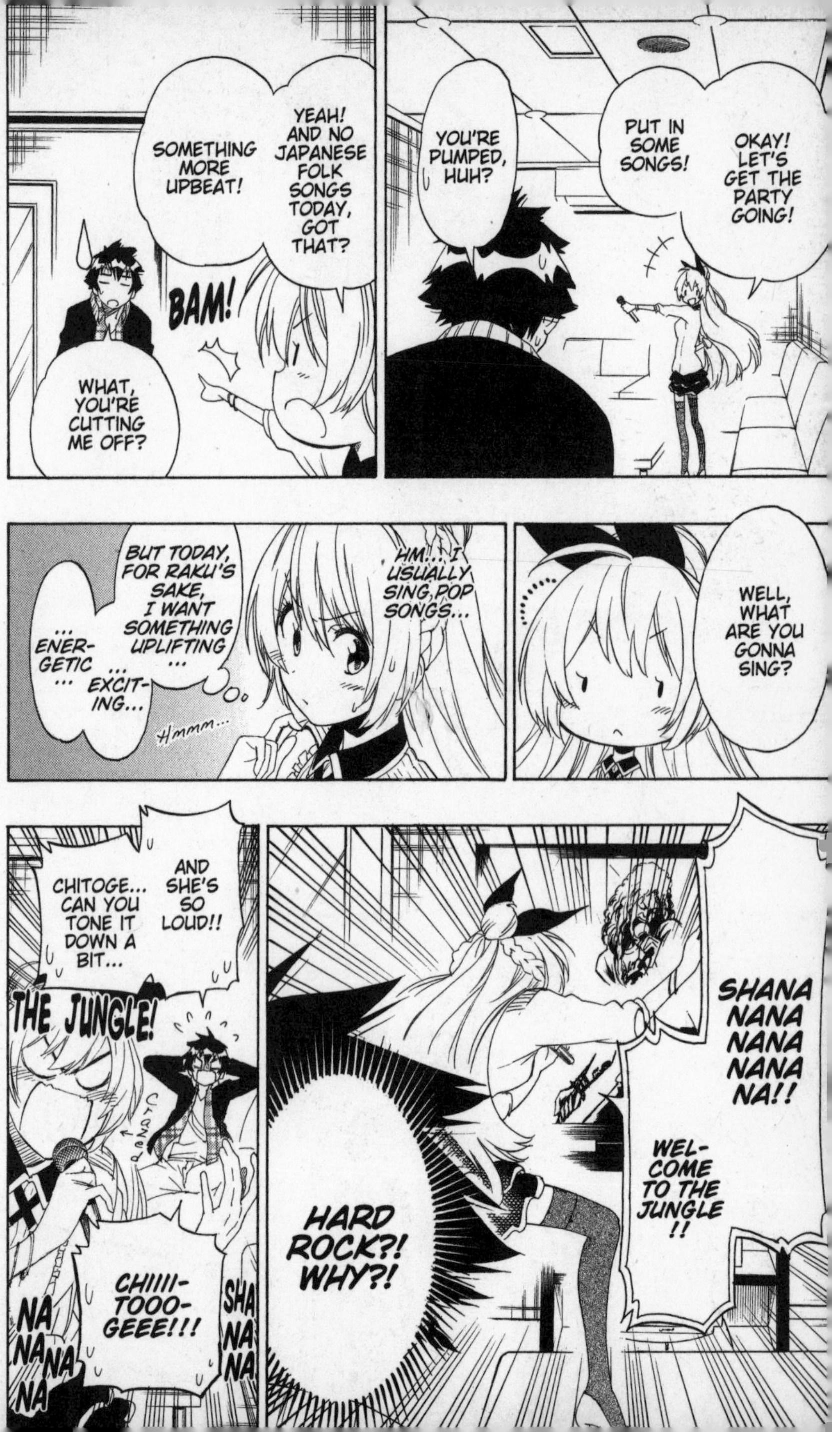
OKAY! LET'S GET THE PARTY GOING!
PUT IN SOME SONGS!
YOU'RE PUMPED, HUH?
YEAH! AND NO JAPANESE FOLK SONGS TODAY, GOT THAT?
SOMETHING MORE UPBEAT!
BAM!
WHAT, YOU'RE CUTTING ME OFF?
WELL, WHAT ARE YOU GONNA SING?
HM... I USUALLY SING POP SONGS...
BUT TODAY, FOR RAKU'S SAKE, I WANT SOMETHING UPLIFTING ...
... ENERGETIC ... EXCITING...
Hmmm...
SHANA NANA NANA NANA NA!!
WELCOME TO THE JUNGLE!!
HARD ROCK?! WHY?!
AND SHE'S SO LOUD!!
CHITOGE... CAN YOU TONE IT DOWN A BIT...
THE JUNGLE!
Crazed
SHA NA NA
NA NA NA NA
CHIIII-TOOO-GEEE!!!

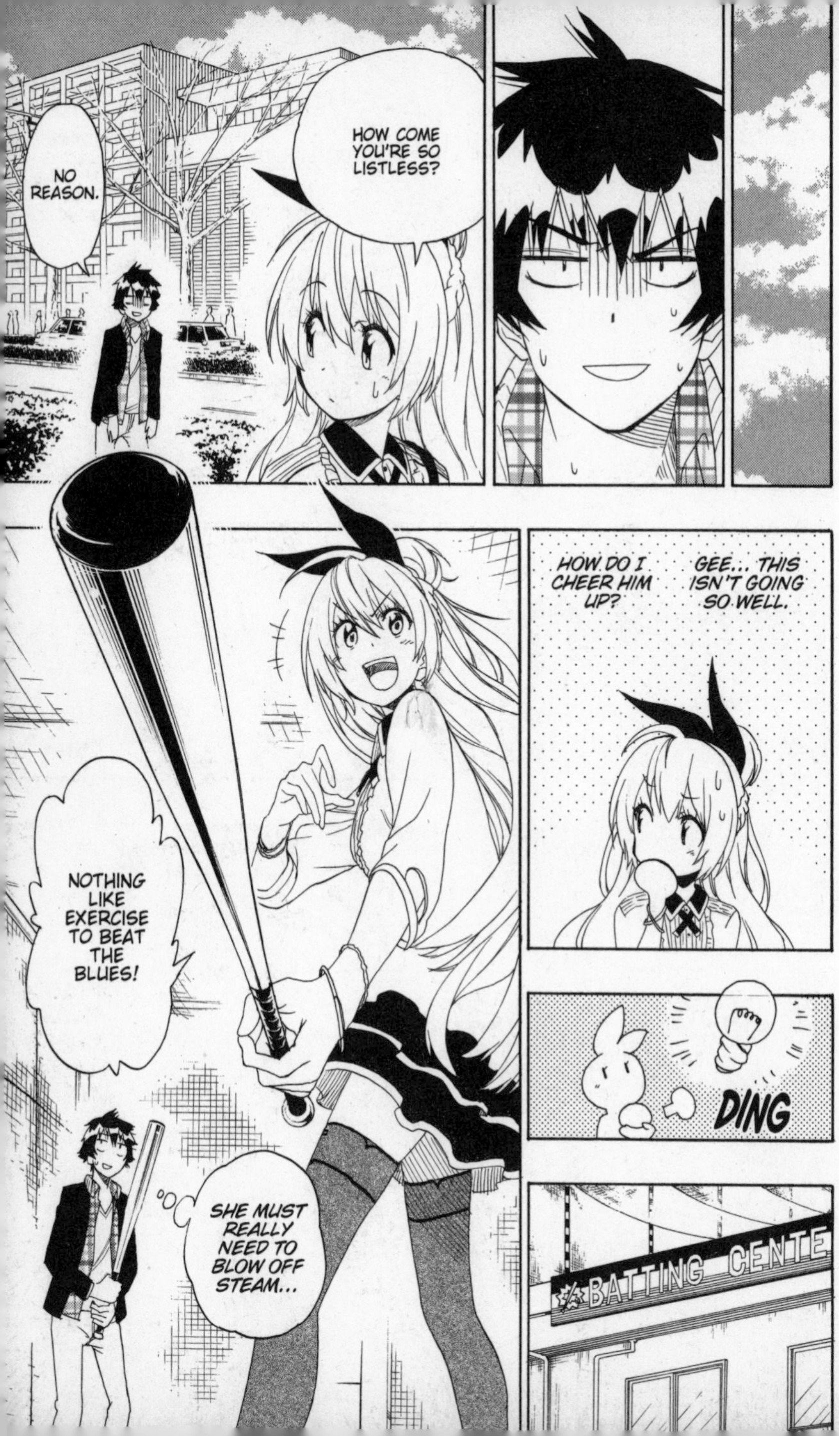
HOW COME YOU'RE SO LISTLESS?
NO REASON.
GEE... THIS ISN'T GOING SO WELL.
HOW DO I CHEER HIM UP?
DING
BATTING CENTE
NOTHING LIKE EXERCISE TO BEAT THE BLUES!
SHE MUST REALLY NEED TO BLOW OFF STEAM...

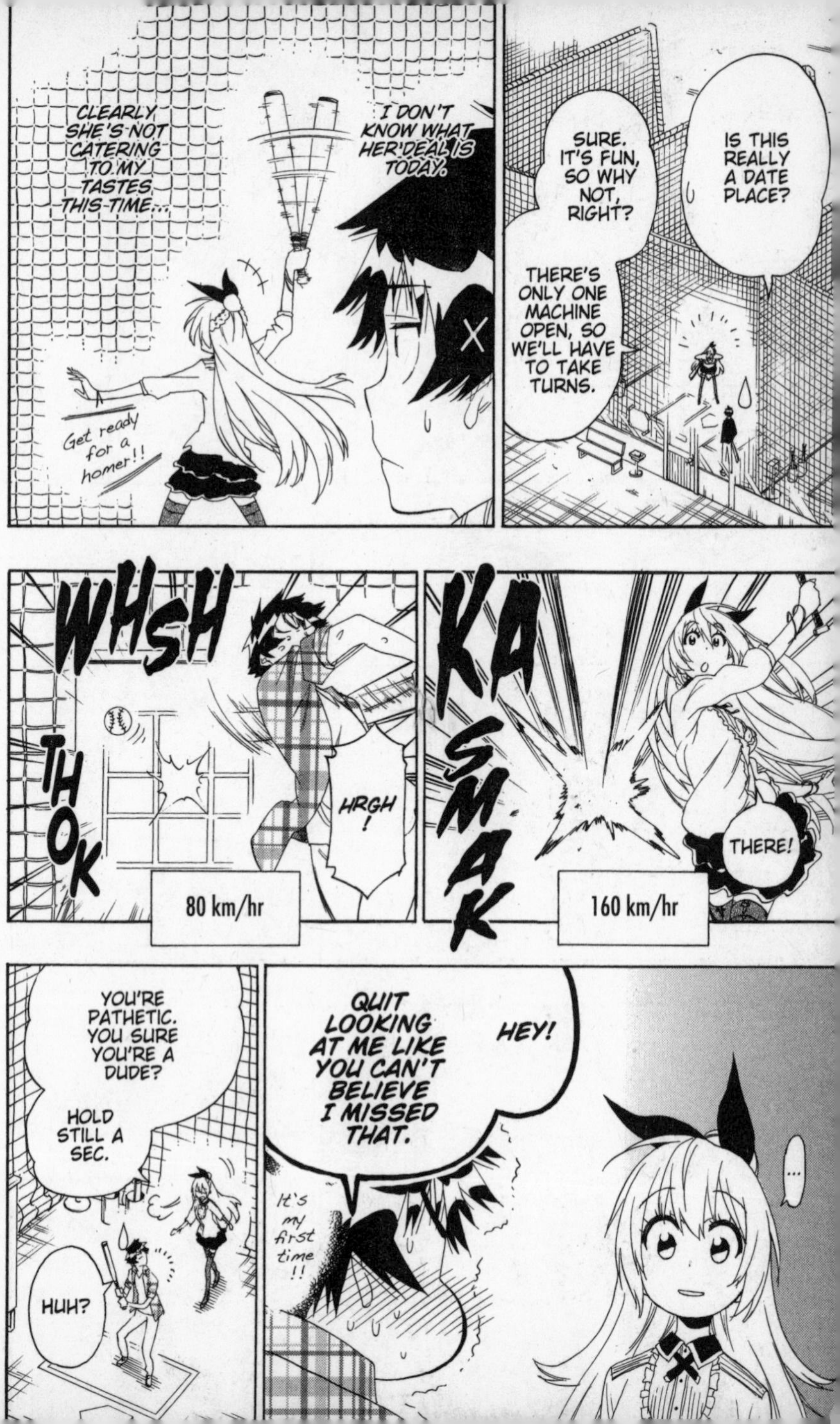
IS THIS REALLY A DATE PLACE?
SURE. IT'S FUN, SO WHY NOT, RIGHT?
THERE'S ONLY ONE MACHINE OPEN, SO WE'LL HAVE TO TAKE TURNS.
I DON'T KNOW WHAT HER DEAL IS TODAY.
CLEARLY SHE'S NOT CATERING TO MY TASTES THIS TIME...
Get ready for a homer!!
KA SMAK
THERE!
160 km/hr
WHSH
HRGH!
THOK
80 km/hr
HEY!
QUIT LOOKING AT ME LIKE YOU CAN'T BELIEVE I MISSED THAT.
It's my first time!!
...
YOU'RE PATHETIC. YOU SURE YOU'RE A DUDE?
HOLD STILL A SEC.
HUH?

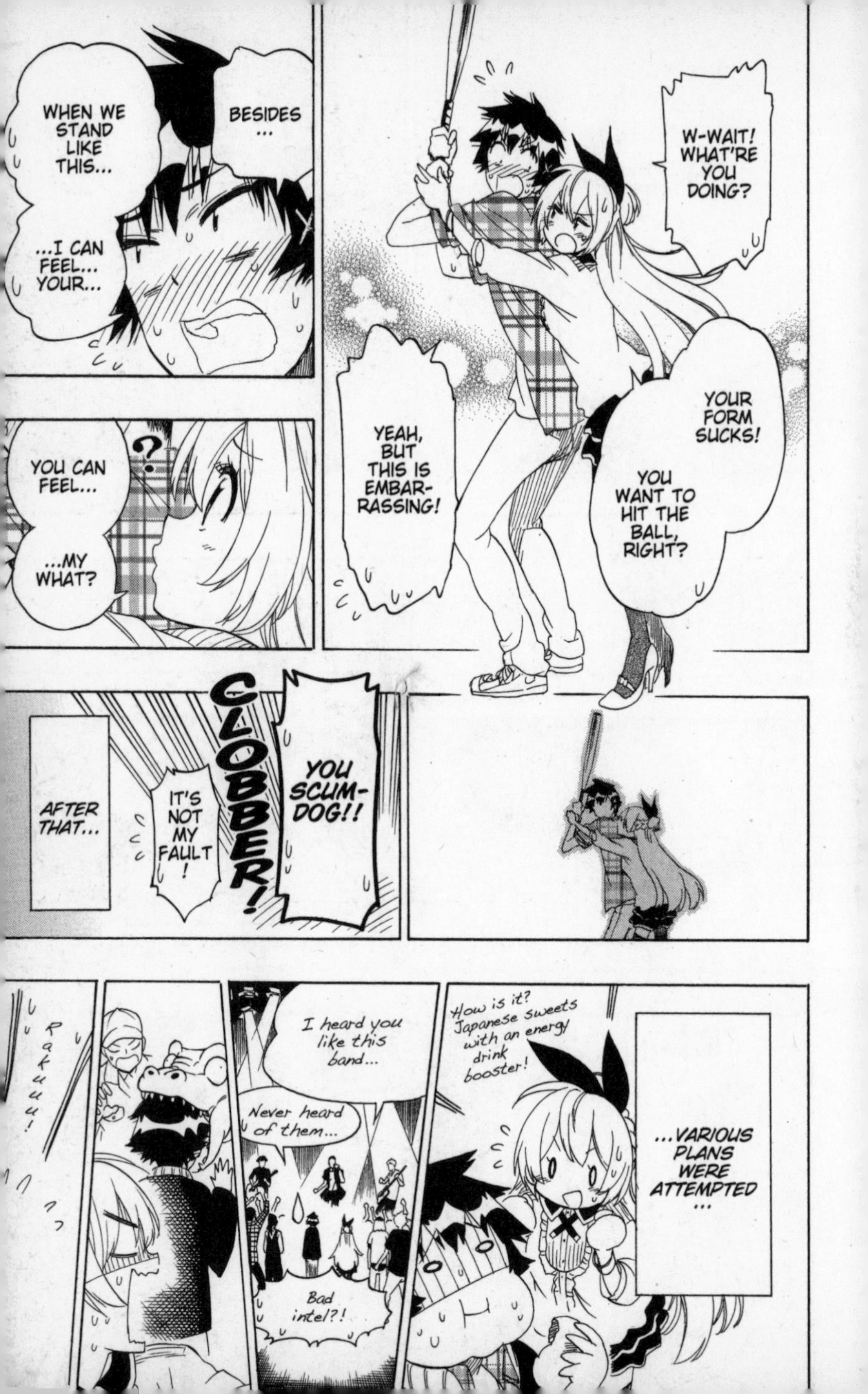
W-WAIT! WHAT'RE YOU DOING?
YOUR FORM SUCKS!
YOU WANT TO HIT THE BALL, RIGHT?
YEAH, BUT THIS IS EMBARRASSING!
BESIDES...
WHEN WE STAND LIKE THIS...
...I CAN FEEL... YOUR...
?
YOU CAN FEEL...
...MY WHAT?
YOU SCUM-DOG!!
CLOBBER!
IT'S NOT MY FAULT!
AFTER THAT...
...VARIOUS PLANS WERE ATTEMPTED...
How is it? Japanese sweets with an energy drink booster!
I heard you like this band...
Never heard of them...
Bad intel?!
Rakuuu!

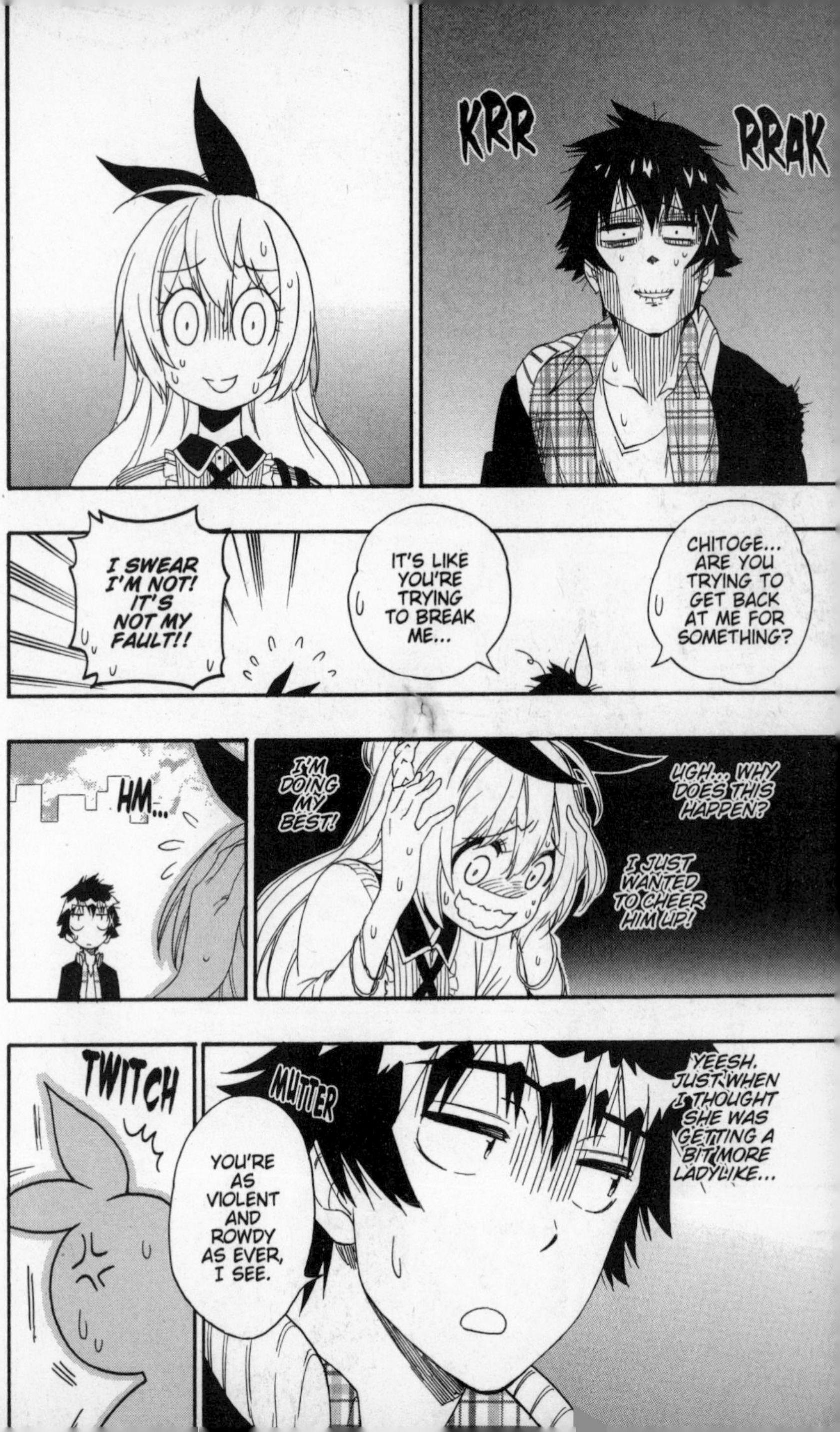
KRR
RRAK
CHITOGE... ARE YOU TRYING TO GET BACK AT ME FOR SOMETHING?
IT'S LIKE YOU'RE TRYING TO BREAK ME...
I SWEAR I'M NOT! IT'S NOT MY FAULT!!
UGH... WHY DOES THIS HAPPEN?
I JUST WANTED TO CHEER HIM UP!
I'M DOING MY BEST!
HM...
YEESH. JUST WHEN I THOUGHT SHE WAS GETTING A BIT MORE LADYLIKE...
MUTTER
YOU'RE AS VIOLENT AND ROWDY AS EVER, I SEE.
TWITCH

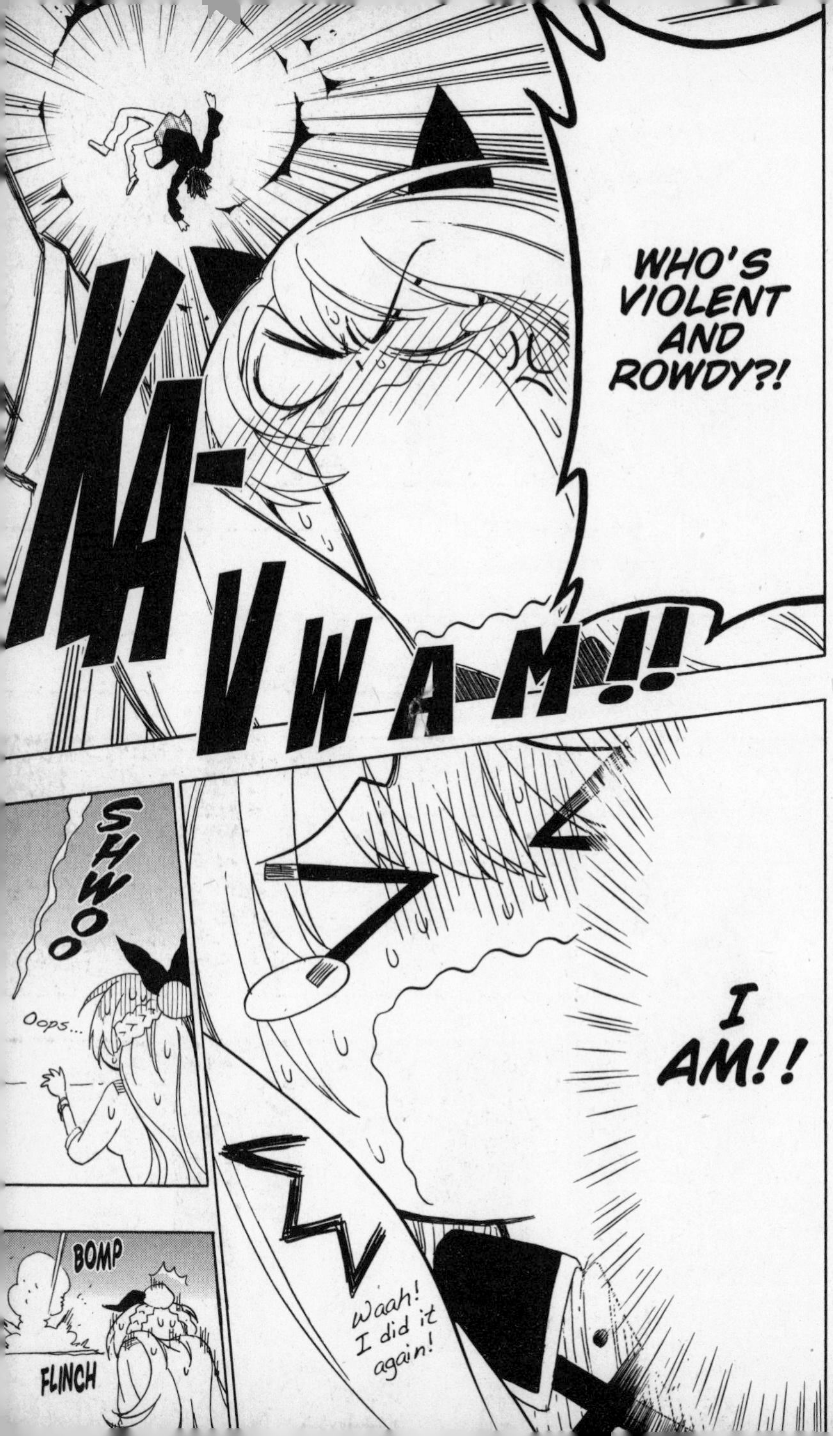
WHO'S VIOLENT AND ROWDY?!
KA-VWAM!!
I AM!!
Waah! I did it again!
SHWOOO
Oops...
BOMP
FLINCH

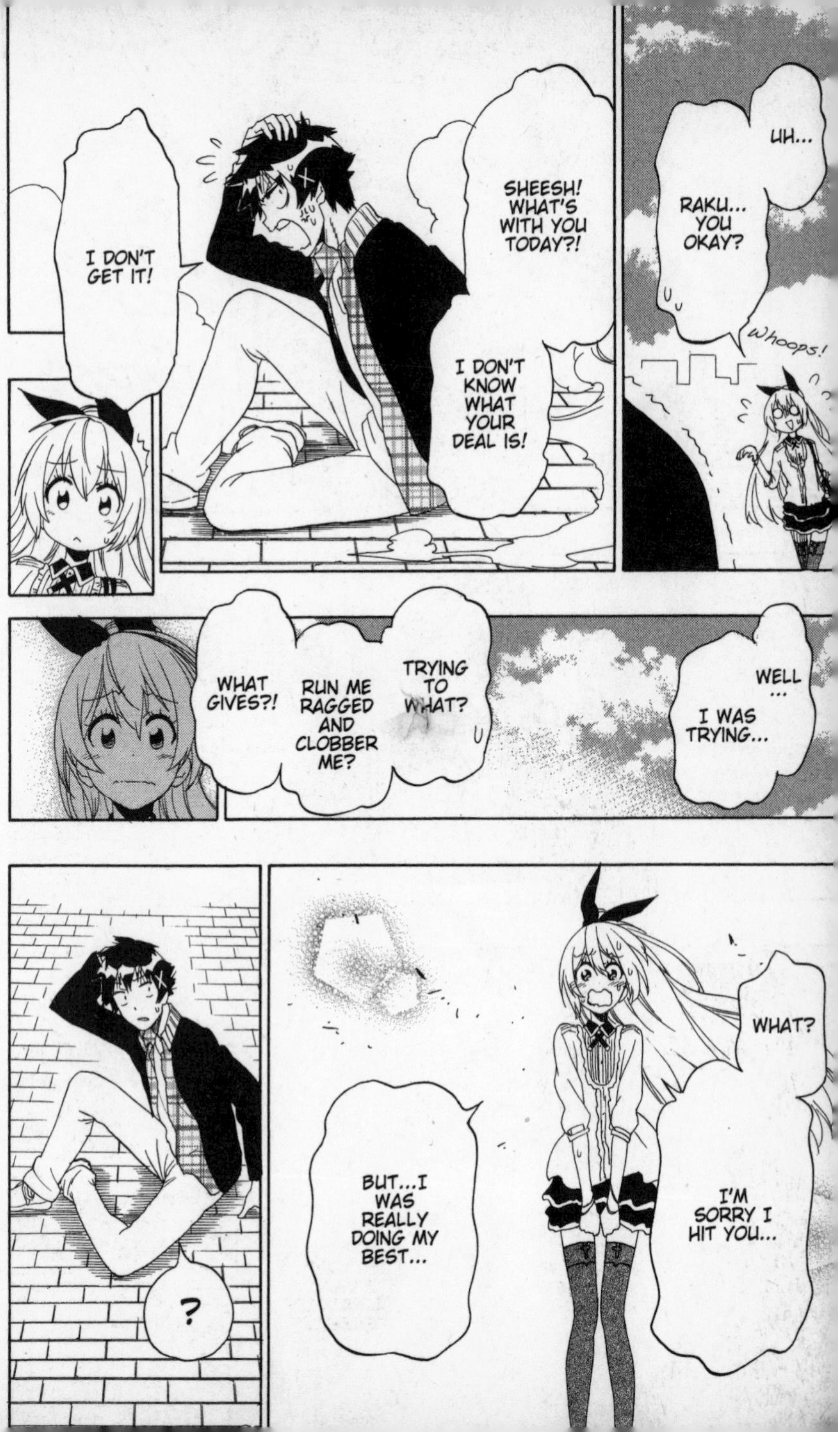
UH...
RAKU... YOU OKAY?
Whoops!
SHEESH! WHAT'S WITH YOU TODAY?!
I DON'T KNOW WHAT YOUR DEAL IS!
I DON'T GET IT!
WELL... I WAS TRYING...
TRYING TO WHAT?
RUN ME RAGGED AND CLOBBER ME?
WHAT GIVES?!
WHAT?
I'M SORRY I HIT YOU...
BUT...I WAS REALLY DOING MY BEST...
?

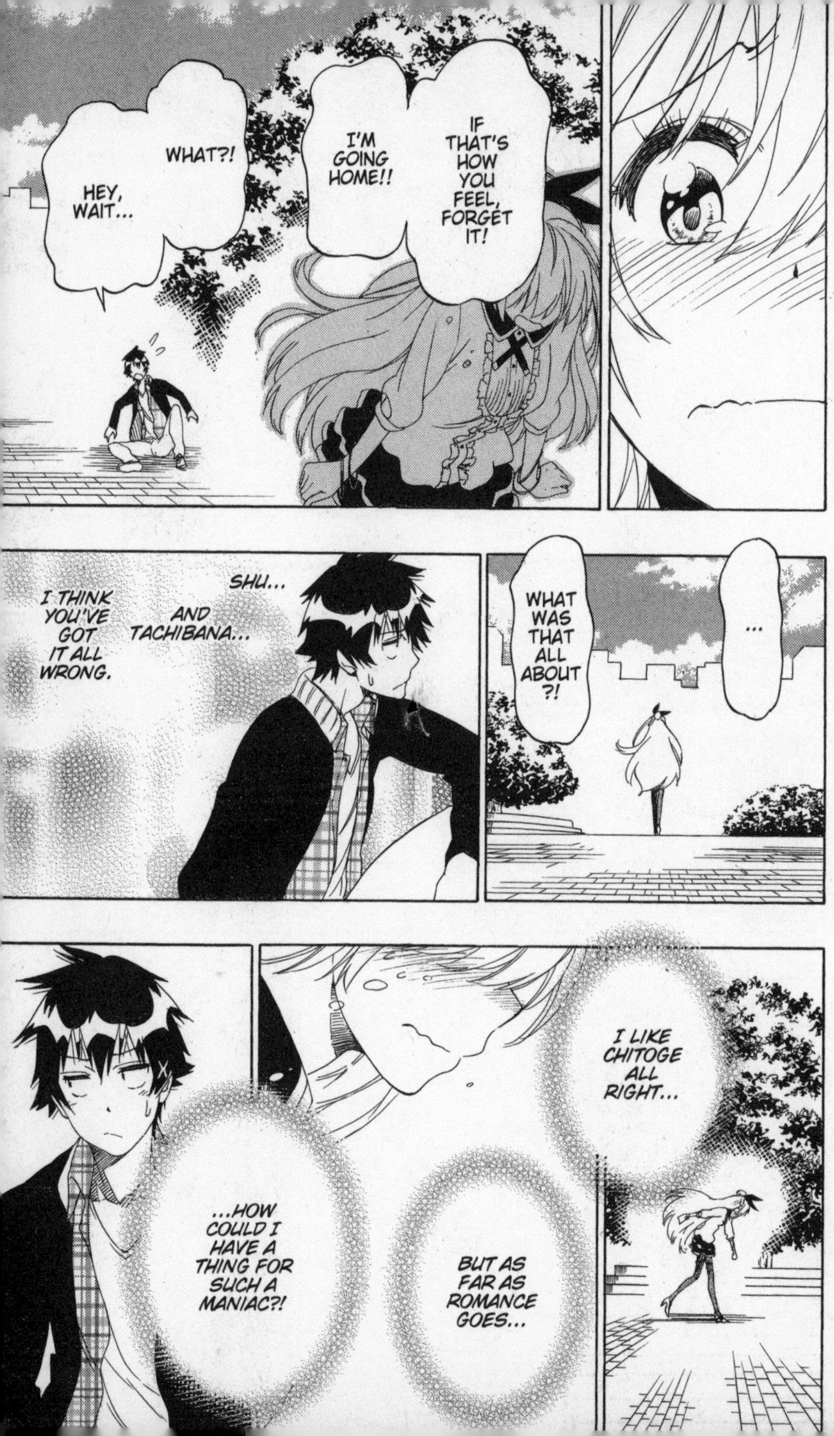
IF THAT'S HOW YOU FEEL, FORGET IT!
I'M GOING HOME!!
WHAT?!
HEY, WAIT...
...
WHAT WAS THAT ALL ABOUT?!
SHU... AND TACHIBANA...
I THINK YOU'VE GOT IT ALL WRONG.
I LIKE CHITOGE ALL RIGHT...
BUT AS FAR AS ROMANCE GOES...
...HOW COULD I HAVE A THING FOR SUCH A MANIAC?!

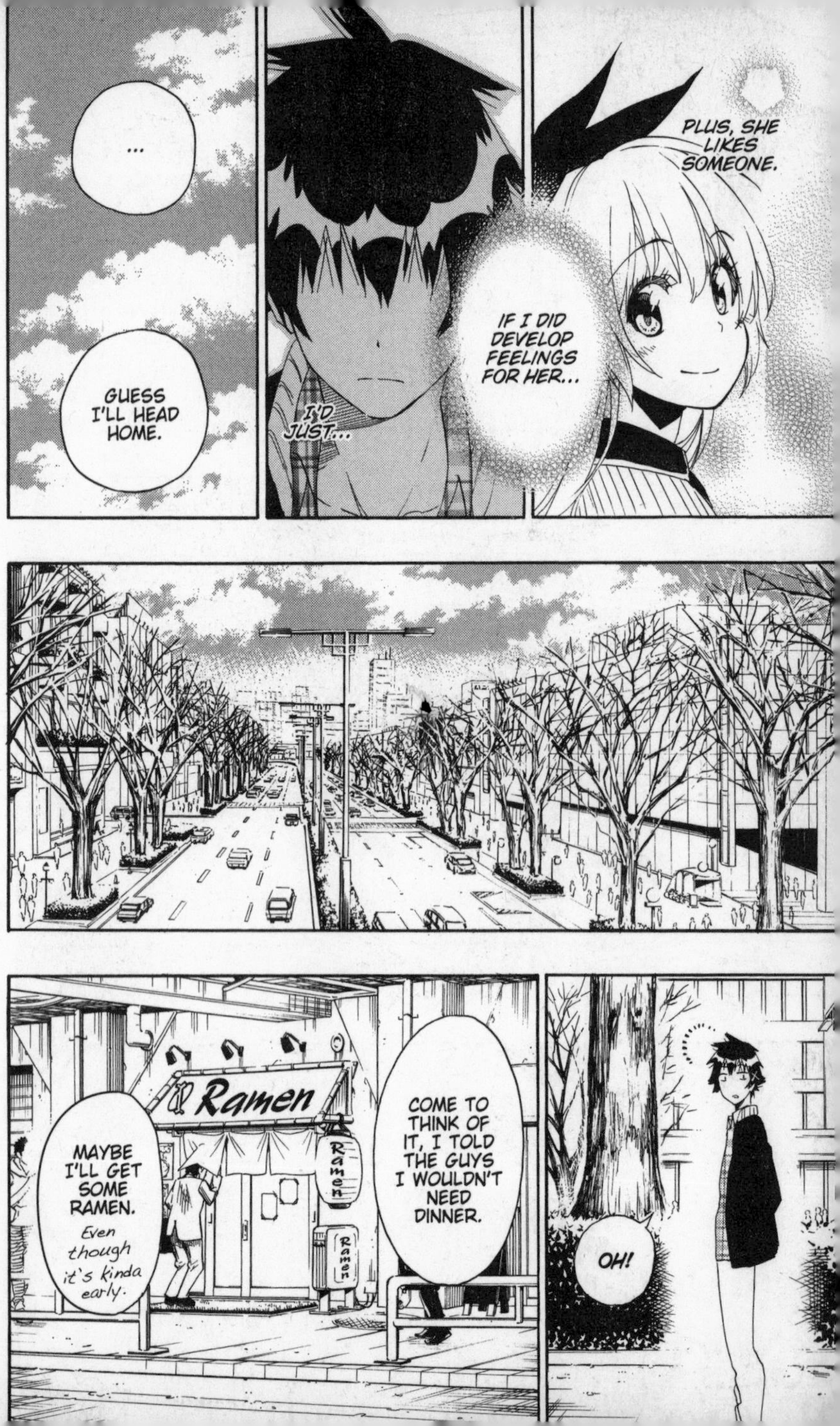
PLUS, SHE LIKES SOMEONE.
IF I DID DEVELOP FEELINGS FOR HER...
I'D JUST...
...
GUESS I'LL HEAD HOME.
OH!
Ramen
Ramen
Ramen
COME TO THINK OF IT, I TOLD THE GUYS I WOULDN'T NEED DINNER.
MAYBE I'LL GET SOME RAMEN.
Even though it's kinda early.

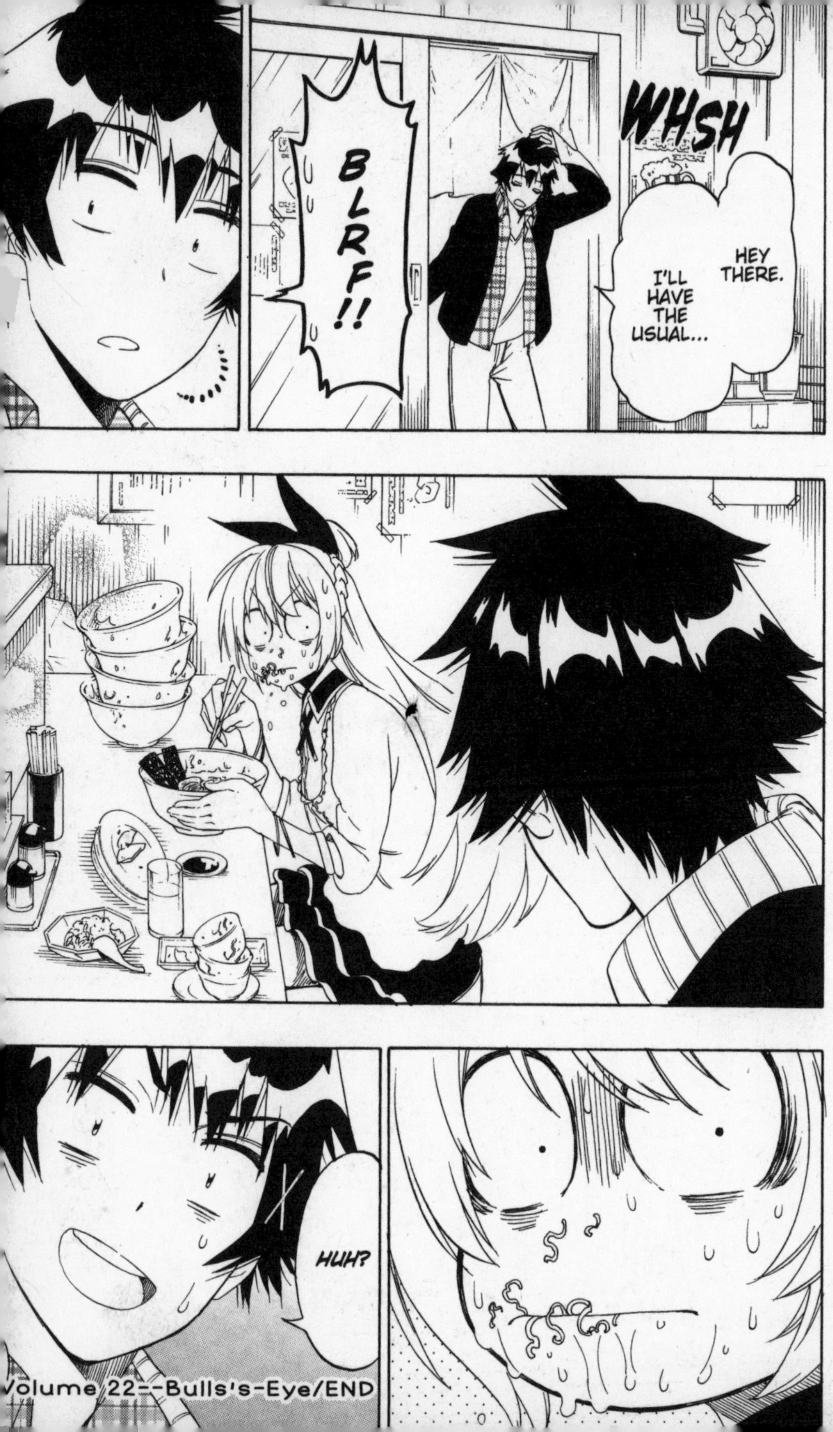
WHSH
HEY THERE.
I'LL HAVE THE USUAL...
BLRF!!
HUH?
Volume 22--Bulls's-Eye/END

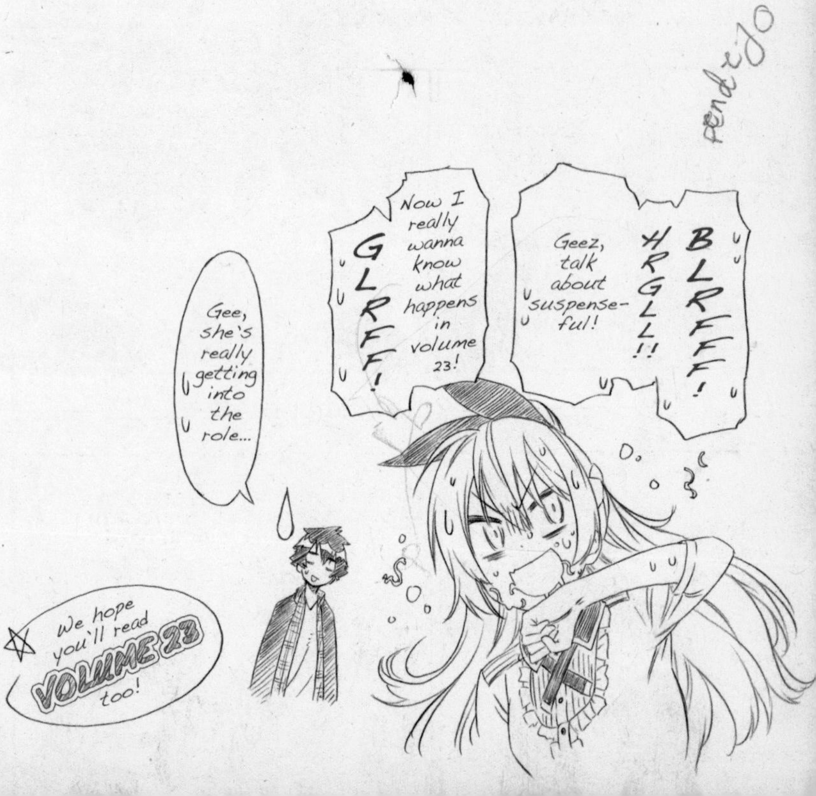

BLRFFF!
HRGLL!!
Geez, talk about suspense-ful!
Now I really wanna know what happens in volume 23!
GLRFF!
Gee, she's really getting into the role...
We hope you'll read VOLUME 23 too!

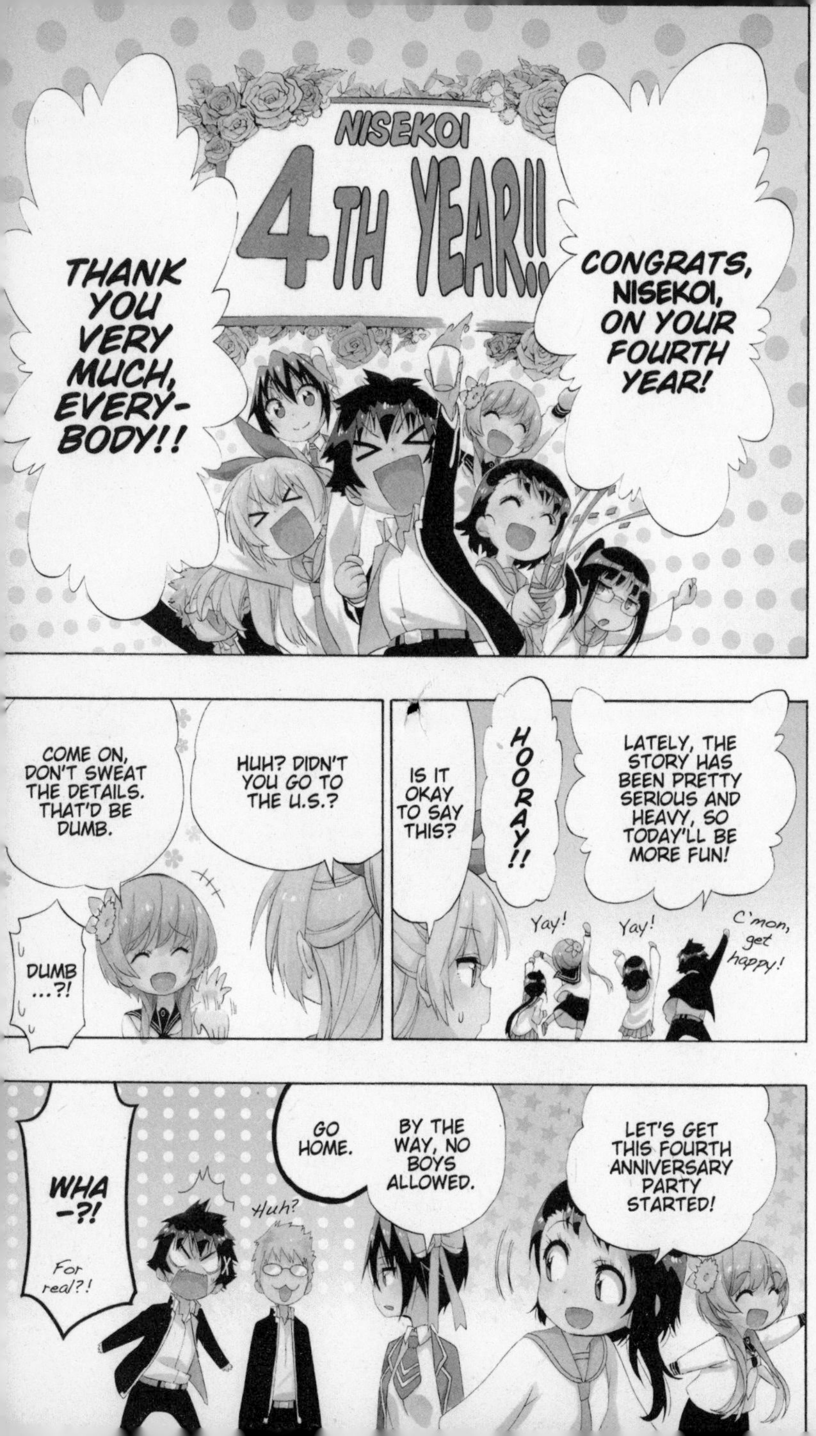
NISEKOI
4TH YEAR!!
CONGRATS, NISEKOI, ON YOUR FOURTH YEAR!
THANK YOU VERY MUCH, EVERY-BODY!!
LATELY, THE STORY HAS BEEN PRETTY SERIOUS AND HEAVY, SO TODAY'LL BE MORE FUN!
HOORAY!!
C'mon, get happy!
Yay!
Yay!
IS IT OKAY TO SAY THIS?
HUH? DIDN'T YOU GO TO THE U.S.?
COME ON, DON'T SWEAT THE DETAILS. THAT'D BE DUMB.
DUMB ...?!
LET'S GET THIS FOURTH ANNIVERSARY PARTY STARTED!
BY THE WAY, NO BOYS ALLOWED.
GO HOME.
Huh?
WHA-?!
For real?!

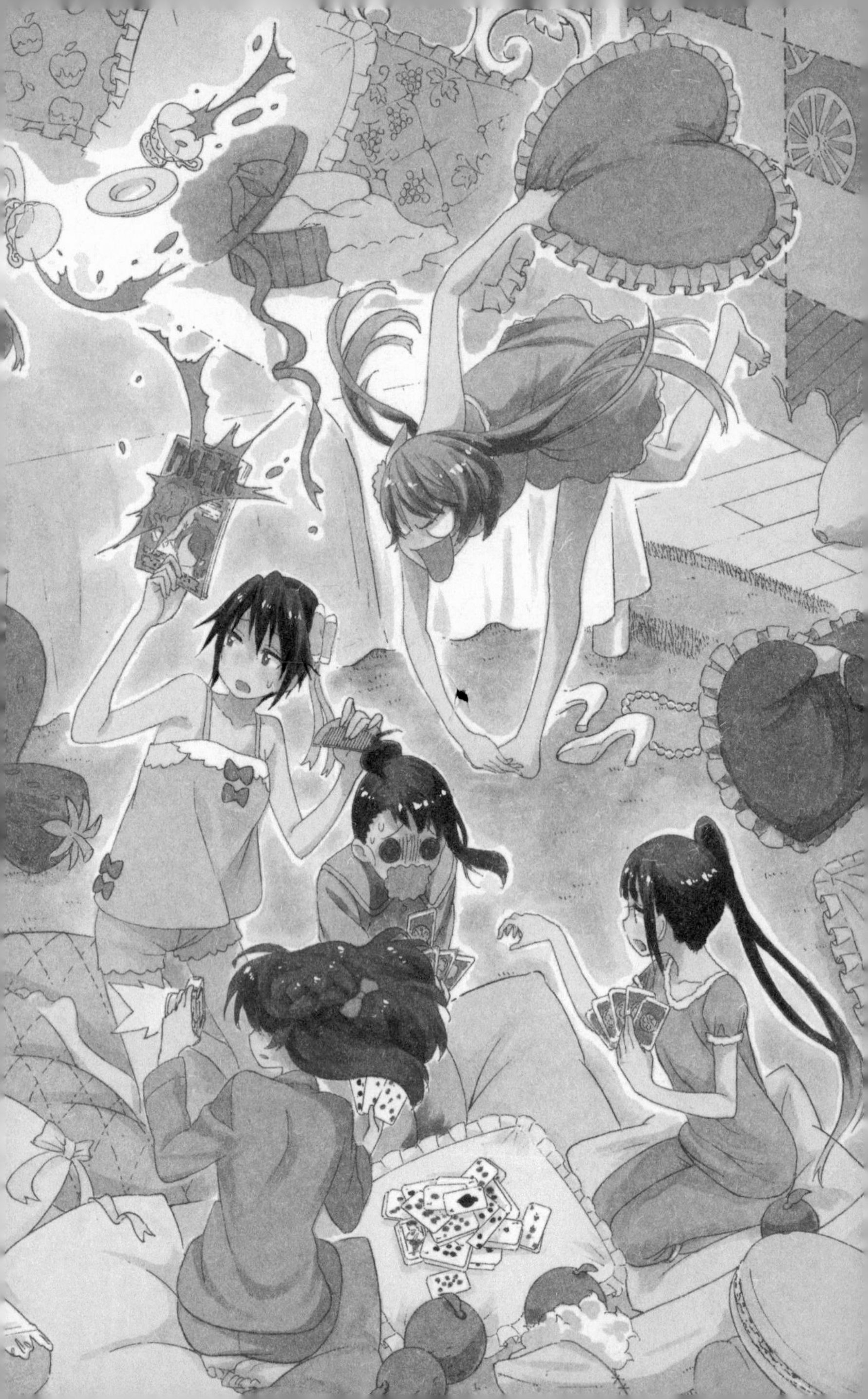

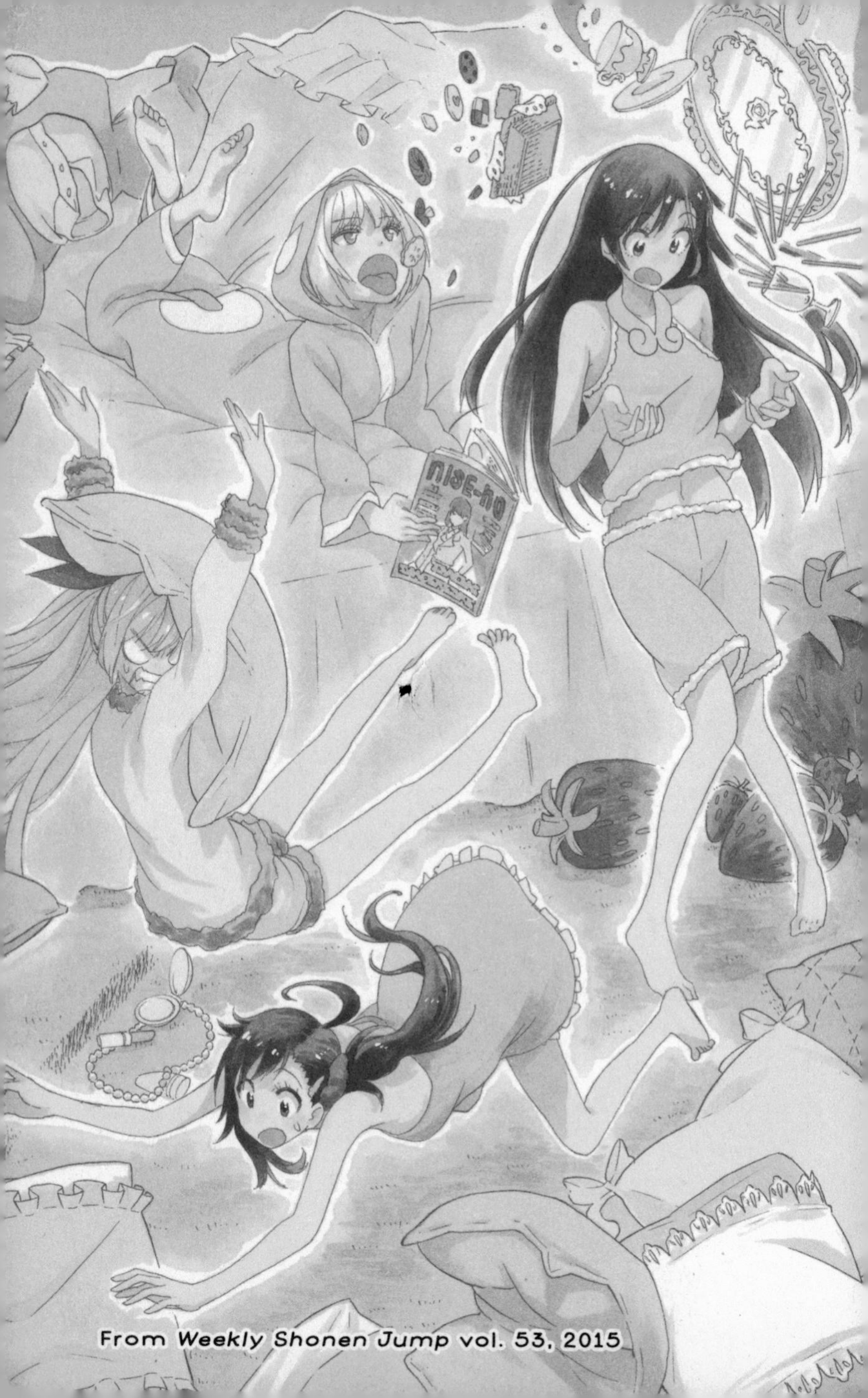

From *Weekly Shonen Jump* vol. 53, 2015

A monster's been reported in Battari Town!
You're to report to the site immediately, Haru!
Roger that, Windle!
These days when I reach the site, the monster's already been defeated.
I suppose it must be the work of that legendary trio...
Yes, probably.
We'll just have to try harder!
Magical Chocolatier Haru!!
But if I show my face too often, my family might find out about my double life!
I know it's an important job, but it's embarrassing! I mean, when I transform...
How will I ever explain it to my sister?
Listen, you can't keep letting that sort of thing get to you if you want to make it big!
Guess I'd better transform. Close your eyes, please.
There's nobody around, right?
Sure! The coast's clear!
FLASH!!
Okay, then! Traaansform!

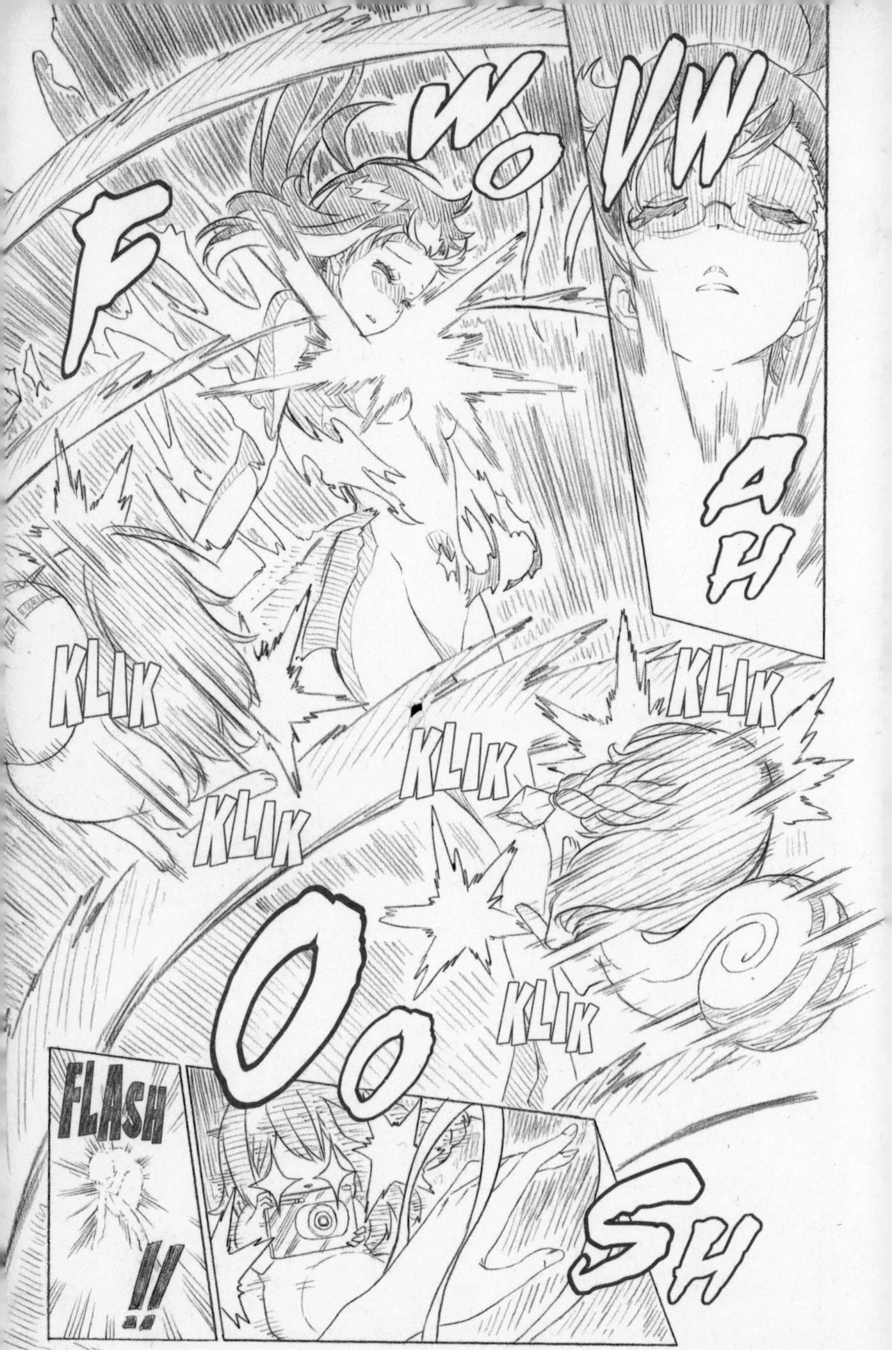
FWOVW
AH
KLIK
KLIK
KLIK
KLIK
KLIK
OOSH
FLASH
!!

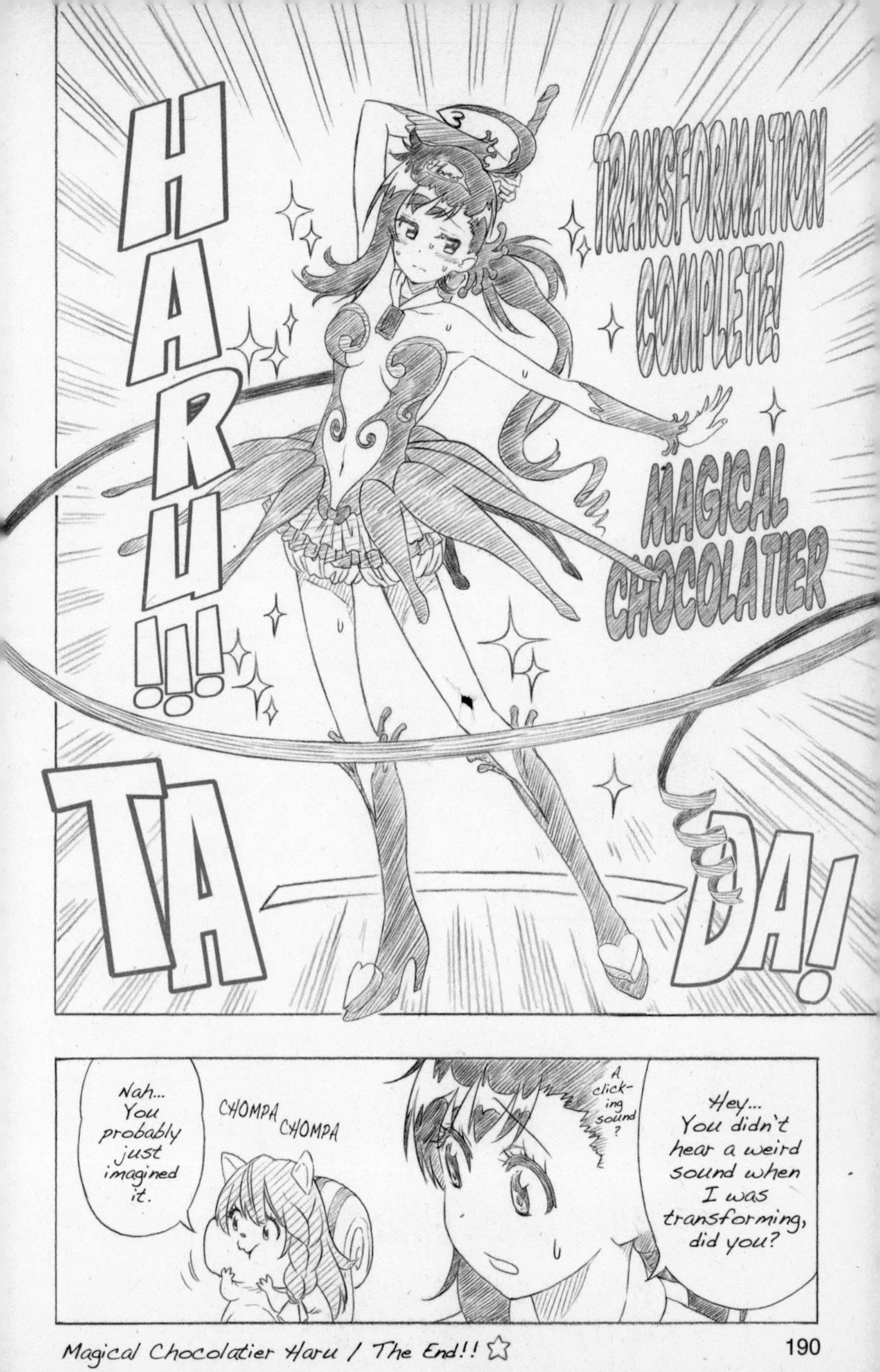
TRANSFORMATION COMPLETE!
MAGICAL CHOCOLATIER
HARU!!!
TA-DA!
Hey... You didn't hear a weird sound when I was transforming, did you?
A clicking sound?
CHOMPA CHOMPA
Nah... You probably just imagined it.

Magical Chocolatier Haru / The End!! ☆

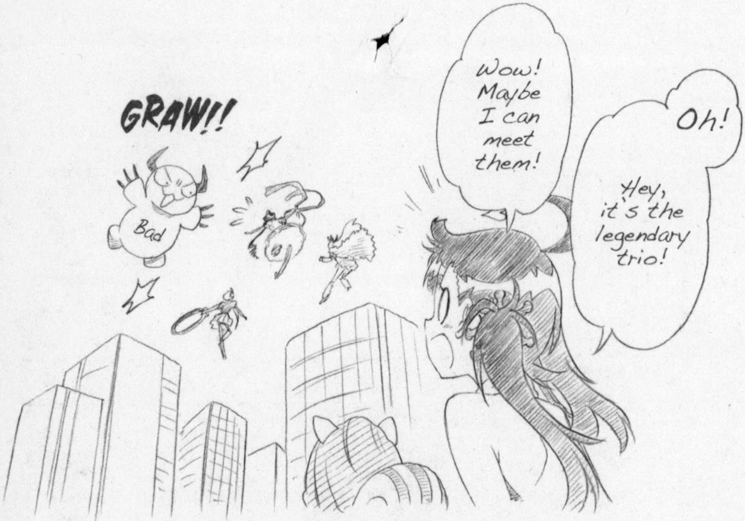
Oh!
Hey, it's the legendary trio!
Wow! Maybe I can meet them!
GRAW!!
Bad

THE FATEFUL CHANCE ENCOUNTER!

FIVE-SECOND COUNTDOWN!!

You're Reading the WRONG WAY!

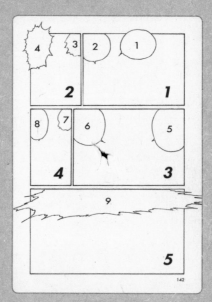

NISEKOI reads from right to left, starting in the upper-right corner. Japanese is read from right to left, meaning that action, sound effects, and word-balloon order are completely reversed from English order.